SISTERS
IN LAW

SISTERS
IN LAW

*How Sandra Day O'Connor
and Ruth Bader Ginsburg Went
to the Supreme Court and
Changed the World*

LINDA
HIRSHMAN

HARPER

An Imprint of HarperCollins*Publishers*

HarperCollins books may be purchased for educational, business, or sales promotional use. For information, please e-mail the Special Markets Department at SPsales@harpercollins.com.

Image credits: Part I: Columbia Law School; Part II: Collection of the Supreme Court of the United States; Part III: © Bettmann/CORBIS; Part IV: Richard W. Strauss, Collection of the Supreme Court of the United States; Part V: David Hume Kennerly/Getty Images.

FIRST EDITION

Designed by Fritz Metsch

Library of Congress Cataloging-in-Publication Data
Hirshman, Linda R. author.
Sisters in law : how Sandra Day O'Connor and Ruth Bader
Ginsburg went to the Supreme Court and changed the world /
Linda Hirshman. — FIRST EDITION.
pages cm
Includes bibliographical references and index.
ISBN 978-0-06-223846-7
1. O'Connor, Sandra Day, 1930—Biography. 2. Ginsburg, Ruth
Bader. 3. Women judges—United States—Biography. 4. Judges—
United States—Biography. 5. United States. Supreme Court. I. Title.
KF8744.H57 2015
347.73'2634—dc23
2015002577

15 16 17 18 19 ov/rrd 10 9 8 7 6 5 4 3 2 1

To my sister, Judith R. Collen, who, in 1948, taught me how to read, and has been here for me ever since. And to my daughter Sarah Shapiro, Philadelphia lawyer, and her daughters, Sylvie and Sydney, who will live, thankfully, in a new world.

Author's Note

❧

Women's names and titles matter. They are so hard won. The convention in journalism is to add the title Justice when introducing a Justice or when the role is particularly meaningful to the content of the text. Otherwise, Justices are referred to by their last names—Rehnquist, Burger—like any other public figures being discussed. Obama. Biden. I have followed this custom except where another speaker refers to them in some other way.

Unlike the male figures who shape the norm, my subjects had different names when they were young—Day and Bader, rather than O'Connor and Ginsburg. When discussing the youthful Sandra Day and Ruth Bader, I usually use their first names. Even Supreme Court justices were kids once.

Contents

✦

Introduction: Ruffled Collars   XI

PART I:
Sandra and Ruth Come into Their Own

1. Country Girl, City Kid   3
2. The Lawsuit of Ruth's Dreams   32
3. Goldwater Girl and Card-Carrying Member
   of the ACLU   45

PART II:
Chief Litigator for the Women's Rights Project

4. Act One: Building Women's Equality   69
5. Intermission: Abortion   78
6. Act Two: Equality in Peril   84
7. Act Three: The Stay-at-Home Dad to the Rescue   94
8. Finale: Boys and Girls Together   105

PART III:
FWOTSC

9. Sandra O'Connor Raises Arizona   117
10. Welcome Justice O'Connor   126

11. Women Work for Justice O'Connor   156

12. Queen Sandra's Court   174

13. No Queen's Peace in the Abortion Wars   184

PART IV:
Sisters in Law

14. I'm Ruth, Not Sandra   199

15. Ginsburg's Feminist Voice   215

16. The Importance of Being O'Connor and Ginsburg 246

17. Justice O'Connor's Self-Inflicted Wound   255

PART V:
Absolute Legacy

18. The Great Dissenter   273

19. Notorious R.B.G.   289

20. Our Heroines   298

Acknowledgments   303

Notes   305

Bibliography and Sources   353

Index   375

Introduction: Ruffled Collars

By the time the nation celebrates the birth of its democracy each Fourth of July, the nine justices of the Supreme Court have mostly left town. But before departing the capital for their summer recess, they must first decide all the cases they have heard since their current term began the previous October. The hardest, most controversial cases, where the unelected Court orders the society to change in a big way, are often left to the end. As the days for decision tick away in late June, the tension in the courtroom is as hot and heavy as the Washington summer air.

On the morning of June 26, 1996, Justice Ruth Bader Ginsburg, the second woman appointed to the high court since its founding, slipped through the red velvet curtain behind the bench and took her seat at the end. Five places along the majestic curve sat Justice Sandra Day O'Connor, since 1981 the first woman on the Supreme Court, or the FWOTSC as she slyly called herself. Each woman justice sported an ornamental white collar on her somber black robe, but otherwise there was no obvious link between the First and Second, any more than between any of the other justices. On that day, however, the public got a rare glimpse at the ties that bound the two most powerful women in the land.

Speaking from the depths of the high-backed chair that towered over her tiny frame, Justice Ginsburg delivered the decision of the Court in *United States v. Virginia*. From that morning in June 1996, Virginia's state-run Virginia Military Institute, which had trained young men since before the Civil War, would have to take females into its ranks. The Constitution of the United States, which required the equal protection of the laws for all persons, including women, demanded it.

Women in the barracks at VMI. Women rolling in the mud during the traditional hazing, women with cropped heads and stiff gray uniforms looking uncannily like the Confederate soldiers VMI had sent to the Civil War a century before. Six of Ginsburg's "brethren" on the Court agreed with her that VMI had to admit women, but the case was much more contentious—and momentous—than that robust majority of seven reflects. Until that day, VMI had been the shining symbol of a world divided between men's and women's proper roles. Before the case got to the Supremes, the lower federal courts had supported VMI's sex-segregated ways. For years, opponents of feminism used the prospect of women in military settings as the prime example of how ridiculous the world would become if women were truly treated as equal to men. VMI was one of the last redoubts. And now *Justice* Ginsburg, who, years ago as Lawyer Ginsburg, had been the premier advocate for women's equality—the "Thurgood Marshall of the women's movement"—was going to order the nation to live in that brave new sex-equal world.

Few people listening knew that Ginsburg got to speak for the Court that morning, because her sister in law, O'Connor, had decided she should. After the justices voted to admit women to VMI at their regular conference, the most senior member of the majority had the right to assign the opinion to any justice who agreed. He assigned it to the senior woman, Sandra Day O'Connor, but she would not take it. She knew who had labored as a Supreme Court lawyer at the American Civil Liberties Union from 1970 to 1980 to get the Court to call women equal. And now the job was done. "This should be Ruth's," she said.

On decision day, justices do not read their whole opinions, which can often run to scores of pages. That morning, Ginsburg chose to include in her summary reading a reference to Justice O'Connor's 1982 opinion in *Hogan v. Mississippi*, which had prohibited Mississippi from segregating the sexes in the state's public nursing schools. O'Connor's opinion for the closely divided court in *Hogan*,

Ginsburg reminded the listeners, had laid down the rule that states may not "close entrance gates based on fixed notions concerning the roles and abilities of males and females." And then Ginsburg, the legendarily undemonstrative justice, paused and, lifting her eyes from her text, met the glance of her predecessor across the bench. She thought of the legacy the two were building together, and nodded. Justice Ginsburg resumed reading the opinion.

Every woman in America was in the courtroom that June day in 1996. Whether you were a Supreme Court lawyer or a stay-at-home mom, pro-choice or pro-life, single or married, having sex in the city or getting ready for a purity ball, in their journey to that day, and on that day, these women changed your life. And so of course changed the lives of men as well. Justices O'Connor and Ginsburg have a stunning history of achievement in a wide range of legal decisions. But *Sisters in Law* tells the story of how together at the pinnacle of legal power they made women equal before the law. They argued for equality, they were the living manifestations of equality, and, because they took power before the revolution was over, they were in the unprecedented position of ordering equality. When women are treated as equals, as Gail Collins memorably said in her bestselling book, "everything changes."

When I graduated from law school in 1969, one of seven women in a class of 150, to start my career as the only female associate in my firm of sixty, the world of the law was the last place where I expected to see change. Interviewers had felt free to tell me their firms did not hire women and did not care if I had made law review. When I stood up to argue my first case in the Supreme Court seven years later, there were just the Nine Old Men. But starting with the admission of serious numbers of women to law school in 1967 and certainly by the time of the Supreme Court decision in *Reed v. Reed* in 1971, which was decided thanks in part to Ginsburg's work at the ACLU, the world had begun to change. Laws saying that women were not equal to men (or that men were not as worthy as women) were struck from the statute books, and part of the stereotyped thinking about women's lives went down the drain with them. In 1981, ten years after Ginsburg began her crusade at the ACLU, President Ronald Reagan appointed an obscure Arizona appellate judge, Sandra Day O'Connor, to the Court, and the campaign for women's equality picked up a doughty and determined role model. It was okay to be first, said O'Connor when the word of her appointment came. But you don't want to be the last.

As they litigated for and modeled the possibility for women to succeed—at the law and in the larger world—my world changed exponentially. I went from being an exotic token to a pretty normal player in the world of law. Of course, they were not personally responsible for the explosion of women entering the legal profession in the 1970s. But they probably mattered more than anyone else. The next time I stood before the Supreme Court, in 1982, Justice O'Connor looked back at me. She did not rule my way, but I was still glad she was there. When I began to write about the women's movement, as a law professor and a philosopher, I had Ruth Bader Ginsburg's stirring invocations to women's equality as the raw material of my analysis.

All movements have heroes. Who gets to the pantheon is often in dispute. But not in this case. Neither of them is perfect, of course, but Justices Ginsburg and O'Connor are unambiguous heroines of the modern feminist movement. And everyone needs heroes. My journey to the Supreme Court began when I found my models in the little public library behind my elementary school in Cleveland, Ohio. To my eternal good fortune, the library carried a whole bunch of biographies for girls. Florence Nightingale; Jane Addams; Julia Ward Howe, who wrote "The Battle Hymn of the Republic"; Anne Carroll, who helped devise military strategy for U.S. Grant; Lucy Stone and then all the suffragettes. By the time I finished the story of Susan B. Anthony, my life course was set. Sandra Day O'Connor and Ruth Bader Ginsburg are the Jane Addamses and the Susan B. Anthonys of the succeeding generations.

Each had a long, hard journey to the place where their stories peaked. Forty-plus years before the announcement of the decision in the VMI case, Justice O'Connor, then a new law school graduate, had been offered a position as a legal secretary. When Justice

Ginsburg arrived at Harvard in 1956, the Law School's dean asked all nine women students in her class to explain how they justified taking up a place that would otherwise have gone to a man. In the intervening forty years, O'Connor and Ginsburg traversed that hostile world to the highest point in the profession. To learn what they did, and how they did it, is to view two very different—and surprisingly similar—journeys to a flourishing life.

O'Connor was appointed in 1981 by a Republican president swept in by a landslide; Ginsburg was put on the Court by a centrist Democrat who had not even won a majority of the popular vote. They came from completely different backgrounds: Republican/Democrat, Goldwater Girl/liberal, Arizona/Brooklyn. Ginsburg, the brunette, opera-loving New Yorker, used to call her blond colleague the Girl of the Golden West. When O'Connor was appointed, Ginsburg, after ten years in feminist activism, did not even know who she was.

They were not soul sisters. O'Connor, the uncomplaining, open-faced, cheerful, and energetic westerner, was easy for her brethren to accept in 1981. As Justice John Paul Stevens said four decades later, "she never complained or asked for special treatment. And she got her work in on time; she never held us up." Ginsburg, the brilliant, solitary alumna of the feminist movement, brought an unwavering vision of the Constitution and a lifetime of experience in movement politics when she arrived. She chose chambers on a different floor than all the other justices, in order to get nicer digs. If she didn't get what she wanted from the Court, she openly pitched an appeal to Congress or, using the media, to public opinion.

But they were sisters in law. Ginsburg has said a thousand times how glad she was that O'Connor was there to greet her in 1993. And how lonely she was after her colleague retired twelve years later. This is the story of how such an unlikely pair came to nod at each other from the highest tribunal in America, as they finished the work of transforming the legal status of American women.

How did they do it? First, they were lawyers. They did not lead a social movement in the conventional sense, marching and sitting in. O'Connor's only formal "feminist" affiliation was with the exceedingly mainstream Associations of Women Judges. Ginsburg, the Thurgood Marshall of the women's movement, was not a conventional movement activist either. She was nowhere to be seen in the legendary Women's Strike for Equality in 1970 or, indeed, marching for anything. When she spoke or wrote, it was almost always in a professional context—women judges, women lawyers, the bar association, law school events, essays in law reviews. Ironically, toward the end of her life, she became an icon on that most populist of mediums, the Internet.

They chose to become lawyers when there was not even a whisper of a women's legal movement, but their choice of career placed them perfectly to make a social revolution through the law when the opportunity arose. Social revolution through law is a particularly American phenomenon. As the preeminent commentator on American democracy, Alexis de Tocqueville, put it two centuries ago, "Scarcely any political question arises in the United States that is not resolved, sooner or later, into a judicial question." Since the Civil War, most American social movements have relied on the potent equality-enforcing constitutional amendments passed in the wake of that engagement. In the 1940s and '50s the lawyer (later Justice) Thurgood Marshall had led the most successful such initiative—using the Civil War amendments to enforce racial equality through the courts. When Congress passed the Civil Rights Act in 1964, the racial legal movement gained another arrow for its quiver. All succeeding legal movements to some extent emulated Marshall's strategy of social change through legal revolution.

Both O'Connor and Ginsburg were part of the American elite—they went to Stanford and Harvard and Columbia Law Schools. Unlike mass social movements, legal social change movements are heavily top-down. They invoke the most unrepresentative institutions, the courts, often the life-tenured federal courts, and they are carried out by people, like both the women justices, of a rarefied mind-set and privileged social class.

When O'Connor and Ginsburg emerged from their private worlds of practice and teaching onto the public stage in the early 1970s, the women's movement was actively moving to become the next legal social movement. The Civil Rights Act of 1964, passed in the wake of the racial social movement, also barred discrimination on the basis of sex, and women's movement lawyers were starting to bring cases under it. The resurgent women's movement even revived an old project from the 1920s. Right after women won the vote in 1920, the most radical of the suffrage leaders, Alice Paul, proposed an Equal Rights Amendment for women as the only way to attack the whole web of discriminatory laws at once. Despite Paul's half century of effort, the ERA had gone nowhere. Then, in the heady days of the 1970s, anything seemed possible.

The two rose to be leaders in the movement, at first Ginsburg directly and O'Connor by example. When a moment is ripe for legal social change, there are often many lawyers who would like to lead it. Only some ascend to positions of power, and only some who ascend lead the movement itself to success. These two did ascend and did succeed. Ginsburg was a self-conscious legal movement leader. From 1972 to 1980, she ran the preeminent women's legal group, the Women's Rights Project of the American Civil Liberties Union, and she taught courses in women's rights at Columbia. Even after she became a federal judge in 1980, she continued to speak and write on women's rights. During those years, Justice O'Connor advanced women's equality in politics, although without embracing the women's movement formally as Ginsburg had. After O'Connor was selected for the Supreme Court in 1981, however, she became the most famous symbol of a lived feminist existence on the planet. And she was the owner of a precious vote on every Supreme Court decision on women's rights, starting with the crucial fifth vote in *Hogan v. Mississippi* in 1982. In 1993, Ginsburg joined her at the pinnacle of power. In the years following O'Connor's retirement in 2006, when the conservative Court turned its back on women's rights, Ginsburg, the eighty-something feminist, became the icon of resistance to the backlash.

Neither their ascent nor their leadership was an accident. They succeeded because they had "what it takes." Together, their differences made them stronger by giving them a wider reach. Starting at least as early as the election of Ronald Reagan in 1980, the country was increasingly divided to the core between Republican conservatism and Democratic liberalism. O'Connor, the youthful Republican campaign worker and sociable president of the Phoenix Junior League, who announced at speaking engagements in the '70s that she had "come with her bra and her wedding ring," covered one part of the political and social spectrum. Ginsburg, the youthful ACLU lawyer and introverted law professor, whose mild manner disguised her laserlike legal mind, brought different strengths and constituencies, including her highly connected and devoted husband, Martin Ginsburg. When the Democrats briefly held the Congress after retaking the White House in 1992, it was the liberals' turn to appoint a woman. It's hard to imagine Ruth Bader Ginsburg having much in common with Ronald Reagan. It's hard to imagine Sandra Day O'Connor swapping life stories with Bill Clinton. Each one was better off for the other being there.

Helpful as their superficial differences were, in their strengths they were actually a lot alike. Each possessed a firm belief that she was naturally and by virtue of her talents entitled to run the show. Expressing her comfort in her success as a legislator, O'Connor always said she never had a moment's trouble on the job once the gatekeepers got past their aversion to women and let her in to govern. The governing class was where she belonged and she calmly set about acting as if she was totally entitled to be there. When one of Ginsburg's female faculty colleagues wound up with a big Washington job shortly after Ginsburg went to the Court in 1993, she asked her pal Ruth if she could believe the two of them were in such high places. Actually, Ruth said, she had no trouble at all believing it.

Where did this extraordinarily rare degree of self-confidence come from? The critical moment of any social movement comes when someone who can think outside the box figures out that other people, rather than, say, nature, or even nature's God, are the source of their oppression. O'Connor and Ginsburg each figured that out. If they had internalized the low opinion of the people around them, Justice O'Connor might have been a legal secretary, and Justice Ginsburg might have learned to cook, instead of being the heroines of the feminist movement. O'Connor's father was an intellectual, trapped on an isolated ranch by family obligations. Domineering and opinionated, Harry Day used to spend hours talking politics with his firstborn child. During her critical early years, there simply was no society to teach her her place. After the tragic early death of an older sister, Ginsburg *was* the only child of a gifted woman, who had seen her brother go off to college while she stayed home. All her first-generation immigrant dreams rested on her bookish, beautiful daughter.

Believing they were entitled to rule, O'Connor and Ginsburg treated their opponents—from conservative Republican legislators who served with O'Connor in the Arizona Senate in the '70s to snarky titans of all-male law school faculties when Ginsburg was teaching—as if they were all members of the same club. Reminiscing about the famed jurist Learned Hand, who had refused to hire her when she graduated in 1957, Ginsburg, years later, was fulsome in her praise. Completely ignoring his blind spot on the subject of women, she wrote only about what a great jurist he was. This is not a matter of the oppressed identifying with their masters. In praising him, she sets herself up as someone whose opinion matters in the elite circles where they both, she assumes, belong. The lawyer who offered to give O'Connor a hand when she became the first woman at the Arizona attorney general's office later remembered embarrassedly how little she needed his assistance! She had no problem with the task of being an assistant attorney general in Arizona at all.

When pressed to admit they were inferior, they took offense. In 1952, the law firm of Gibson, Dunn & Crutcher interviewed a young Sandra Day fresh out of Stanford Law School and suggested she might find employment with them as a legal secretary. After all, they would never hire a woman lawyer. Three decades later, O'Connor, now Justice O'Connor, gave a wicked get-even speech at the firm's hundredth-anniversary celebration, a speech she called the most fun talk she'd ever delivered. Ginsburg so often told the story of the law school dean asking her what she was doing taking a seat at Harvard from a deserving man that the dean finally went public asserting it had been a *joke.*

But self-esteem is not enough to change the world. If the two had thought that they were the only women worthy of governing, they would have been useless to the movement. They might even have been harmful, like oppressed people who gain access to power and then pull the ladder up after them. Instead, the two jurists' clarity about their rightful place among the legal elite actually enabled them to see the injustice of women's inequality in general. If Gibson, Dunn had no business relegating O'Connor to the job of secretary because of her sex, why would they be any more justified in turning down another woman?

Where did this combination of self-respect and regard for others come from? In addition to their unique family histories, they sprang from cultures of empowerment. O'Connor came from an open western culture that placed a high value on volunteering. Frontier communities such as the American West had no manpower to waste. This unique culture allowed women a robust public role despite their exclusion from high-level formal employment. In institutions such as the Junior League and museum boards that fell from favor after feminism opened paid jobs to women, the women in O'Connor's world demonstrated their worth to anyone who was noticing. And O'Connor was noticing. She once said that she went back to practicing law after a few years of tending to her family in order to get some respite from the demands of the Junior League! Her reliance on voluntarism was a constant theme in her life, public as well as private.

Ginsburg came of age in the early years of the liberal revival. At college, she was the protégée and research assistant of a legendary liberal, Robert Cushman. Her professors at Cornell, like the men who taught her at Harvard, recognized at once that her talents entitled her to claim the goods of liberalism—equality, self-fulfillment—and they advocated for her tirelessly. By the time Ginsburg got her law degree in 1959, the dam was about to break in American culture. It would be the '60s. When the time came, both O'Connor and Ginsburg were prepared by their upbringing and culture to see the injustice of women's inequality.

Not only did O'Connor and Ginsburg recognize that they and

other women were being treated unjustly, they recognized that a lot of the problem and, therefore, the solution, lay with the legal system. The laws of all fifty states (and the federal government) treated women and men differently. Inequality was such a given at the time that it demanded a profound clarity of vision for women to figure out that it was wrong. The two arrived at this similar insight by somewhat different paths. O'Connor had been inspired to study law by a desire to make a difference, any difference. Since she was very capable of recognizing her own value, laws treating women differently from men struck her as unjust immediately. Ginsburg came to law with a clear liberal legal agenda. One of the touchstones of American liberalism is that the Constitution exists to protect people against an unjust state. Liberalism suited her perfectly for her future role as a crusading lawyer. Of course, neither O'Connor nor Ginsburg graduated law school with a visible commitment to the then nonexistent women's movement. Their deep commitments to making a difference and to equality, however, predisposed them to be useful when the movement came.

They also shared a capacity to take their revenge, cold. After her new colleague Justice William Brennan insulted Justice O'Connor in an over-the-top dissent during her first year on the Court in 1981, he found her mysteriously immune to his vaunted political charms, charms he used to get the five votes he needed on the nine-justice court. She never *said* anything. But he called his dissent "the worst mistake I ever made." When, at the beginning of her activism in 1970, Ginsburg was trying to get a piece of the action in the first women's Supreme Court case of the new era, *Reed v. Reed*, her contact at the ACLU, Mel Wulf, did not respond enthusiastically to her offers to help. So she and her husband reached out to other contacts at the ACLU who were more excited about her talents. Ginsburg and Wulf appear together on many briefs in women's rights cases after she came to the ACLU in 1972. But six years later, when he was ousted from his staff job as legal director in an internecine battle, Ginsburg, by then one of four powerful ACLU general counsel, "didn't say a word," he says, to save him.

When they could not get even, they would act as if they were not mad at all. As Ginsburg often told her avid audiences, on the eve of her wedding, her mother-in-law bequeathed her a pair of earplugs and shared the secret of a good marriage: "sometimes you have to be a little deaf." The liberal Justice Ginsburg's decades-long odd-couple friendship with her ultraconservative colleague Justice Antonin Scalia is famous. Less well known is that for years after she became the lead litigator for women's equality she corresponded in the friendliest tones with the legendary antifeminist University of Chicago law professor Philip Kurland. O'Connor was a visible supporter of the women's Equal Rights Amendment, yet she maintained a lifelong friendship with the conservative Barry Goldwater, an early and vocal opponent. Perhaps their firm belief that they were natural members of the formerly all-male elite explains why they could turn a deaf ear to powerful colleagues who were making life so much worse for women. After years of correspondence, when Ginsburg wanted Professor Kurland to help her daughter, then a student at the University of Chicago, she simply wrote him an adorable note describing her daughter's merit, just as men in power have always done. When anti-abortion activists tried to keep O'Connor off the Court in 1981, Barry Goldwater, still powerful, announced that anyone who opposed her should be spanked. It pays, sometimes, to be a little deaf.

Like all disempowered individuals, women tend to be viewed generically. When Ginsburg was appointed to the Supreme Court in 1993, the National Association of Women Judges had a party. They gave each of the two women on the Supreme Court a T-shirt. Justice O'Connor's said, "I'm Sandra, not Ruth." Ginsburg's said, "I'm Ruth, not Sandra." Sure enough, every term for years after Ruth's appointment, some hapless lawyer called them by the wrong name. But although they were similar, they were not generic. Similar and different, once acquainted (they met shortly after O'Connor was appointed) they formed a productive relationship. From her appointment in 1981 until right after Ginsburg joined her, O'Connor took more law clerks from Ginsburg's D.C. Circuit chambers than any other source. Neither bosom buddies nor mean girl competitors, as the moment of acknowledgment in the VMI decision perfectly reflects, the two justices hit the sweet spot of affectionate alliance. For anyone who aspires to lead a social movement, their relationship alone is an inspiration.

Barriers didn't stop them, mockery didn't faze them. While researching this book in the Arizona state archives, I was approached by one of the librarians. She wanted me to know that she had gone on a field trip with Justice Sandra Day O'Connor years before. A lawyer was writing an article about a historic case that originated in Arizona mining country, and he was leading an expedition to the sites where the dispute arose. By chance Justice O'Connor was in Phoenix, where she maintained a home. When she heard that one of her pals, an Arizona State Supreme Court justice, was going on the trip, she decided to go, too. As the vans rumbled across the high desert en route to lunch at a local ranch, they came to a gully that was running with floodwater too deep to cross. They were marooned for several hours. The situation worsened rapidly when Justice O'Connor revealed that she had to pee. As the organizers sat looking stunned and helpless, the justice clambered out of the van.

"Don't worry about me," she told the assembled barristers. "I'll just find a mesquite bush to go behind." Seeing their reaction, she added, "I grew up on a ranch!" And so she did. "I'll never forget it," said the archivist, "a justice of the Supreme Court of the United States dropping trou behind a mesquite tree."

When Ginsburg was nominated to the Supreme Court in 1993, someone sent her a fax relating that one of her old law school classmates told a meeting of his Rotary Club that the guys in her law school class used to call her by the nickname "Bitch." "Better bitch," Ginsburg responded, looking back on her journey from the derisive Harvard Law School scene to the highest court in the land, "than mouse."

Part I

Sandra and Ruth
Come into Their Own

Ruth Bader Ginsburg in 1972, the year she became the
first female tenure-track faculty member at Columbia Law School.

I

Country Girl, City Kid

❦

GROWING UP ON A RANCH

Sandra's father, Harry Day, wanted to go to college. He thought he'd go to Stanford after serving in World War I. But just as he set out for college, his father, H. C. Day, died, leaving his parched and dusty family ranch in southeast Arizona in terrible financial straits. Harry had to leave California to see if he could rescue the cattle-raising operation. He never got to go to college. It was one of the regrets of his life.

But he was lucky in love. In 1927, on a cattle-buying trip to El Paso, he met Ada Mae Wilkey, from an El Paso ranching family, whom he had once known as a girl. Ada Mae, a college grad married briefly and abruptly divorced in the 1920s, had a checkered past. Still, her family didn't want her marrying Harry Day and living on that primitive ranch with no power and no water. So the couple eloped.

Ada Mae was a trouper. She planted a garden around the little adobe house in the dry landscape. She played the piano and cooked huge meals, for the help or for parties. Biographer Joan Biskupic describes Sandra's parents as presenting a decidedly mixed message, the father "a Gary Cooper individualist" can-do type, the mother a stockinged woman in a frock in the '30s dust bowl, always "a lady."

When, in 1930, Ada Mae was ready to give birth to the baby girl who would become Justice O'Connor, she went to El Paso, where there were modern health services. After a time, Harry Day came to visit his firstborn, Sandra.

DA, as she calls him, is the unrivaled star of O'Connor's

childhood memoir *Lazy B: Growing Up on a Cattle Ranch in the American Southwest.* The justice's brother, Alan Day, who wrote the book with her, vividly recalls his oldest sibling as the favorite. His father "was on his best behavior when she was around, because Sandra would bring up stimulating subjects that he would want to talk about. And they would mentally head down the path together." (There was also a sister, Ann, eight years younger than Sandra.) Harry Day was a vociferous conservative of the pure free-market variety. Self-reliance and individual responsibility were his touchstones. When Sandra was six, her parents sent her away to El Paso to live with her grandmother during the school year and go to proper schools. She found her grandmother totally annoying: "My grandmother was a nonstop talker. If her eyes were open, her lips were moving. It created quite a problem for all of those years, but somehow we survived." Despite her pleas to return, with the exception of a single year in local schools, that's where she stayed. There were simply no schools anywhere near the enormous cattle ranch.

It was not easy being Harry Day's favorite kid. When she was fifteen, she was driving the ranch truck across the unmapped terrain of the huge isolated ranch to bring lunch to her father and the crew when she got a flat tire.

"I knew," she recalls in *Lazy B*, "no one would be coming along the road either way to help. If the tire was to be changed, I had to do it."

But when she jacked it up, the lug nuts were stuck and she could not get the tire off.

"Finally I decided I would have to let the truck back down until the truck rested on the ground again. . . . I pushed with all my might, but the lug nuts would not loosen. Finally I stood on the lug wrench and tried to jump a little on it to create more force. Joy! It worked. . . ."

"I started the engine and continued on."

But "it was late."

When she arrived at the work site, "I could see DA but he didn't acknowledge my presence." She set out the lunch she had brought and "then I waited." The crew finished branding and came over to eat.

" 'You're late,' said DA. 'I know,' I said. 'I had a flat tire . . . and had to change it.' 'You should have started earlier,' said DA. 'Sorry, DA, I didn't expect a flat.' . . . I had expected a word of praise for changing the tire. But, to the contrary, I realized that only one thing was expected: an on-time lunch."

Justice O'Connor says that she learned the value of no excuses from the incident. She must have quickly figured out that no excuses applied even when the incident was actually excusable. No matter how unfair, she would be better off not to directly defy the male authority figures in her life with demands for just treatment. As an only child for eight years and treated like a son, she had also internalized a sense of entitlement normally associated with straight white men. For the rest of her life she would combine her confidence in her own equal value with a unique ability to absorb a high level of injustice without complaint.

Within a year of the flat tire incident, Sandra left the ranch for Stanford. Sandra Day cut quite a swathe when she appeared in 1946 at the ripe age of sixteen. One of her dorm mates tells the story of how the girl from a remote Arizona ranch by way of an obscure El Paso private high school quickly rose to the top of the social order. "She had the most gorgeous clothes." And, "after the first school dance . . . she came back with this *cute* guy, Andy, a returning vet, who had a red convertible. We were blown away."

The Lazy B must have been a powerful experience. Even though after she turned six she lived on the ranch full time for only one year, all these years later, Justice O'Connor still calls herself a "cowgirl."

BROOKLYN BORN AND BRED

Until she went away to college in 1950, Ruth Bader lived on the first two floors of 1584 East Ninth Street, in Brooklyn. It was a pretty, rectangular house. But it was a modest home. Ginsburg's father, Nathan, had come from Russia and followed the classic

Jewish immigrant path of going into the garment business, first as a furrier and then as a haberdasher. He never achieved much material success. When Ruth was two, her older sister Marilyn died of meningitis, leaving her an only child.

It's a short block and a half from 1584 East Ninth Street to P.S. 238, on East Eighth, just across Avenue P. Seven years after P.S. 238 opened in 1930, tiny five-year-old Ruth Bader approached the high yellow brick building, pushed open the heavy doors, and walked across a terrazzo foyer to a big classroom with a hardwood parquet floor and high windows. There were a thousand children in this intimidating, enormous school, grades K–8, and classes often had thirty students in them.

Before she could read on her own, Ruth would sit in her mother's lap while Celia Bader read to her. Her mother, who had been raised Orthodox, taught her more about the tradition of justice than the more rigid rules of the Jewish faith. When Ruth was older, she and her mother had a ritual of weekly outings, Ruth to the children's section of the library, which was above a Chinese restaurant, and her mother to get her hair "done."

Even in grammar school, the future Harvard student was already distinguishing herself. When she was appointed to the Supreme Court in 1993, P.S. 238 invited her to a celebratory breakfast. The principal gave Ruth her record card from the 1930s showing practically all A's. The new justice reported very happy memories of her time there.

When she got to James Madison High School nine years later, she took up baton twirling and became a cheerleader. No mere bookish nerd, the honor society member and secretary to the English Department chair joined the orchestra, the school newspaper, and the pep squad.

It all sounds quite idyllic, except that her mother was dying. Celia Bader had her first treatment for cervical cancer just as the fourteen-year-old began her freshman year, and she died the day before graduation. Ruth used to sit in the sickroom, doing her homework. More than forty years later, Ginsburg stood in the White House Rose Garden with President Bill Clinton to accept her nomination to the Supreme Court of the United States. After the future justice thanked all the people who had made her nomination possible, she concluded, "I have a last thank-you. It's to my mother. My mother was the bravest and strongest person I have known," she recalled, "who was taken from me much too soon. I pray that I may be all that she would have been had she lived in an age when women could aspire and achieve and daughters are cherished as much as sons."

Ruth graduated sixth in her class in 1950 and went to Cornell, one of two Ivy League schools that admitted men and women to classes together, and where smart girls abounded. Although her mother had managed to squirrel some money away for her daughter, who knew she was valued as much as a son, Ruth got lots of scholarship help. Ginsburg was participating in one of the greatest transformations in American history: the college education of the female children of immigrants and the working class. Ginsburg's mother, "the strongest and bravest person" Ginsburg knew, had gone to work at age fifteen to send her *brother* to college. But like millions of girls in the postwar prosperity, her daughter, Ruth, went to college herself.

Ruth ("Kiki") Bader was, to all appearances, a conventional college coed. She appeared in her sorority (AEPhi) house picture dressed in a buttoned-up cardigan over a straight skirt topped off with a trendy little knotted scarf. A pretty, popular sorority girl in the outfit du jour, Ruth already understood very well what it took to get along.

ROLE MODELS FOR A MEANINGFUL LIFE

One otherwise unremarkable night at Stanford, Sandra's dorm mate, Mary Beth Growdon, invited her to a discussion at the home of her uncle, a professor at the university. When they arrived at Harry and Emilia Rathbuns', Uncle Harry, a nonpracticing lawyer and engineer, was conducting a seminar on the meaning of human life. "What am I? Who am I? Where am I bound? What is my destination?" Sandra was mesmerized. Growing up as she had on a remote ranch and educated at a small-town boarding school, the new ideas she met at Stanford were a revelation for the bright and curious youngster.

And inspiration was Rathbun's strong suit. He had read an undergraduate letter to the Stanford paper, expressing apprehension about venturing into an unknown world, and responded with a lecture to his next class. "My lecture that day was spontaneous," Rathbun later recalled. "It was an outpouring. I couldn't help myself. I had to tell those kids that the meaning of life was up to them, that no teacher and no school and nobody else could hand it to them like a diploma."

As Rathbun had it, human evolution produced an ever-evolving "deepening of consciousness, awareness, our ability to perceive the nature of reality." The goal of a human life was to continue that process, "overcoming our ignorance, seeing reality, dispelling illusion." (Against all scientific thinking about the pace and causation of actual evolution, he concluded that if people would follow the clues he unearthed, they could actually move to the next stage of "evolution.") Rathbun invoked what he called a natural human drive to evolve toward self-realization, which he defined as "realizing your potentialities" and "seeing things as they really are." His lectures about the meaning of life often culminated in Rathbun reciting Rudyard Kipling's paean to heroic individualism, "If" ("If you can trust yourself when all men doubt you," et cetera).

Heady with inspiration, the young undergraduate may not have noticed that Rathbun's theories about finding personal meaning could support almost any outcome. Indeed, in addition to generating a variety of social and religious experiments, including an association with the early northern California LSD scene, the Rathbuns spawned an antinuclear movement, a movement devoted to saving the earth, and one for the application of science to religion. As time went by, the Rathbun enterprises got increasingly weird, culminating in their frank admission that they were starting a "new religion." The social historian Steven Geller, who, with the religion professor Martin Cook, wrote a book about the Rathbuns' movement, says he was astonished to learn "how lightweight it was. Poof," he says, "and it would blow away."

But it is hard to overestimate its influence on the young Sandra Day. She credits Harry Rathbun with helping to shape her "philosophy of life." The lectures on the meaning of life, which finally had to be moved to a huge auditorium, went on for decades after she left Stanford. More than a half century after her encounter with Rathbun, O'Connor, then a retired Supreme Court justice, returned to Stanford to deliver the inaugural speech in a series honoring him. She called Rathbun "the most inspiring teacher I had ever had."

Rathbun's loose commitment to bettering the world without a firm picture of what a better world would look like is visible throughout Justice O'Connor's career. Although Rathbun's teachings seem strangely empty, this openness to a multitude of ideas was something she emulated during her tenure in collective decision making in the Arizona legislature, where she began her political career. It was also brilliantly useful later, as the Court became more conservative during her tenure from 1981 to 2005. As she gradually became the crucial fifth "swing" vote between the four mostly conservative and the four mostly liberal justices, she was open to compromise. She would solve the problem before her without worrying about what big principle she was laying down. Like the American public's opinion on contentious issues, Justice O'Connor's decisions were mostly patchwork compromises that almost never set down any principles to guide future decision making. Her 1989 opinions in the closely divided cases about government Christmas displays, for example, drew an incomprehensible line between Christmas displays on courthouse steps (not allowed) and on a public lawn (allowed). But her "ineffable gift" for the social sweet spot and ability to take a position quite free of any singular theory steered the Court safely down a treacherous path for a long time.

Ruth, too, met a mentor at college when her government professor Robert Cushman asked her to be his research assistant. As Ruth arrived at Cornell in 1950, Cushman was heavily engaged in the most contentious political issue of the time: the anti-Communist crusade of Senator Joseph McCarthy. Cushman is legendary among political scientists for having sounded the alarm against what would become McCarthyism early, and, as the darkness fell, often. In 1944, when it was starting to become actively dangerous to call out society on its repression, he had spent his capital as president of the American Political Science Association sending out a warning, "Civil Liberty After the War."

Cushman taught his young protégée that "our country was estranged from its most basic values." Americans have a history, he wrote, of assuming that constitutional democracy is "the true way of life" and that all societies will, in the long run, come to recognize that. If this were true, even the most generous scheme of freedom of speech, press, and assembly would "involve no actual danger to the public security or the stability of our institutions." But, Cushman continued, vested interests, in particular the vested interest of "our traditional capitalistic system of economic life," were making "dangerous assaults" on "freedom of opinion and public discussion." The would-be oppressors, Cushman accused, are after not merely Communists, but, under the guise of a threat to public security, they pursue "any reformer who proposes any change in our economic system."

By 1948, Cushman was supervising the overtly anti-McCarthyite Studies in Civil Liberty, funded by the Rockefeller Foundation. As the red-hunting reached fever pitch, one of the series authors, Robert Carr, recommended that the prosecutorial House Un-American Activities Committee should be abolished for having "encouraged a widespread witch-hunting spirit both in government and in private life."

Unlike Rathbun, Cushman left his protégée not only with a charge to make the world better but with a clear idea of *how* to make things better. He was an articulate spokesman for the value of traditional liberal freedom. A trained political scientist, he focused on a problem endemic to liberalism: how to protect the liberal regime of freedom against people, such as Communists, who use freedom to advance ideas that attack freedom itself. His solution was to be faithful to freedom even in the face of such an assault. Too often, he taught, people purported to be defending liberal democracy when they were really defending economic privilege. Life would be "better," to Ruth's mentor, if people stopped using the language of patriotism to defend their privileges and the less powerful were free to speak against them.

During her time with Cushman, the future justice learned that "there were brave lawyers who were standing up and defending people before the Senate Internal Security Committee and the House Un-American Activities Committee, and reminding legislators that this nation is great because we respect every person's right to think, speak and publish freely, without Big Brother government telling them what is the right way to think." Inspired, she got "the notion that lawyers could earn a living at that business, but could also help make things a little better for their community, both local—state, national—and world." She saw "a trade plus the ability to use your learning, your talent, to help make things a little better for others."

The young Cornellian left Cushman's service with a broad commitment to liberal politics. A Jewish girl from Brooklyn in the 1940s, she's unlikely to have been raised with conservative beliefs as O'Connor was. But as she describes it, her encounter with Professor Cushman enabled her to put a frame around her beliefs and inspired her to a life in the law, not a common dream for a female in 1952. As liberalism has done throughout its long history, the theory ultimately empowered her to see the grievances of a disempowered group, in her case, women like herself. Moreover, her later interest in women's rights, while primary, was embedded in an overall commitment to equality for all disempowered people. Although she did not fall into the trap of taking up every cause that came along, when she got to the bench and began addressing cases of all sorts, she followed a coherent liberal line.

As a liberal, then, the young graduate had her principles. When she got a chance to apply them as a Supreme Court justice years later, she did not have to reinvent legal theory. She was not, like William Brennan or William Douglas—or Antonin Scalia—a cutting-edge legal thinker. Once she took offense at the status of women, she took the existing liberal jurisprudence of equality under law and deployed it in the interests of women. As she saw it, the arc of American history bent toward including all marginalized groups into equal participation in national life. Her strength lay not in inventing overarching new approaches, but in her meticulous command of the game by the rules set down. It would be a masterful performance.

LAW SCHOOL AND LIFE

Inspired by Rathbun, Sandra too set off to study law. Starting her senior year, she managed to condense the three years of graduate study into two, graduating from Stanford Law School in 1952. Stanford was, for Sandra, a conservative decision. She'd been an undergraduate there, so this western institution did not require her to adjust to a strange culture. Yet, in choosing Stanford Law School, as in so many instances in the rest of her working life, Sandra Day's conservative decision put her at the cutting edge of social change.

Just three years before she arrived, Stanford Law School, a respectable, but not outstanding, institution, had hired a transformative dean, Carl Spaeth. Spaeth had credentials from teaching at Yale and Northwestern, and came from a high post at the Department of State. Before Spaeth, Stanford had no national law review, that peculiar institution where outstanding students judge and edit the scholarly writings of their teachers (and teachers from all over the academy) as well as learn to write legal articles themselves. By the time Stanford got its law review, just before Sandra arrived, *Harvard Law Review*, founded in 1887, had published definitive works on everything from the right to privacy to the meaning of the rule of law itself. All ambitious law students aspire to be selected for law review, a traditional stepping-stone to prestigious clerkships with prominent judges, lucrative and high-status careers. Prior to 1949, Stanford had never placed a single one of its students in the pinnacle of clerkships, a Supreme Court position. In 1949, just before Sandra arrived, Warren Christopher, later secretary of state, arrived from Stanford to clerk for Justice William O. Douglas. Stanford was on the move.

Young Sandra Day checked all the boxes at the newly rising

Stanford Law School. She was an editor of the law review; she was elected to the honorary society Order of the Coif. Popular, a fearless questioner in class, she seems never to have realized that being a woman would pose a problem for her as she sought to realize her potential (as her old mentor Rathbun would say). Although there were only four women in her class, and only two on the law review, there are no stories from her Stanford years of faculty hazing and rude questions about taking up a place a man would want.

Everybody loved Sandra, particularly John O'Connor III, the dashing, handsome son of a San Francisco physician. John, a year behind his future wife, spent an evening with her in the romantic pursuit of proofreading and citation checking for a law review article. Having the bright idea that a beer would lighten their labors, they took the draft to Dinah's Shack. And they never dated anyone else.

Coming out of Stanford Law School, then, the young rancher's daughter had no reason to suspect that being a woman was a problem. Her early life had prepared her to expect to do anything as long as she, no excuses, did the work. Embedded in an isolated family life and educated in the rising waters of the postwar West, she was raised outside of society's prescribed hierarchy—a sort of wild child.

As graduation loomed, seeing law firm jobs posted on the bulletin board at school, she started to phone around.

—This is Sandra Day. I saw your job posting on the Stanford
   bulletin board, and I'd like to apply.
—Well, we didn't mean women. We don't hire *women*.

After forty or so such exchanges, the young lawyer made a signature move—she rattled her network, and asked a college friend to arrange an interview with the friend's dad, a big deal at the California law firm Gibson, Dunn & Crutcher.

"This firm," her friend's father told her, "has never hired a woman lawyer. I don't see the day when we will. . . . Our clients wouldn't stand for it.

"Well, now," he continued, seeing her disappointment, "would you like me to explore whether we could find a place for you here as a legal secretary?"

"No, I don't think so. Thank you."

As O'Connor has told it a thousand times since, even after forty other rejections on the phone, she was still shocked. She was going to have a long uphill journey to get to the place she had thought so blithely was hers by right.

Just as O'Connor got the bad news about the status of women in the legal profession, Ginsburg started down the same road. She was going to go to Harvard, where her husband was already a year ahead. Although Ruth selected her life partner, Martin Ginsburg, long before either went to law school, like the O'Connors, their professional ambitions meshed. Martin Ginsburg was the only young man she dated, she always said, who cared that she had a brain. (Of course, she was only seventeen when she met him.) Fast friends from their first blind date at Cornell, they became engaged in two years and arranged to marry when Ruth graduated, a year after Marty got out. Fortunately, Ruth, who was first in her class at Cornell, had no trouble getting into Harvard Law School too. But in good '50s fashion the future feminist leader put her legal education on hold when Marty was drafted out of Harvard, and the young married couple headed off to Fort Sill, Oklahoma.

Ruth got a full blast of the illiberal world outside of Cornell University when she took a modest job at the local Social Security office near the base. When her supervisor discovered she was pregnant, he said, "Well, you can't fly to the training session [for the promised job promotion] pregnant. So you can't be promoted." The ever-observant Ginsburg noted that another woman, who kept her pregnancy a secret, did not suffer a similar fate. The de facto demotion cost the young clerk real money. But of course she didn't sue. In 1954 the Supreme Court told the nation that states could not segregate the races. But nothing the government supervisor did to *women* was considered illegal in 1955. Ginsburg gave birth to her first child, a daughter, Jane, that year.

She did make strides on the home front, though. When Marty,

who had been a chemistry major at Cornell, sat down to a meal prepared by his new bride early in their long married life, he immediately concluded that he had to spend some of his time mastering the art of French cooking. Someone had given the young couple a copy of *The Escoffier Cookbook*, and Martin Ginsburg began making every dish in the several-hundred-pages-long tome one meal at a time.

Marty turned into a legendary amateur chef. His spouses' dinners for the justices of the Supreme Court evoked such warm memories that when he died the Court published a cookbook in his memory (*Chef Supreme*). He also made sure his birdlike wife actually consumed something once in a while, hovering over her to be sure she ate. Ruth's kitchen saga says much about her overall strategy of obliquely offering the narrowest target in making social change. "The children," Ruth always contended, "banished" her from the stovetop after tasting some of her offerings. Ruth Bader Ginsburg didn't make a thing out of it. She just didn't learn to cook. Sometimes it pays to be a little hungry.

A few months after Jane was born, the Ginsburgs returned to Harvard Law School, Marty to resume his second year and Ruth as a lowly 1L. Unlike the upstart western Stanford University, Harvard had its gender hierarchy firmly in place. The only ladies' room at Harvard was in the basement of one of the two classroom buildings.

Erwin Griswold gave a dinner party to find out how the women justified taking a place a man would otherwise have had. Following a well-established tradition, each of the women students was escorted by a male faculty member. Ginsburg's date was the constitutional law scholar Herbert Wechsler, who, she thought, "looked more like God than any man I ever saw." It was an ironic pairing. When he squired the young lady law student to the dean's dinner, Harvard's godlike Wechsler was about to become the point man in the scholarly resistance to the Supreme Court's 1954 desegregation decision. His rabid criticism of that case made him the father of harmfully retrograde attacks on every subsequent move to equality: extending the Fourteenth Amendment to women, abortion rights, gay marriage. Unknown to her, Ruth Bader Ginsburg's life work would have been a lot easier if her dinner companion had choked on his hors d'oeuvres. In due course, Griswold called on Ginsburg to justify her presence in the law school. To her lifelong unending astonishment, the future feminist icon answered the dean, "it's important for wives to understand their husband's work." Harvard concluded its hostile treatment when, a couple of years later, Ruth Ginsburg, who had predictably gotten good enough grades for law review, asked Harvard Law School to grant her a degree if she finished her third year satisfactorily at Columbia. She wanted to keep her family together while Marty started practicing law in New York. They said no.

Years later, the law school announced that students in "significant relationships" could carry their Harvard degree after transfer. Marty, ever the advocate for his talented wife, immediately shot off a letter to the school newspaper. "In 1958," Marty wrote, "the administration's response was uncomplicated. Ruth was not asked if she was 'seriously involved' with spouse or child or both. No one inquired as to the likelihood of divorce on the one hand, or marital stability and even additional children on the other. No one speculated as to the quality of third year legal education at Columbia. It was all irrelevant. To bestow the crowning accolade of a Harvard degree, Harvard required the third year be spent at Harvard. Career blighted at an early age, Ruth transferred her affections to Columbia and satisfactorily completed the third year. After reading that transfer by reason of marriage now is viewed more kindly in Cambridge, I asked Ruth if she planned to trade in her Columbia degree for a Harvard degree. She just smiled."

When they published the letter, the editors of the 1977 *Law Record* added a note to tell their readers that the "Ruth" in question was at the time a professor at Columbia and head of the ACLU Women's Rights Project. Think, they speculated, of what she might have accomplished with a Harvard degree. In Ginsburg's files, the article appears with an annotation in her writing: "or had been a male." Harvard's policy fell hardest on its female students, usually the ones who left their career path to follow a male mate.

She never missed the real lesson. And she always thought she was entitled to anything available to any other human of any gender.

GRACE UNDER FIRE

Ruth had more than the usual reasons to stick close to Marty in 1958. The year before, Martin Ginsburg, twenty-four years old and in his third year of law school, had been diagnosed with testicular cancer, metastasized into the lymph nodes. At that time, about 90 percent of testicular cancer patients died of the disease. Looking back, Ruth Bader Ginsburg does not even allow herself the luxury of the 10 percent: "At the time, there were no known survivors," she says flatly.

As Martin Ginsburg underwent two surgeries, "the second massive," and eight weeks of radiation—the only treatments at the time—his wife continued caring for him, their young daughter, and attending her own law school classes. And working on the law review.

"That's one of the reasons I have such fond memories of law school," Ginsburg says. "Our classmates rallied around us and kept us going. We got some good person in each [third-year] class to put a carbon paper in their notes and give me a set of notes." Incredibly, Marty graduated with his class. At some point the story morphed into a tale of Ruth attending both Martin's classes and hers, as well as working on the law review, where she was the only woman. The actual version is heroic enough as is.

A third surgery, two years later, showed no further evidence of cancer. "We survived that year," Ruth Bader Ginsburg says, and learned that "nothing could happen that we couldn't cope with." Everyone who saw them together over the half century of their marriage reports the intensity of their attachment.

But even after Marty finished his cancer treatments, the doctors said there would be no more children, and they were not "out of the woods" until the traditional five years had passed. Although Ruth Bader Ginsburg gave a million speeches after she came to prominence in the early '70s, she didn't talk much about her husband's illness. When she mentioned him, it was mostly about how he did the cooking. In 2010 she finally owned up to what drives many women to cling to their work: "[F]rankly we didn't know how long Marty was going to live, and I might end up being the sole supporter of Jane." Of course, Ginsburg's story has a happier ending: "By the time we were out of the danger zone and it was past the five-year mark of his surgery, I was so hooked on my job that I would not give it up." Ginsburg has never said why it took her a half century to divulge that her concern over sheer economic survival partially fueled her brilliant career. Like the harsh emotional landscape of O'Connor's western childhood, Ginsburg's fear of impoverishment would not have fit the sunny narrative they each constructed as they climbed the ranks.

WORKING TO LIVE AND LIVING TO WORK

Like Ruth answering the insulting questioning at the dean's dinner, young Sandra Day showed no sign of indignation at her treatment by the law firms. She did not try to change the society to fit her idea of just treatment in 1953. Like oppressed minorities for generations before, Sandra found an employment opportunity working for the government. She heard that the deputy attorney for San Mateo County had once hired a woman, so she applied to him. As O'Connor later recalled, she was first told that the office had no budget to hire additional attorneys. Sandra agreed to work for free until funds became available. When she was told there was no office for her, she said, "I got along with your secretary pretty well; maybe she'll let me put my desk with hers." (In a graphic demonstration of women's lesser prospects, while she was sitting with the secretary, her classmate William Rehnquist, maybe a place or two ahead of her in class rank, went from Stanford to clerk for Justice Robert Jackson on the Supreme Court.)

O'Connor eventually managed to earn a salary from the county attorney, and when she left to accompany her new husband, John, to Europe, where he was serving with the army's lawyer corps, she found her second professional opportunity as a government lawyer, this time with the Army Quartermaster Corps. Despite O'Connor's plea that she had to work because the young couple liked to eat, money could not have been that tight. After John got out of the army, the couple rented an "adorable" cottage in Salzburg with old Austrian carvings of hearts and birds. They skied every day until the last flake of snow disappeared from the mountains. Then, having "run out of money," they reluctantly came home, establishing their first household in the burgeoning sun belt city of Phoenix, Arizona. John O'Connor quickly got a job at Fennemore, Craig, von Ammon, McClennen & Udall.

The community was made for them. The wife of one of their army pals wrote to her brother John Driggs, already a pillar of the community and later the mayor of Phoenix, to tell him to take care of their friends the O'Connors. William Rehnquist was already in town. He worked at the law firm of Denison Kitchel, the Harvard grad and constitutional law expert who would run Barry Goldwater's presidential campaign.

Phoenix grew seven times in population in the two decades before John and Sandra arrived, attracting soldiers who had learned to love the sunny climate during their war years, stationed at the various Arizona air force bases, and midwesterners fleeing the frozen cities of the snow belt. Many of the newcomers were Republicans. O'Connor's 1957 Arizona was a perfect microcosm of what would soon happen to politics in America. The Democratic Party was complacent, old, tired, and corrupt. The conservative revival generated a right-to-work law that made union membership optional, which then disemboweled the unions. Then the newcomers started a network of Young Republican clubs and presented themselves as the party of modernization. With the purchase of the *Arizona Republic* and the *Phoenix Gazette* by the conservative publisher Eugene C. Pulliam, the Republicans effectively took over the state media. In the next election, heavily assisted by the Pulliam papers, a Republican, Howard Pyle, won the governorship. His campaign manager was a young Barry Goldwater. The O'Connors fit right in. John joined the Rotary and the up-and-coming Young Republicans.

Typical of a western community, the reborn Republican Party rested on a robust network of volunteers. When she saw that conventional career opportunities were closed to her, the astute young Sandra O'Connor opened her own law office. A few years later, when the babysitter for her two young sons quit, O'Connor left her practice to stay home, but threw herself into Republican campaigns, becoming a precinct committeeman and eventually county vice chairman. She continued a lifelong practice of being at once a man's man and a girl's girl, joining at the same time the tony all-female Junior League. The Phoenix Junior League did major community service, and O'Connor quickly rose to become president of this powerful voluntary organization.

Her version of her time at home does reflect that life away from the workplace generated a certain unused capacity for her legendary energies. One year of her stint as a stay-at-home mom, she decided to cook something different every single night for 365 nights. In 1963, the O'Connors and the Driggses gave a party for two hundred people to inaugurate Legend City, the mini Disneyland that some Phoenix developer had decided was just what the growing city needed. The gala, scheduled for the night before the theme park opened, involved a chicken dinner, a pie bar, and every amusement, up to and including the ASU Marching Band. Elaborate private entertainments were an O'Connor hallmark.

In contrast to the sex-segregated law firms in Phoenix, by 1958, the summer between Ginsburg's second and third years in law school, the supposedly liberal New York law firm of Paul, Weiss, Rifkind, Wharton & Garrison had steeled itself to endure a woman hire. Since, as Ginsburg later recalled, they just wanted to check the woman box, her interviewer, the partner Lloyd Garrison, did not actually pay much attention to her in the interview. Paul, Weiss hired her as a summer associate, but, despite her having the highest grades in the entire third-year class at law school, it was just a summer fling. When she got out, Paul, Weiss did not offer her a permanent job.

Her teachers Professor (later Dean) Albert Sachs of Harvard and Columbia's famed constitutional law scholar Gerald Gunther thought their brilliant former student should aim higher than Paul, Weiss, anyway. They recommended her for a Supreme Court clerkship with their closest connection, Justice Felix Frankfurter. Frankfurter quickly answered. "I'm not hiring a woman."

Frankfurter was hardly alone. The legendary federal appeals court judge Learned Hand also turned Gunther down, supposedly because he feared a woman would inhibit his salty style of speech. None of the other Supreme Court justices, including that liberal avatar William Brennan, would hire a woman. In 1973 Brennan would author the first opinion to suggest treating sex discrimination as harshly as race, but in 1959, Ginsburg could only find a clerkship with Edmund Palmieri, a judge on the lowest rung of the federal court system, the district court. By chance, Palmieri chauffeured his colleague from the Court of Appeals, Learned Hand, home from the federal courthouse they shared, rides filled with talk in Hand's usual expressive style. One night, on the way home, the young law clerk in the backseat mustered the temerity to ask Hand why, since he had rejected her application to be his clerk on linguistic grounds, he felt free to swear as much as he liked in the car with her. "Young lady," he answered, speaking to the windshield, "I'm not looking at you."

"It was," she recalled decades later, "as if I wasn't there."

Buoyed by Palmieri's robust support in 1961, Ginsburg received several offers from law firms but decided instead to stay in academic life for a while. She signed on with a project at Columbia that was studying the procedures of foreign court systems. Professor Hans Smit, her mentor and sponsor on the project, was notorious for running "ladies day" in his class, calling only on his handful of female students one day and ignoring them the rest of the year. There is no record of her ever saying a word about it.

In 1961, leaving Jane with her father for several weeks, Ginsburg took off to study court procedure in Sweden. She landed in the middle of the Swedish feminist revolution. It started with a clarion call from a woman journalist, Eva Moberg, much in the same way that *The Feminine Mystique* set a fire under the woman's movement in America. Unlike Friedan's work, however, Moberg's article, "The Conditional Emancipation of Women," made a more radical argument—that women could not be emancipated simply by entering men's spheres; instead, men must also enter the women's sphere. Or, as Moberg put it, both would be "people." Moberg's approach soon became the conventional wisdom in Swedish thinking, public policy, and law. Sweden made parental leave available to men, began to plan its public transportation and zoning to make it easier for both parents to work outside the home, and generally attacked sex-role stereotyping. In 1961, Sweden was the future, and Ginsburg was there to see it work.

By 1970, Prime Minister Olof Palme was lecturing Americans in "The Emancipation of Man." "Men," he said, "should have a larger share in the various aspects of family life, for example, better contact with the children. The women should become economically more independent, get to know fellow-workers and to have contacts with environments outside the home. The greatest gain of increased equality between the sexes would be, of course, that nobody should be forced into a predetermined role on account of sex, but should be given better possibilities to develop his or her personal talents."

Despite her exposure to the Swedish experience at the beginning of the '60s, Ginsburg spent most of the rest of that tumultuous decade minding her own business, teaching civil procedure at Rutgers Law School. In keeping with her low profile, when she became pregnant again, she made no demands on her employer; she simply hid her second pregnancy with her mother-in-law's larger clothes, lest she be penalized again for reproducing on the job. Being pregnant at all was something of a miracle for the Ginsburgs, in light of the doctors' warnings that Marty's treatment for cancer meant no more children. "James's safe arrival in 1965 showed that they misjudged," she crowed.

Her first day of teaching in 1963, Ginsburg looked out from behind the podium at the former newspaperman Frank Askin, one of the many returning adult students Rutgers attracted in those '60s days of self-realization. "She delivered an endless boring monologue," Askin, now a professor at Rutgers himself, recalls.

At the end of her first year, the students performed a skit about her at their annual faculty send-up. A student playing their introverted civil procedure teacher gave a monotonal lecture while being stripped of her clothing. "She's completely oblivious to the whole thing," Askin recalls, "until she's down to a bra and panties." Ginsburg's abstracted affect did not make her a favorite among students hungry for entertainment—or colleagues looking for a little academic bonhomie. Marty Ginsburg—bluff, hospitable, hilarious, athletic—quickly became the stand-in for his unforthcoming spouse.

Sandra O'Connor apparently wasn't paying all that much attention to the feminine mystique either. She thought practicing law was a lot easier than running the Junior League. No need to hang out a shingle this time. The Republican state attorney general Bob Pickrell was hiring assistants, and, as the future justice forthrightly admitted, "since I had been active in Republican activities, that no doubt helped." She set herself up in the little office she was assigned as an assistant attorney general, hanging on the impersonal walls pictures her children had drawn.

Although everyone realized she was the first woman assistant in the office, ever, it posed no problem. Her new colleague Paul Rosenblatt thought his female coworker was "a pleasure. First of all she was *very* attractive! And then she was so pleasant. And we had a great bunch of people in the office and we really needed the help, we were so busy." The newcomer lost no time in exercising her traditional social skills in the new work environment either, inviting her helpful colleague Paul to dinner, which she hosted with her usual fabulous hospitality and delicious cooking.

In 1969 the state senator representing O'Connor's aptly named Paradise Valley neighborhood left the Arizona Senate to work for the Nixon administration, and O'Connor decided that she "would try to obtain appointment to that position" by the county board of supervisors. She knew the Republicans through her party volunteer activities, so she went to them and, surprise, they appointed her to the vacant seat. Relentlessly sociable and bent on a public life, the transition to the legislature was natural for a woman who never seemed to recognize how uppity she was.

Even though O'Connor and Ginsburg were leading relatively conventional lives, the '60s *were* happening. In 1963, Betty Friedan published *The Feminine Mystique.* Congress passed the Civil Rights Act, forbidding sex-based discrimination in employment. Casey Hayden and Mary King started circulating "Sex and Caste: A Kind of Memo" among the Students for a Democratic Society. Betty Friedan and others called for a new organization, the National Organization for Women. The new movement revived the old call for an amendment to the Constitution, the Equal Rights Amendment, protecting women, just as the Civil War amendments protected black Americans (*Equality of rights under the law shall not be denied or abridged by the United States or by any State on account of sex*). The Senate began hearings on proposed legislation.

The currents of change even reached the conservative heartland in Barry Goldwater's Arizona. As O'Connor would later demonstrate on a larger stage, the tirelessly hardworking, superficially conventional new legislator provided the Republican leadership in the state legislature with an easy way to integrate women. "Many women around the nation were claiming more in terms of their desire to be treated equally and to have equal opportunities at work and I was the beneficiary, really, of a lot of that sentiment," she forthrightly admits. The Republicans engaged in a bit of affirmative action and made her chair of the powerful State, County and Municipal Affairs Committee, unprecedented for a newbie state senator. In 1972, O'Connor ran for the second-highest post, majority leader, and became the first woman in America to sit in the leadership of her state's lawmaking body. "Once I got in," she proudly remembers, "I never had a further problem."

O'Connor later said that a woman's success comes easier if "both partners" understand "that the wife intends to pursue her separate career," because "there is less likelihood of subsequent disappointment by the husband who experiences a greater share of responsibility for child care as a result." But while Sandra O'Connor was leading the majority of the Arizona state senate, she came home every night to cook dinner for their three sons. O'Connor was famous for her Mexican dinners, at which, she says, legislators from both sides of the aisle resolved their differences and did the people's business.

Across the nation, social change was coming at a somewhat faster pace. In 1967, the University of Chicago Law School tripled the number of women in its entering class from seven to twenty-one, and, in 1968, with the Vietnam War siphoning off male applicants, the law school admitted forty. That year, when a firm said it didn't hire women, the ungrateful female Chicago students did not move a desk in with the secretaries at some obscure government job. They sued the law school for violating the Civil Rights Act by maintaining a discriminatory hiring hall.

Under pressure from women students, NYU's law school, followed quickly by Yale, started a course in Women and the Law. Rutgers was inundated with second-career women coming back to law school under the influence of the feminist revolution. When Ginsburg—one of a handful of women law teachers—and the women students at Rutgers got wind of the development across the Hudson, they immediately planned a course of their own. "The students coopted her," her colleague Frank Askin remembers. "There were only two women on the faculty and the other one wasn't interested. She's still teaching property somewhere."

In typical Ginsburg fashion, her first act of feminist insurgency was to visit the library and gather all the materials there were on the subject of Women and the Law. It was an easy task, she noticed, because there was so little written. But as she examined the failed efforts to achieve equality, her "consciousness was awakened, and she began to wonder: 'How have people been putting up with such arbitrary distinctions? How have I been putting up with them?'" The grudges she had been carrying just got a lot heavier.

Her warm recollections of the gender ferment during her Swedish sojourns make this maiden foray into feminism something less of a Road to Damascus story. Within a year after Olof Palme delivered his 1970 address in D.C., Professor Ruth Bader Ginsburg, then of the Rutgers law faculty, was citing his speech in letters to each of the members of the Senate and House Judiciary Committees in support of the Equal Rights Amendment. As the Swedes had been saying, Ginsburg avowed that men were as constrained by sex-role stereotyping as women were. "The traditional arrangement sometimes exacts a heavy toll from the dominant sex," she wrote. And in a later speech at Duke: "A sharp line between the sexes, while generally functioning to confine women's opportunities, occasionally yields a male victim." When she took the time to organize her insights into a larger theory, what she called "Realizing the Equality Principle," she cited Eva Moberg's essay: "In it, she deplored the state of affairs existing in her country, as in this one, that women in the work force were nonetheless expected to maintain their traditional function inside the family." Happily married to her master chef husband, this small, reserved woman brought her deep love for her spouse to any man who struggled to escape the double bind of gender roles. One of her favorite Supreme Court clerks won her attention when he applied, because he was a stay-at-home dad during law school.

She was, as her earliest feminist work reflects, committed to social change. But Ruth Bader Ginsburg was no Betty Friedan. Her strength lay in her razor-sharp mastery of the unromantic subjects of civil procedure and, as she immediately realized, constitutional doctrine. Even her rabble-rousing first speech after her awakening is a compendium of cases, past, present—and to come. She does not just rail against the gilded cage; she recites the facts of cases such as *Goesaert v. Cleary*, the 1948 Supreme Court decision that allowed women to be cut off from bartending in the interest of social morality. She predicts the impact of the cases feminism has thrown up, which are coming down the pipeline. As she began her feminist journey in the early Rutgers years, the monotonal lecturer turned her powerful analytic mind to the problem of using the equality language of the Constitution to destabilize the wall between men's and women's roles.

The Ruth Bader Ginsburg archive at the Library of Congress contains the papers from the crucial couple of years of the feminist heroine's consciousness-raising. Despite her lifelong diffident, lady-like demeanor, the files are revealingly radical. They include all the essential elements of her brilliant career. From Moberg she got that inequality in the home would always keep women down, and things that looked like protection—such as alimony and shorter work hours—only made matters worse. "Few women," she said in an early speech, "who have considered the effect of special protection in the past seek advantaged treatment today." The revived feminist movement was pushing an Equal Rights Amendment, which would make all legal distinctions unlawful. Until they succeeded in passing a new constitutional Equal Rights Amendment, however, legal feminists were going to have to fight trench warfare to extract legal equality from the existing, race-based constitutional provisions.

Early on, Ginsburg obtained an essay by the feminist writer Alix Kates Shulman, "A Marriage Agreement," in a short-lived publication with the über-'70s title *Up from Under*. Shulman's "Marriage Agreement," written with her then husband, was perhaps the most radical document of the explosive feminist revolution. "After I had been home with the children for six years," it opens, "I began to attend meetings of the newly formed Women's Liberation Movement in New York City." Next thing you knew, Shulman and her spouse had signed a two-page single-spaced contract addressing eleven items of domestic labor—children's mornings, transportation, help, nighttime, babysitting, sick care, weekends, and household cooking, shopping, cleaning, and laundry. He had the dishes on Tuesday, Thursday, and Sunday and she did them Monday, Wednesday, and Saturday. Friday was split "according to who did extra work during the week."

Like the 1960s Swedish movement to pull men into the private sphere, the fact that Ginsburg kept a copy of "A Marriage Agreement"—of all the manifestos, articles, and volumes the '70s feminist movement produced—reflects her lifelong and profound commitment to the most radical goals of feminism: private justice.

Americans reacted to Shulman's suggestion of domestic equality with near-fatal fury and devastating mockery. Two decades after "A Marriage Agreement" was published, the sociologist Arlie Hochschild wrote an entire book, *The Second Shift*, about how the feminist movement was derailed by the failure to embrace the principles in Shulman's little essay. But Ginsburg never wavered from her principles. It might take years or even generations, but in Ginsburg's ideal world, women were not going to have to bring home the bacon and fry it in the pan; as in the Ginsburg household, the jobs would be divided fairly.

She collected the sociologist Lenore Weitzman's legendary article on how divorce impoverishes women and enriches men, yielding the second plank of Ginsburg's feminist platform—that the gilded cage of protective dependency is more cage than gilt. That realization fueled her relentless war on protective legislation for women, as "treating women as less than full persons within the meaning of the Constitution." Protective labor legislation, such as maximum hours for women workers when there were no such "protections" for men, split the feminist labor activists from the so-called liberal feminists for a long time. There was serious infighting over the feminists' proposed Equal Rights Amendment, which would make such laws unconstitutional. But Ginsburg never wavered in her belief that most laws and practices that supposedly protected women actually did more harm than good. As a lawyer, she never argued for special protection. The petite and soft-spoken radical proposed to expose all women to the icy winds of the market and individualist politics, starting with being able, for example, to tend their own bars. "All I ask of my brethren," she constantly repeated, quoting the long-dead radical abolitionist and suffragist Sarah Grimké, "is that they take their feet off our necks."

The government could hurt women in so many ways. When Ginsburg left the Rutgers library, she had learned that laws excluded women from countless human activities. Women could not or need not serve on juries, and, therefore, they would never be judged by juries of their peers. They could not tend bar in unhealthy saloons and so the would-be barkeeps could not earn their keep. They would be protected by marrying and so their parents' duty of support for, say, college tuition, ended sooner for them than for their brothers.

She did not only haunt the library. One day that year, a handful of female law students met in some feminist's walk-up apartment in Greenwich Village to discuss life and law. Small and retiring, Professor Ginsburg of Rutgers Law School had a story to tell the group. "When I was a first-year student at Harvard," she began, "the dean had a dinner for all the women students. . . ." It was the first time she shared the story in a political setting and it would not be the last. Ginsburg set up the seminar on Women and the Law and began working on the first ever casebook on the subject.

But the classroom would not confine her. Within months of her life-altering trip to the Rutgers library, Ginsburg was standing before a meeting of the newborn National Association of Law Women at Duke University. "Technology," she told the assembled women, "and society's drastically curtailed child production goals," make the division of labor between the sexes, assigning women to domestic labor, obsolete. "Feminism is an idea whose time has come." The problem, she continued, was that "nothing is more ubiquitously pervasive than an idea whose time won't go." Even she could not figure out how to litigate to force married couples to abide by the marriage agreement. Most women weren't lucky enough to be married to Martin Ginsburg.

Ruth Bader Ginsburg, of Harvard and Columbia law review pedigree, knew where to turn. What feminists could do, she told the audience, is make the government stop putting the weight of law behind the sex-role stereotypes that drove the injustice in the private realm. Legal sex-role stereotyping was worse than private behavior, she believed, because a "popular, but unproved assumption enshrined in law, deprives women of the opportunity to prove it false." Everything about the revived women's movement conspired to present Ginsburg with the first leg of her journey to fame and power. Arguing for the Equal Rights Amendment, which dated back to the 1920s, motivated the movement to focus on the web of laws that expressly kept women down. The flood of women into law schools pressured these institutions into regularizing the focus on Women and the Law into academic channels and credits. The same women provided a brilliant resource for the work of identifying legal issues and devising ways to challenge them.

Within months of starting the research for her seminar, Professor Ginsburg was writing to the members of the relevant congressional committees urging them to pass the suffrage-era Equal Rights Amendment. If passed, the ERA, forbidding the government to discriminate on grounds of sex, would have made it close to impossible for any law to distinguish between male and female. Like the laws against race discrimination, any law treating men and women differently would have to serve a compelling government interest. Practically, almost no law ever passes that test.

Ginsburg first framed her letters to Congress as coming from her and from the students in her seminar. Soon, she stepped out of her cocoon of collective action and began asserting the arguments simply as coming from herself. The letters from the lady professor triggered hilarious efforts to address her. They called her Professor, Mrs., and the then newly conceived "Ms." One Rep. Charles Sandman addressed her as "M's." (Ginsburg famously refused to take the bait on how she should be addressed then or in her many appearances in the Supreme Court.) But as one of the few female law professors in the country, she was a natural advocate for the new legal order.

The task was great and the resources scant. Had the Equal Rights Amendment passed, Ginsburg would have taken a very different path from the long march she was now undertaking. While she waited and hoped, she knew she had to try to use the existing Constitution to free women from the sex-role stereotypes enshrined in law. From her perch on the Rutgers faculty, she started working on women's rights cases with her local New Jersey ACLU.

The problem with her campaign for constitutional equality was that all the equality language in the Constitution was rooted in the American struggle with slavery and racial inequality. By the early '70s, activists had succeeded in expanding the enforcement of equality beyond race—to protect aliens, and religious and ethnic minorities, for example. But by the time Ginsburg started her quest in 1970, any hope of getting women the same protections from discrimination as blacks ran right into the powerful backlash that had formed after the wave of social change we call the '60s. Just as women took their place in the long march of American equality, the society—and the Court—were getting more conservative. It would be an exquisite task.

2

The Lawsuit of Ruth's Dreams

⁂

No one was better suited for the exquisite task of radical politics than the diminutive, immaculate, soft-spoken thirty-seven-year-old denizen of the Upper East Side. By 1970, Brooklyn's Kiki Bader was living in a luxurious coop apartment at Sixty-Ninth Street and Lexington Avenue, in a building designed by Emery Roth and Sons, the same firm that produced some of New York's landmark apartments and hotels. Although she later dined out on the tale of how her son's school always bothered her alone until she reminded them that James actually had "two parents," most bourgeois New York parents would have killed to be annoyed by the elite Dalton School. Martin Ginsburg, well into his career as a renowned tax lawyer by then, was not only a good cook, he could bring the bacon home.

In a scene right out of Hepburn and Tracy's battle-of-the-sexes movie *Adam's Rib*, Professor Ginsburg was working in her home office in their upscale apartment one night in 1970 when Marty waltzed into her sanctum with a tax advance sheet. Greeted with an impatient "no time for tax cases," Marty persevered. This one she had to read.

Marty's case involved a lifelong bachelor, Charles Moritz, the sole support of his eighty-nine-year-old widowed mother. He tried to collect the $600 deduction the tax code provided for caretaking costs while he was out earning a living as a medical editor. The Internal Revenue Code, having no truck with lifelong bachelors and their mothers, allowed only the dependency deduction for caretaking women, widowers, and the unlucky married man whose wife is "incapacitated."

The line separated men from women, full stop. There were no distracting issues here, unless the court was willing to say that it was unnatural for men, rather than women, to care for their mothers. From Ruth Ginsburg's strategic point of view, it did not matter whether the plaintiff was male or female. The only issue was whether, in 1970, the government could treat one sex unequally simply because . . . it could. Civil rights lawyers are always looking for the perfect case, one that squarely presents the injustice of the distinctions, with no distracting side issues and with a very appealing plaintiff to represent the cause. The Ginsburgs decided Charles Moritz was the plaintiff for them. (When Moritz first got their call, he thought someone was playing a joke. Why would fancy New York lawyers be bothered with him?) Unlike *Adam's Rib*, where the defense attorney played by Katharine Hepburn was at war with her prosecutor husband (Spencer Tracy) in the case against Judy Holliday's bloodthirsty wife, in the Moritz case the Ginsburgs were on the same side. Moritz was, of course, ecstatic to have them. Since he had lost before the tax court, the next step in his case was to appeal the decision to the local federal court of appeals in Colorado, where he lived. The Ginsburgs wrote the papers to start the appeal and began working on the brief. When it was done they sent some copies around to lawyers they thought might be interested.

CARD-CARRYING MEMBERS OF THE ACLU

The liberal NYU professor Norman Dorsen was sitting in his faculty office at the Law School when the Ginsburgs' brief arrived. Dorsen, who was an important general counsel at the national office of the American Civil Liberties Union, thought it was a great job. "Marty doing the tax side and Ruth making the equal protection argument, I wrote her and said it was an absolutely brilliant piece of work." Dorsen—and the ACLU—mattered. That's why the Ginsburgs sent him their brief. They were looking for help with the thousands of dollars of expenses they knew they would incur representing Charles Moritz in the federal court of appeals.

By 1970, anyone who was anyone in social change was banging on the door of the ACLU. Ruth and Marty Ginsburg, however, weren't just anyone. At Rutgers, Ruth was already starting to take sex-discrimination cases for the New Jersey ACLU. One day that fall, she opened her office door at Rutgers and who should be standing there but Mel Wulf, the dining hall waiter at her old summer camp, Camp Che-Na-Wah. Wulf, the legal director of the national ACLU, was visiting Ruth's former student and present colleague Frank Askin, who was already a member of the ACLU board. After the customary chat about Swedish civil procedure, Ginsburg told Wulf she was doing a sex-discrimination case for the New Jersey ACLU. He was not impressed with her little local litigation, although he later called this the moment he "plucked Ruth Bader Ginsburg from obscurity." As usual with Ginsburg, it was more like she did it herself (backwards and in high heels). She sent Wulf a follow-up letter with an appeal for help with the Moritz case. Getting no response, Ruth deployed her second arrow—a clever, musically themed letter to Wulf about the value of the Moritz case, in the form of a play on Gilbert and Sullivan, familiar from their camp productions.

Her interest in Wulf intensified when she read that the ACLU was already in charge of *Reed v. Reed*, the first constitutional sex-discrimination case to go to the Supreme Court since 1961. The Reeds, separated and then divorced, were in court because the state of Idaho had a law preferring men over women as the administrators of dead people's estates. When the Reeds' son died, Cecil Reed was appointed executor, over the mother, Sally. Sally Reed's sense of injustice may have been fueled by the tragic circumstances of her son's death. A judge had ordered Sally to turn her son over to his father under the then-standard doctrine that a child old enough to need education about the world should be transferred to his father, once the "tender years" spent with his mother were over. Right after she relinquished him to his father, the boy had killed himself. Now his father was going to administer their son's estate.

Ginsburg asked to see the papers Mel Wulf was drafting to appeal *Reed v. Reed* to the high court. Her reading was that Wulf wasn't moving aggressively enough to change the legal landscape for women. She wrote to Wulf again and suggested that perhaps he could use a woman's touch with his brief to the Supreme Court on behalf of women's rights. Teaching a course and trolling for relevant cases, skinny, bookish Ruth Bader Ginsburg took a look at *Reed v. Reed* and decided to stand on that lever and move the world.

But first a word or two about that world.

EVERYTHING YOU ALWAYS WANTED TO KNOW ABOUT THE CONSTITUTION BUT WERE AFRAID TO ASK

The Constitution, c. 1970: No Girls Allowed

There's a reason Ginsburg was in favor of women having a constitutional amendment of their own, the Equal Rights Amendment. The Fourteenth Amendment to the United States Constitution, which mandates the equal protection of the laws, like all of the amendments passed after the Civil War, was interpreted to apply to discrimination on the grounds of race (or servitude). If a law discriminated on the basis of race it was suspect, and had to be justified by a compelling state interest. After all, that's why the Civil War was fought.

Until Ruth Bader Ginsburg started her crusade, trying to get constitutional protection against discrimination for any human person other than a black person was almost impossible. Legislatures "discriminate" all the time in the ordinary course of making laws. Driving fifty miles an hour, illegal; forty, legal. Voters at twenty-one, disenfranchised at twenty; employers of more than fifty covered by the labor law, those employing fewer than fifty not covered. Judges and scholars worried that once these legislative decisions to divide the population could be challenged in court, where would the challenges stop? It's one thing to say schools couldn't be segregated into black and white, but demanding the legislature to justify all classifications would lead to anarchy.

Almost four decades before the reborn feminist movement, the

Supreme Court had said that the standard for review of most laws would be whether they are rational. Only a tiny category of laws would be looked at hard, what the Court called a strict-scrutiny standard of review. Those were laws that discriminate on race or alienage and laws that impact the explicit protections of the Bill of Rights, such as freedom of speech and religion. Otherwise, all the law required was that the legislature have some rational basis for distinguishing between its citizens, including its male and female citizens. Rational basis was the lowest standard of judicial review of legislation.

When Ruth Bader Ginsburg took pen to hand for the mother who wanted a fair shot at administering her dead son's estate, the Court had repeatedly turned back pleas to stop the states from treating women differently from men. Just ten years before, in *Hoyt v. Florida*, the Court had said it was okay to discourage women from serving on juries. Between 1961 and 1971, however, lay the earthquake we call the feminist movement. Now seminars full of newly enrolled female law students around the country were turning up examples of how the discriminatory laws hurt women. They wanted the equal protection of the laws applied to them, too. Could the feminist law professor Ruth Bader Ginsburg persuade the Court to apply the race-based Civil War amendments to the altered landscape of sex?

Even Liberal Lawyers Are Conservative

Paradoxically, the American legal system is as conservative as the American Revolution was revolutionary. Despite the revolution, America inherited its legal system from the mother ship, England. In our mutual system of common law, which developed over centuries, deciding one case at a time, courts can make law. But because courts are usually not elected, when they make common law, they are reluctant to make it seem as though they are legislating from the bench. They pretend they're just applying what the prior cases required. The federal courts, which mostly interpret the U.S. Constitution, are also not elected. The Constitution is so old, and the language so broad, that when a court lays down new rules, it appears to be just making stuff up. So the courts try really hard to convince themselves that what they are doing is just discovering what the Constitution meant.

Asking a court, conservative by nature and history, to make the leap from protecting the constitutional beneficiaries of the Civil War to applying equality to their wives was a big jump. At that time, Justice William Brennan, the liberal judge Ginsburg was counting on, wouldn't even hire a female student to be his law clerk.

In 1969 the "liberal" *Harvard Law Review* published a 150-page article on equal protection, the very constitutional doctrine Ginsburg was invoking. The word "sex," as in "sex discrimination," appears four times—three to distinguish it from genuinely suspect categories such as race and once in a footnote to ask whether "experience teaches that the biological differences between the sexes are often related to performance." The brainiacs at Harvard then offered their ultimate argument against constitutional equality for women: Who could imagine gender integration in the military?

Ginsburg had her work cut out for her.

WOMEN'S LIB AT THE LIBERTIES UNION

The American Civil Liberties Union invoked by Ginsburg in 1971 was almost as white and male as the Arizona legislature O'Connor sought to join. Of the ACLU National Board, which had the authority to dictate policy, 91 percent was male. The leaders of both staff and board were all white, male, Ivy League–educated lawyers: Executive Director Aryeh Neier (New York, Cornell J.D.), Legal Director Melvin Wulf (New York, Columbia J.D.), General Counsel Osmond Fraenkel (New York, Columbia J.D.), Marvin Karpatkin (New York, Yale J.D.), and Norman Dorsen (New York, Harvard J.D.).

Until just a few months before Wulf ran into Ginsburg at Rutgers, the ACLU was not even on record as supporting the Equal Rights Amendment. Board members with ties to organized labor had long opposed the equality provision because it threatened the labor laws that gave special protections to women. More regrettable was the attitude reflected in the *Harvard Law Review* article, that women's rights simply weren't worth more than a footnote. The Congress on Racial Equality's Floyd McKissick, who served on the ACLU Equality Committee, was forthright: CORE would work on black male power. Women could wait until "tomorrow." As women began demanding legal equality more loudly in the early '70s, a lot of liberal men decided that the civil liberty of equality, like the Civil War amendments, really should apply only to race. Dorothy Kenyon and Pauli Murray, the two intrepid women who had been trying to liberalize the ACLU, in some cases for decades, were starting to have "tantrums."

Relief came from an unlikely source. In the wake of the feminist movement, the women from ACLU chapters out in the hinterlands formed a woman's caucus. They threatened to quit, called the organization on its founding principles, and started asking for surveys of everybody's salaries in the ACLU itself. Fortunately for them, the ACLU had made the fundamental error of holding biennial conferences with representatives from all the affiliates gathered together with the overwhelmingly white male national board. In June 1970 the women made their move, presenting the conference with a resolution to make women's rights a priority. With one dissenting vote, the board did a 180-degree turn and endorsed the Equal Rights Amendment. And they elected Kentucky's Suzy Post, a Berkeley grad and an old activist in the racial civil rights movement, to the board.

Abigail Adams once predicted that if the Framers left women out of the new republic they were founding, the "ladies" would "foment a rebellion." Here it was.

While Ginsburg was trying to get Mel Wulf's attention to let her in on *Reed v. Reed* in the fall of 1970, Suzy Post went to the next level. Why, she and her caucus asked in a fiery letter, were there not more women in a position to decide whatever issue came along? Why was the ACLU National Board 91 percent male? The women began to use dirty words like "quota."

Just then, Ginsburg and the caucus women caught a break from two men at the top of the ACLU. The newly elected executive director, Aryeh Neier, adopted a strategy he had developed at his former post, the New York Civil Liberties Union, which involved identifying a problem and putting a civil liberties frame around it. One such problem was the society assigning groups to enclaves of inequality. Neier and the other NYCLUers included women high on the list of groups with a history of unequal treatment, now making a claim to equality as a matter of civil rights. At the ACLU, the volunteer general counsel Norman Dorsen, also a law professor, readily endorsed the concept of equality as a civil liberties issue and assigned a student to make the argument for the ERA. Under their leadership, the ACLU weighed in on the feminist revolution.

THE GRANDMOTHER OF ALL BRIEFS

When they didn't hear back from Mel Wulf, the Ginsburgs rattled their network a little harder. When Norman Dorsen found a copy of the Ginsburgs' brief for Charles Moritz in his mail, he didn't just write to Ruth, he copied Wulf. Within days, Ruth's phone rang. It was Wulf. Would his old camp buddy like to help him on the *Reed v. Reed* brief?

Ginsburg hung up and called her girls: Janice Goodman and Mary F. Kelly, the NYU students who had carried the word about the Women and the Law class across the river to Rutgers; Ann Freedman, one of the three student authors of the authoritative *Yale Law Journal* article on the merits of the Equal Rights Amendment, who was just finishing up at Yale; and Ginsburg's own student Diana Rigelman, who had just graduated.

Okay, hotshots, now's your chance. This could be our *Brown*. Rigelman, Freedman, Goodman, and Kelly had all been in college in the hottest years of the '60s, yet, as the era drew to a close, these women had chosen law school rather than joining the SDS and mobilizing against the Vietnam War. Although Freedman, for example, was deeply involved with the New Haven Women's Liberation Union, defending Black Panthers and protesting the Vietnam War, she was still attending Yale Law School. In their dreams they were Thurgood Marshall, circa 1954. The racial civil rights movement had given birth to the women's movement. Now the racial legal rights movement would give rise to the women's legal rights movement.

To the twenty-something law students, Ruth Bader Ginsburg, at thirty-eight, was an emissary from another generation. "She was not somebody who wanted to dismantle capitalism, the master's house," says Ann Freedman. "But she also wasn't an apologist for the existing order. She saw the harm that sexist rules did in ordinary people's lives. But in her generation, what attracted people to the law was the process. She was always a lawyer's lawyer." The movement lawyers were going to a Supreme Court that still had no women clerks. A lawyer's lawyer was just what the movement needed.

The highest goal was obvious: get the court to see sex like race. Ginsburg's team of young legal activists turned to the research that feminist law students had been gathering about Women and the Law for the courses they were creating out of whole cloth and to support the movement for an Equal Rights Amendment in Congress. James Madison's wife, Dolley, they found, had written letters in the eighteenth century comparing women's status to that of slaves. The man widely credited with doing the spadework to support the civil rights movement, the great sociologist of race Gunnar Myrdal, had compared slaves to women. In law school, they had all learned the heroic narrative of how progressive lawyers such as Louis Brandeis, later the first Jew on the Supreme Court, had broken the ban on protective labor legislation by drowning the court with social science data on the terrible conditions in factories. In *Brown*, Marshall used scientific studies about black children in segregated schools choosing white dolls over black toys when offered a selection to convince the Court that separate could never be equal. So it was no surprise that the students gave Ginsburg a draft brimming over with data about the changing place of women in society—their workforce participation, their rising levels of education, their long march to suffrage.

From her office at Rutgers Law School, Professor Ginsburg

added the legal argument. The Court should treat sex distinctions like race, she argued—something people are born with and which should not determine their fates. If she won that argument, the entire structure of discriminatory American law would buckle. Like the society at large and the *Harvard Law Review*, much of the American legal system was built on the assumption that women were different from men, and usually not in a good way. When the Supreme Court reporter Nina Totenberg saw Ginsburg's brief in *Reed*, she was stunned to see the comparison between sex and race. She'd always thought the Fourteenth Amendment was for African Americans. So she shut herself in the little phone booth the Court provided for reporters and called the professor at Rutgers. Only after she got an hour-long lecture on Professor Ginsburg's view of the deep similarities between the two examples of exclusion did she understand completely what the feminist intellectual was after. Ginsburg, Totenberg says, may not like the press, but she has always known how to use it.

Ginsburg had another arrow in her quiver. The rising tide of opposition to the Equal Rights Amendment pending in the Senate reflected the culture's ambivalence about equating sex equality with racial equality. Strictly speaking, Ginsburg did not need the Court to go that far. She could win just by getting the Supreme Court to say the law was so unjustified as to be irrational, the lowest standard that any legal distinction must meet. Any application of the Fourteenth Amendment to sex would be a move forward. She could try for the larger victory later.

Reed v. Reed, challenging the Idaho law that automatically chose men over women to administer dead people's estates, should be easy to win under this low standard, Ginsburg hoped. It was a weird moment in Court history. By the time of the argument in *Reed v. Reed*, the Court was down from nine to seven. Chief Justice Earl Warren, who gave his name to the Court that made the legal civil rights revolution, and the liberal Abe Fortas both left the Court in 1969, and were replaced by Warren Burger and Harry Blackmun. Right before *Reed v. Reed*, Hugo Black and John Marshall Harlan left. President Nixon was considering their replacements.

Of the remaining seven, William O. Douglas, once the young Turk of the New Deal, could still be counted on to vote for an equality claim, as could William Brennan, the old Democratic pol and the premier theorist of the Warren Court, and Thurgood Marshall, the iconic leader of the racial civil rights movement. Since the Court was down to seven, technically, Sally Reed needed only one more vote. Chief Justice Warren Burger and Associate Justice Harry Blackmun, the leading edge of the Republican backlash against the Warren Court, were not invariably conservative. Eisenhower's Potter Stewart and JFK's appointee Byron White were considered centrist. Somewhere in those four, the ACLU thought it could harvest at least one vote. By 1971, it was unlikely that four members of the Court would rule that women, by virtue of their sex, were presumptively unfit to do the simple task of administering their dead sons' estates.

Looking at the Court to come, however, Ginsburg knew the justices and their likely successors would not find many other laws discriminating against women too silly and irrational to pass constitutional muster. Assumptions about the fundamental differences between the sexes were deep and broad. Nixon had taken office vowing to put an end to social experimentation under the guise of constitutional fiat. He was about to make two more appointments, for a record four appointments in one term. All the Women and the Law seminars in the world could not change the fact that given the Court's present—and future—mind-set, most laws based on assumptions of sex differences would probably meet the low standard of mere rationality. Ginsburg had to find a way to jazz up the process of thinking about women's equality far enough to produce real results for future cases but not so far as to scare Stewart and White, the crucial two centrist old horses on the Supreme Court at the time. She needed a middle road between mere rationality and equating sex with race.

If you look hard enough in the American legal system you can find precedent for almost anything. No one was a harder looker than Ruth Bader Ginsburg. As Ann Freedman, a coworker on the *Reed* brief, put it, she had an amazing "ability to zero in on the task at hand."

Working on the original *Moritz* appeal, the Ginsburgs had found *F.S. Royster Guano v. Virginia*, the fifty-year-old unfortunately titled "bird shit" case. In *Royster Guano*, the Court struck down a state law that taxed different kinds of corporations differently, saying the distinction in the law did not advance the state's purpose enough to justify discriminating between mostly in-state and mostly out-of-state companies. Even in light of the states' broad discretion in local tax matters, the Court said, a discriminatory law must at least fairly and substantially advance the legislature's purpose in passing it. To a normal person, the difference between "rationally related to a legitimate state interest," the conventional low standard for reviewing discrimination, and "fairly and substantially" advancing the interest, the *Royster Guano* standard, does not seem world-altering. And in the half century since the Court decided this obscure equal-protection case in 1920, it had played no role in the Court's evolving equal protection jurisprudence. No one actually cared whether it was unconstitutional in 1920 for Virginia to favor Virginia corporations with entirely out-of-state business over corporations with only some out-of-state business.

But in interpreting the Fourteenth Amendment of the United States Constitution, the difference between a law that is merely "rational" and one that must be "fair and substantial" creates an opening big enough to drive a legal revolution through. The ACLU brief in *Reed* offered the Court bird shit, aka an opportunity to look a little harder at lines between the sexes.

With exquisitely careful legal analysis for the court and a working relationship with the Supreme Court press, Ginsburg was on her way. She did not argue *Reed v. Reed*; that honor went to the Idaho lawyer who started it (the argument was, by all reports, a complete disaster). She merely spearheaded the ACLU's brief, detailing the history of women's suffering and invoking *Royster Guano*.

The Court did not equate sex with race when it decided *Reed v. Reed*. But when the Supreme Court issued its unanimous opinion striking down the Idaho law that preferred men to women in November 1971, it carried the loaded language Ruth had excavated from the avian fertilizer case. The days of assuming automatically that women were different from the standard citizen were over. From then on, the hundreds of remaining laws the movement had identified as preferring men—or women, as it turned out—would have to show a "fair and substantial" reason for distinguishing between them. The government could no longer assume for its convenience that women, the little darlings, would be too ditsy to administer estates—or anything else. Even the conservative Warren Burger signed on to that.

Professor Ginsburg was about to start taking down those laws. There have been many female lawyers in America, a few before and many after Ruth Bader Ginsburg. And many of them have devoted themselves to the feminist legal movement or served, as Sandra Day O'Connor would, as incomparable role models, with stunning results. But the constitutional scholar Geoffrey Stone, who was clerking for Justice William Brennan when Ginsburg made her own first oral argument in the Supreme Court, calls her "simply the most important woman lawyer in the history of the Republic."

3

Goldwater Girl and Card-Carrying Member of the ACLU

❧

DEMOCRACY AND DISTRUST

Professor Ginsburg wasn't the only young woman lawyer cataloguing laws that made unwarranted distinctions between men and women. So, as it happened, was newly elected State Senator Sandra O'Connor.

O'Connor's files from the early 1970s, like Ginsburg's, might be titled "The Unexpectedly Radical Feminist Clippings File of an Apparently Unthreatening Professional Woman." In 1971, O'Connor was reading about the edgy new feminists of Los Angeles and single-by-choice New York radicals in filthy Greenwich Village walk-ups.

Most strikingly, State Senator O'Connor obtained—and kept— the 1970 special issue on women from the distinctly cosmopolitan *Atlantic Monthly*. Why, the introduction to the special issue asked, were "American women, while enjoying more material, political, and social advantages than any other women in history . . . nonetheless so discontent with their lot?" And the editors got an earful. The writer Catherine Drinker Bowen speculated that the Revolution was imminent, in light of the falling birthrate, since, surely, "no woman can devote a life to the raising of [only] two [kids]." Paula Stern, fresh out of graduate school at Harvard, described marriage as a refuge from a hostile world and an agency in making sure it stayed bad in the future: "Once married she can stop fighting cultural stereotypes and start teaching them to her children."

Sociologist and women's rights activist Alice Rossi told the magazine the insulting stories she had been gathering from working women, stories that must have been resonant and reassuring to the Stanford law grad who was offered only a secretarial berth when she applied. "I never wanted to teach grade school children," one woman had told Rossi. "But I found so much prejudice and resentment against me in my first job in an architectural firm . . . that I couldn't take it. I left and switched to teaching art. At least I feel welcome in a school." Another reported that she "had the experience last year of seeing a job I had filled for two years upgraded when it was filled by a man, at double the salary I was paid for the same work. College-trained women are lumped with the secretarial and clerical staff, while college-trained men are seen as potential executives. A few years of this and everybody is behaving according to what is expected of them, not what they are capable of."

Rossi's article included this now-commonplace but then-revolutionary insight: "If [women] are vital and assertive, they are rejected as 'aggressive bitches out to castrate men.' If they are quiet and unassuming, they are rejected as 'unlikely to amount to much.'" O'Connor struggled visibly to thread that same needle. She ran for office, but she ran home to make dinner every night for her husband and three sons. In an early speech to women students at the local university, she extolled the virtues of dependence on a male spouse: "Those women who are fortunate enough to have husbands or other means to support them can truly enjoy the freedom of choice to select that work which is most satisfying to them, and to select work of a part time or occasional nature." She repeated without irony John O'Connor's joke about her career in speeches about how to combine love and work. "I think it is a tribute to American democracy," O'Connor's lawyer husband said, "when a cook, who moonlights as a janitor, can be elected to high public office."

When O'Connor wrote to President Nixon in 1971 on the subject of the two Supreme Court nominations he had before him, it was merely "to encourage [him] to consider" for appointment "one of the well-qualified women lawyers in our country today." But

she hastened to reassure him that she was "confident that [his] se-
lections will be well-considered and wise." After all, "Chief Justice
Warren Burger has already proven himself to the American people
to have been a splendid choice." (Unknown to O'Connor, Burger
had made his opposition to a female nomination clear to the president, threatening to resign if the president polluted the Court with
a woman.)

O'Connor may have read the *Atlantic* articles on What Women
Want, but she turned down the page corner at the piece that cata-
logued the laws at every level of American government that treated
women differently. The Equal Rights Amendment–fueled attack
on the web of legal discrimination against women suited her perfectly. Exactly like Ginsburg at her feminist awakening, O'Connor
began creating a hit list of such laws in her case in the state she was
helping to govern and set about having them changed.

The first task was a no-brainer: repeal the state law limiting
women to an eight-hour workday. Here, the Republican legislator's conservative free-market principles and her commitment to
women's equality overlapped perfectly. (She did not know that
Ginsburg always saw protections such as the eight-hour-day law as
an excuse to keep women out of better jobs.) As at the ACLU, the
forces of liberalism were divided on whether it was more important
to make women equal—by letting them work the same hours
as men—or to protect them. The liberals for protection—unions,
liberal Democrats—were against O'Connor in the Arizona legislature. Even though these forces of liberalism were receding in
Arizona by then, she prevailed by only a single vote.

The Equal Rights Amendment, then being heard by the U.S.
Senate Judiciary Committee, would have struck down all state
laws that discriminated on the basis of sex. But despite her later
claims to support the equality measure, she initially told students
at ASU, "I'm not sure the equal rights amendment is necessary. I
am inclined to believe that a few well-chosen cases brought before
the federal courts would establish the equality of women under the
equal protection clause of the Fourteenth Amendment, and the
civil rights act, in a meaningful way."

Thousands of miles away, of course, Ruth Bader Ginsburg was pounding on Mel Wulf to let her in on the first well-chosen case. In any event, O'Connor had another idea about how to make the world a better place for women. If women wanted the world to change, she advised the students, they would have to use their electoral power more wisely and run for public office. She thought social change should come from the bottom up. And she thought the presence of women in public life—working hard and asking no favors—would change the society like nothing else.

Two years after her remarks, O'Connor, by then majority leader of the state senate, got her chance to do as she had advised the ASU students and help women through her electoral power. On March 22, 1972, the Equal Rights Amendment passed the U.S. Senate. Accompanied by a halo of bipartisan goodwill, it arrived at Majority Leader O'Connor's Senate Committee for hearings on ratification by the state. State legislatures were falling all over themselves in a race to ratify. When the women's activist Irene Rasmussen, then the wife of one of John O'Connor's associates, went to Senator O'Connor to urge her to get it passed, O'Connor assured her it was a done deal. She had already been thoroughly lobbied to heat up her lukewarm support for the ERA by a pal from her Phoenix social circle, the chair of the White House Women's Commission, Jacqueline Gutwillig.

Wanting to see it happen, Rasmussen took herself down to the meeting of the Senate committee that had the ERA in its power. As Rasmussen remembers, "The Equal Rights Amendment came up on the agenda in the Judiciary Committee. And John Conlan [Republican committee chairman] said something very mild like, 'You know, this is a big national deal, I don't think we should rush into this, I think we should study it, and hold some hearings, and talk about it, what do you think Majority Leader O'Connor?' And, without batting an eye," Rasmussen remembers, "she gave in."

The delay was a death knell for the ERA in Arizona. In the early years of ERA revival, the measure had bipartisan support. President Nixon's own Citizens Advisory Council on the Status of Women, led by O'Connor's pal Gutwillig, had generated the legal theory that most supporters used to defend the amendment. But O'Connor's mentor and inspiration, Barry Goldwater, had already signaled the position of the party's conservative wing by voting against it in the U.S. Senate. On April 10, right after O'Connor introduced the measure in Arizona, he wrote her a letter to share his concern that the amendment would try to "change the design of the Lord by making men and women identical." Led on the ground in Arizona by State Senator Conlan, O'Connor's Republican Party followed Goldwater to the right. Across the country in St. Louis, Missouri, Phyllis Schlafly, an old-fashioned red-baiting woman lawyer with a beehive hairdo, weighed in to STOP, as her signs brilliantly stated, the ERA. Schlafly, who had self-published a book in support of Goldwater in 1964, had become a force to be reckoned with in the increasingly conservative Republican Party. Despite herself being a female lawyer and an activist, when she got wind of the ERA, she saw red.

Flogged by Schlafly, who formed a prescient alliance of fundamentalist religious groups, the Republican Party rescinded its commitment to the women's amendment. Republican state legislators started to oppose its ratification. For the next year, O'Connor was caught between her ambitions in a conservative Republican Party and her professed concern for women's rights. When asked, she sent a mealymouthed "on the other hand" letter about how reasonable people could differ on the merits of the ERA. While she did not believe it threatened family life or women's freedom, "many sincere and genuine questions have been raised," she wrote. She tried to get rid of the politically inconvenient amendment by sending it to the people to vote on directly in a referendum. When that did not work, she voted to send it to the Senate floor. But it was too late. The motion to report the ERA out of committee to the whole Senate lost 5–4. The easy days of feminist principles and conservative politics were over.

O'Connor was not working in a private study on the Upper East Side of Manhattan or out of an academic office. She was in the trenches of the Arizona state legislature. And when it came to the ERA, the Arizona soil was as hostile a landscape for women as the desert O'Connor's family tried to ranch. Comparing her inability to get traction on women's equality with the comparative ease of Ginsburg's litigation initiative in the same years illustrates the appeal of a top-down strategy rather than state-by-state legislative battles. The ACLU litigator Ginsburg was addressing life-tenured federal judges. And life-tenured federal judges don't have to worry about being reelected.

Rasmussen and other feminist activists blamed O'Connor squarely for advancing her political ambition instead of using her power to push the ERA. "Justice Sandra Day O'Connor," Rasmussen says, "had a lot of mileage ever since then as being an Equal Rights Amendment supporter, and so forth, and in fact, she was not and she had the power and she didn't exercise it, and she allowed an ambitious man to overwhelm her . . . she was pointless from that time on."

From that point on, O'Connor got the reputation of being someone who didn't pick losing battles, not necessarily a bad thing in someone seeking to make a political career in an entirely male world increasingly beholden to the revived conservative movement. Ginsburg was famous for picking her battles, too. But she was picking among various claims for litigation within an overall commitment to the movement for women's equality, not weighing women's equality against unrelated ends.

As it turned out, despite Rasmussen's disillusionment, O'Connor's self-advancement advanced the movement. Years later, when Irene Rasmussen brought her young daughter Rachel to Washington, she went to visit her old friend at the Supreme Court. Justice O'Connor gave them a grand tour and took them to lunch in the justices' dining room. It was good, Rasmussen admits, for Rachel to see a successful woman making it at that elevated level. Perhaps O'Connor had put her career first, but, had she not been so strategic, would she have been there to show Rachel it could be done at all?

WITH LIBERAL FRIENDS, WHO NEEDS ENEMIES?

While O'Connor was struggling with her competing loyalties in Arizona, Ginsburg was working her constituency: the lawyers.

Although they were not as conservative as the Arizona Republicans with whom O'Connor was contending, the organized bar wasn't exactly falling all over itself for sex equality either. In April 1971, as Congress was considering the Equal Rights Amendment, the *American Bar Association Journal* published an article by a lawyer's wife: "Don't try to have the last word in an argument," the distaff side of the profession advised. "Be prepared to serve scrambled eggs with a smile at 10 p.m. Women's lib notwithstanding, be sure his sox match."

At its annual meeting in 1971 the American Bar Association held a mock arbitration, which they titled, to their own immense amusement, "Will London Bridge? or Women's Lib?" The convention theatricals apparently centered on an imaginary dispute over whether the women's movement in New York created such a state of social unrest that a project to build a transatlantic bridge from London would have to be scrapped. When the good fun was reported in the bar association's magazine, it elicited the predictable response from the handful of female members. According to a furious letter to the editor, the ABA presented as witnesses for women a hussy who had abandoned her husband and children and was a *lesbian*, of all things. One could not imagine, the letter writer suggested, that the ABA would amuse itself with such a treatment of, say, the racial civil rights movement.

Ginsburg responded to the deployment of mockery in typical fashion with a dry, scholarly article in the same publication, arguing that the ERA was necessary because of the gender-biased federal and state laws that might take forever to undo, one at a time. (In protected environments, Ginsburg was a lot more forthright and a lot funnier. Speaking of the ABA article to a gathering of women activists, she noted that the Bridges and Libs matter had been argued exclusively by men, none of whom "claimed any expertise regarding women or bridges.") Early on, Ginsburg suggested that decisions about women might have better outcomes if women were involved in making them. Not only would the experience of women doing demanding jobs well change men's minds about their inclusion, they would also make better decisions.

Smarmy mockery in bar association magazines was the least of her problems. Just before the ERA went to the states, a bomb-throwing article by the prestigious constitutional law scholar Philip Kurland, "The Equal Rights Amendment: Some Problems of Construction," gave Schlafly and her troops all the legal ammunition they needed. Kurland, who, with Ginsburg's old Harvard Law School dinner-party companion Herbert Wechsler, had led the scholarly assault on the desegregation decisions of the Warren Court, was a natural for the job of arguing against women's equality.

He had already testified against the ERA in hearings before Senator Sam Ervin. Like the Republican Barry Goldwater, Ervin saw the equality amendment as a frivolous fashion intended to upset the Lord's order. (Before taking up the cause of inequality for women, the North Carolina senator, who became sort of a folk hero when he presided over the Watergate hearings, was a legendary opponent of racial civil rights.) Claiming no agenda, Kurland presented himself as merely alerting people to possible consequences of the new law, using the tried-and-proven strategy of masking arguments against social change in the seductive guise of scholarly and constitutional purity.

The Equal Rights Amendment was an outright amendment, not a judicial interpretation of the existing text, so Kurland could not claim, as he had in the *Brown* debate, that the Court had overstepped the constitutional language and imposed its own values. He had to take a different tack. As with his attack on *Brown*, Kurland professed to be sympathetic to the *goal* of eliminating some forms of sex discrimination. But he was worried about the social disruption that would ensue. Protective labor legislation (limits on the hours women could work, for example) and protective domestic labor legislation like alimony would be swept away, leaving housewives and workers exposed to the chill winds of equal rights, he feared. The law might no longer require women to change their names upon marriage. Women would be drafted. They might have to go to the same public colleges or use the same toilets as men. Anyway, if women are aggrieved, why don't they just use their majority status and change the laws? They're not like black people, he argued, a real minority (whose constitutional rights Kurland had also resisted in his rabid criticisms of the school desegregation decision). Kurland always managed to come out against equality, and always from the purest of motives.

Regardless of the purity of Kurland's motives, his article did something a fundamentalist religious alliance led by a former Bircher like Schlafly could never do. Because it came from a prestigious constitutional law professor, it made opposition to the ERA respectable. When social change depends on legal change, law professors, usually rather marginal to politics, matter a lot. Kurland's most incendiary charges—unisex toilets, women drafted—turned out not to happen, and much of the equalization of employment practices would happen as a result of the coverage of women in the 1964 Civil Rights Act even without the ERA. But Kurland was correct about the demise of single-sex public colleges and he was right that real legal gender equality changes society a lot. That warning, in the hands of the conservative firebrand Schlafly, was enough to doom the ERA.

Liberal constitutional scholars, including Ginsburg's ACLU colleague Norman Dorsen, lined up ten deep on the other side. But it did not help. People expected scholars at the ACLU to support the ERA. That Kurland, a respected faculty member at a major law school, weighed in *against* disruption of the universe of sexual stereotypes was unexpected and therefore powerful. Although they ultimately voted to support the Equal Rights Amendment, even the ACLU board of directors, when pressed by the new social developments, also fretted over the possibility of women in men's prisons and toilets.

In classic Ginsburg style, even in the heat of battle she wrote politely to her colleague Philip Kurland and her old Harvard professor Paul Freund, who had joined him in opposition: "I am so sorry," she penned, "to see you used this way." Never one to give offense unless strictly necessary, in a speech published a few years later she mildly described it as "Curious" to hear such opinions from "gentlemen with extraordinary minds, and rare talent for making relevant connections."

As Ginsburg was well aware as the ERA went down, not only did these male scholars help defeat the ERA, their prior criticism of the racial civil rights decisions made any ensuing effort to achieve equality through the existing Constitution much harder to pull off. The Court, these professors contended, overreached in reading the racially motivated Fourteenth Amendment's equality language to forbid segregation by race. How much greater was the violation in applying the equality principles to women, who weren't even mentioned in the Civil War amendments? Legal feminists were damned by these law professors if they did try to change the Constitution and damned if they tried to use the Constitution as it was. Truly, an "extraordinary mind" is a terrible thing to waste.

But Ginsburg was a soldier. She re-upped, writing, speaking, providing others with arguments. From 1970, when she wrote to the members of the Judiciary Committees of both houses of Congress, to the day she first became a federal judge in 1980, she was working for the enactment of the ERA. Trying to buck up her colleague Professor Joan Krauskopf, who had apparently met with a screamer at an appearance in 1974, Ginsburg instructs that she must "meet irrational arguments with facts and cool reason." She was anointed to defend the amendment by the powerful gatekeepers who ran the opinion page at *The New York Times*. She gave ammunition to the League of Women Voters. She wrote a letter to the *Times* after some rabbi predicted the world would end. As befitted a woman already legendary for her focus, she prepared notes to deliver "Three Minutes on the ERA" on NPR.

Almost certainly at the same time the Arizona legislature was voting to kill the ERA, she stood at NYU with Norman Dorsen, addressing a huge rally in favor of the amendment. After her rousing speech to the crowd, Dorsen leaned down, as everyone does, to address the diminutive attorney, and said, "You know, this is never going to pass." She really didn't want to hear that, he recalled.

Like Sandra Day O'Connor, Ruth Bader Ginsburg wasn't much for picking losers. Although she never faltered publicly in her support of the Equal Rights Amendment, she was not a legislator, so she didn't have to choose between the amendment and her personal ambitions for her career. While the nation pondered an Equal Rights Amendment, cases like *Reed v. Reed* and *Moritz v. Commissioner of Internal Revenue* were her idea of a good plan to move women's equality along. Congress stripped her of the *Moritz* appeal by changing the unjust law and mooting it out. But cases were breaking out everywhere.

THE WOMEN'S RIGHTS PROJECT HAS A THOUSAND MOTHERS

As she turned to the ACLU as the focus of her activism, Ginsburg was keenly aware of the organization's checkered feminist past. Although they had nothing to do with the brief in *Reed v. Reed*, she put the names of the two women, Dorothy Kenyon and Pauli Murray, who had fought the ACLU board for decades to recognize women's claims, on the cover of the brief. She knew whose shoulders she stood on. (Kenyon died within months.)

After the 1970 ACLU Biennial Conference had teed up the issue of women's rights, the newly formed Equality Committee began flooding the board with policy positions. "Sex," along with "race, color, religion and national origin," should be included in all civil rights legislation; the Fifth and Fourteenth Amendments require equal treatment regardless of sex, and legislation and education to "combat" discrimination against women should be pursued full throttle.

The ACLU board set limits on its commitment to equality broadly defined. Sex discrimination in employment would be opposed, but, even with the exception for "reasonable bases for differentiation," the board could not accept the idea of women in combat. When they voted, the ACLU agreed to leave the military out of their policy position. It would take more than forty years until the U.S. military removed the last barriers for women in the armed services. The academic freedom committee resisted the proposal that all private colleges should become coed, fretting over men's and women's freedom to associate only with their own kind.

While the solons of the civil liberties union dithered over

Harvard and Wellesley, Professor Ginsburg simply moved forward to integrate her own school. Rutgers University was a sex-segregated public college, with Rutgers College, a men's school, and Douglass College, a smaller, separate school for women. After the board of directors refused to dismantle this structure, then dean Richard McCormick appealed for help to his feminist colleague at the law school. On April 13, 1971, Ginsburg wrote to acting Rutgers president Richard Schlatter, informing him that a recent federal decision ordering the University of Virginia to integrate women "renders Rutgers College vulnerable" to a similar action. And so Rutgers admitted women to the men's school and disbanded Douglass College.

Worse than the threat to private single-sex colleges, from the standpoint of the ACLU old guard, the 1970 conference took direct aim at the ACLU itself. The ACLU must, it recommended, "take affirmative and vigorous action . . . to increase significantly the representation of women on all policy making bodies and committees of the organization. *Token representation will no longer be acceptable.*" The ACLU, the rebels of 1970 resolved, had "underutilized the potentialities and talents of women in its organization."

In October 1971, the ACLU board voted unanimously to add women's rights as a new priority. On December 4, a panel of women appeared before the board to argue for a women's rights project. One of the presenters at the December meeting was "Prof. Ginzberg [*sic*] Rutgers University and Harvard University law professor." (In her presentation, Ginsburg told her now-routine story about the century of Supreme Court decisions against women— that they could be discouraged from serving on juries in *Hoyt v. Florida* or, in *Goesaert v. Cleary*, forbidden to tend bars—a sorry history punctuated by the victory in *Reed v. Reed* a month before the ACLU board met.)

This laconic note of her Harvard status in the ACLU minutes speaks volumes. Some years into the feminist movement, during the fall semester of 1971, Ginsburg was visiting at Harvard Law School, which had just noticed it had no permanent female faculty. When the ACLU board met, it was not at all clear that Harvard would offer the lowly Rutgers professor a permanent position. In fact, when Harvard Law School hesitated and asked her to come back for a second term visit, she spurned them, accepting an offer from Columbia instead. When the exquisitely status-conscious directors of the ACLU surveyed the women before them, Ginsburg was the closest thing to a tenured Harvard professor. If the ACLU was going to wrap the civil liberties mantle around the unruly feminist revolution, it would at least have a clubbable spokesman. By the time the December board meeting adjourned, the budget for 1972 included the additional legal costs of a Women's Rights Project.

Executive Director Aryeh Neier often set up special projects addressing issues of paramount importance to him with employees answerable directly to him. At an earlier time he believed that the black civil rights struggle was the driving force in other struggles for civil rights. Now he believed women's rights had taken the lead. And he had identified Ginsburg as his designated hitter.

He had good reason. When hiring, he always asked for a writing sample. And once he saw hers, he knew he didn't need to look any further. Not only was she a brilliant thinker and writer, Neier thought, she was someone who commanded sober attention. "I wanted someone who would take an issue which at that moment was the subject of a certain amount of mockery and who would deal with it with the gravitas which it deserved."

As the Rutgers student skit had shown, if there's one thing Ruth Bader Ginsburg had, it was gravitas. And she had theory. No Separate Categories. That was her overriding and lifelong message. There was another advantage, too. Picking Ginsburg out of the pool of women lawyers available in 1971 did not trigger the angry jealousy that often erupts when a movement leader emerges. As the activist Ann Freedman put it, "When that person is as talented and exceptional as everyone acknowledges Ruth always has been, it's not surprising that when opportunities open up people want her to play those roles. No one says, 'You're making *Ruth* the head of that?'"

Within two months of the 1971 presentation, Neier reported

to the board that the Women's Rights Project would begin, and Ruth Bader Ginsburg would be the director. Since she was going to move from Rutgers Law School to Columbia, the ACLU would split her time with her new employer.

Despite the founding of the Women's Rights Project, the ACLU had hardly turned into a female paradise. In the wake of the 1970 meeting, the women's caucus devised a plan to survey the affiliates for their female ranks and numbers and actively recruit women for the highest-ranking jobs. Most radical of all, they proposed to expand the heavily male, insular national board and establish quotas for female representation.

The female activists triggered two years of gender conflict at the liberal organization. A committee to implement the women's representation policy produced a robust proposal accompanied by an unsigned "supporting memorandum." The memorandum, prepared by the newly founded ACLU Women's Rights Project, has Ginsburg's fingerprints all over it. It begins with an excerpt from her brief for the ACLU in *Reed v. Reed*. Moving, as usual, from one dry case citation to another in a businesslike way, the memo innocently inserts the ACLU's own policy on racial affirmative action into the middle of the argument. One of Ginsburg's favorite themes—that women are socialized such that they cannot "push on an open door"—answers the argument she saw coming that a majority such as women don't need quotas.

This time even Ginsburg's friendly persuasion did not work. Good limousine liberals, the ACLU board members declined to apply their own quota standards to themselves. The histories rarely record that the Thurgood Marshall of the women's movement failed to convince her own institution to move affirmatively on gender. By 1974, women finally began to make a substantial appearance in the national and local ACLU boardrooms.

Faced with a battle she couldn't win, Ruth, typically, turned a deaf ear. Despite the ACLU's reluctance to serve as a role model for other institutions, the Women's Rights Project, designed to force gender change, worked beyond anyone's fondest dreams. Ruth Bader Ginsburg had a gift for partnerships, and her relationship with the ACLU was no exception. They even had a honeymoon suite. Neier, a legendary fund-raiser, had spotted the offices of the bankrupt Johns Manville Company in midtown Manhattan and got the lease for a song. For perhaps the first time in history, the civil rights organization challenged the establishment from "wood paneled offices," Neier remembers with glee. "Ruth was there more than she was at Columbia. After all, she lived on the Upper East Side. And it didn't hurt that the surroundings were so pleasant."

Aware of Ginsburg's weaknesses as well as her strengths, Neier hired a second woman—the movement activist Brenda Feigen Fasteau, right off the masthead of the new *Ms.* magazine. The ACLU was the ideal location for Ginsburg's careful, incremental strategy. Most social-change law firms have to root around for plaintiffs, using their informal movement connections to identify the issues that are appropriate for litigation and hoping for appealing individuals and fact patterns. In its national network of chapters with a well-established reputation for litigating peoples' grievances, the ACLU had a built-in pipeline to every imaginable potential plaintiff. It didn't hurt that the chapters were part of the national women's initiative, and that the ACLU had charged its chapters with developing women's initiatives of their own. Feigen Fasteau was busy identifying a laundry list of areas for action: employment, credit, public aid to discriminating private institutions, education, training—and, what turned out to be a nonstarter for the project, reproductive control.

The trove of litigation possibilities turned up by the Women and the Law movement paled beside the population of aggrieved American women. Once the lens of gender equality was put on American law, complaints arrived with alarming speed. Letters, they got letters. "I have paid into Social Security for twenty-five years," writes Mary Ferrari of Richmond, California, "and was denied Social Security Benefits for my husband." Shelly Lutzker made scores of telephone calls for jobs after an airline laid her off for being pregnant, but the New York employment office did not believe her efforts were sincere. She was, after all, pregnant. Toni Strausbaugh, nine-year marine veteran and single mother of two, wanted to enlist in the National Guard but was barred because of her dependent children. Air force second lieutenant Carol Pyles wanted her commission reinstated after being discharged for pregnancy. Debra Monsoor was trying to make it at a strip mine in Wyoming. She was paid less, harassed physically and verbally, and denied any chance at training or promotion.

Angry women who couldn't get promoted, couldn't find out the criteria for promotion, suspected unequal pay, couldn't see the collective bargaining agreement, were qualified but rejected—all wrote to the ACLU, which could not handle even a small percentage of the grievances that came pouring in. This posed a big problem for the orderly Professor Ginsburg, who wanted to follow Thurgood Marshall's example and bring the most obvious cases to the Supreme Court first, paving the way for the more radical issues to follow. Thus, discrimination between sexes for who could administer estates, case *Reed v. Reed*, came before cases with real social heft, challenging pregnancy discrimination or the male-only draft. Ginsburg had her capable hands full trying to ride herd on the "uppity women" who wanted to sue everyone and take their places in the ranks of the equal.

One problem she did not have to deal with (and therefore could not control) was the core feminist issue, abortion, which the Supreme Court ultimately would decide in *Roe v. Wade* in 1973. Indeed, Justice O'Connor, then state senate majority leader, had a much closer, and politically more perilous, relationship to this hot issue than Ginsburg, the feminist icon. In 1970, three years before *Roe v. Wade*, O'Connor had supported an unsuccessful bill to repeal the sweeping Arizona criminal prohibition against abortion. After *Roe*, which struck down all such laws, she resisted state efforts to pass a stricter law than the Court would allow and to petition Congress to stop the practice. Although O'Connor was hardly a champion of choice—she supported efforts to stop the state from funding abortions for poor women and supported laws allowing hospital workers to refuse to participate in them—Arizona abortion opponents still tried to stop her appointment to the Supreme Court when the time came.

The ACLU was legal counsel in one of the two companion cases that go by the name *Roe v. Wade*, but Ginsburg was protected from the abortion problem for a crass reason. Aryeh Neier was eager to tap into the resources of the Ford Foundation for the ACLU, and, he says, Ford, while explicitly open to appeals from the burgeoning feminist movement, would not fund anything related to abortion. Ginsburg's separation from the abortion issue was thus an accident of history but one with profound consequences. She might never have been confirmed to the Supreme Court had she been involved in the ACLU's extensive efforts to secure abortion rights for women. On the flip side, the abortion litigation, which was spun off to the nascent ACLU Reproductive Freedom Project, did not benefit from Ginsburg's theoretical grounding, discipline, and strategic bent.

Maddeningly, to Ginsburg, she came within a hairsbreadth of presenting the issue in the perfect case for female self-determination, deliciously, a case of forced abortion. In 1970, the air force sent Captain Susan Struck home from Vietnam, on the grounds that she was pregnant. Take a free government abortion, the air force offered, or we'll discharge you. Instead, Struck sued. Tossing her out of her government job because she had a baby instead of the proffered abortion violated the Constitution, she claimed. While litigating, Struck, a Catholic, had the baby and gave it up for adoption. In 1971, the Supreme Court agreed to hear her plea. Boy, did Ginsburg want to argue that one.

It is unimaginable that in 1972 the Supreme Court would have allowed the government to force an abortion on a woman as a condition of her keeping her job and military career. People have largely forgotten, but all the reproductive rights cases including *Roe* go back to a 1947 decision forbidding the government to sterilize criminals. Despite the abortion opponents' propaganda, the seminal reproductive rights decisions did not involve bead-wearing hippies wanting to have sex without consequences in the mud of Woodstock. It was the right to *have* a child that the Court protected first, in a time perilously close to the Nazi era of racial sterilizations. From that principle sprang the decisions that the government could not force people to reproduce any more than it could forbid them from doing so.

Struck had everything. In addition to proposing the forced abortion, the air force then punished Susan Struck for having had a baby at all, even though she was no longer responsible for it, treating pregnancy, which happens only to women, differently from any other disability. Men with drug and alcohol disabilities were treated better than women who got pregnant. And the government said it was for their own good! So the Struck case could have given birth to a sound, equality-based abortion decision and it also could have forestalled the risible later cases where the Court denied that pregnancy discrimination was a woman's issue.

But Ginsburg's nemesis from Harvard, the former "what are you women doing here" dean, Erwin Griswold, got in the way. By 1972, Griswold was serving as the chief government lawyer, the solicitor general of the United States. He thought the government was about to lose the *Struck* case, in the highest court in the land, weakening its ability to discriminate against pregnant women in other contexts. So he pressured the air force to repeal its policy and reinstate Captain Struck. Then he told the Supreme Court the case was moot; there was no dispute left. The Court dismissed Struck's case.

Within a few years the justices decided two cases in ways that were less favorable to women than Ginsburg hoped to have achieved. They decided *Roe v. Wade*, the abortion case, on sweeping privacy grounds instead of as an extension of the principle of women's equality. Resting on the fragile concept of "privacy," the abortion decision was politically vulnerable to claims that the "private" decision was just an arbitrary "private" choice, rather than a path to women's equality under the law. In two other cases the year after *Roe v. Wade*, the Court allowed the government to exclude pregnancy from disability benefits to save the government money.

Other than abortion rights, for the rest of the decade and for years after Ginsburg left to go on the federal bench in 1981, the ACLU Women's Rights Project was the go-to place for women's legal rights. The 1970s—the Neier years—may have been the high-water mark of the ACLU's social power. In the late stage of the Vietnam War, the Pentagon Papers and the Nixon impeachment catapulted issues of rights onto the front burner and kept them there. And Neier was by all accounts a gonzo fund-raiser. The ACLU got money from Ford, from Carnegie, and from Neier's personal piggy bank, the Playboy Foundation. The WRP had four full-time lawyers, social activists, staff, and a country full of volunteer cooperating attorneys.

By 1980 the ACLU women's initiative had gotten over a million dollars from the Ford Foundation alone. Susan Berresford, a program officer at Ford, was at the forefront of moving the foundation into its role as a funder of the feminist revolution. The ACLU brought its new "star" Ginsburg to meet the folks at Ford, and Berresford took an instant liking to her, because "she had a calm, clear, powerful argument . . . and she was compelling and smart and calm in a way that added to her certainty, she was so confident about it." Berresford's boss at Ford, Michael Svirdoff, was a wise-cracking guy with a limited tolerance for what he called "sensitivity meetings." The clear, calm Ginsburg was perfect for him.

Ginsburg's imperturbability was to be sorely tested when, in 1973, the Ford Foundation funded a meeting that Ginsburg convened along with Sylvia Roberts, the head lawyer from the National Organization for Women. Their agenda was to bring all the lawyers doing women's rights litigation around the country to a hotel conference room and try to set some priorities and divide the work. Ginsburg was always very concerned that the cases reach the Court in the order most likely to generate a growing structure of favorable decisions.

The conference is a textbook example of Ginsburg's finesse in managing the women's legal revolution. Everyone should agree, Ginsburg and Roberts decided in the early days of conference planning, that litigation would be their method and they wouldn't spend all their time at the conference reinventing the wheel. In her characteristically tidy way, Ginsburg suggested how the participants should think about the issue. Should they set priorities on issues? Should they present issues in a particular order? How should they publicize, share, support their efforts? Buried right in the middle of the list was the thing she actually cared about: "Identification of cases ripe for Supreme Court adjudication and of cases in which Supreme Court resolution should not (yet) be sought."

But the left is never tidy. When the answers to Ginsburg's questions came back, one of the participants, Mary Eastwood, suggested that the first night be devoted to the "legal philosophy of feminism" with a special emphasis on "factionalism in the women's rights movement." Ginsburg, by contrast, had hoped that the time would be spent on "what they wish to come from our meeting." But when the feminist lawyers arrived at the basement conference room of the Sheraton Russell Hotel, on the first night of the conference, April 26, they received a case study to discuss: "Daisy, Sheryl and Joan," who "live in a lovely big house in the country with a dog and three cats" and wished to adopt some children, but "the county adoption agency turned them down because of a rumor (true) that Daisy and Sheryl were a Lesbian couple, and in any event, 'three adults is not a family but a commune.'" Is lesbianism a feminist issue, Eastwood asked. And the movement lawyers were off to the races.

"Everything that concerns women is important," Ginsburg's co-moderator Sylvia Roberts suggested. "Lesbianism allows greater freedom for alternative life-styles and thus helps women and men break out of sex roles," the newly minted law professor Barbara Babcock added. "In New York," the old movement hand Janice Goodman volunteered, "many women say lesbianism is the forefront of the movement."

Ginsburg was a liberal, but she did not espouse the '60s mantra that no one is free until everyone is free. "Not all feminist issues should be litigated now," she said, "because some are losers, given the current political climate, and could set back our efforts to develop favorable law. For example, it's the wrong time to challenge veterans' preferences." As to litigating lesbianism, she innocently reminded the gathering, "A student note in a recent Yale Law Journal deals with the impact of the ERA on same-sex marriage. The note takes the position that a ban on them [same-sex marriages] would be unconstitutional under ERA. That note is now being used by opponents of ERA to scare off supporters." (The 1973 note writer was prescient; in 1993 the first court to legitimate same-sex marriage, in Hawaii, made its decision based on the Equal Rights Amendment to the state constitution.) Same-sex marriage did not concern Ginsburg at that moment. Until the day it stopped twitching, passing the Equal Rights Amendment was always her priority. Being Ginsburg, however, she put her argument in the mouths of others, in this case the Yale law student.

Ginsburg's soon-to-be project director Kathleen Peratis disagreed with her future boss. "[I] reject the idea of not doing something because it would get us a bad name in society," she contended; "there's a value in the lunatic fringe."

The ACLU board member Pauli Murray, who had been through the glory days of the NAACP Legal Defense Fund, reminded the group that picking and choosing cases was central to Thurgood Marshall's effectiveness. Why, she told the group, Marshall even turned her down when she was rejected for college in 1938 because he thought her case would not be a good-enough precedent. "One bad decision of the Supreme Court has a terrible impact," she reiterated. The participants were having none of it. Why should lawyers be deciding what issues get priority, one lawyer asked. We don't control what cases we get anyway, another asserted. Faction was the name of the game in '70s social movements.

As the '70s feminists went about their anarchic ritual, someone suggested that they simply turn to the next proposal on the agenda, a well-funded national center patterned on the model of the NAACP. Ginsburg was already a year into running the center, midwifed by Pauli Murray, and setting most of the priorities for legal feminism. With Ford Foundation support, her students at Columbia were gathering litigation through the ACLU in an effort to realize her equality agenda. Yet she said almost nothing about her role, confining her remarks throughout the conference to bland inquiries about timing and reporting on factual matters such as recent decisions.

Since Ginsburg was not leading a conventional social movement, she did not need to have many such meetings to sustain the momentum and keep the troops in line. Her razor-sharp professional skills and self-possession had already earned her a powerful position in the feminist legal movement. She just had to avoid giving offense.

"If someone else had been in that position," the ACLU's Neier believes, "I doubt they would be able to secure that degree of cooperation from other litigators in the field. . . . [S]he tended to inspire collaboration and respect rather than competition. She was not a person who was vain in any way. She did not try to capture the limelight. This was a self-effacing person who was on the one hand very disciplined in her thinking and on the other hand very kind to the people she worked with." "She has this soft little tiny voice," the NPR Court expert Nina Totenberg notes, "and she can say really devastating things in that quiet voice."

Her newfound status in the power elite did not silence the quiet voice. No sooner had she arrived at Columbia and the ACLU than she was urging her colleagues to stop their sexist antics. Right out of the box she wrote to the president of Columbia, forwarding him the wonderful Rutgers affirmative action plan for getting more women on the faculty. In classic Ginsburg fashion, she starts the letter by reminding President McGill that they had already met at a parents' night at the Dalton School. Just us natural elites here, President McGill. She wrote to the New York County Bar Association objecting to the use of the word "brethren" in light of the large participation by women in bar functions. She fussed privately and publicly about the professors and activists holding professional meetings at all-male clubs, as the Century Club was in the '70s. She comes down hard on the ACLU. Why didn't they pay more attention to my huge Supreme Court victories in their annual reports? she asks. The American Bar Association didn't give the progressive section on rights and responsibilities a big-enough room at its meeting. "Ruth got away with a lot," Janice Goodman recollects. "If I could figure out how she did it, I'd have done it myself."

Part II

Chief Litigator for the Women's Rights Project

Ruth Bader Ginsburg during the summer of 1977, when she was a scholar in residence at the Rockefeller Foundation in Bellagio, Italy.

4

Act One: Building Women's Equality

꘎

Mozart had, by many accounts, five operatic masterpieces. Jane Austen's reputation rests on five novels. As the chief litigator for the Women's Rights Project from 1971 to 1980, Ruth Bader Ginsburg argued in five great Supreme Court victories (and one loss). In five landmark cases over less than a decade, she largely transformed the constitutional status of women in America. *Reed v. Reed*, the 1971 women as administrators of estates case, might make it six, but she did not argue that one. She merely wrote the brief the Court adopted as its opinion.

DEBUT

On a cold Wednesday afternoon in January 1973, Ruth Bader Ginsburg rose to make her first argument in the United States Supreme Court. Although she was on for only ten minutes, she had not eaten lunch; in her anxiety she was afraid she would throw it up. The case, *Frontiero v. Richardson*, had come from the federal court in Alabama, where it was handled by the founders of the brand-new Southern Poverty Law Center, Morris Dees and Joseph Levin. Levin first offered to let Ginsburg argue at the Supreme Court. But, as the case progressed, Levin decided he was too attached to the matter—and his first opportunity to appear before the Court—to let it go. So Levin argued first, graciously ceding ten minutes to "Professor Ginsburg."

Frontiero v. Richardson arose because Sharron Frontiero, an air force medic, challenged the military presumption that servicemen's wives were dependent on their husbands for support, but servicewomen's husbands were not. With a husband as a spouse, she had to prove that he needed her to survive in order to get the housing and medical benefits that married male servicemen got for their families as a matter of course. The dependent spouse rule was just one of myriad rules assuming female dependency and male independence that the women's legal movement had turned up since its awakening.

GINSBURG THE SNEAKY LITIGATOR

But *Frontiero* was a great vehicle to use in asking for a more demanding standard of review of such discriminatory laws (to move sex discrimination into the category of those things, such as race discrimination or restraints on speech, that the Court had long ago said it would look at very hard). When the Court decided *Reed v. Reed*, Ruth's first effort, it barely moved the standard of review for sex discrimination above the standard that applies to all legal distinctions: Was the law rational? After *Reed v. Reed*, a sex-discriminatory law must fairly and substantially advance the legislature's purpose in passing it. *Reed* was huge because it was the first case where the Court refused to accept legal distinctions between the sexes as self-evident. The *Reed* standard is better than the low standard of mere rationality, but not close to Ginsburg's aspiration to have the Court treat distinctions based on sex the same as race. In race cases, the government must prove that the discrimination is necessary to achieve a compelling governmental interest. Since the decision striking down segregated schools in 1954, almost no distinction has met that heavy burden.

Ginsburg was consciously following a well-established strategy. Even though aroused women all over the country were deluging the ACLU with complaints, a legal social change movement always wants to start changing big issues in the law like the standard for sex discrimination with cases that cause minimal disruption in the real world. The facts in the case revealed that making the few servicewomen prove that their husbands were dependent on

them while letting servicemen claim benefits for their wives without proof served no purpose of substance for the air force. It just
made the military's administrative lives a little easier, by relying on
an unattractive social presumption that women were always dependent on their spouses—and men were not.

Since there were so few women soldiers, the Court could help
women out a lot by undercutting that destructive presumption at
very little cost to the government. But once the Court changes the
law enough to accommodate the small social change, it turns on
the big engine of change in the legal precedent. The laws of the
land were shot through with presumptions that women were dependent and men were not; indeed, shot through with all kinds
of presumptions about women. Legal systems make presumptions
all the time. It's the presumptions about women that Ginsburg
was after. Change the standard for reviewing presumptions about
women and you change the entire body of law.

Ginsburg and her colleagues fought valiantly to control the
Frontiero case. They did not want to see another inept provincial
lawyer screw it up like the awful oral advocate from Idaho had
done in *Reed v. Reed*. When Frontiero's lawyers from the Southern
Poverty Law Center asked the ACLU for help with their Supreme
Court filings, General Counsel Mel Wulf believed they had an understanding to give it to Ruth to argue. She began framing the
brief by asking for stricter scrutiny. Levin reneged on his offer to
let her argue in October, three months before argument. Worse, as
the briefing proceeded, it became clear that the Southern Poverty
Law Center had decided to present the case as a modest application
of the low standard of review Ginsburg had won in *Reed v. Reed*.
The discrimination was simply arbitrary, they would argue, done
for the air force's convenience, which is just what the Court had
forbidden in *Reed*.

The ACLUers were apoplectic. It was one thing to have a lawyer botch an oral argument as Sally Reed's attorney had done.
But Levin now proposed to change the legal strategy! As Ginsburg envisioned it, each case was supposed to build on the prior
case, just like the NAACP had done, not simply repeat what they

had already achieved. It was particularly maddening that the new unambitious Levin strategy came from a colleague, one Charles Abernathy, then a lowly 3L, albeit at Harvard, who thought he understood how to manage the Nixon Court. Apparently Feigen Fasteau imperfectly concealed her impatience with the upstart's new strategy, because he wrote her a huffy letter about how his team was more "sophisticated" than she perceived. Her lack of respect made them, he threatened, disinclined to attend to any of her suggestions on anything.

Jockeying for position in presenting Supreme Court cases is standard operating procedure in the elite section of the bar that regularly appears there. Cases can begin with local disputes in almost any town in the nation, where people like Sally Reed or Sharron Frontiero are grateful for a lawyer like Joseph Levin to pay attention to their grievances at all. At the other end of the food chain, there is a well-established group of lawyers centered in New York and D.C. who specialize in the prestigious work of presenting cases to the Supreme Court. Unlike the original client's dedicated representatives, these high-powered law firms and organizations, such as the NAACP Legal Defense Fund or Ginsburg's ACLU, are often most interested in seeing the constitutional law that governs the entire nation develop in a certain way. They frequently employ people who clerked for the justices and know the inside scoop at the Court. They are sometimes seriously obnoxious to the rubes they perceive to be in the way. The local lawyers, often with warm relationships with the actual parties, don't want to turn their cases over to the fancy pants at the big shops. A case like *Frontiero v. Richardson* looks to a lawyer just starting out like his first—and perhaps only—shot at glory.

Ginsburg's people tried everything to get Levin to back off. As would often be her practice, after lesser voices like Feigen Fasteau's failed to work, Ginsburg wrote to Levin directly. Having a woman argue was important, she asserted. "I am not very good at self-advertisement," she continued, "but believe you have some understanding of the knowledge of the women's rights area I have developed over the past two years." Levin responded almost by return mail. He didn't think sex mattered for oral argument purposes. "I am normally the easiest guy in the world to get along with and find it very uncomfortable to engage in squabbling of any sort, petty or otherwise."

The exchange of letters looms large in Ginsburg lore, because she is so rarely caught on the record boasting about her abilities. But her second letter to Levin a week later reveals the steel-trap mind behind the velvet modesty. "I suppose it is hard for either of us, at this stage, to see each other as we describe ourselves," she opens disarmingly. Then Ginsburg puts in the shiv. "The 'easiest guy in the world to get along with,' in my book, would not *renege on an understanding*. On the other hand, *my attempt to bring you back to where we stood on the oral argument from May-October* probably does not seem to you to have been penned by someone who is, by nature, rather modest [emphasis added]." In two lines she tags him as doing something wrong regardless of how nice he is, while she describes herself as just trying to enforce a contract, however immodest that makes her. And all in a tone of sweet reason: "I suppose it is hard for either of us . . ."

Ginsburg's mysterious appeal to fractious lefty lawyers normally worked in part because she took the position that "we all want to do the right thing here." In this case, it didn't work, and the two groups canceled their meeting to work on the brief. At the oral argument in January, Levin took the lion's share of the argument time, arguing only that the air force scheme was so irrational it failed the modest standard of *Reed v. Reed*. Even if they won the battle, then, the larger war would not be advanced. Ginsburg was reduced to making her argument for the Court to scrutinize sex discrimination strictly, as they did to race discrimination, in a brief as a friend of the Court and to speak briefly after Levin finished.

Although the Court has unyieldingly resisted any possibility of video coverage for decades, oral arguments, including Ruth Bader Ginsburg's debut in *Frontiero v. Richardson*, are recorded. For anyone who has heard her flat, halting presentations in interviews, the recording is a revelation. The familiar, Brooklyn-inflected voice was the same. But the Pinteresque pauses that once caused a job candidate to leave her office in the middle of his interview, thinking it had concluded, were nowhere to be heard. For ten solid minutes, she articulated the argument for comparing sex with race and imposing strict scrutiny on any distinctions between male and female. All the hesitation, as Nina Totenberg has observed, disappears "when Ruth starts to perform."

The argument she made is by now familiar. Women have a long history of oppression, could not even vote for most of the nation's history, and were, in 1972, almost unseen in corporate boardrooms or the halls of representative government. The justification for treating women differently—protecting them—excludes them from important arenas of civic and human life, such as from serving on juries and often from holding better jobs. Assuming they are dependent beings who belong in the home, as the air force scheme assumed, confines both sexes to stereotypes that limits their opportunities and imagination.

In a drumbeat of simple declarative sentences, she made raising the standard seem not just simple, but inevitable:

"Amicus [the ACLU]," she begins, "urges the Court to recognize in this case what it has in others, that it writes not only for this case and this day alone, but for this type of case. . . . To provide the guidance so badly needed and because recognition is long overdue, amicus urges the Court to declare sex a suspect criterion.

"This would not be quite the giant step appellee [the air force] suggests."

Why not, she explains:

"Sex like race is a visible, immutable characteristic bearing no necessary relationship to ability. Sex like race has been made the basis for unjustified or at least unproved assumptions, concerning an individual's potential to perform or to contribute to society."

Her opponents say that race was the special concern of the Fourteenth Amendment. And it was. And again she asks the Court to consider not the what but the why:

"But why," she then asks, "did the framers of the Fourteenth Amendment regard racial discrimination as odious? Because a person's skin color bears no necessary relationship to ability."

And then she drives in her point: "similarly as appellees concede, a person's sex bears no necessary relationship to ability."

The argument makes unavoidable a ruling that sex is as suspect as race. Had she succeeded, much of the rest of the drama of women and the Court would have been unnecessary. Uninterrupted by even a single question, her oral argument reveals graphically the woman who "treats everyone as if they were as smart as she is." Although the argument has a simple structure, she does not dumb down her language. Women don't make less money, they receive less "remuneration." Distinctions are not just illegal, they are "odious." Perhaps imperfectly aware of the inner life of the nine men before her, she ended her maiden voyage with a ringing invocation of the suffragist Sarah Grimké: We do not ask men for special treatment, she intoned, "All we ask is that they take their feet off our necks."

She was brilliant. At their conference, seven justices voted to strike down the air force scheme. And she converted Justice Brennan to strict scrutiny, treating sex like race. (Actually, her argument that sex was like race persuaded Brennan's clerk Geoffrey Stone, who left his justice with two drafts late one night, the narrow one applying *Reed v. Reed* and a broad opinion raising the standard for sex discrimination. When Stone got to work the next day he found Justice Brennan had come on board for the bold move.)

But Brennan had an uphill battle getting a majority. Although you wouldn't know it from the unanimous decision in *Reed v. Reed*, the Court changed foundationally when the nation elected a Republican president in 1968. Although the seven justices from *Reed v. Reed* remained, Nixon had filled the two remaining vacancies. He added William Rehnquist, O'Connor's old Stanford friend and the most conservative justice in decades, and a courtly Virginia lawyer from a corporate firm, the former ABA president Lewis Powell. The new justices were not what you would call feminists. Even the least conservative Nixon justice, Harry Blackmun, had already expressed disdain for the seriousness of legal feminism. "The ACLU," he had written of Ginsburg's legendary brief in *Reed*, had filed a "very lengthy brief" in this "simple little case."

"I hope we don't get into a long and emotional discussion about women's rights." In fact, Ginsburg's brief was, at sixty pages, long, but not unusually long. In some of the back and forth between the justices during the consideration of the follow-up case, *Frontiero*, Burger asked Powell to be harsher on Brennan's liberal effort, describing himself as trying to "mute the outrage of Women's Lib." As Aryeh Neier had figured out at the founding of the Women's Rights Project, men often thought women's rights were frivolous. Even his serious brainiac Ruth Bader Ginsburg failed to persuade Harry Blackmun or Warren Burger of the seriousness of her cause.

So Brennan had his work cut out for him. He was sure of the support of his liberal colleagues William Douglas and Thurgood Marshall for giving Ginsburg her strict scrutiny. He had even captured the somewhat unpredictable fourth Democratic appointee, Byron White. Justices Warren Burger and William Rehnquist were never in play to raise sex discrimination to the level of race. Brennan then went to the "centrists" to try to get to five. Justice Harry Blackmun, who seemed to be waffling politically, seemed like a possibility for a while. But Blackmun was impatient with Ginsburg's pitch, again calling her briefs overly long and giving her a churlish C-plus for her brilliant oral argument in *Frontiero* ("very precise female," he noted in his habitual reviews of the various lawyers' performances).

When Blackmun finally came out on the conservative side, Brennan turned his sights on the old Eisenhower centrist Potter Stewart. But at that moment Nixon's latest appointee, Lewis Powell, just a year into his tenure, surfaced as Brennan's adversary. In a memo to the Court, and ultimately in his concurring opinion, Powell argued that the Court should not elevate sex to race while ratification of the Equal Rights Amendment was pending in the various states.

Powell's papers, which have become public since the decision in *Frontiero*, raise the question of whether his ERA argument is just pretext. His notes to self actually reveal that he, a very conventional Virginia gentleman, was unsympathetic to Frontiero from the beginning and might even have dissented altogether. "Close case," he noted right out of the box. There are so few women in the military and the statistics indicate very few dependent husbands, he reasoned. The law requiring women to prove their spouses' dependency "may well," he thought, "be rational." Certainly, he noted, "women" do not "constitute a suspect class." *Reed v. Reed* did not say so, he reminds himself.

"Women are not fungible with men (thank god!)" he wrote to Brennan. He voted for Frontiero in the end, but he persuaded the Court that they ought not to raise the standard for sex discrimination. As long as Lewis Powell, the persuadable fifth vote in a heavily divided Court, held sway, the government would never have to produce a compelling reason why it treated women differently from men.

The story of the near miss at getting the standard of review changed in *Frontiero* illustrates perfectly what Ginsburg and the Women's Rights Project were up against. The Supreme Court, just starting on its journey away from the legendary civil rights victories of the 1950s and '60s to becoming one of the most conservative in history, was not going to treat women like black Americans. The Court decided the case for Sharron Frontiero—women in the armed forces would now get their automatic benefits—by a vote of 8–1, with only the conservative Rehnquist dissenting. Brennan wrote an opinion equating sex discrimination with race. But four of the eight justices in the majority joined Powell in writing separately from Brennan, leaving the liberal Brennan with a minority of but four votes. The decision in *Frontiero* looked like a victory, but it was more like a placeholder.

It would seem all the more surprising, then, when, a month after the argument in *Frontiero*, the Court, in an opinion by Justice Blackmun, struck down every one of the nation's abortion laws.

5

Intermission: Abortion

꠸

Justice Blackmun later called *Roe v. Wade*, the abortion decision, "a necessary first step in the emancipation of American women." Maybe. But, in the form of Blackmun's opinion in *Roe v. Wade*, the abortion decision looked more like an intermission in the drama of the feminist legal revolution than the next development. Although women were 100 percent of the people seeking abortions, Justice Blackmun spoke of the pregnant woman's "right of privacy" and concluded that abortion, "a medical decision," must also respect the "right of the physician." As many feminist critics, including Ruth Bader Ginsburg, later noted, instead of addressing why imprisoning women in their pregnancies excluded them from equal social opportunity, the decision imprisoned them in their individual "privacy," making the decision seem like an arbitrary act of will. While the country was in gender upheaval, and Ginsburg and her troops were challenging the court to undo legal presumptions about gender, the abortion decision managed to sidestep all that.

The separation of abortion from feminism is not all that surprising. The doctors who started the abortion reform movement in the 1940s were the furthest thing from feminists, radical or mainstream. One thing about doctors—they don't like to see their patients die, especially when it's not nature that's killing them. It's the law. Once abortion became safe—indeed, safer than childbirth—after World War II, doctors started noticing that almost half of maternal deaths were from botched illegal abortions. A privileged few women managed to secure hospital-committee-approved "therapeutic" procedures.

Women would try to abort, doctors knew. The only question was whether they died—or became infertile—from it. The most liberal specialists—the psychiatrists—began to talk about the issue. In 1955, Planned Parenthood held a secret conference on the subject for health professionals, and the conference produced an actual statement. Doctors needed more freedom to decide what their patients needed, the statement said. Coincidentally, in 1959 an essentially all-male group of ultra-establishment lawyers and law professors, the American Law Institute, began devising a Model Penal Code to reform all American criminal law. Responding to the doctors' increasingly vocal concerns, the code proposed to modify the criminal prohibition of abortion by urging that it be performed in licensed hospitals in situations where doctors determined that it was required to save the life or preserve the physical or mental health of the pregnant woman. The ALI's codes carry great weight among lawmakers, and reform-minded legislators in many states began adopting the liberal provisions of the new abortion protocol.

A year later, the pregnant Arizona TV star (*Romper Room*) Shari Finkbine found out the sleeping pills her husband brought her from England contained thalidomide and would likely cause her to give birth to a baby with deformed or missing arms or legs. Since abortion was criminal in Arizona and most of the United States, she went to Sweden. She also went public. Support for legal abortion soared. Even the Equal Rights Amendment foe and conservative icon Barry Goldwater and his wife, Peggy, were mainstays of Arizona Planned Parenthood.

There was no way this issue was going to stay in the hands of reformist male doctors and children's TV stars after the rebirth of the feminist movement in 1963. As early as 1962, a California medical technician started the Society for Humane Abortion; a group around the Chicago civil rights activist Heather Booth founded Jane, the women's collective that actually performed abortions; NOW had a Conference on Reproductive Rights; and NARAL, the organization to Repeal, not Reform, the laws was born. The women of the women's movement did not want to beg their doctors for understanding or submit to powerful hospital committees to determine the state of their mental health. They saw the issue as a pure question of women's liberty, and they thought the laws, including the reformed laws, should be repealed.

That abortion would, as Tocqueville said about all American conflicts, surface in the Supreme Court quickly became inevitable. Ultimately two cases arrived. *Roe v. Wade*, the case that came to stand for abortion rights, was put together by two green female University of Texas law grads to challenge the state's nineteenth-century criminal prohibition. The companion case, *Doe v. Bolton*, was carefully crafted by the ACLU to challenge the limits on abortion that remained even after Georgia had liberalized its abortion law to the American Law Institute model. The Texas lawyer Sarah Weddington made her reputation on the case and went on to a long career advocating for women and other liberal causes, including the successful initiative to score a federal judgeship for Ruth Bader Ginsburg in 1980.

By 1971, when the case was heard, every imaginable interest group had weighed in. All the arguments in the evolving and diverse resistance to abortion laws—from the doctors' interest in proper practice of medicine to the right to privacy to women's unique burden in the childbearing arena—had been presented to the Court.

In voting 7–2 to strike down the laws against abortion, the refined old WASPy gentlemen of the United States Supreme Court, circa 1973—and their lukewarm Catholic brother William Brennan—embraced the conventional, doctor-centric analysis. The establishment was clearly on the side of the Court, and the society was completely fed up with dying women arriving at emergency rooms after botched illegal abortions. Neither Justice Blackmun nor his brethren, however, were prepared to concede that women were simply entitled to abortion as a means to an end in a flourishing life.

Ginsburg later shared her unhappiness with the abortion decision. Abortion was not the business of the Women's Rights Project, but, from the sidelines, she developed a much more radical theory about abortion. To this equality advocate, abortion prohibitions stereotyped women as breeders and kept them from realizing their full potential in life. Hence, the laws violated the equality provisions of the Constitution.

She said nothing at the time. In her remarks a decade later she took issue with the decision. All decisions involving female reproduction were about women being equal, meaning women, not the government, and not Justice Blackmun's beloved mostly male physicians, ought to be making decisions about whether women should "bear or beget a child." Pregnancy was no different from any other sex-linked category, even where dressed up as benign. "Exaltation of woman's unique role in bearing children," she wrote, "has, in effect, restrained women from developing their individual talents . . . and has impelled them to accept a dependent, subordinate status in society."

Not only was *Roe v. Wade* too conservative, according to Ginsburg, but it was also too radical! It cut off the political process, which had been slowly liberalizing the laws state by state. Contrary to what some would like to believe, Ginsburg was hardly saying the draconic Texas law making abortion criminal should have been sustained. She just thought the Court should strike down that law as unconstitutional and leave it up to the states to keep trying instead of striking down the laws of all fifty states as it did. The backlash to *Roe*, she speculated, might have been avoided or minimized with this incremental strategy. Unsurprisingly, the article, coming from a liberal activist, was widely used by conservatives to argue against court action in the social-change arena, most pointedly in the ensuing litigation for same-sex marriage. Conservatives never referred to Ginsburg's radical criticism of *Roe*, which appears in the same article.

But regardless of how you looked at it, the Court's decision in *Roe*, which looks like a feminist victory, violated every tenet of Ruth Bader Ginsburg's social movement strategy: keep your eye on the ball of *equality*

and

slowly kick it down the field.

She was probably wrong about arguing abortion in 1973 as a matter of women's rights. The equal-protection argument she advocates was clearly presented to the Court in the amicus brief from a women lawyers' coalition, a document written by the able women's advocate Nancy Stearns of the Center for Constitutional Rights. It is extremely doubtful that the Court would have threatened the laws of fifty states, on the grounds that the burden on women of bearing children sets them up as forever unequal, much less reached that decision by a 7–2 majority. Just after ruling in *Roe*, the Court heard a couple of cases about whether women's pregnancy must be treated like any other disability in the law. It ruled repeatedly in support of discrimination against pregnant women. Denying disability benefits for pregnancy, the Court said, isn't sex discrimination. It divides pregnant people from nonpregnant people, not men from women. They just didn't get it that pregnancy was a uniquely female problem and a central issue in the movement toward equality.

Ginsburg understood full well how destructive it was to assign the full burden of reproduction of the species to women. After the second bad pregnancy disability decision, she turned to the op-ed pages of *The New York Times*, asking Congress to intervene and amend the Civil Rights Act to make pregnancy discrimination illegal. Which it did.

Ultimately, she said, a European system of income and medical benefits for pregnancy and childbirth was essential to avoid a "drop out period that may have devastating effects on a woman's lifelong earnings and self-fulfillment potential." No constitutional interpretation, however generous, could achieve that goal. But getting Congress to recognize that pregnancy discrimination is sex discrimination was a good first step toward a political solution to the financial burden of pregnancy. Ginsburg always knew the order of change.

Maybe it's a good thing the Court did not realize its abortion decision was a landmark in what some of the key justices condescendingly called "Women's Lib," emancipating women from their stereotyped role as units of reproduction. When people do figure this out, the response is often backlash against abortion rights, rather than endorsement. Ginsburg's strategy of presenting very unthreatening facts such as the trivial discrimination in *Reed v. Reed* or cases with male plaintiffs such as *Moritz* was not going to conceal forever the socially transformative impact of undoing sex-role stereotypes.

Indeed, well before the decision in *Roe*, feminism's archenemy Phyllis Schlafly had begun to proselytize against abortion on the grounds that motherhood *is* a woman's career. She correctly figured out that making abortion (like day care) available would deal a direct blow to what Ginsburg would call "sex role stereotypes," but which Schlafly called "the basic unit of society." There is robust evidence of resistance to liberalization of abortion in the political realm for three years before the decision in *Roe*. In this rare instance it seems Ginsburg was wrong on both counts. It wasn't judicial usurpation of the legislative function that provoked the backlash. It was in powerful measure that abortion represented the leading edge of women's liberation. So the decision certainly wouldn't have fared better if the Court had admitted it was doing the dreaded equality thing.

6

Act Two: Equality in Peril

❦

With her usual laserlike focus, Ginsburg kept lining up her cases. And boy, were there cases. One by one, the entire structure of American law, built blindly on antique assumptions about women's role and behavior, came under the scrutiny of the women's movement lawyers. In the decade after *Reed v. Reed*, more than twenty cases challenging sex discrimination reached the highest court. Aryeh Neier was right; it was the civil rights movement of the era. And Ginsburg got the lion's share for herself.

Even as she was in the midst of her career as an advocate, some people were already planning for her to be making the decisions, rather than merely arguing for them. In her high school yearbook in 1973, her daughter, Jane, listed her "ambition" as seeing "Mother appointed to the Supreme Court." Jane was farsighted, considering that there were almost no women on any court. When President Richard Nixon floated the name of the California judge Mildred Lillie for a Supreme Court vacancy in 1971, the American Bar Association lost no time in finding her to be unqualified. But, as Nixon's uncharacteristically progressive suggestion of Lillie reflects, change was in the air. (When word of Nixon's openness to suggestion leaked out, he heard from a then-obscure Arizona state senator, Sandra O'Connor, urging him to move to the distaff side!) As Jane—and Sandra—dreamed, two of Ginsburg's colleagues at Columbia, Professors Philip Schrag and George Cooper, were working Governor Nelson Rockefeller to appoint the rising female star on their faculty to the highest court in New York. Nothing came of it, but the suggestion, surfacing just three short years after she turned her attention to litigating women's equality, shows the force field she created.

Still, if Ginsburg was going to be in front of the bench, rather than on it, she at least wished she could be the one deciding what cases she'd be arguing. But she couldn't even control her own ACLU! One unpleasant morning in the fall of 1973, she opened the Supreme Court edition of the lawyers' weekly newsletter and learned that a Florida man was using the equality language of the Constitution to take money from poor widows. Under Florida law, widows, but not widowers, were entitled to a tiny break on their state taxes. The widower Melvin Kahn thought that was sex discrimination, and he wanted it stopped. To Ginsburg's horror, Kahn's unappealing case was going to the high court. When she called the lawyer who brought Kahn's challenge to the widows' tax break, *Kahn v. Shevin*, he expressed delight at hearing from another lawyer from the sponsoring organization, her very own ACLU. No one had told her.

She grabbed it to handle at the Supreme Court, but her heart was heavy. Protection was always the Achilles' heel of the movement for women's equality. When the Equal Rights Amendment resurfaced in the 1960s, women's liberal allies from the labor movement dragged their feet about supporting it, because they saw that formal equality was incompatible with laws mandating maximum hours and the like for women, but not men. The whole body of pension law was shot through with little special concerns for old ladies, as was the law of alimony for wives. The draft law contained a blanket exemption for all females. Conservative adversaries of the Equal Rights Amendment such as Professor Philip Kurland and Phyllis Schlafly relied heavily on the loss of protections such as alimony and exemption from the draft to drive support away from the equality law. Ginsburg was at ground zero in these debates. She understood that there might be circumstances where affirmative action for women was required to remedy specific bad practices from the past. But at the beginning of the movement toward legal equality, she was much more concerned that the law's assistance was more cage than gilt.

Both her prior cases had directed the Court's gaze toward women as competent administrators or women as soldiers. The last thing she wanted was to ask for the expansion of the equal-protection clause to sex by challenging something that protected widows and tugged on the heartstrings of justices such as William O. Douglas, whose widowed mother had struggled mightily to survive. As a technical matter, the Florida law was discriminatory and it did rest on presumptions about women being dependent, just like Ginsburg's other cases. But the challenge was unappealing.

It was her only defeat. On April 24, 1974, Justice Douglas sustained the widows' tax preference. His opinion was the first setback to Ginsburg's strategy of challenging laws that assumed a subordinate role for women. Ginsburg's argument against protective laws such as the widows' tax break and protective labor laws was that the good they did to women in the short term was offset by the harm they did by locking women into a dependent stereotype in the long run. Everyone knows single women are poorer than men, Douglas wrote, in a direct rebuff to her position, and they need protection. Preferences such as the widows' tax exemption were beneficent, Justice Douglas continued, not a short-term patch destined in the long term to harm women by excluding them from the risks and rewards of the larger world. And, Douglas continued gratuitously, gender is not necessarily suspect in constitutional law anyway. After all, no one's talking about drafting women, are they? Poor, unprotected women exposed to equality, which will inevitably end in their being drafted, sounded just like the horrible picture Professor Kurland painted to defeat the ERA. Well, not while Justice Douglas was around.

With *Kahn*, the number of justices willing to subject sex discrimination, like racial segregation, to strict scrutiny, went from the four who had supported Justice Brennan in *Frontiero* to two. Marlo Thomas's feminist TV special, *Free to Be You and Me*, might have appeared to enormous acclaim just the month before the decision in *Kahn v. Shevin* (and a subsequent Emmy Award), but most of the Nine Old Men thought the impoverished widow was closer to the truth of women's lives than That Girl. They did not see their decision perpetuating the helpless-widow image as harmful; they thought they were helping the poor old lady out.

Ginsburg was alarmed. The upcoming Supreme Court term would truly be the Term of the Woman. When the Court opened for business the first Monday in October 1974, it would consider cases involving almost every aspect of women's equality: women on juries; women as soldiers, defending their country; women as workers, earning Social Security; and even parents' obligations to their girl children. What the Court did in 1974–75 could determine the course of the women's legal movement for decades. Ginsburg was well aware: she was arguing half the cases. And now she was starting that momentous year deep in the precedential hole. Curse Melvin Kahn.

But there was an ace in that hole. For the first time in its history, as the Supreme Court addressed the issue of whether to turn back the clock on sex discrimination following *Kahn* or to move forward building on *Frontiero*, the 1974–75 Court included among the elite rank of Supreme Court clerks *four women*. That was almost as many women clerks in one term as the Court had experienced in its entire history. Justices Marshall and Blackmun had female law clerks. More important, so did Justice Powell, and, for the first time, Justice Brennan.

Therein lies a tale. Despite his liberal opinions, Justice Brennan did not go willingly into the new world of gender equality. "Send me someone else," Brennan had said abruptly in 1970, when his informal network of clerkship sources at Berkeley Law School called to recommend Alison Grey, first in her class. The mortified law professors had to tell their star student she would not be Brennan's pathbreaking first female clerk after all. Three years later, in 1973, Berkeley professor and former Brennan clerk Stephen Barnett tried again, with the equally well qualified graduate Marsha Berzon. This time Barnett would not take Brennan's immediate no for an answer. He courageously wrote to Brennan that the justice was taking a serious chance of public embarrassment or, worse, a lawsuit. "I cannot believe that, on reflection," he wrote to this

most powerful man, "you will continue a policy that is both unconstitutional and simply wrong. . . ." Brennan caved. A few months
later, Marsha Berzon arrived, complete with child-care responsibilities, having to leave chambers each afternoon at five to retrieve her
baby, Jeremy, from day care. In a delicious irony, Justice Brennan
was also running out. His daughter had gotten divorced and she
and her baby were living with him. It was Grandpa Brennan's job
to fetch his granddaughter from day care while his daughter rebooted her career.

Before the 1974 term opened in October, Justice Powell's new
female clerk, Penny Clark, decided her justice should get a little
help with the Term of the Woman. Clark knew her customer. In
his view of the world, "there are all kinds of good reasons why
you would differentiate between men and women and there was
no way he was going to make the government prove there was a
compelling reason for those differences." She decided to write him
a memo, a preterm overview of three pending sex-discrimination
cases. She opened with a bland neutrality: "I have attempted to
outline an approach to sex discrimination that will harmonize with
your opinions on equal protection, with special attention to the role
the Court should play in this controversial area." The Clark memorandum looks even-handed and actually sounds quite conservative.
Clark cast the proponents of equal rights such as the ACLU lawyer Ginsburg as immoderate and describes their position as "eliminating all, or virtually all, distinctions between the sexes." In a
gratuitous aside, she described the "moderates," including outright
opponents of the Equal Rights Amendment, as fearing to put their
opinions in print, presumably because of an oppressive climate of
political correctness from the left. Worse still, the "activists" see the
job of rectifying relations between the sexes as the business of the
Court! The "moderates" prefer the more flexible political process,
so much better suited, she advises, to solving exquisite problems of
a changing social order.

She also laid out in detail why the activists were wrong in
equating sex with race: women had been voting for a half century,
they were not ghettoized away from the governing sex, indeed they

were sleeping with the electorate, so to speak. Many measures were for their "protection," and they counted on such protection and "participated" in its enactment. Since sex is not suspect like race, Ginsburg's pet plaintiffs, men, who always had the upper hand, had no standing to ask for social neutrality in the few areas where the society helped women; indeed no one had standing to ask the society to just act better, sexwise. So much for Ginsburg's theory that sex-role stereotyping hurts everyone, and plaintiffs could as easily be men as women. (When, some years later in 1978, Powell explicitly said sex was not like race in an affirmative action case, Ginsburg died a little. Maybe time constraints made him terse, she speculated, and when the Court had a sex case it would understand why women sometimes need affirmative action too.)

Despite the unattractive tone, Clark laid out a theoretical framework that allowed her justice, Powell, to remain faithful to his retrograde social vision and still vote to strike down laws that either hurt women or benefited men or were ambiguous in their effect. The precedents since *Reed v. Reed* and the incontestable social changes in women's roles made it impossible to simply rubber-stamp sex discrimination in the law, she says. "The touchstone," in the brave new world of reviewing sex-based legal classes, she concluded, "should be injury to women." In case he might miss the injury, she gave him a little cheat sheet on questionable sex distinctions. "Laws that use sex as a classifying device without good reasons (preferably factual) should fall. Laws that discriminate against women will usually be invalid" because they don't serve a "legitimate state interest" standard. When looking for a state interest, she warned, you should look carefully, even at laws that seem to help women, because "legislative assumptions about women's proper role" are often just old-time stereotypes and simply not reliable.

And so, Clark told Justice Powell, here's what you ought to do in the first three cases coming down the pike in the Term of the Woman. In *Schlesinger v. Ballard*, a disgruntled male soldier is suing the army because it gives the handful of women in the armed services extra time to qualify for promotion. Turn the guy down, she recommended. After all, women don't get much chance to show their stuff in the sexist and old-fashioned army, so the rule just protects them a little bit against the effects of the prior discrimination. Sort of like affirmative action or the widows' real estate deduction in *Kahn*; no harm to women, no foul.

Second, duck Ruth Ginsburg's case, *Edwards v. Healy*, on behalf of all of Louisiana's women discouraged from jury service by the requirement that, rather than be called, they must volunteer to serve. Louisiana just changed its offending jury arrangements anyway, so you have an easy out, because you can say the Louisiana women's gripe is met and the case is moot. But strike down Louisiana's old jury law by another route, using *Taylor v. Louisiana*, a case brought by a male defendant challenging his conviction by an all-male Louisiana jury. His case is definitely not moot, as he is rotting in jail now. The race cases established long ago that a criminal jury must resemble the community from which it is drawn, and Louisiana is definitely not all male, so the convicted criminal's case is pretty much a slam dunk. When ruling in the criminal case, she continues, you'll probably have to overrule your 1961 decision in *Hoyt v. Florida*, which allowed such female volunteer jury arrangements in Florida. However, without any serious women's lib taint, you can take out Louisiana's law, because the standards for a fair jury are particularly demanding since the Court struck down all-white juries years ago. In a democracy with women common on the voter rolls, being tried by a jury with no women on it may not be as bad as the all-white juries, but it is still pretty raw.

And it worked. Criminal defendants being so much more important to the Supreme Court than women citizens, Clark could get Powell to move the law toward eliminating sex discrimination in jury selection without confronting what he was doing in the sex-role arena. Once the Court said discouraging women from jury service was questionable, the society would stop doing it. The social belief that women did not belong on juries would no longer be buttressed by the law. Thus this canny female law clerk accomplished with a flank attack what Ginsburg's direct litigation strategy might have failed to do on its own.

Powell represented the slice of Supreme Court opinion that

Ginsburg had to win. Justices Rehnquist and Burger mainly opposed the women's legal revolution, and Justices Brennan and Marshall were mainly in favor. Justice Douglas was sick. The critical swing voters—increasingly conservative old-school members of the court—tended to go where Powell went. Only one of Ginsburg's five cases was close. The four central members of the Court either sniffed out social revolution and opposed her or they felt safe enough to go along. Powell seemed to be the bellwether, and Penny Clark had given him every reason this crucial term to take a narrow but not entirely hostile stance. It's not like Powell was naturally progressive on women. "This was not the first or the only time in our chambers that one of us persuaded him away from his first inclination," she recalls with satisfaction decades later. "He told his clerks I'll discuss anything until I vote."

Unknown to her then, when Ruth Bader Ginsburg donned a bright red suit and put a matching ribbon around her ponytail two weeks into the term to present the oral argument in the case against Louisiana's stereotyping of women jurors, in *Edwards v. Healy*, the Court was already primed to duck the case as moot. Too bad. She had been waiting to overturn the Court's 1961 decision in *Hoyt v. Florida* since she read it the first time. The all-male jury in *Hoyt* had convicted the defendant, Gwendolyn Hoyt, of killing her unfaithful husband. They rejected her plea of temporary insanity, which was the only defense available to a beleaguered and abused woman at the time. The unspoken assumption was that a woman on the jury might have recognized the legitimacy of that defense. Dismissing Hoyt's challenge to the all-male jury, the Supreme Court had announced unanimously that women were "the center of home and family life," which was reason enough for the state to keep them from the jury pool.

Ginsburg hated *Hoyt v. Florida*. When she was testifying at the hearings for her own confirmation to the highest court in 1993, she reached back to *Hoyt* to explain to the Senate why it was so important to change the way the Courts treated women:

"The Court said," Ginsburg told the members of the Senate Judiciary Committee, "Florida's scheme was pure favor to women.

They had the best of both worlds. They could serve if they wanted to. They had only to sign up in the clerk's office. They didn't have to serve if they didn't want to, so what was the complaint about? Women were treated better than men. Apparently, little thought was given to Gwendolyn Hoyt and the murder charge affirmed in her case."

Maybe Ginsburg hated *Hoyt* because the 1961 decision coincided with her experience of not standing a chance in the world of all-male faculties and Supreme Court clerkships even as valedictorian of her law school class. What could have been a charming anachronism like *Bradwell v. Illinois*, the nineteenth-century case allowing states to exclude women from practicing law, was instead about women of her own time. In describing the case to the Senate, she uncharacteristically dripped resentment that such a decision would come from "the liberal Warren Court." From the awakening of her feminist consciousness in 1970 on, almost all her speeches referred to the astonishing survival into modernity of a decision that assumes women had no civic duty to judge—or right to be judged by—their peers.

The Court held Ginsburg's case for months until the new Louisiana law repealing the special treatment of women jurors came into effect and then dismissed it as moot. Thus Ginsburg did not get the ringing condemnation of the sex-segregated society she sought. However, as Clark's memo anticipated, the Court could not avoid the issue entirely, because it had also agreed to review the criminal defendant Billy Taylor's challenge to his conviction by an all-male jury—the product of Louisiana's not calling women unless they volunteer.

The Court reversed Taylor's conviction. We don't have to decide, Justice White wrote for the near-unanimous Court in *Taylor*, whether protecting women is a good idea or not. Protecting women against having to serve on juries is just not a good-enough idea to justify nearly sending someone to death with a jury that does not remotely resemble the community he comes from. In deciding the jury rights case, Justice White did say that the hated precedent, *Hoyt v. Florida*, was no longer good law: "If it was ever the case that women were unqualified to sit on juries or were so situated that none of them should be required to perform jury service, that time has long since passed. . . . What is a fair cross section at one time or place is not necessarily a fair cross section at another time or a different place."

Ginsburg should have been cheering the decision. The problem, of course, was that the Court ignored Ginsburg's ambitious equal-protection argument for respect for women's citizenship and the end to sex-role stereotypes. Instead the Court issued a narrow decision about a criminal defendant's highly protected right to a representative jury. While White's opinion was not a perfect outcome, every time a Supreme Court opinion recognized the altered social landscape for women, Ginsburg moved closer to her goal of an outright prohibition of all gender distinctions. In a system that runs on guidance from the past, such as the American legal system, every favorable word in an opinion is a potential building block.

7

Act Three: The Stay-at-Home Dad to the Rescue

✦

WOMEN ARE WORKERS, MEN ARE PARENTS, BABIES ARE BABIES

Talk about appealing plaintiffs: in 1972, Stephen Wiesenfeld's wife died in childbirth, leaving him the sole parent of an orphan son, Jason. Wiesenfeld made up his mind. He would be both mother and father to Jason. With government survivor benefits, he could stay home and raise the child. But Social Security said no. The United States government gave such support only to female people, like Justice Douglas's mother.

Had Stephen Wiesenfeld not existed, Ruth Bader Ginsburg might have had to invent him. He was the perfect plaintiff. As one of Ruth's student assistants put it, "a man whose wife died in childbirth, something that doesn't happen a lot in the latter part of the twentieth century, with a BABY . . . WIDOWS AND ORPHANS—you can't get any better than that!" With an MBA in business, Wiesenfeld ran a little business, but mostly he had stayed home and run the household while his schoolteacher wife, Paula, earned the income subject to Social Security. Now Social Security was depriving him of the benefit of Paula's labors. Wiesenfeld was no Melvin Kahn, an unpleasant representative of what seemed to be men's lib, looking for a tax break on the back of Justice Douglas's mother. Stephen Wiesenfeld was her favorite client.

When Social Security turned him down, Wiesenfeld knew exactly what it meant. After all, he grew up in a "liberal, free thinking home and was part of equality for all." He wrote a letter to the editor of his local paper in New Jersey, asking if Gloria Steinem knew about what was happening to him! He was not trying to be facetious; he was actually hoping to attract some help. Wiesenfeld hit the jackpot. A colleague of Ginsburg's from Rutgers saw the letter and sent it on to her. "Meeting [her] was exactly what I had in mind when I wrote the letter," he crowed.

After months of correspondence and telephone calls, Stephen actually did meet Ginsburg, laden with document cases, on the train to the lowest-level federal court in Trenton for the first argument in his case. Can I help you with all those papers? he asked. "I learned a little lesson," he recalls from that first encounter, "and I never asked her again!" He should have known. From their first telephone call, "She was always very much in control and knew exactly what she wanted to say. Very bright, very alert person, very sharp. You could talk to her and . . . and she knew exactly what she wanted to ask and she was able to describe to me exactly what the procedures would be." Very precise female, as Justice Blackmun had noted. Ginsburg of the ACLU won the case in the Trenton court. Indeed, the court held that such sex discrimination was like race, and only a compelling governmental interest could justify it, giving Ginsburg the decision she had missed by one vote in *Frontiero*. The judges struck down the Social Security law as unconstitutional. But nothing, as she told Wiesenfeld, mattered except what the Supreme Court would do when the government appealed its loss.

A NOTE ON GATEKEEPERS

As she predicted, the federal government appealed the Wiesenfeld decision to the Supreme Court. The Court sets up a lot of barricades against the tide of appeals that washes over them every term. Since the Court has a lot of power to refuse to hear cases, it winds up turning down most of the initial requests. In 1973, in an effort to cut back on the amount of work they did, Justice Burger set up a pool of clerks to look at the requests for Supreme Court review. All the justices but Stevens, who was unwilling to rely on the opinions of others, assigned one of their law clerks to the pool. Under the pool procedure, which continues to this day (Justice Alito is currently the only holdout), each of the petitions for Supreme Court review goes randomly to one of the eight law clerks, who writes a preliminary memo about the case, rather than each of the nine justices having a clerk look at every request separately. The preliminary memos advise whether the Court should consider addressing the case in full, or whether it should refuse to hear the appeal at all or deal with it summarily, without briefs and argument.

Since the creation of the pool, complaints have surfaced periodically that a case's fate—whether it even gets heard at all—depends too heavily on the luck of the draw. The single clerk of a liberal judge, the research reflects, will treat a liberal claim very differently than a single clerk from a conservative judge. All the justices may, of course, review any appeal themselves, but their natural reluctance to invest the time means the pool plays a substantial gatekeeping function in determining what the Court hears.

The Court's deliberations in Stephen Wiesenfeld's case, preserved in Justice Powell's papers, give an inadvertent look into the politics of the pool and the gender politics at the Court at this crucial moment. Because a three-judge federal court had struck down a federal law as unconstitutional, the United States government was the defendant, and the government had a right to appeal to the Supreme Court. Unlike most requests for review, where there is an appeal of right, the Court could not refuse to address the merits of what the three judges did. However, it could still summarily affirm (good for Ginsburg's case) or reverse (bad) the lower court without full briefing and argument. Or, of course, hear it in full.

Ginsburg had the bad luck to have the government's appeal drawn by John E. O'Neill, the pool clerk from the chambers of the most conservative justice sitting on the Court in 1974, William Rehnquist. Rehnquist had cast the sole negative vote in her near-unanimous victory in *Frontiero*, the air force spouse case. O'Neill's pool memo suggested the Court do the worst possible thing for Wiesenfeld—reverse the favorable opinion summarily, on the authority of the Court's hostile decision in *Kahn v. Shevin*. Since any judge or clerk reading the memo would have to ask about the Court's recent favorable decision in *Frontiero*, O'Neill innocently adds a line: "Cf. *Frontiero v. Richardson*." The letters "Cf." in Court talk mean, "of course, you might want to take a look at your other sex-discrimination decision before you toss Ginsburg out."

O'Neill's recommendation is a little startling, in light of the Supreme Court's two essentially inconsistent decisions on sex discrimination in two years. In *Frontiero*, the Court saw the woman as the soldier, getting benefits for her husband that were not as good as those that male soldiers got for their wives. That looked like sex discrimination. In *Kahn*, the Court saw the woman as a widow, getting a little more than a much more fortunate man. That just looked like good sense. The name of the game in a legal movement such as the women's movement is to get the Court to lay down as much law as possible in your favor rejecting distinctions before a distinction the Court likes—such as widows needing a property tax break versus greedy widowers like Melvin Kahn—comes up in a case. Ginsburg was the world champion at hooking the Court into voiding laws that distinguished between men and women before they realized the unpleasant social consequences of the unisex world they were setting up. She got the hook into the Court when she got it to say that wives could not be presumed to be the dependents in *Frontiero*. But she could not stop the Court from saying that widows could be presumed to be needy old folks in *Kahn*.

Unless the Court is prepared to reverse one of the inconsistent cases, it usually ignores one as it goes about making the ensuing decisions. O'Neill's memo assumes the Court had chosen to follow the discriminatory decision in *Kahn*, and that Ginsburg's victory in *Frontiero* was a dead end. The Court, he advised, did not even have to hear Stephen Wiesenfeld's case. Had the Court followed his advice, that decision would have seriously threatened Ginsburg's careful campaign to apply the equality amendments to women.

O'Neill failed to stop the Court from taking a good look at *Weinberger v. Wiesenfeld*. At their conference, a majority of the justices, including O'Neill's boss, Rehnquist, voted to move the case to full briefing and argument. This was not necessarily good news for

Ginsburg, as the Court may well have been thinking of hearing it to undo her victory in the court below, but it was better than what O'Neill had suggested. Justice Powell noted in his papers that he wanted to hear the case in part because he doubted the correctness of the trial court decision "in view of *Kahn*." He was okay with Social Security preferring widowed mothers to widowed fathers. He was not even about to say it was irrational for the government to make it harder for Stephen Wiesenfeld to care for Jason than if he'd been a widow.

In his notes for the case, Justice Powell speculated that a stay-at-home dad must be "indolent." Justice Blackmun, too, thought at first that *Kahn* should carry the day. After all, if it's constitutional for Florida to favor widows a little, why isn't it constitutional for Social Security to favor female survivors a little? Despite the victory in the lower court, Ginsburg knew her days of asking the Court to treat sex like race were over. So she walked away. Just give us a little more of a hard look, she suggests in her brief. Not as seriously as if the law confined benefits to white people, say, but a harder look than just asking if the law is crazy.

In the run-up to oral argument, Powell got another memo from Penny Clark. She knew how hard her task would be: "His wife was in charge of his household, and his assumption was that almost no man would choose to stay home and take care of his children. [Jo Powell] lived the gracious life of the wife of a noted lawyer in Richmond, Virginia. His view was, okay, we men are in the office and this frees up our wives to do what they do and maybe if a man would do that it would seem indolent." To Powell, stay-at-home parents were tennis-playing Virginia matrons, not harried single dads trying to keep a babysitter so they could supplement their income a little. So much for Stephen Wiesenfeld.

In her preterm memo on sex discrimination, Penny Clark had advised Powell that men should not be allowed to sue to invalidate legal schemes that benefit women. But this time, the Social Security scheme's beneficiary was not so clear. Widows gained over widowers under the scheme, it was true, but at the same time dead women workers lost out to dead male workers in terms of what they left to care for their families. So, in some way, the dead Paula Wiesenfeld was the real plaintiff, just like the female soldier in *Frontiero*.

Justice Powell might be sympathetic, Clark thought, to the argument that the law was plain-and-simple discrimination against the women now venturing into the workplace. And so she wrote in her memorandum to the justice, this was not about widows and widowers. This law discriminated against female wage-earners, who paid Social Security but didn't leave as much to their families to use as male workers did. After all, her memo continued, among workers, there was a "widespread practice of taking Social Security benefits into account in calculating life insurance needs." "True," Justice Powell wrote in the margins, seeming to soften slightly from his initial response to the case. When he went to oral argument, he specifically recorded in his notes that Ginsburg did argue that the discrimination was against the working schoolteacher Paula Wiesenfeld.

Brennan's female law clerk took a different tack. Clued in by the extensive history of law of surviving parents' benefits set out in Ginsburg's brief, Marsha Berzon framed an argument for Brennan that the law was really intended to protect families. Hence, the damage to baby Jason Wiesenfeld by depriving him of the support of whichever parent survived was the key to the outcome.

Ruth Bader Ginsburg did not care which of the many Wiesenfelds the Court chose to protect; she just wanted to win the case. She took time out from contemplating the "blue skies and snow-capped mountains" while visiting "Wyoming, the Equality State" to answer a worried letter from Wiesenfeld. "The Florida widowers' case [Kahn] was mine," she wrote, but "your situation is clearly distinguishable. . . . Perhaps if the Supreme Court had heard your case first, the Florida case would have gone in our favor," the canny strategist fretted. She was even ready to settle for a tie for Wiesenfeld. Justice Douglas was at death's door and not sitting, leaving eight justices on the bench, and a 4–4 split would have left the favorable lower court opinion standing, allowing her to fight the terrible precedent in *Kahn* another day. When she sat down at the table reserved for counsel on January 20, 1975, she had at her side Stephen Wiesenfeld. Baby Jason would be Ginsburg's pet for the rest of her life. In the ensuing years, she guided his steps to law school and flew to Florida to perform his wedding ceremony.

When the justices met to discuss Stephen Wiesenfeld's case, Brennan was ready with Berzon's family-centered history of the Social Security survivors' law. "Goal of statute is to provide for children," he argued at the justices' conference. "This accords with statutory intent." Brennan attracted the other three justices from before Nixon started appointing—Marshall, White, and Stewart— but it was Lewis Powell, Penny Clark's justice, who provided the crucial fifth vote at the conference. Social Security would no longer discriminate between widows and widowers based on their sex.

Brennan, being the senior justice in the majority, assigned the opinion to himself. Again, as in *Frontiero*, his draft opinion went further than the votes at conference would have suggested was allowed. Exactly as Ginsburg had envisioned five years before, he used the invalidation of a minor discrimination in law not just for Baby Jason Wiesenfeld, but to strike a blow at sex-role stereotypes across society. "It is no less important for a child to be cared for by its sole surviving parent when that parent is male, rather than female," Brennan wrote. "And a father, no less than a mother, has a constitutionally protected right to the companionship, care, custody, and management of the children he has sired and raised, [which] undeniably warrants deference and, absent a powerful countervailing interest, protection." Brennan's far-reaching opinion attracted the agreement of Justice Blackmun, who had initially voted against Wiesenfeld, so Brennan had his five votes and didn't care when Powell surfaced with a quibble, which ultimately became a concurring opinion.

The quibble is revealing. Powell found the impermissible discrimination in Paula Wiesenfeld, the working mother's inability to provide a survivor benefit for her husband. As Powell saw it, Paula therefore accumulated fewer Social Security benefits while working than a comparable male worker. But what Powell really wanted to say in writing a separate opinion from Brennan's was that it was clear to him who *should* stay home with a baby. No using the law to attack sex-role stereotypes for Powell: "I attach less significance to the view emphasized by the Court that a purpose of the statute is to enable the surviving parent to remain at home to care for a child. In light of the long experience to the contrary, one may doubt that fathers generally will forgo work and remain at home to care for children to the same extent that mothers may make this choice." Men should not stay home.

So appealing was the Wiesenfeld family that in the end even Justice Rehnquist cast one of his few votes for women, going along with striking down the discriminatory law because it hurt the "child of a contributing worker." To the end of Rehnquist's life, he occasionally asked Ginsburg about Jason Wiesenfeld, who would always be the "baby" to Rehnquist.

And so the all-male Supreme Court managed to reproduce the entire history of the feminist movement. Justice Brennan's opinion for the five-man majority reflected the "activist" (and Ginsburg's) position that men and women could work for wages or stay home with babies, without being tied in to a stereotypical sex role. But he knew he could never get a majority of his Court to say that any distinction was suspect, as he had come within one vote of doing in *Frontiero*, before the Court started retrenching. The argument that sex discrimination was as constitutionally illicit as race was over for the moment. Justice Powell advanced the Betty Friedan formal equality argument that if women work for wages, their wages should be the same as a man would make. Of course, he reminded his audience, women should also be culturally burdened with caring for the home. And Justice Rehnquist foreshadowed the postfeminist argument that children are the most important concern in any decision.

Ginsburg never got the Supreme Court to say that sex was like race. However, except for the hardest cases, war and sex, never again would the Supreme Court say that an American law could treat women differently from men simply because they were women. The cultural issues—male caregivers as "indolent," babies as the most important job—would remain like little land mines ready to explode the movement once Ginsburg's job of establishing formal legal equality was done. But culture was not Ginsburg's task: she would change the law. Without the law telling people that women are different and destined for domestic life, the culture had the chance to change women's roles. After that, as she wrote in one of her many speeches, housewifery should be "freely chosen, not thrust upon them 'willy-nilly.'"

Ginsburg was not the only one who recognized the Term of the Woman. As the Court deliberated over *Weinberger v. Wiesenfeld*, she got a letter from her ERA opponent Philip Kurland, who edited a scholarly journal about the Supreme Court. Kurland would be delighted if Ginsburg would write about the "slew of sex discrimination cases" on this year's docket. She responded with a warning that she could hardly be objective, since she was the lawyer in the main ones! As long as she had his attention, however, on another subject entirely, she felt obliged to warn him that he was in danger of missing out on the opportunity to have an extraordinary student in the "excellent quality course" he offered at the University of Chicago. Jane Ginsburg was having "difficulty getting permission to take [Kurland's seminar] in the spring quarter," fancy that. Two weeks later, Kurland wrote to tell Ruth that his class was studying the opinion in the *Weinberger v. Wiesenfeld* case, since one of the students, her daughter, was kind enough to share her copy. Somehow Jane got the necessary permission to take Professor Kurland's course.

When Ginsburg agreed to comment on the several women's cases for Kurland's review, she had been worrying about the decision in Wiesenfeld's case. "I'm hoping for four votes," she told Stephen in a phone call. On March 19, 1975, Wiesenfeld's phone rang again. It was Ruth at a pay phone at the side of the highway. The news had come over the radio that she had won their case. "What was the vote?" she asked anxiously. (He did not know either.) She soon learned it was unanimous. "She gave the best oral arguments we heard the entire term I clerked," Penny Clark remembers, "extremely articulate, very self-possessed, not a hint of nervousness or uncertainty, she stated her case very clearly and made persuasive arguments. For all of the years from that time, whenever I heard of her, I have a mental picture of her in a red suit—that very petite person standing very straight at the podium and making this really high-quality argument. And it was huge because there weren't very many woman mentors around, to pattern my conduct as a lawyer and an oral arguer on. So what it said to me as a young woman lawyer starting out is that there are women lawyers working at the height of their profession and I can do the same. It was inspiring!"

A few weeks later, the Ginsburgs had a party to celebrate the victory in the Wiesenfeld case. Forty or more student helpers, funders, and the Wiesenfelds, father and son, gathered at their huge apartment on the Upper East Side. Jason Wiesenfeld was three. The Ginsburgs' young son James, then eight, was waiting for him with toys and presents. After the party, Ginsburg wrote to Wiesenfeld to tell him what a wonderful child Jason was and how proud he should be. And so the stay-at-home dad and the future Supreme Court justice began a lifelong correspondence. You'll find a good babysitter, Ginsburg reassures Wiesenfeld in an early note. Sometimes it takes several tries to find the right person. He describes his job to her as "motherhood," and then, catching himself as a "sexist" because he should have said "parenthood," he confesses, "I feel as oppressed as any mother who stays home with a baby all day." No "indolent" life for single dad Stephen Wiesenfeld.

The law, especially Social Security, was still riddled through with widows' preferences way beyond the surviving-parent benefit at issue in *Weinberger v. Wiesenfeld*. The most expensive benefit was that widows who did not have Social Security benefits could collect their spouse's benefits without proving they were dependent on the spouse. Widowers who did not have Social Security had to prove dependency on their dead wives. Since most men at the time worked and accumulated Social Security to the maximum allowed, they wouldn't have qualified for spousal benefits anyway. The only exception was that male public employees, who have their own pension plan separate from Social Security, could technically claim Social Security widowers' benefits under the precedents Ginsburg had established. Sooner or later, Ginsburg was going to have to perform at the high court for a greedy widower who was getting, say, a teachers' pension and was not dependent on his dead wife's Social Security benefits, but who wanted to collect anyway. But for his sex, he would be eligible. In a trice after *Weinberger v. Wiesenfeld*, Leon Goldfarb, a public employee himself not eligible for Social Security, sued to collect a widower's benefit from his wife's contributions without proving he had depended on her. And he asked the ACLU for help.

Goldfarb had no minor children. He just wanted to be treated like a widow for Social Security purposes: Wiesenfeld without the "baby." Ginsburg won it, but barely. The justices just hated the situation this small, clever woman had put them in, but five of them thought they were caught. Unless, as Justice Brennan opined at the conference, they wanted to overrule "*Weinberger* [*v. Wiesenfeld*] and *Frontiero*," they had to give Goldfarb his windfall. "The Court has gone too far," the newly appointed Justice John Paul Stevens thundered; he was "not content with the present state of the law, yet [felt] bound by cases already decided—[*Weinberger v.*] *Wiesenfeld* and *Frontiero*." As the opinions circulated, Stevens voted for Ginsburg and then against and then again for her. Justice Stewart thought the distinctions in Social Security should have been left to the legislature but conceded that Ginsburg had driven the gender issue in the other direction. "If the slate were clean," Powell grumbled, "I would certainly leave it to Congress . . . [but *Weinberger v.*] *Wiesenfeld* and *Frontiero* . . . certainly strongly support the decision [in Ginsburg's favor]." The government estimated a decision for Goldfarb would cost hundreds of millions of dollars, which would all go to men who did not need the money. The justices went back and forth for months trying to figure out an escape hatch. But brick by brick, one favorable word in one opinion at a time, Ginsburg had changed the law's presumptions about sex distinctions. In five short years, she had built a structure of women's equality using appealing litigants as much as she could. It is the ultimate testament to her architecture that now even unlikely occupants like Leon Goldfarb were sheltered by her work.

8

Finale: Boys and Girls Together

⁎

If treating widowers the same as widowed mothers was hard for the Court, equal protection for college girls and boys should have been easy. The rising generation of young females was changing at warp speed. The same 1974 term as *Weinberger v. Wiesenfeld* and the jury cases, the Court had heard a case, *Stanton v. Stanton*, from a divorcee in Utah who was trying to undo a divorce agreement that cut off child support for her eighteen-year-old daughter. Utah law held that girls did not need support because they were all grown up (and ready to marry) at age eighteen. Utah boys needed support until twenty-one, presumably so they could go to college. Preparing Justice Powell to address the case of unequal child support, Penny Clark asked her justice to "Pardon my outrage. This kind of assumption about behavioral differences between men and women, and especially the assumption that women do not have to support themselves, is at the heart of economic discrimination against women." In 1975, without any help from Ginsburg, who was not involved in the case, the Court held the Utah law unconstitutional. Only Justice Rehnquist disagreed.

As she was preparing the hard work of representing Goldfarb in the term after *Stanton*, Ginsburg got wind of another girl case coming up without her careful stewardship. Girls in Oklahoma were allowed to drink 3.2% beer at eighteen, while guys had to wait until they were twenty-one. The Hoot and Holler drive-through supermarket sued. *Craig v. Boren*, as the near-beer case came to be called, should have been easy, too. The kinds of protective justifications for sex discrimination that dogged the widows' cases were not at issue when young females were involved. Ginsburg thought the law was "ridiculous." Justice Powell's clerk Christina Whitman thought the case was "silly." But the case turned out to be much headier than the 3.2% subject matter predicted, because this time the state had a defense to justify discrimination: boys drive drunk a lot more than girls do. And technically the law discriminated against boys, who were hardly a victim class. How exactly did a law that treated young females as sober citizens harm them anyway? The local federal court upheld the Oklahoma law, and Ginsburg asked if she could help the beer drinkers' lawyer.

Ginsburg went a little easier on Craig's Oklahoma lawyer, Fred Gilbert, than on prior locals. She offered to take the friend of the Court role if he didn't want her to write his brief for him and disclaimed any intent to elbow him out of the fun of oral argument at the high court. The two civil rights lawyers engaged in a long-distance politeness contest, in which he hid behind the difficulty of brief writing at a distance and she conceded his point while continuing to try to write his brief from a distance. By the time they got to the third round of briefs, she was engaged in such tactics as sending him "the idea of an appropriate reply." She actually arranged for oral argument in *Craig v. Boren* to take place before oral argument in her case, *Califano v. Goldfarb*, which was, fortuitously, scheduled for the same day, October 5, 1976. He did a horrible job. Since she did not argue the Oklahoma case, the justices simply waited until Ginsburg stood up to argue her own case to ask her the questions they had left from the one before. No matter. Under her tutelage, Gilbert focused his efforts on getting the Court to recognize that it had in fact established a higher standard for laws that discriminated on the grounds of sex—maybe not as high as the barrier for laws based on race, but not where Ginsburg started in 1970 either.

And a palpably more searching review of sex-discrimination laws is exactly what she got from the "silly" near-beer case. The very unpersuasive statistical evidence the state of Oklahoma could muster about road safety failed to convince the Court that such an antiquated and "silly" law should make bad constitutional doctrine in the area of sex discrimination. Brennan, the senior liberal, had at least seven votes—everyone but the conservative Rehnquist and Chief Justice Warren Burger—to strike it down. (Burger, newly converted to opposing sex equality, and Rehnquist continued to inveigh against creating *any* special standard for sex discrimination, proposing to roll back the clock to where Ginsburg stepped in, *Reed v. Reed* in 1970.) Brennan again assigned the opinion to himself.

And so, although he never got five votes to treat sex differences as harshly as race, Brennan continued to slowly raise the standard for laws that discriminate on grounds of sex. We know exactly how far Brennan pushed the envelope, because Powell's clerk Tyler Baker was on it like a heat-seeking missile. In a draft, Brennan proposes to rule that "To withstand constitutional challenge, previous cases establish that classifications by gender must serve *important* governmental objectives and must be substantially related to achievement of those objectives." Wait a minute, Baker noted in a memo. Where did that "important" standard come from? That did not appear in any language they'd used before. But Brennan carried the day, simply by lining up Ruth Bader Ginsburg's great cases (and the non-ACLU case of the Utah teenager). One by one, he pointed out, the Court had rejected justifications for distinguishing between the sexes. In *Reed* it rejected administrative convenience, in *Frontiero* it rejected overbroad generalizations, in *Weinberger v. Wiesenfeld* it protected working women, and finally, in protecting *Stanton*'s daughter in Utah, it rejected misconceptions about women's place in the home. If you added up all the moves the Court had ruled out, you'd see it was almost impossible for a law that discriminated on sex to be upheld. Somewhere along the line, the tiny advocate with the precise voice had raised the standard for constitutional scrutiny of laws that separate male from female. Powell wrote a separate opinion, concurring to say he didn't like it, but "candor compel[led] him to admit" that something like a legal change had been achieved.

Having set the hook in the now faraway case of Sally Reed, Ginsburg even won for the greedy widower in *Goldfarb*. Six months after *Craig v. Boren*, she learned that the Court had handed down its opinion in her favor. Goldfarb was 5–4, much closer than her other victories, but widowers were always a harder sell to the Nine Old Men. Woo hoo, wrote the advocate to her favorite client, Stephen Wiesenfeld, on March 2, 1977. "Won Goldfarb 5–4! . . . Without the precedent in your case, we would never have achieved this success."

IF MY FRIENDS COULD SEE ME NOW

A week after the decision in *Goldfarb*, Ginsburg appeared in *Time* magazine as one of "Ten Teachers Who Shape the Future," alongside such luminaries as Harvard's legendary constitutional law guru Laurence Tribe, later of *Bush v. Gore* fame, and the man who suspended the death penalty, Anthony Amsterdam. She argued the cause of the Equal Rights Amendment in *The New York Times*. She testified before the United States Senate on the constitutionality of extending the ratification deadline for the ERA. She wrote (on the ERA) for *Cosmo*! Her daughter, Jane, having duly impressed Philip Kurland with her paper in his seminar at the U of C, made it to Harvard Law School, where she followed in her mother's footsteps onto the all-powerful *Harvard Law Review*. Even James, who had been the subject of annoying phone calls from school all those years, found computers a compelling subject and spent a happy summer on a student exchange to France. She and Marty celebrated their twenty-fifth wedding anniversary, "a rare thing these days," she thought.

In 1977 she won a month's residency at the Rockefeller Foundation's famed Bellagio Center, in a castle perched high above Lake Como, Italy. She was supposed to write an article about the impact of her litigation on constitutional equality. "Heavenly," she wrote to Stephen Wiesenfeld. Looking out over the towering pine trees and manicured lawns from the antiques-filled magisterial rooms, "It is," she told her ACLU boss Aryeh Neier in a postcard he never expected to see, "a place not to work on a law review article but to write poetry to your lover." But Ginsburg was always more than a "mind in a vat" to the men who understood her. "She was an attractive woman," Neier remembers fondly. "I could very well imagine a romantic attachment to her."

While Ruth was hanging out with the movers and shakers on the op-ed page of *The New York Times* and dreaming among the murmuring pines, people, including her devoted husband, were mobilizing to move her up to the next career plateau. Marty, whose tax prowess made him emminently employable, left his law firm to take up a job teaching tax at Columbia. So they were colleagues. He was also portable.

Once Jimmy Carter, a Democrat, was elected in 1976, he was committed to integrating the federal judiciary with racial minorities and women. And women's expectations went way up. The path was tortuous. First the Carter White House had to wrench the job of finding nominees from the members of the white and male United States Senate. Carter achieved this early in his term, creating citizens' nominating committees to suggest names for the all-important courts of appeals. Then the women's advocates on staff at the White House had to wrench access to the Carter committees from the clueless Justice Department, which would normally have had responsibility for justice-related matters such as nominees to the federal courts. The department, led by Attorney General Griffin Bell, whose longtime law firm, King & Spalding, was later successfully charged with illegal sex discrimination, was not a hotbed of diversity. And then, the newly enlightened White House had to fight off the American Bar Association, which still demanded fifteen years of legal experience to be labeled qualified to be a judge. That rolled the clock back to women who graduated law school before 1962, a group who could essentially be counted on one hand.

From the moment of Carter's election, Ginsburg's name started appearing in articles on the list of likely nominees. By 1978, Congress had voted to create dozens of new federal judgeships, and it looked like the logjam for female and minority appointees was about to be broken. Surely, of the handful of arguably qualified women to start integrating the federal bench, Ruth should have been on everybody's list. Marty Ginsburg, until 1979 a very influential tax lawyer at the powerhouse New York law firm Weil, Gotshal & Manges, began a letter-writing campaign. His well-connected partner Ira Millstein wrote in support of Ruth to a close Carter connection at Griffin Bell's law firm. Unknown to her, a throwback to her original interest in foreign law brought her useful attention. She was chosen to be part of an eleven-person delegation from the American Bar Association to China, which she described as "a country of many millions without any lawyers." Such trips were invaluable for the networking that is essential to ascending a high federal bench. Blessedly, she reports, as the lone woman she had her own room. "My colleagues were required to double, and constantly complained of each others' snoring." Regardless of the banality of the conversation, her companion on that China trip, Chesterfield Smith, an immediate past president of the ABA, wrote to his successor, the *chairman* of Carter's Citizens' Commission for Appointments to the Second Circuit, Lawrence Walsh. "Without reservation," Smith told Walsh, he was "confident that Ruth Bader Ginsburg would make a perfectly splendid appellate judge."

Judge Patrick Higginbotham, the prodigiously talented, youngest sitting federal judge, got one of his pals to write directly to Michael Egan, the guy at Justice responsible for vetting the appointments. Marty used every occasion, including the not obvious occasion of the meeting of the American Law Institute Federal Income Tax Project, to buttonhole well-connected acquaintances. Not satisfied with his surrogates, Marty Ginsburg wrote to Associate Attorney General Michael Egan himself. If Egan needed a reference for Ruth, her husband wrote, his exceedingly well-connected friends would be "happy to supply it." And in case the Justice Department did not have a full-enough file on her, Marty was sending Egan some newspaper and magazine articles.

Despite its origin in Carter's desire for more diversity, the Second Circuit commission produced an all-male list of potential nominees. When Carter filled all the vacancies on the Second Circuit with men, women's groups, which had organized robustly to penetrate the judicial selection process, were very unhappy. And vociferous. Susan Ness, the well-connected Washington insider running the process for the National Women's Political Caucus, went public with her criticisms of the old boys' networks set up by Senators Javits and Moynihan of New York. Javits's panel, all men! Moynihan's panel, one woman, not a lawyer! And that from New York, which had the highest concentration of women lawyers in the country. Ness specifically called the Carter administration on the failure to appoint Ginsburg, who, as usual, was more circumspect, letting her aggressive feminist shock troops do the work. "A federal appellate judgeship is not in the cards for me, it seems," she wrote to her chum William Spann, president of the ABA, in 1979, "—a disappointment, although in retrospect I suppose my expectations were unrealistic."

By now Ginsburg, in her mid-forties, was a little fried. In a 1977 speech to the American Trial Lawyers Association, she advised future Supreme Court advocates to "feed the Court" what it needs, in the form of "chunks" of text in the brief "they can lift verbatim" into their opinions. "Dress conservatively," she cautioned, and "prepare for their lack of manners"! Nor did brilliance excuse the rudeness: "No justice ever asked better or harder questions than my colleagues at Columbia did in the moot court" rehearsals they held beforehand; indeed, she told her audience, the justices make terribly annoying and mistaken statements from the bench. She shared with her colleagues a few of the worst examples, especially the reflexive sexist wisecracks that she deafened herself to ignore. The impolitic tone of the speech reflects her desire to be done with the work of persuading her intellectual inferiors to do the right thing.

As she looked longingly across the bench, she had one more case to argue, *Duren v. Missouri*, a follow-up to the attack on eliminating women from juries, this time by allowing them to request an automatic exemption. She won handily (8–1) in light of the big jury cases from earlier in her campaign. On May 31, 1979, she wrote to Stephen Wiesenfeld that if the forces for women's equality won one last case, *Califano v. Westcott*, she would be "satisfied that we have reached the end of the road, successfully, on explicit sex lines in the law." *Westcott*, which was not her case, challenged the distinction in welfare law between families with unemployed fathers, who got welfare, and families with unemployed mothers, who did not. Not surprisingly, when confronted with such a raw distinction in the law, after all Ginsburg's spadework, the Court struck the welfare law down. In her own words, she was at "the end of the road."

A LONG JOURNEY

Marty kept working the phones. One day toward the very end of Carter's one term, as more judgeships started opening up, Marilyn Haft, then counsel to Vice President Walter Mondale, looked up from her desk to see Martin Ginsburg, a friend of Haft's ex-husband, standing in her office. The new judges bill had produced a vacancy on the prestigious federal Court of Appeals for the D.C. Circuit, and, although the family would have to move away from New York, he was lobbying the people in the White House to consider Ruth for the next opening. Haft had been at the ACLU at the same time as Ruth, so she was all for it and did everything she could to make it happen.

Despite the existence of Citizens Commissions and Pipeline Projects, federal judgeships ultimately come down to a small group of informal White House decision makers. In December 1979, the presidential assistant Sarah Weddington, of *Roe v. Wade* fame, Attorney General Benjamin Civiletti, and the congressional liaison Frank Moore were looking at the lists of candidates. Weddington was lobbying hard for Ginsburg, whom she had known for almost a decade through their mutual interest in women's rights. Civiletti was unenthusiastic. Finally, in a bald exercise of log-rolling, Weddington traded her support for two of the attorney general's male candidates in exchange for his vote for Ginsburg. But Weddington was not so certain that Civiletti would stay true to the deal, so she went directly to Carter—her office was just above his in the White House—after the meeting. "I never leak," she reminded him, "but this time I need to leak this appointment before anyone changes his mind." Then she called Ginsburg to tell her the news. Two days later, *The Washington Post* ran a scoop: "Feminist Picked for U.S. Court of Appeals Here." "Informed sources," the *Post* reports, revealed the selection.

Ruth Ginsburg was still very jumpy. Her nomination had been prematurely leaked, she groused, and she had a long, anxious wait. Carter's people took a long time to send her name to the Senate. Then the Senate Judiciary Committee took a really long time even setting a hearing. "People at the right end of the political spectrum" were going to "attempt to paint [her] as a wild-eyed radical," she feared. Learning that a feminist colleague, Lynn Hecht Schafran from the NOW Legal Defense Fund, had talked about her campaign against men meeting to do their business at all-male clubs, the nominee wrote to caution her friend. "In the future be very careful about anything that might be attributed to me. Things are not going as well as they might," she fretted, "and I must be super cautious about defusing charges against me on the ground of my 'militant feminism.'" Time was slipping by, and a presidential election loomed in November.

Who should ride to the rescue but Martin Ginsburg's well-connected law partner Ira Millstein. Fortuitously, Millstein "had some prior dealings" with the ranking minority member of the Senate Judiciary Committee, the Republican Orrin Hatch. So the well-connected lawyer organized a little lunch for the conservative Mormon Utah senator and the head of the ACLU Women's Rights Project, who was hoping to ascend to the bench. Millstein urged the senator to hear her out and make up his own mind about her being an ideologue, biased and unsuited for broader judicial responsibilities. He says he doesn't remember what she said at lunch. But whatever she said to Senator Hatch that day, after the lunch the "opposition seemed to have melted away." Nobody, as Nina Totenberg reminds us, performs as well under pressure as the small but steely Ruth Bader Ginsburg.

Martin Ginsburg sold all the stocks in his investment portfolio so Ruth would not have to recuse herself from cases involving his companies, and the family moved to an apartment in the luxury Watergate condominium.

On June 30, 1980, Ruth Bader Ginsburg put on her judicial robes. Her days of imploring the courts were over. Now she would be doing the deciding.

Part III

FWOTSC

Sandra Day O'Connor with Chief Justice Warren Burger immediately
before she was sworn in as the first female Supreme Court justice, September 25, 1981.

9

Sandra O'Connor Raises Arizona

⁂

WHAT COULD SHE HAVE BEEN THINKING

In 1971, just as people were beginning the push that would ultimately put her and Ruth Bader Ginsburg on the bench, State Senator Sandra Day O'Connor wrote to President Richard Nixon to suggest he use the vacancy that had just come up to place a female on the Supreme Court. Your other choices have been just wonderful, she begins flatteringly. Now it would be a great time to add a woman.

He did not. Instead, President Nixon's selection, O'Connor's Stanford classmate and Phoenix friend William Rehnquist, was the furthest thing from the candidate she had suggested. First and foremost, Rehnquist was at the cutting edge of the conservative legal campaign to roll back the civil rights movement at its racial foundation. This campaign had devastating implications for the women's movement, because the movement for women's legal equality had always rested on the foundation laid by the racial civil rights movement. That's what President Clinton meant when he called Ruth Bader Ginsburg the "Thurgood Marshall of the Women's Movement" at her nomination in 1993. Without the expansive interpretation of the Fourteenth Amendment that started with the racial movement, none of the other equality movements could have gotten off the ground.

During his confirmation battle, Rehnquist was found to be the author of a memorandum to Justice Jackson, for whom he had clerked in 1952, outlining why Jackson should vote against school desegregation in *Brown*. "I realize," Rehnquist admitted, "that it is an unpopular and unhumanitarian position, for which I have been excoriated by 'liberal' colleagyes [*sic*], but I think Plessy v. Ferguson [the 1877 decision approving racial segregation in the South] was right and should be re-affirmed." (Ignoring the advice, Jackson joined the unanimous decision ordering desegregation.) When Rehnquist, along with his law school friends Sandra and John O'Connor, settled in Phoenix after his clerkship, he continued his opposition to racial civil rights. As the city of Phoenix contemplated passing a civil rights ordinance in 1964, Rehnquist, then a lawyer in private practice, testified at the hearings. He had no client in the matter, he told the city council. But he wanted the legislators to know that a law forbidding merchants from discriminating on the grounds of race sacrificed shopkeepers' rights in order to protect the rights of racial minorities. In such cases, Rehnquist held, property rights mattered more than racial justice.

Despite Rehnquist's substantive opposition to every aspect of the women's legal movement, Sandra O'Connor flung herself into the campaign for his appointment. Her passionate advocacy of Rehnquist's confirmation for a seat she had proposed for a woman neatly presents the question of how serious a feminist she was.

At first glance, it might seem that she was just like the many conservative women activists who surfaced as the Republican Party definitively broke with the feminist movement in the '70s. The anti-ERA activist Phyllis Schlafly was an early example of the type. Outstanding women, they preached, would do just fine without any change in the law. They did not need the Equal Rights Amendment, which would hurt their more traditional sisters. Certainly they did not need anything like access to abortion, with all its moral hazard. O'Connor followed in the Schlafly mode when she busily volunteered her services, living off the income of her lawyer husband, to endear herself to the Republican establishment and then asked her party to appoint her to the overwhelmingly male legislature. She sounded a lot like Schlafly when she boasted that once any discriminatory all-male institution let her in the door, she never had another moment's difficulty. If O'Connor were a Phyllis Schlafly type, her advocacy of Rehnquist would not be puzzling at all.

But even as early in her career as 1971, her request that Nixon appoint a woman is somewhat at odds with conservative feminism. The long-standing practice of discrimination in the legal profession meant that, in 1971, there was no woman competitive with the male candidates for a Supreme Court appointment by any neutral standard, especially compared to someone with the credentials of a William Rehnquist. And, endearingly, O'Connor knew it. Later, long after President Reagan's political strategy motivated him to appoint her in 1981, she defended affirmative action to her conservative colleague Antonin Scalia. Interrupting his diatribe against it at conference in an affirmative action case, she asked, "Why, Nino, how do you think I got here?"

Moreover, immediately after she went to bat for Rehnquist she actively pursued women's equality through legal change on all fronts. Like Ginsburg, she recognized that women could use the law to pry open realms of life foreclosed to them by historical practices of exclusion. She did not just think they should volunteer for the Republican Party and then ask for favors. So her advocacy of a man whose efforts would undermine that progress remains a puzzle.

Another possible explanation is that despite her recognition of the value of law as an instrument for women's advancement, she might have decided that the conservative agenda she shared with her good friend—favoring the states over the federal government and business over government at any level—was more important than her concerns for women. Certainly, once she got to the Court, she voted with Rehnquist on federalism and regulatory issues almost all the time.

Or she may have felt that Rehnquist—by all accounts a great friend and a fair-minded individual in his private dealings—was suitable to serve on an important institution like the Court. His character and administrative capability made him "attractive" in her eyes, a highly personal evaluation she used throughout her life.

High-minded governance—merit selection of judges, civic education—was a consistent theme for her. When O'Connor came of political age in Arizona in the 1950s and '60s, decades of one-party rule by the Democratic Party had produced a corrupt and factionalized pattern of governance by rulers fearful of economic change. If Arizona was the state of the three C's (Copper, Cotton, and Citrus), people used to say, lobbyists ran the Democratic legislature with the three B's—Booze, Beefsteaks, and Blondes. The newly arrived Republican migrants from places like Kansas quickly captured the language of political rectitude, portraying themselves as the energetic reform-minded proponents of useful economic growth. Just before Rehnquist was nominated, O'Connor played a lead role in getting the legislature redistricted to favor Republicans. (When Dems squawked, Gene Pulliam's *Arizona Republic* editorialized that any self-respecting political party would do the same.) There is no evidence that, despite her disagreement with the Republican Party on women's issues, she ever stopped thinking of the Republicans as the better governors.

She opened her drive for Rehnquist with an unsolicited letter to the chairman of the Senate Judiciary Committee offering to testify for her friend. Days after the nomination, she was making speeches on the floor of the Senate and to the socially powerful Phoenix Kiwanis about Rehnquist's merits. Her efforts were in keeping with her lifelong political strategy to know a lot of people and work the people you know. A relatively obscure state legislator, she had uncharacteristically easy access to the confirmation process. Rehnquist's and O'Connor's mutual friend the former Arizonan Richard Kleindienst, then an assistant attorney general, was responsible for Rehnquist's selection. She made a list of all the people she thought could help and gave them their "assignments," mostly to contact the people *they* knew. Being a board member of a big Arizona bank, she recruited its president, Sherman Hazeltine, to work the bank presidents' network around the country to contact their senators. It was a great idea: bank presidents know a lot of senators, and she collected scores of letters from the local bankers to their representatives in Congress. She printed up the roster of Stanford classmates and pursued the ones she knew would be supportive and willing to reach their representatives. The O'Connors' household was soon covered with paperwork.

The Rehnquist forces thought the two U.S. senators from

Arizona were sufficient for witness purposes and turned down O'Connor's offer to testify. They did, however, use her heavily to defend against the charges that Rehnquist, in his role as Republican poll watcher, had harassed black voters by asking them to demonstrate their literacy. Apparently anxious that the charges not catch fire, Kleindienst sent O'Connor on research missions for exculpatory material. In November 1971, in the middle of the debate over his nomination, Rehnquist himself sent her a memo recalling a legal opinion from the Arizona attorney general forbidding poll watchers from demanding literacy. Could she find the opinion? It would bolster his defense that he didn't do any such thing. His pal on the scene duly produced the opinion.

When her researches turned up damaging documents, such as a legal article filled with incendiary rhetoric that the nominee had written for a local rag, she recommended to Rehnquist that the article "not come out." Rehnquist had called the highest court of the United States a "bleeding heart" in criminal procedure, and quoted with admiration an old Supreme Court opinion: "there should be no appeal permitted in a criminal case; if the jury said a man was to be hanged, he was hanged." The article, O'Connor reassured him, had not come out so far. It emerged only after Rehnquist was long confirmed.

As the confirmation process wound down, Rehnquist wrote her and John a note of warm thanks for all their efforts. She wrote to each of the people who had helped campaign for his confirmation. The investiture, which they attended, was "an emotional moment" for her, "in view of the significance which it holds for the future of the Court," which would now have a member who had opposed desegregation. His appointment was certainly significant in one arena: for the next nine years, as the ACLU's Ginsburg appeared before the Supreme Court to establish the foundation of legal equality for women, Rehnquist almost without exception voted no.

KEEPING HOUSE AND KEEPING STATE HOUSE

A few months later, the regional office of the Committee to Re-Elect the President began pressing the Arizona campaign chair,

Sam Mardian, to recruit a woman to help head up Nixon's 1972 election effort. Even if the president wasn't going to integrate the Court, the politicos at least felt that the reelection operation shouldn't be 100 percent male. The energetic and resourceful O'Connor was a natural. In her efforts to help reelect President Nixon, she visited the local offices, organized events, encouraged the Young Republicans at Arizona State University, coordinated polling between local and national campaigns. One of her proud accomplishments was the establishment of identity groups within the campaign, such as blacks, Spanish-speakers, and the elderly. There were thirteen in all. Despite her concern with equalizing the Arizona laws applied to women, women did not appear on the political list of interest groups in the Republican campaign. After the election, her lively and competent campaign performance elicited the predictable inquiry about her availability to join the administration, but she declined. Her family was ensconced in Phoenix, John in practice, the boys in school, she said.

In the Arizona world where she elected to remain, the 1972 election returned the Republicans to power in the statehouse, and Senator O'Connor promptly unseated the Republican majority leader. For the next two years, she would be at the center of power in the local legislature. She was keenly aware that she "was in a position of power. I got the things I wanted enacted." She describes her years in the legislature as a time of bipartisan cooperation for the good of the people, and her record does include advancing laws both liberal and conservative. She took the Republican line on gun control, the death penalty, and school busing, but she swung the other way on environmental issues and bilingual education. She even tried for a middle-of-the-road approach to welfare.

And she made real efforts on women's equality. This was not as independent of party as it now looks. Although Justice Rehnquist's record was a leading indicator, Republicans did not bail on women's equality all at once. Only in 1980 did the party formally revoke support of the Equal Rights Amendment in its platform. Throughout the '70s, nonpartisan "law reform" movements out of professional institutions such as the Commissioners on Uniform

State Laws were recommending nondiscriminatory schemes in areas like family law, where ancient divisions survived. In 1973, O'Connor was able to lead a bipartisan effort to repeal the web of Arizona laws that discriminated against women. She was visibly behind the revision of Arizona's community property law to allow women rights of management over marital property and to remove male-only language that sometimes carried a real sting, for instance, that only fathers could sue for the death or injury of a child.

Despite her mixed ideological record, her most robust initiative was a core conservative agenda item: putting a cap on taxes. She started, in 1973, by convening a meeting of prominent citizens. By the next year, she had submitted a proposal for a referendum to amend the state constitution to limit state expenditures to a fixed percentage of the total personal income of the state. O'Connor pulled out all the stops to get the measure passed. She wrote to the party icon Senator Barry Goldwater, asking him to contact recalcitrant House members, Republican and Democratic, to pass the measure out. "It is my belief that placing this measure on the ballot for November [1974] elections would be a boost to the Republican cause in November," she implored Goldwater, and "passage of it in Arizona would pave the way for similar action in other states." Two days later, Senator Goldwater, who usually avoided state legislative battles, responded by sending a telegram to Arizona House Majority Leader Burton Barr. O'Connor's measure even came to the attention of Governor Ronald Reagan, who saluted her at a meeting of the Arizona Republican Party's Trunk 'n' Tusk Club. It was probably the first time Reagan had ever heard of her.

The tax limitation movement was of a piece with the revival of conservative politics in general. Analysts widely credit the passage of tax-cutting Proposition 13 in California in 1978 with giving a major boost to Ronald Reagan's stature as a presidential contender. So in making her big legislative initiative out of an effort to limit taxes, O'Connor was aligning herself with the most conservative developments on the national scene. Barr, then majority leader of the Republican State House of Representatives, says of his relentlessly hardworking colleague, "With Sandra O'Connor, there ain't no Miller Time."

QUITTING AGAIN

But O'Connor would not be on the ballot with the measure she had worked so hard to pass. Several months before the election of 1974, Majority Leader O'Connor announced she would not run for reelection, once more turning her back on the career she had laboriously built. It wasn't that her babysitter quit, which had preceded her previous retirement from the world of work. This time she quit, she says, because she thought people shouldn't stay in the legislature too long. They get a big head. Or maybe she was just fed up. Just before she announced her resignation, she snapped at one of her colleagues, who had said, "If you were a man, I'd punch you in the mouth." "If you were a man," O'Connor uncharacteristically responded, "you could." Years later when asked about her time in the mostly male Arizona statehouse, she sighed, "I was never one of the boys." The tax limitation referendum failed to pass.

And once again she resigned without a plan for her future. But luck was with her this time. A month after she ended her stay in the legislature, a state judgeship became available. Under Arizona's system of electing judges, first she had to win the Republican primary. It seems an odd comedown for the powerful legislative leader, but after a hard election battle she found herself in the basement of the courthouse presiding over ordinary criminal trials. By all accounts she very much enjoyed her obscure position, with its exposure to a range of human emotions and experiences. Despite their modest positions, the sixty or so members of the Arizona judiciary managed to make a good time for themselves. O'Connor reunited with Paul Rosenblatt, her old colleague from the AG's office, now himself a state trial judge, at various judicial conferences. There was always a big dinner, and Mary Fran Ogg, one of the judges' wives, led long evenings of drink and song around the piano. Rosenblatt disagreed with Burton Barr's quip about it never being Miller Time with his hardworking colleague in the legislature. Barr wouldn't think that, Rosenblatt says, if he had seen O'Connor singing around the piano at "Ogg/judicial Miller Time."

Welcome Justice O'Connor

As O'Connor embraced and then retreated from real political power, other, similarly situated Republican women, who had also married "wealthily," were making a flank attack on the world of politics, straddling the divide between women's claims and the party's increasing conservatism. The most brilliant success was Anne Armstrong, born into money even before she married the Texas rancher Tobin Armstrong. The Armstrongs had essentially revived the Republican Party in Texas, which had been a Democratic stronghold since the Civil War. The gonzo fund-raiser and organizer Armstrong did not run for office, but, rather, followed the traditional fund-raiser's route to the Republican National Committee. She was the first female co-chair of the committee in history and then went on to become an advisor to Richard Nixon. This made her the go-to girl for female candidates for high office. In 1972, when the southwest regional campaign director wanted to recommend O'Connor for such a position, it was Armstrong he asked. One week before Nixon resigned in 1974, Armstrong suggested Patricia Lindh, wife of the oil executive Robert Lindh, to be White House special assistant for women.

In the palmy days of establishment Republican support for women's causes like the ERA, Armstrong and Lindh moved smoothly into position under Nixon's successor Gerald Ford. The women worked on women's interest in matters such as credit discrimination and education. As the ERA faded from favor, it was the women candidates who commanded their attention. Unlike Ginsburg the litigator and O'Connor the legislator, when it came to women's issues, Lindh described her undertaking as "nagging a lot." On the rare occasions when the White House personnel office asked, she "inundated them with women."

One woman on Pat Lindh's list was the Maricopa County trial judge Sandra Day O'Connor. Lindh suggested Gerald Ford consider her to replace Supreme Court justice William O. Douglas in 1975. Proposing a lowly state trial judge for the Supreme Court is not as crazy as it sounds. There simply were almost no women on the bench at all in 1975, so Lindh's list included low-ranking judges from the local D.C. trial court and a Florida state trial judge in a position like O'Connor's. (That year also marks the first appearance of Ginsburg's name on a list, predictably, from the National Women's Political Caucus; she was certainly not an obvious contender for the attention of a Republican White House.) It all came to naught when Ford appointed the federal appeals court judge John Paul Stevens to take Douglas's place.

As usual with her, O'Connor would rise along a much less traditional path than the women's advocates in Washington could dream of. And once again, her connections played a role. To her everlasting good fortune, in 1979, her pal the teetotal Mormon—and former Phoenix mayor—John Driggs wanted to spice up his social life. "We go to all these other people's cocktail parties and dinners," John said to his wife, Gail, "and we can't do the same." Searching for a way to make a party special without violating the tenets of their religion with alcohol, John asked his wife, "Who do we know that's important that might come in and give a speech and that would be our twist at the party?" "Well," she said, "what about Mark Cannon?" Cannon, a distant relative, was the administrative assistant to the chief justice of the United States, Warren Burger.

Driggs immediately picked up the phone. "Hey, Mark," he asked, "any chance that you're going to be in Arizona?"

"Well, as a matter of fact, in August," Cannon replied, "the chief and I are going to Flagstaff for a meeting."

Flagstaff, three hours north of Phoenix, is a couple of hours south of the Grand Canyon area, including the gorgeous Lake

Powell, created by a dam on the Colorado River. For years a favorite summer pastime of Arizonans was to rent houseboats and motor around the lake, swimming in its crystalline waters and admiring the stunning scenery. The Driggses had just gone to Lake Powell with a neighbor the year before and they were totally enamored with the experience. Without missing a beat, John Driggs asked Cannon whether the chief justice had ever been on Lake Powell. Cannon thought not. "What if," Driggs inquired, "we tried to put a trip together after your conference?" A month later, the chief justice accepted the houseboat invitation. Driggs arranged to bring the Driggs kids, and the houseboat owner's son offered to pilot them for a chance to meet the Big Chief.

Then Driggs had another problem: What to do to entertain the chief justice of the United States for three days? Gail and John Driggs weren't even lawyers! They'd better expand the party, John decided. Reviewing the list of their acquaintances, John said, "Let's just invite the O'Connors." Even though Sandra was marooned in the humblest courtroom in Phoenix, John and Gail just felt totally comfortable with their good friends, and they knew the O'Connors were lively company. So John Driggs called his pal John O'Connor at his law firm and asked him if he'd like to help host Chief Justice Warren Burger of the Supreme Court after his conference in Flagstaff. "Would we ever!" John O'Connor replied.

A few months later, the chief justice walked onto the deck of a houseboat in northern Arizona. "Call me Chief," he said in his trademark humble way. The little party swam, they explored the canyons, they ate the wonderful meals the Driggses and O'Connors had painstakingly planned. At the table, the chief justice took the opportunity to share with the assembled families his personal history, his interest in American history, and any other matters they cared to discuss. Indeed, if anyone asked Burger a question away from the assembled seven or eight passengers, he would always defer the answer until he had everyone's full attention.

Several times the guests lingering over the table after dinner would notice that the chief—and Superior Court Judge Sandra Day O'Connor—had vanished. When John Driggs went looking he found the two of them sitting in a remote corner of the upper deck, chatting away like old friends. On several occasions, they spent until the wee hours of the morning talking. No one knows what they said. Gail Driggs speculates they were discussing stories from history.

"Wouldn't it be great," Gail said to her husband as they drove back to Phoenix after the vacation, "if someday Sandra went on the Court?"

"Don't be silly," he replied. "Never happen."

Six months later, Governor Bruce Babbitt elevated O'Connor out of the basement and onto the intermediate state court, the Arizona Court of Appeals. The woman she replaced, Judge Mary Schroeder, the first woman partner in a major Phoenix law firm, had just been appointed to the Federal Court of Appeals for the Ninth Circuit by President Carter. Schroeder was the beneficiary of the same lobbying and organizing that put Ginsburg on the D.C. Circuit, and she was the Arizona Democrats' candidate for the pathbreaking Supreme Court slot, should the opportunity arise. At the time, O'Connor's appointment to replace her on the Arizona court just looked like insurance to Governor Babbitt, who was planning a run for reelection and did not want the popular female ex-legislator O'Connor as his Republican opponent. But he wasn't the only one with his eye on the compelling Sandra Day O'Connor. When the Driggses reached O'Connor in the receiving line at her investiture ceremony as an appellate judge, she drew John Driggs aside. "Guess what!" she whispered. "The chief just invited me to go to London with an American delegation to a legal conference."

Whatever the occasion, she always rose to the occasion. Bill Bryson, who went on to become a judge on the U.S. Court of Appeals for the Federal Circuit, was then a low-level employee in the Justice Department and, coincidentally, the boyfriend of Justice Powell's former clerk Penny Clark. He was also one of the staffers to the delegation Burger assembled. When he returned from London he reported to Penny that there was this amazing woman on this trip, who had added so much to the discussions with her perspective as a legislator. What a brilliant person, and most of all, unlike other notables on the trip, this stranger from Arizona was "kind and considerate to the staff who were making their trip comfortable and took note of the efforts the people who were organizing all of these things were making."

FWOTSC HAS A THOUSAND FATHERS

By 1980 the bipartisan consensus on women—that the laws should not discriminate on grounds of sex and that qualified women should be allowed to compete for jobs at every level—had seriously unraveled. There was no more room for good-government Republicans to agree to disagree on matters such as the Equal Rights Amendment while well-heeled women such as Anne Armstrong and Pat Lindh "nagged" long-suffering men in the White House for a token appointment here and there. At its 1980 convention, the Republican Party, firmly in the hands of the conservative wing, and about to nominate Ronald Reagan, repudiated its support for the Equal Rights Amendment and allied itself publicly with the opponents of women's abortion rights. Polling revealed that women were starting to peel off from the Grand Old Party. Four years later, the gender gap, wherein women disproportionately support the Democratic candidate and men the Republican, would emerge as a constant in American politics.

There are more women, and they vote in higher numbers. Once in a while the candidates' insecurity in face of the electoral process yields social change. One such moment was 1980. Disabled by his party's conservative turn, Reagan could only offer female voters a symbol. Urged on by his somewhat liberal campaign advisor Stuart Spencer, Reagan announced that if elected he would fill the next Supreme Court vacancy with a woman. Almost immediately after he took office, Justice Potter Stewart decided it was time to step down.

Many men have claim to the role of godfather to the future Justice O'Connor. After Reagan won, her houseboat pal Warren Burger invited White House counsel Fred Fielding for lunch to tout her candidacy. O'Connor's biographer Ann McFeatters asserts that her relationship with William Rehnquist was crucial in getting her on the list. Others cite the long and warm partnership with Barry Goldwater. As luck would have it just as her candidacy heated up, O'Connor did the honors at Goldwater's nephew's wedding. She delivered a paean to family values, which Goldwater later used to defend her against attacks from right-to-life activists in Arizona. But in all of this historical inquiry almost no one focuses on the obvious Godfather—Reagan himself. Before he died, Attorney General William French Smith, who was undoubtedly at the center of any Supreme Court nomination process, told an aide that in 1980 Reagan had given him a short list with O'Connor's name written on it in Reagan's own hand. Knowing now that Reagan had noticed her as early as 1974 for her tax-ceiling efforts in Arizona makes this explanation a lot more convincing. The White House decided to send a scouting party to O'Connor's Edenic home in Paradise Valley.

She might have been the only woman at the time who could have pulled it off. Despite Republican feminism's promising beginning as a ladylike request for simple justice, by 1980 the feminist movement was pretty distant from the Republican Party and vice versa. Richard Nixon had vetoed the only serious effort to provide public funds for child care, Republicans provided most of the votes to cut off public Medicaid funding for abortions, and the convention that nominated Ronald Reagan also withdrew party support for the ERA.

The kinds of women who broke the entry barriers to law school and were beginning to be discussed as judicial candidates looked a lot more like Ruth Bader Ginsburg than Sandra Day O'Connor. Even the women on most lists Smith gathered for Reagan were Democrats! They understood that being a better cook *and* a better lawyer was still no weapon against a world of discrimination and stereotyping, that the coercive power of the law was going to have to be brought to bear on women's inequality, that publicly funded day care would be a huge help and abortion rights were foundational.

Appellate Judge Sandra Day O'Connor thought women mostly just had to get a foot in the door, so she was a perfect candidate for the role of symbolic Republican appointment. If people only got to know her, she believed, they would recognize her extraordinary talents and her keen social skills. In the small western community that sparsely populated Arizona still was, volunteers as disciplined and talented as Sandra Day O'Connor were rare. That people might persist in sacrificing women's talents in order to keep their universe all male did not seem to occur to her.

When the vetting committee arrived at O'Connor's house, she did the now-familiar bra and wedding ring routine; after discussing the ins and outs of federal/state relations with Kenneth Starr and the White House team, she fixed them a lovely lunch of salmon salad and iced tea. She had everything, Starr reported back: the right age, philosophy, and political support. Besides, replete with salmon salad, he said, "I liked her." The fact that she'd never heard a federal case—indeed, her docket was heavily filled with the most banal workman's compensation disputes, Mary Schroeder recalls—was of no consequence. Once Reagan met her, he felt the same way. Horses, ranching—their get-acquainted meeting produced a perfect union of two independent spirits from the sun-drenched West. No need to bring anyone else, he told his team. Shortly after meeting her and before the opposition could mobilize, Ronald Reagan acted to nominate her. If she could get through the confirmation process, the next Supreme Court justice would break the glass . . . portico and ascend to the highest court in the land. When Judge Ruth Bader Ginsburg of the D.C. Circuit Court of Appeals got the news on her car radio in Washington, she was glad to hear it, even though she had never heard of the nominee.

O'Connor returned home from her interview with Reagan just in time for her husband's firm's Fourth of July party. "We didn't think she would get it," John O'Connor's protegée and Sandra's admirer Ruth McGregor says. But when, contrary to their speculation, her nomination was announced, John's firm was all in. The Justice Department sent briefing notebooks, and McGregor and a handful of John O'Connor's partners spent a weekend at the firm's library going over the material to prepare her for her hearings.

While she went through the process, she dealt with the stress in her own way. One Sunday morning that summer, John Driggs got a call. "John," Sandra asked, "what are you doing today?"

"Just going to church, why?"

"May I come?"

"Of course you can."

"John O'Connor was a Catholic," Driggs confirms, "but neither of them was much of a churchgoer." So, although she was not a Mormon, off she went to the Mormon services that Sunday in the middle of a stress-filled summer. Of course the Driggses were thrilled, called everyone in the family, and made sure the sermon and lesson were suitable for the exalted occasion. By chance, the sex-segregated ladies' service meeting that day included a recipe from the renowned local cook Judge Sandra Day O'Connor. She was uncharacteristically fidgety, rooting around in her purse for something during the service. But she said nothing about the reason. And no one asked.

Despite her initial nervousness, when O'Connor actually appeared in the Senate, her trademark combination of stunningly industrious preparation and western charisma swept the field. She had studied not only the answers to questions about the law but also the senators' personal histories and interests. Bystanders observed the social intelligence that had drawn fellow legislators and judges to her home in Paradise Valley for Mexican dinners for decades past. The biographer Joan Biskupic tells the story of her visit to Edward Kennedy, not the most obvious supporter of a Reagan appointee. "Senator Kennedy," she reportedly began, "how is your mother?" And Kennedy responded with an intimate anecdote about his mother's loss of her short-term memory.

As a female nominee, she was the beneficiary of enormous good feeling about landmarks and breakthroughs. Representatives of the whole female-lawyer industrial complex weighed in. Eleanor Smeal, representing the National Organization for Women, testified in favor of the nomination: "We do not contend that the National Organization for Women agrees with all of the legal and political views of Judge O'Connor. As a matter of fact, we know that our own State organization, Arizona NOW, did oppose Judge O'Connor in some of her positions in her career as a Senator. However, we do not think that total agreement is necessary and we believe that there has been overall a commitment and an understanding of discrimination." Public opinion polls on her were through the roof.

As a female in public life, she had left a paper trail of support for women's issues that alert conservatives insistently raised. There was the little issue of her support for a bill to repeal Arizona's criminal abortion law in 1970 and her advocacy of the Equal Rights Amendment. But at the moment of her confirmation hearings, she managed to present a blank slate. Partly, this turned out to be an accurate reflection of her commitments, or lack of commitments. Partly it was simply false: either she or her advocates in the White House put out the story that there was no recorded 1970 vote on repealing Arizona's criminal abortion law, when there clearly was. She adopted the now-uniform stance of the successful Supreme Court nominee, decrying the reality of abortion—O'Connor said she now thought the procedure "abhorrent" and would of course never use it herself—and steadfastly refusing to opine about what she would do with *Roe v. Wade*. When Senator Biden reminded her of her historic duty to be an advocate for women, he too was met with a steadfast silence.

Confirmation was 99–0. *Ms* magazine published a warm and optimistic article by the NOW Legal Defense and Education Fund's Lynn Hecht Schafran, perhaps the most authoritative spokesperson for women and the judiciary. No woman, feminists hoped, could have come of age with O'Connor's obvious ambitions and interests in the 1950s and not be shaped by the experience of discrimination. If nothing else, her presence should curtail the Court's inclination to treat women as thought experiments when ruling. Sometimes the justices' obliviousness to women's value did not affect their decisions; for example, Justice Brennan advocated the most robust attack on sex discrimination while discriminating in hiring. But at other times, the justices' ignorance was more of a threat. Assuming women were all privileged Richmond matrons like his wife, Powell came perilously close to voting against Stephen Wiesenfeld in the Social Security case.

The symbolic impact of the appointment was manifest at once. Sandra Day O'Connor's swearing-in was the hottest ticket in town. "The pressures for attendance at the ceremony," the administration-oriented Chief Justice Burger groused, "are far beyond our capacity. This has given rise to a good many problems." The justices could have no more than their usual allotment of guests. People, including the unprecedented number of press, would be standing in the hall. Even the outdoor reception would be "wall-to-wall guests." Two hundred of those prospective guests came from the new nominee, who asked every member of the sixty-something Arizona court system she had just left to attend her ascension. And so, when the first female justice descended the marble steps of the Supreme Court building on the arm of her self-appointed escort, Warren Burger, the crowd was thick with friends and family. Reflecting her usual uncanny understanding of social dynamics, while everyone else took pictures of her, she asked a friend to take a picture of the reporters taking the pictures.

She understood and accepted that she was going to be a role model. As she famously said, "It was okay to be first. But I did not want to be the last." Even her elevated brethren wanted to introduce her to the girls in their lives. In the years since Lewis Powell wrote his special opinion in *Weinberger v. Wiesenfeld* to assure the public that he knew women would mostly tend to the family, he had, of all things, acquired a lawyer for a daughter-in-law. One of his first acts as O'Connor's new friend on the Court was to introduce "Mims" Powell, Esquire, to the FWOTSC. He arranged for his daughter-in-law to attend the swearing-in. And O'Connor never missed a beat. "Although Justice O'Connor shook hands with hundreds of people," he reported in one of his family letters after the occasion, "she remembered Mims and complimented her."

A LITTLE HELP FROM A NEW FRIEND

Sandra Day O'Connor hates mess. "Messy" is one of her harshest terms for anything—laws, politics—that displeases her. While she was still going through the confirmation process, her Arizona pal Mary-Audrey Weicker Mellor (Senator Lowell Weicker's sister) wrote to her friend Lewis Powell. "I just could not wait to write you concerning my good friend Sandra O'Connor . . . she is so un-asssuming and has such simplicity and dignity." So, she continues, "I'm writing to you to ask if you might watch over Sandra." The Powells found the O'Connors a place to live, through a friend who had an apartment in the Watergate.

At work, when she arrived, "There were files just piled on the floor all around the chambers," recalls her first clerk, Ruth McGregor. (MacGregor, in her late thirties, had taken a leave from her partnership at John O'Connor's law firm to give the FWOTSC a hand. After all, she thought, how many chances like this come along in a lawyer's life?) And with all their hard work to get O'Connor ready to attend her first meeting of the Court, which had the daunting task of addressing the cases that had piled up over the summer, they did not know that the Court took up matters in a different system the justices had devised. The newcomer's precious briefing book was all out of order, so, at the lunch break, she rushed back to her chambers to try to get it reorganized for the second half of the meeting so she wouldn't have to keep trying to find her place in her notes. Powell gave her his experienced secretary, Linda Blandford.

Although media speculated that O'Connor would be pair-bonded with her old friend William Rehnquist, Lewis and Jo Powell turned out to be her natural cohorts. The two couples went together to visit Justice Powell's pet Virginia project, Colonial Williamsburg, a re-creation of the original colonial town, complete with staff in hoop skirts and knee breeches. "It is," Justice O'Connor wrote in the thank-you, "the most exciting living museum in the world . . . to make that visit in the company of Virginia's most distinguished and kindest family . . . Virginia is at the core of our history as a nation. We have loved seeing it partly through your eyes."

Although the Lazy B Ranch was thousands of miles from Colonial Virginia, the correspondence reveals that the two families were strikingly similar. When the O'Connors went to their first Supreme Court dinner party at the Powells' house they found themselves in the company of the retired Justice Potter Stewart (who, as one wag had it, "gave up his seat for a woman"); Ronald Reagan's chief of staff, the Republican heavy-hitter Jim Baker, and his wife; and old friends of the Powells, Fitzgerald and Margaret Bemiss. Typical of Powell's social circles, Bemiss, an old-school Virginia conservative Democrat, businessman, and bank director, was a conservationist and had also been involved with worthy causes such as figuring out how to get Virginia schools to comply with the desegregation orders in *Brown*. "What a special treat," O'Connor wrote in her customary thank-you note to her hosts. "A delicious meal, good company and good conversation—an unbeatable combination." When O'Connor reciprocated, she prepared her colleague in advance for the pillars of the WASP establishment who would join them at table: "Jean and Les Douglas [executive vice president at the investment firm Folger Nolan Fleming Douglas], Phyllis and Bill Draper (he is head of ex-im Bank), Sheila and Ebersole Gaines (he is deputy director of OPIC) [the overseas private investment corporation, steering private U.S. investment to developing countries], Daphne and Bob Murray of Houston Texas [where he was chairman of the executive committee of Pinemont Bank], and Gail and Harry Holes (he is president of the Pebble Beach Corp and Aspen Corp.)."

They shared an unspoken assumption about the virtue of the country club elites. When O'Connor was nominated there was a mild flap about John O'Connor's membership in clubs—the Phoenix Country Club, Paradise Valley Country Club—that would not have women as members. Arizona social power was concentrated in those clubs; other members included Senator Goldwater, the Pulliam heir Dan Quayle, U.S. Senator Paul Fannin, and most of the named partners in Phoenix law firms. Later, in 1990, Lincoln Ragsdale, a prominent African American Phoenix citizen, raised a fuss about the exclusionary racial behavior of the PVCC.

Covering the flap, the Arizona papers tried and failed to reach Justice O'Connor, explaining that "Mrs. O'Connor" was in Montana and could not be reached for comment. Unlike Powell, who finally quit the whites-only clubs he belonged to in Richmond, including the Commonwealth Club and the Country Club of Virginia, the O'Connors never quit theirs.

In 1983, shortly after Ruth went on the bench, the Ginsburgs resigned from their golf club, Woodmont Country Club in Rockville, Maryland. Moving to D.C. in 1980, they had joined Woodmont, which had a policy of waiving the steep $25,000 initiation fee for high-ranking Washington pols, such as judges of the court of appeals. Marty played golf there, and, in 1983, the Ginsburgs brought in Ruth's colleague Judge Harry Edwards, an avid golfer and an African American. Out of a clear blue sky, when confronted with an African American member, the club rescinded the policy of waiving the fee. And the Ginsburgs left.

O'Connor still golfs at the PVCC. Just after the election of 2000, she scored a hole in one.

O'CONNOR BREAKS THE TIE

As the new lady justice settled in, feminists held their breath. They did not have long to wait. Only weeks after O'Connor took her seat, she was confronted with the ultimate test: a pathbreaking case of sex discrimination. The lower court had ordered the oldest women-only public college in America, the Mississippi University for Women, to admit men to its nursing school. Mississippi appealed.

In a dramatic coincidence, O'Connor's clerk, thirty-eight-year-old Ruth McGregor, who had lived through some of the inequities of lawyering while female, drew from the clerk pool the job of recommending whether the Court should hear Mississippi's appeal to the Supreme Court. She recommended that they take it. The existing law on sex-segregated schools was "messy," she wrote; the only Supreme Court decision on the subject issued from a reduced court of eight, which split 4–4, and the cultural consensus had not yet formed on whether women's schools helped women or hurt them.

When she sat down at the October conference, one month into her duties, O'Connor faced an ideologically riven tribunal. The three Republican-appointed conservative justices—her staunch advocate Chief Justice Burger, her law school pal William Rehnquist, and the unpredictable Harry Blackmun, along with the increasingly conservative Democratic appointee Byron White—enough to grant review—all wanted to take the case, likely with an eye to reversing and allowing Mississippi to segregate the sexes. The liberals remaining on the Court—William Brennan, Thurgood Marshall, and the increasingly liberal Ford appointee John Paul Stevens—wanted to deny review, affirming the lower court order to admit men. Her closest friend on the Court, Lewis Powell, also voted with the liberals not to review the case, which would leave the lower court order integrating the school in place, although his reasons were completely opaque.

Since Ginsburg left the field in 1980, the Supreme Court justices had been subtly backtracking from applying the high standard for discriminatory laws she had so laboriously achieved. They did not overtly overrule her great cases, but in one case they approved a law with tougher penalties for male perpetrators of statutory rape, and they passed on an opportunity to disallow the male-only draft registration. Moreover, integrating the Mississippi women's university represented a big bite of social change, after Ginsburg's exquisitely careful small change cases. The Court had experienced firsthand what happened when it ordered racial integration of the schools, which had also started with a request to desegregate public universities.

One thing about Justice O'Connor: she never had trouble making decisions. All those years as the only child on an isolated ranch had produced a woman singularly impervious to social pressure. O'Connor voted to hear the case.

The Mississippi University for Women was the oldest single-sex college in the United States. For years before it was founded there was no state institution of higher education for white women in Mississippi at all. The University of Mississippi and Mississippi State had always been male. During Reconstruction, the federal government had forced upon Mississippi *two* schools for black Mississippians, one for each gender. By the time *Hogan v. Mississippi* reached the Supreme Court in the fall of 1981, all the colleges but MUW had integrated the sexes, regardless of the degree of racial integration in the other Mississippi schools.

In *Hogan*, as was often the case, sex and race were devilishly intertwined. The code of proper ladylike behavior, conveyed by all-female schools such as MUW, had traditionally been reserved for women who happened to be white. Schools for African Americans taught working skills such as farming. The "W," as the Mississippi University for Women was called, all white until 1966, taught its white women students skills like "drawing, painting, designing, and engraving." As a contemporary scholar put it recently, the single-sex colleges "taught white women to be ladies."

Throughout the South, sex segregation was also used as a weapon against racial integration. After the Supreme Court ordered the schools racially desegregated in *Brown*, school districts in the South suddenly initiated programs of sex-segregated schools. And in the W, Mississippi already had a women-only school. Even after racial integration came to the W, the fight to defend sex segregation looked hauntingly similar to the fight for racial segregation. In 1971, ten years before Joe Hogan tried to study nursing, another (white) man, Charles Perkins, had applied for art classes at the W. He dropped his quest after a rock shattered his living room window. Maybe Mississippi could not legally separate the races, but, through sex segregation, at least it could keep its white women away from black men. Wilbur Colom, the African American lawyer for the would-be male coed in *Hogan*, got the case because, when Joe Hogan decided he was entitled to get his nursing education at a public college in his own hometown, every white lawyer in town turned him down. No white lawyer would take on the Mississippi establishment. It wasn't white men the W was afraid of, as Colom put it bluntly: "Miscegenation. That was the traditional fear."

None of this retrograde social context appears on the surface of the *Hogan* case. Instead, the case appears as a pure sex-discrimination matter: How to justify public money for a women-only college? The state invoked the mantle of women's schools such as Vassar and Wellesley. Women learned better, became better leaders, and deserved a school of their own since they had been discriminated against for years, the state's lawyer maintained. Justice Powell's clerk John Wiley found these arguments rather comical, in light of the subjects the W offered its would-be Sandra Day O'Connors: "the MUW's 'contemporary Women' course series (which is 'designed to prepare young women for the very active roles demanded of them in the Twentieth Century') consist of the following: 'Fashion, Introduction to Modeling, [Advanced] Modeling, and Personal Development [which] presents various methods of self-improvement in appearance and acceptable procedures in social situations.' "

Justices don't always act predictably. When it came time to decide *Hogan*, White, who had voted to take the case, voted to affirm, and Powell, who had voted to leave the lower court decision undisturbed, disturbed it by voting to reverse. That left the newbie, O'Connor, deciding the outcome between the four jurists of the conservative Republican-appointed faction who saw no illegal discrimination and the leftover liberals and the centrists, Brennan, Marshall, White, and Stevens, who would strike it down. At conference, O'Connor joined the left, but with less than a ringing endorsement for sure. "The record here," she said flatly, "does not show the benefit of unisex schools." William Brennan, the senior justice in the majority, cannily assigned the new female justice to write the sex-discrimination opinion.

Six months later, Martin Ginsburg walked into his wife's study and put O'Connor's opinion down on her desk. "Did you write this?" he asked.

She might well have. Until the last paragraph, Justice O'Connor's opinion in her first sex-discrimination case read like a monograph on the career of Ruth Bader Ginsburg. "We begin our analysis," O'Connor began, "aided by several firmly established principles. Because the challenged policy expressly discriminates among applicants on the basis of gender, it is subject to scrutiny under the

Equal Protection Clause of the Fourteenth Amendment. *Reed v. Reed.*" *Reed v. Reed* was of course Ginsburg's first Supreme Court case.

"Our decisions," O'Connor continued, "also establish that the party seeking to uphold a statute that classifies individuals on the basis of their gender must carry the burden of showing an 'exceedingly persuasive justification' for the classification. Kirchberg v. Feenstra . . . The burden is met only by showing at least that the classification serves 'important governmental objectives, and that the discriminatory means employed' are 'substantially related to the achievement of those objectives,'" she concluded, citing more recent cases applying the exact language of Ginsburg's standard-setting breakthrough in the near-beer case, *Craig v. Boren.*

Although she did not name Ginsburg, O'Connor's opinion advanced the project of Ginsburg's legal crusade to change the sex-role stereotypes that imprisoned members of her sex: "the test for determining the validity of a gender-based classification . . . must be applied free of fixed notions concerning the roles and abilities of males and females. Care must be taken in ascertaining whether the statutory objective itself reflects archaic and stereotypic notions. Thus, if the statutory objective is to exclude or "protect" members of one gender because they are presumed to suffer from an inherent handicap or to be innately inferior, the objective itself is illegitimate. See Frontiero v. Richardson, *411 U.S. 677,* 684–685 (1973) (plurality opinion)." *Frontiero* was Ginsburg's second case.

In case anyone missed the real social revolution embedded in *Frontiero,* Justice O'Connor made it explicit. If we agree that enabling women to develop is a legitimate goal for the state to pursue, we would still have to see if the system of women's colleges is the best way to help women to excel. When we decide that, we have to use our reason, rather than *"the mechanical application of traditional, often inaccurate, assumptions about the proper roles of men and women."* After all, she continued, warming to the subject, just look at all the offensively backward-looking arguments the states and federal government have advanced to justify the long list of state schemes we've already struck down. Both in its concocted objective and in the inadequate link between sex discrimination in school and its objective, Mississippi failed to provide the exceedingly persuasive justification for its discrimination.

O'Connor took the opportunity to remind the world of how harmful protective institutions such as all-female nursing schools could be. Stereotyping nursing as women's work harms women, O'Connor suggests: "Officials of the American Nurses Association have suggested that excluding men from the field has depressed nurses' wages. . . . To the extent the exclusion of men has that effect, MUW's admissions policy actually penalizes the very class the State purports to benefit. Cf. *Weinberger* v. *Wiesenfeld, supra*." If men don't do it, it doesn't get paid well, the tough-minded daughter of the West sets out. Stereotyping harms women in every conceivable way. Of course Marty Ginsburg asked his wife, "Did you write this?"

Justice O'Connor's new Supreme Court BFF, Lewis Powell, had been assigned to write the dissent for the four justices who disagreed. When he received the draft of her opinion, he must have hit the roof. The draft is covered with his handwritten notes, punctuated with exclamation points and indignant rhetoric. He started by challenging the premise that the case even involves sex discrimination. That is just "Absurd," he scribbled in the margins. It's a *man* complaining, he continued. Justice Powell almost seems to have forgotten that men were complaining in many of the decisions he supported in sex-discrimination cases—men such as the widowers Stephen Wiesenfeld and Leon Goldfarb, the aspiring beer guzzler Curtis Craig. And what's Hogan complaining about, Powell asked? That he has to travel to Ole Miss to study nursing instead of conveniently doing it in his hometown. Convenience! Justice Powell exclaimed. Since when did that get to be a constitutional right? This is indeed a bizarre argument. Civil rights litigation often involves test cases over trivia. One is hard-pressed to imagine him saying that the African American Rosa Parks having to stand for a short bus ride in the bad old days of segregated transportation was trivial.

Powell's internal memos paint a vivid picture of a "Southern gentleman," as Penny Clark describes him, who has finally had enough social change. Okay, women workers should get spousal benefits for their husbands, and women should not be discouraged from jury service. But integrated schools are a serious social change in a settled society that suits him just fine. He believes in single-sex education, he wrote. "I have experienced it myself through a wife and three daughters." To argue that no substantial state interest is being served, he continues, is to condemn the educational judgment that for most of the history of this country has justified the great women's colleges. (Apparently Powell's clerk's merriment over the curriculum offered by the W did not make that big an impact on the justice.) Women who want to go to great segregated colleges should be able to make that choice. The fad for coeducation recently, he grouses, is just fashion. Justice Powell didn't just want to tell people about how his wife and daughters flourished in a sex-segregated system, he told his clerk, he wanted to remind the world about the wonderful girls' schools in his state. "Hollins College, Mary Baldwin College, Randolph Macon Woman's College and Sweet Briar College remain all women's, and each has a proud and respected reputation." Powell's beloved women's colleges are all private, and thus less beholden to constitutional requirements of equal treatment, but that's not his point at all. For centuries, girls' schools have been good for females, full stop. And so, concluded Powell, the public women's schools are good too and pass the constitutional test.

The extent to which Justice Powell was over the moon in this case is reflected in an astonishing note to the hapless clerk. The clerk was trying to get away from the unavoidable comparison between sex-segregated schools and the touchstone of modern political immorality, racially segregated schools. He suggested, "Because racial segregation was the product of hostile discrimination against blacks, segregated facilities were offered, not as alternatives to increase the choices available to blacks, but as the sole alternative." "It [racial segregation] was not hostile in my state," Powell wrote in the margins of the memo. "It was unreasoning acceptance of a system that had prevailed for centuries and approved by Plessy [*v. Ferguson*, the 1896 case that was overturned in *Brown*]."

Justice Powell's sanguine description of race relations in Virginia is more than a little hard to understand. Even in Powell's beloved Virginia, in every year before *Brown*, there were at least one or two lynchings.

So Powell dissented. Following receipt of O'Connor's draft opinion, he circulated his dissenting opinion, with its vision of a "proud and respected" network of southern women's colleges. In her ultimate opinion, O'Connor deftly dealt with Powell's justification of segregation on the basis of women's "choice." Every segregated institution gives the favored group a choice, she wrote, like white people wanting to choose to go to all-white schools. It's the excluded people like the plaintiff who are stripped of their choice. And that's what the Fourteenth Amendment forbids.

As the various drafts were circulating, a weird thing happened, but one fraught with meaning for the development of O'Connor's contribution to the Court—and women's equality. Chief Justice Burger noticed that Powell had described O'Connor's draft as striking down all single-sex education at the Mississippi University for Women. Apparently there had been some talk at conference of the case involving only the nursing school, although the liberal justices had all signed off on O'Connor's broad opinion by the time Burger noticed. Maybe, Burger wrote to Powell in a private letter, we can confine the decision, which we lost, to apply only to schools of nursing. Uh, Powell writes back, I don't think so. "It is true that Sandra refers primarily to the school of nursing . . . but the rationale of her opinion applies with equal force to every other school or department." (Burger referred to O'Connor's draft majority decision as the "Court's opinion" while Powell described her throughout as "Sandra.") Burger must have written to O'Connor anyway, because two days later she wrote to Powell, offering to cut back on the scope of the opinion.

Powell properly attacked O'Connor's offer as incoherent: "The logic of the Court's entire opinion, apart from the aforementioned statements, appears to apply sweepingly to the entire university." But she stuck with the narrowing language. And so, in a footnote in the middle of a brilliant and unprecedentedly sweeping assertion of the rights of and wrongs to women in her first term on the Court, Justice O'Connor limited her decision to the narrowest possible situation: the school of *nursing* at the MUW. It was, as Powell correctly sniffed out, narrow, all right, but completely incoherent.

"She only ruled about the nursing school!" Wilbur Colom snorted. Within days of the opinion, Colom recalls, "men flooded the other departments at the W with applications. And the administrators decided they had spent enough money defending a lost cause. The MUW was integrated in every department within a year." It was the first of many O'Connor opinions that made major social change and then limited the decision to the particulars of the case at hand, leaving everyone who had to make decisions afterward somewhat in the dark. In this case college administrators decided on their own what they should do. In later cases, plaintive requests for guidance reverberated up the food chain in the federal courts: "Justice O'Connor, now what do we do?"

The women of the "W" were horrible to Joe Hogan. He did not even last long enough to get his degree. As boys began to flood into the Mississippi University for Women, however, stereotypes fell like levees. The girls, who had been "living like nuns, shut up in dormitories with mandatory hours," Colom observed, moved out! "They joined the guys living in apartments in town," like most college kids in the 1980s. "And then," Colom reports gleefully, "the college became sort of a center for lesbians. It's widely thought," he says, "that a lot of the girls aren't distracted by the guys at all, as the state said they would be if the college were coed."

ROLE MODEL

O'Connor's role in the *Hogan* decision turned out to be a harbinger. She would be a force for progress and a force of caution and compromise. However conservative her self-image, she had no choice. From the day she was sworn in, she was a light and a lightning rod. On the day of her ceremony, she borrowed a robe that was too short, so her dress peeked out from underneath it in photos shot on the Supreme Court steps. In a preview of the decades to come in treatment of women in politics, the inch of pink cloth elicited yards of criticism and comment.

But she was determined not to fail. Proud and competitive—her ferocity on the tennis court was legendary—she was strengthened by an unlimited capacity for work and, as the long-ago incident with the flat tire on the ranch reveals, an intense determination to finish whatever she started. Politician as she had been for so long, she knew that part of her success had nothing to do with making good decisions about cases before the Court. She was a role model.

She started an all-female aerobics class at the Court, innocently saying she had always stopped for aerobics on her way in to work in Phoenix. The command performance early in the morning was a mixed blessing for her female clerks ("while we were up there dancing around, the guys were already working," one complained). But aerobics gave the girls a real chance to bond with their justice and were a vivid contrast to the all-male basketball games in the "highest court in the land." Nor was the lesson lost on the politically savvy young law clerks. Once O'Connor started the aerobics, "Justice White didn't own the athletic franchise anymore," as Justice Souter's clerk David Goldberg observed when he came to the Court a decade later.

After she got her sea legs in the first term, the legendarily energetic jurist began to intersperse her opinion-writing duties with a staggering schedule of speech making and symbolic ribbon-cutting. Expectations in the gorgeous glassed-in auditorium at the Wingspread Center in Racine, Wisconsin, could not have been higher when she rose one April day in 1982 to address a meeting of women judges, organized by two prominent feminist academics and two prominent judges' associations. Deploying her usual combination of optimism about women's prospects and the bra and wedding ring routine that had served her well in years of Arizona politics, O'Connor was not a hit. During the Q and A someone asked her about work/family balance, a question far newer then than it is today. "Women should always put their families first," O'Connor answered. Barbara Babcock, the first female professor at O'Connor's alma mater, Stanford Law School, was not pleased to hear this. O'Connor's reflexive family-first answer was insulting to a room full of women, many of whom had sacrificed family in whole or in part to be where they were. O'Connor hadn't yet learned, Babcock remembers, how to do the woman thing.

But she was always a fast learner. She was also possessed of an almost perfect photographic memory, hugely useful for both her role model duties and for the mountains of paperwork in her job. One day, she got on an elevator with the Arizona lawyer Mary Schroeder, the power went out, and all the buttons went dark. When it came back on, Justice O'Connor remembered perfectly which floor everyone in the crowded elevator had chosen.

For the most part, in those early days, she tried her best to sidestep the problem of women entirely. When she started giving speeches, she tried to position herself simply as an authoritative voice to speak about the administration of justice. She went to her alma mater, Stanford, and gave a talk, "What Individuals Can Do to Improve the Courts." She opened the new Vanderbilt Law Library with the talk "Professional Competence and Social Responsibility." These exhortations to individual virtue, like volunteering, satisfy the Rathbun-like injunction to improve the world without actually upsetting the existing social order in service of a better world. Like O'Connor's narrow, fact-based opinions, her vision is benign, but threatens little large-scale change.

When a person wields the critical fifth vote at the level of the Supreme Court, however, disproportionate social consequences often ensue, something that the theorists on the Court, right and left, all understood. Regardless of Justice O'Connor's narrow, problem-solving methodology, it was not a big step from the order admitting a man to study nursing to massive partying in coed off-campus apartments at the former women's university. Similarly, although the content was not overtly feminist, her mere presence on the powerful Court was a lesson in itself.

She quickly developed a way of talking about social change without threatening the establishment. It was an exquisite balance.

Celebrating the seventy-fifth anniversary of the New England School of Law, which started as a law school for *women* (Portia Law School!), she said the law school "has continued to demonstrate an admirable sensitivity to those groups underrepresented in the legal profession. . . . Over the next twenty-five years there is no doubt that courtroom benches, law facilities, and law firm partnerships will reflect the increased percentage of women and other minority groups who are now being admitted to practice." All the rest of her presentation is about the gender-neutral subject of a law school's responsibility to train its students in "ethical responsibility" and "practical competence."

Arriving at Fordham Law School in New York to dedicate its new building, she again opened her remarks with an homage to the role of women: "I think I should acknowledge and thank in part for my invitation Fordham's Rector in 1918. That year the faculty faced the issue of women's rights. The minutes of a May 1918 faculty meeting note that shortly before the close of the meeting, the Rector 'asked for a discussion of the advisability of matriculating women in the Law School.' After listening to the opinion of the various faculty members he announced that he would take the 'matter under advisement' and notify the faculty of his decision." A postscript to the minutes adds: "In a letter from the Rev. Rector . . . under the date of July 6, 1918, he writes, 'it has been decided that, owing to objections raised against it, women will not be admitted to classes of the Law School this Fall.'" The minutes, however, contain a terse unexplained amendment, O'Connor continues: "In September 1918 the Rev. Rector authorized the matriculation of women and ordered the insertion of this fact to be put in the newspapers."

And then she delivered the punch:

"I like to think that your former Rector not only helped advance the cause of women in the law, but that he would have been pleased that a woman was invited to give remarks today."

The rest of the speech was the usual gender-neutral call to public service. That a woman was invited to give remarks was sufficient; in O'Connor's case, the medium was the message.

O'CONNOR'S ABORTION ANALYSIS ON A COLLISION
COURSE WITH ITSELF

O'Connor's pleasantly symbolic feminist honeymoon cruise was about to hit the shoals of abortion, the issue that would not die. The Catholic Church had been fighting the liberalization of abortion laws since the 1960s. In 1967, the National Conference of Catholic Bishops had founded a national Right to Life Committee to resist the movement to reform, and the Church was starting to have some success when *Roe* came down. Bill Cox, assistant director of the Missouri Catholic Conference, knew that the Catholic Church alone could not undo what the Court had done. The Protestant clergy in Missouri had been essentially silent in the days after *Roe*.

At the instance of the MCC staff the Missouri bishops approved the formation of a secular pro-life group to be called Missouri Citizens for Life (MCL). Cox began crisscrossing the state, setting up MCL chapters and soliciting help from non-Catholics. MCL started at the Catholic Conference office, but, like the anti-abortion movement in general, it soon moved to an independent identity, Missouri Right to Life, which formed a political action committee and began to endorse pro-life candidates for election.

Within a year of the *Roe* decision, Missouri passed its first post-*Roe* anti-abortion law, which allowed doctors, nurses, and hospitals to refuse to perform an abortion when it violated their moral, ethical, or religious beliefs. In 1974, Missouri passed a bill requiring informed consent by the woman considering an abortion, her spouse if married, and the consent of the parents of an unmarried minor under the age of eighteen. It also banned abortions performed after twelve weeks of pregnancy that involved the injection of a saline solution into the mother's womb.

Early on, the resistance to liberalized abortion transcended the Catholic origins. The 1972 presidential campaign of the Protestant Richard Nixon embraced abortion opposition as a way to attract Catholic Democrats. Although the first Missouri law was introduced by a Catholic legislator, Missouri Right to Life proudly presented the self-identified "Episcopalian" Thomas Eagleton to the public in a massive anti-abortion rally in 1973. As the '70s passed, the Republican Party gradually framed resistance to abortion rights as part of its resistance to cultural and sexual liberation in general. Although the Supreme Court struck down the ambitiously anti-abortion Missouri law, the movement would keep passing laws, looking for holes in the *Roe* decision and for any legal method to restrict abortion. Thanks in part to Cox and his colleagues' efforts, Missouri would be what scholars later called a "challenger" state. And sooner or later those challenges were going to come before the Supreme Court with the first women on it.

No one was more aware of the challenge than *Roe*'s author, Harry Blackmun.

Blackmun really did not like his new colleague. Even before an actual female justice had emerged as a possibility in 1981, the so-called emancipator of women had pettishly argued against the Court dropping the traditional "Mr. Justice" salutation. Justice Stevens had attended a moot court session at Notre Dame alongside the well-respected appeals court judge Cornelia Kennedy. After one of the winning all-female team had addressed her as Madame Justice for the umpteenth time, Kennedy laid it out. "A simple Justice will do," she explained. Justice is an honorable-enough title! In anticipation of a Miss or Mrs. (or Ms.) coming on board at some point, Justice Stevens brought the story to his colleague Potter Stewart, who proposed the change. The Court made it regardless of Blackmun's resistance. Once O'Conner got there the shy, perfectionist, self-deprecating Minnesotan found his outgoing, relentlessly sociable, supremely self-confident colleague altogether too much to take.

Blackmun's behavior was unattractive, but neither gender nor personality was at the heart of his problem with O'Connor. His problem was abortion. As the political pressure to roll back abortion rights rose, the dwindling majority on the Court for Blackmun's signature achievement, *Roe v. Wade*, already had him nervous. President Ronald Reagan presented him with a colleague who told the Senate she found abortion personally "repugnant."

The pace of challenges to abortion rights guaranteed that he'd get to take her measure on his issue soon enough. Driven by people like Missouri's Bill Cox and his organization, states and localities had produced an almost endless stream of regulations to make getting the procedure as hard as possible. In 1982, just a year after O'Connor joined the Court, the justices gathered several cases— from Cox's Missouri, as well as Ohio and Virginia—to set out some standards for what restrictions, if any, they would allow. The states and cities before the Court had demanded that doctors tell women that all pregnancies are "human life" from the beginning and recite a list of dire consequences abortion might produce. They imposed a hospital requirement on abortions after three months and required minors to inform their parents of their plans. Following *Roe*, the appeals courts had duly struck the restrictions down. Justice O'Connor joined her conservative brethren on the court to take the cases for review, under the title *Akron v. Akron Center for Reproductive Health*. It was the first signal she sent out.

When the dust settled in the *Akron* case, *Roe* emerged unscathed. Justice Powell wrote a strong opinion for the majority of six, forbidding states from making abortion harder to come by simply because they didn't want women to get abortions at all. Abortion is a fundamental right, he wrote, and as such may be limited only by a compelling state interest, usually in maternal health.

O'Connor disagreed and wrote a dissent. She admitted that the Court had said the Constitution applies to this so-called right:

"In Roe v. Wade . . . the Court held that the right of privacy . . . founded in the Fourteenth Amendment's concept of personal liberty and restrictions upon state action . . . is broad enough to encompass a woman's decision whether or not to terminate her pregnancy."

As in her confirmation proceedings, she refused to say what she would have done if she'd been sitting on the Court in 1973. The parties did not ask for the nuclear option, overruling *Roe*, she notes, and so the Court would not reexamine the decision. But for the new justice even to recognize that possibility a mere decade after the decision was chilling to Blackmun and the pro-abortion forces.

However, she continued, had she been there, she sure would have done a better job than Harry Blackmun. Blackmun's opinion in *Roe* had extended constitutional protection to choosing abortion according to how far along the pregnancy was. In the first trimester, when abortion is safer than pregnancy, the right to abortion was absolute. Then, up to the point where the fetus can live outside the womb (viability), the state may only impose limitations designed to serve the mother's health. Thereafter the state may still prohibit abortions, unless the prohibition endangers the mother's health. The woman's health is primary throughout and is the exclusive interest until the fetus can live outside the womb.

"[I]t is apparent from the Court's opinion," O'Connor believed, "that neither sound constitutional theory nor our need to decide cases based on the application of neutral principles can accommodate an analytical framework that varies according to the "stages" of pregnancy, where those stages, and their concomitant standards of review, differ according to the level of medical technology available when a particular challenge to state regulation occurs." The standard, O'Connor speculated, was on a collision course with itself. In her scientific understanding, doctors would get better and better at preserving the fetus outside the womb, rolling back the cutoff for viability. Abortion would get safer and safer, pushing the untouchable first trimester further and further forward. "Unworkable," "illegitimate," "unjustifiable in law or logic"—only the timely intervention from one of Blackmun's clerks to his counterpart with O'Connor prevented her from calling Blackmun's framework "unprincipled" in her dissenting opinion.

Justice O'Connor then set out her version of an abortion decision. Contrary to Blackmun's opinion in *Roe*, O'Connor believed that the state had an interest not just in the mother's health, but in the *fetus* from conception. So the government can do anything it wants at any time as long as it does not place an "undue burden" on the woman's decision to terminate. No connection to women's health is required. In this first effort since her appointment, O'Connor served notice that, as an example of the proposed standard, she would uphold every one of the city of Akron's restrictions on women's choice.

Although she is later credited for devising the undue-burden standard for abortion rights, it was not her idea. During the twelve years of Republican administrations after the 1980 election, the Justice Department had played the lead role in rolling back abortion rights. O'Connor's standard comes directly from the Reagan Justice Department's friend of the court brief in the *Akron* case. The brief, which stopped just short of telling the Court to overrule *Roe v. Wade* altogether, was highly controversial. Nine years later, President George H. W. Bush's administration, in a similar role as friend of the Court, would go all the way and request that *Roe* be overturned. The confrontation was inevitable: once the Court conceded the state's nine-month-long interest in the fetus, that interest was on a collision course with women's interest in obtaining abortions. There was no principled stopping place. There was only the establishment distaste for stories of thalidomide babies and coat hangers: abortion couldn't be made criminal enough to go back to those bad old days. Just as difficult as possible short of that.

O'Connor's proposed revision of *Roe* was just a dissent in 1983, and she lost the rematch of the same fight in her second abortion case in 1986. The women's groups, which had been cautiously optimistic, veered sharply away from their first female champion. Unlike Blackmun's clean, time-related test with restrictions grounded in women's health, the squishy language of "undue burden" promised—and later delivered—a mare's nest of increasingly ambitious efforts to cut back on abortion rights.

A DISH BETTER TAKEN COLD

But the First Woman was a better friend than women realized, in the angry aftermath of the *Akron* dissent. In 1983, as she was preparing to embrace the Reagan administration's very hostile position on abortion, she cheerfully went across town to her first National Conference on Women and the Law at George Washington Law School.

The conferences had come a long way since their origins as a scruffy gathering of feminist activists in the 1960s. The 1983 conference involved a thousand lawyers, law professors, and students and merited the appearance of a Supreme Court justice. And who should be at the conference but the famed women's advocate and court of appeals judge, Ruth Bader Ginsburg. Ginsburg, of course, had been going to the conferences since the earliest days, when she toted around her photocopied materials for the Woman and the Law course and exchanged syllabi, all of which she eventually turned into one of the very first casebooks on the subject. Although Ginsburg had never heard of O'Connor when the FWOTSC surfaced as a Supreme Court nominee in 1981, one of Ginsburg's former clerks, Deborah Merritt, was working as a clerk to Justice Potter Stewart, whom O'Connor would replace. When Stewart retired in the middle of Merritt's term as clerk, his replacement took Merritt on. So, in O'Connor's first term, she had a clerk from Ginsburg's chambers. And, of course, when Sandra's opinion in the Mississippi University for Women case came out, Marty Ginsburg asked his wife if she had been O'Connor's ghostwriter. Ginsburg had reason to look forward to making her acquaintance. And there was the new justice, at the fourteenth annual Conference on Women and the Law.

Unknown to Ginsburg, when she ran into O'Connor at the conference, the Court was about to deliver a sweet victory on the subject of Women and the Law (Firm).

Women Work for Justice O'Connor

꙰

The Court's helping hand to women lawyers was sweet, but late. Gibson, Dunn had told Sandra Day O'Connor she could be a secretary in 1952. When Diane Blank and Mary Kelly went to law school in 1968, they surely were not thinking it would take until Justice O'Connor's third term, sixteen years after they were 1Ls, for the Court to tell firms they could not direct female law students to the steno pool. The young law students had a play-by-the-rules mentality. If they worked hard and did well, the status-conscious and highly bureaucratized process of law-firm hiring should waft them up to the Nirvana of big-firm life. They would get hired as summer interns after their first year in law school and then as entry-level associates after graduation. The process turned largely on the grades they received and on their performance on the prestigious and select law reviews at their schools. There seemed little room for the kind of covert distaste for women workers that allowed so much discrimination in less structured environments. They did not think that cosmopolitan New York law firms in 1968 would still act a lot like Gibson, Dunn circa 1952.

FEMALE LAW GRADS SUE PEOPLE

But at the end of the day, they and a handful of other classmates had to sue the biggest firms in New York to get a chance at the brass ring. In 1971, Blank sued Sullivan and Cromwell, and a woman named Margaret Kohn sued Royall, Koegel and Wells. In 1977, Sullivan and Cromwell settled with Diane Blank, rather than let her look at their statistics on hiring women. It should have been a lesson to the firm. But when Justice O'Connor considered the case of law-firm hiring seven years after Sullivan and Cromwell settled, the number of women partners at Sullivan and Cromwell could still be counted on one . . . finger. One. Out of seventy-five partners. Women had been pouring out of the law schools since 1970, but somehow they almost never made it across the magic line to partner.

The woman justice who never made partner—or even associate in 1983—found herself facing this reality from behind the bench. The powerhouse Atlanta law firm King & Spalding, home to Jimmy Carter's former attorney general, Griffin Bell, had turned down a young female Columbia graduate, Elizabeth Anderson Hishon, for partner. King & Spalding had never had a female partner. They had just made their first Jewish partner a few years earlier. To their astonishment, Betsy Hishon, a stereotypically good girl, who had never made waves, filed suit. The firm, she charged, had discriminated against her in employment, in violation of the Civil Rights Act. Unlike Sullivan and Cromwell and the rest, King & Spalding did not deny that they discriminated against women, and they would not settle. Instead they stood on principle: law firms are partnerships, not employers, under the Civil Rights Act, and so in deciding who to take as their partner, they're not hiring, they're choosing partners. They can discriminate as much as they want. Indeed, King & Spalding told the courts, the most powerful engine of freedom in the American political universe, the First Amendment to the Constitution, protects their right to associate—or not to associate—as partners with anyone they choose. If they decide that No Girlz are Allowed in their club, it's their constitutional right.

Actually, King & Spalding had a few females at the firm when they rejected Betsy Hishon. According to *The Wall Street Journal*, right before Hishon's case got to the Supreme Court, one of the Girls of King & Spalding was the prize-winning summer intern "with the body we'd like to see more of." The others participated in a bathing suit contest (they had planned a wet T-shirt contest, but someone must have told them it wasn't a great idea in light of the pending litigation). Bathing suits, wet T-shirts: the media covering the case were over the moon.

No one on the Supreme Court wanted to rule in favor of King & Spalding. O'Connor's law clerk Stewart Schwab, who wrote the pool memo about whether to take the case, thought the firm was wrong about partnerships being exempt from the Civil Rights Act and protected by the First Amendment. He recommended waiting until the lower courts had ruled a bunch of different ways on the matter, what is called in Supreme Court language a "split in the Circuits." All those rejected female lawyers could wait until the lower courts had disagreed among themselves. Not surprisingly, Justice O'Connor, rejected three decades before by every firm she solicited, did not think the young women should wait. She thought the Court should grant review. And so it did, by the minimum requirement of four votes. The legal issue in the case is a technical one. Partners are equals in risk and control, unlike employers and employees, and the legislative history of the Civil Rights Act is unclear about whether the prohibition against race and sex discrimination in employment applies to that more informal and egalitarian relationship. Firms couldn't refuse to hire female associates, but maybe they could refuse to become partners with the women.

Were law partnerships exempt from the Civil Rights Act? At oral argument, O'Connor was unusually aggressive with the lawyer for King & Spalding: "Congress knew full well how to write in exemptions to the Civil Rights Act," she said, "and they put in three (small businesses, religious organizations, state and local government) and you're asking us to create one out of some abstract notion of lawyers. If Congress had intended to have this exemption, wouldn't it have said so?" Answering her, King & Spalding's lawyer, the legendary champion of the racial civil rights movement Charles Morgan, sounded downright testy. Maybe, despite the First Amendment argument, he was embarrassed to be arguing that a law firm could legally say it just would not hire women—or black people. It was certainly the first time Morgan had to answer to a powerful woman lawyer as to why the club said no girls allowed.

The Court ultimately got around the problem of how the act applied to partnerships by focusing on Hishon's situation. She was hired as an associate with the assumption that the firm would consider her fairly for partnership at the end of her probationary period as an associate. Unlike a partner, an associate is unambiguously an employee of the law firm. With the help of the Justice Department's supporting briefs and argument, the Court ruled that the decision about whether to promote an associate, who is clearly an employee, to partner, was an employment decision covered by the Civil Rights Act (and not, they easily concluded, protected by the First Amendment).

The case is interesting to Court buffs, because the archives show Warren Burger overtly engaging in the behavior that drove his colleagues nuts, but which was often hidden from view. He would vote with the majority at the conference when the cases were tentatively decided. Then, as a member of the majority, he could claim his privilege as the chief to assign who would write the opinion. He would then assign it to himself and undermine the decision he did not really support as much as he could get away with without driving his colleagues to produce a competing opinion and steal his majority. So in *Hishon*, which was unanimous, he circulated a draft opinion suggesting that her case against the firm was based on their contractual commitment to treat her fairly rather than the Civil Rights Act requirement that law partnerships as employers treat all employees fairly. Had he succeeded in holding a majority for his opinion, the ruling would have been fine for Betsy Hishon, but so narrow as to be meaningless for the cause of women's equality. Law firms would just start inserting a clause in their hiring contracts that hiring as an associate meant nothing about consideration for partnership.

In a heartbeat, the liberal Justice Brennan jumped all over Burger. The result is right, he says, but that's not the law. I guess I'll have to start a competing opinion. Justice Stevens jumped in with a memo adding a snarky but entirely accurate comment that Burger's theory would not even justify putting the case in federal court. (Ordinary contract disputes go to the state courts. Only the federal Civil Rights Act claim put the case in federal court.)

Even with the other justices piling on, Justice O'Connor felt constrained to add her voice, warning the chief that she would not join the opinion as he suggested it. "I still think the opinion should recognize a recovery under Title VII rather than on simply the contract theory." Burger, realizing he'd gone too far, backed off and wrote an opinion applying the Civil Rights Act to law firms' promotion decisions.

Justice Powell was the only jurist who thought the chief was right the first time. He had aggressively questioned Hishon's lawyer about how law firms could function if their every partnership decision was subject to the Civil Rights Act. Powell didn't think law firms had a sex problem in the enlightened year of 1984: "Discrimination is unlikely to occur certainly at this late date—because it is contrary to a firm's best interest," he wrote in his usual memo to self. "The future of a law firm, like that of a football team, depends on the wisdom and care with which partners are chosen. Neither sex nor race is a negative factor in a modern law firm." He filed a separate concurring opinion to emphasize the limits on the decision. Okay, law firms couldn't discriminate against their associate/employees. But once a person became a partner her civil rights evaporated, he reiterated. Good thing women law partners didn't need the help.

Or maybe they did. Four years after the decision in *Hishon*, the newly formed American Bar Association Commission on Women in the Profession decided to hold hearings on the issue. The first chairwoman, one Hillary Rodham Clinton, was skeptical that the hearings would be productive. Only the losers would show up, she predicted. Instead, leading lights of the bar—Pat Wald, the only woman on the D.C. Circuit, and Brooksley Born, first female president of the *Stanford Law Review* and partner at the powerful Washington law firm of Arnold and Porter—showed up to tell stories of the "problem" women faced trying to succeed in law firms. They got case assignments steering them away from the lucrative big cases and stripping them of the ability to strut their stuff; they were confined to obscure jobs, reviewing documents. The law firms acquiesce in clients' requests not to have women on their matters, and don't invite them to the critical off-premises social networking. Then they are characterized as unable to get new business. Their work, the report concluded, is treated with "a presumption of incompetence."

Hishon v. King & Spalding appears nowhere in the voluminous literature about the Burger Court. The Supreme Court biographies—of Burger, Blackmun, Powell, Brennan, Stevens, even O'Connor—include analyses of hundreds of cases about everything from exhaustion of remedies in habeas petitions to federal power over strip mining. Yet they are silent about the battle for inclusion of this otherwise conventional young woman attorney. The case must have seemed utterly trivial to the historians of the Court. But for the young women struggling to make their way in firms like King & Spalding, with not enough female partners and too many wet T-shirt contests, Betsy Hishon's victory felt like a life preserver.

It wasn't just the young women lawyers who benefited from Hishon's victory over King & Spalding. When the sociologist Barbara Harris studied nineteenth-century professional women, comparing the difficulties they had in entering the legal and medical professions, she found that women faced greatest opposition from the bar . . . the law clearly was an all-male domain, closest to the center of power, that was not to be invaded or changed by females. So the progress of women in legal institutions affected women everywhere.

Justice O'Connor knew exactly how important the decision was. The following year, when the New York State Bar Association asked her to write the foreword to its series on the achievement of women in the legal profession, she opened her piece with the decision in *Hishon*: "Of special interest to women lawyers was *Hishon v. King & Spaulding* [*sic*] decided during the 1983 Term, which confirms that Title VII applies to the partnership decisions of law firms as well as to the hiring and promotion policies of corporations."

As the article reflects, Justice O'Connor had learned a lot about framing "the woman thing" in the three years since her misstep at the 1982 judges' conference. Bemoaning the underrepresentation of women in the judiciary and the partnerships of law firms, she quickly recognized that "tenacious social and cultural barriers" made women's advancement harder, and recognized the benefit from women attorneys' groups acting together to remove the "artificial barriers" that thwart them. Instead of advising her audience to always put their families first, she acknowledged that expecting women to bear the lion's share of domestic responsibilities is an important part of what holds them back at work. She even gave a shout-out to New York State's pioneering females, including one "Ruth Bader Ginsberg [*sic*]" now of the "United States Court of Appeals for the District of Columbia Circuit."

THE WET T-SHIRT CONTEST

Planning a wet T-shirt contest and defending discrimination in law-firm hiring in the same year, *King & Spalding* hit a rare double. It presented the Court with a classic example of sex discrimination pure and simple and gave the nation a glimpse into the devilish connection between sex as in *sex* and sex as in inequality, a much fuzzier concept.

The sex thing had been bubbling up for a while. Stories of male supervisors demanding sex and threatening retaliation were the staples of '70s consciousness-raising. The stories were unattractive. But were they illegal? At first judges and cultural authorities of all stripes were skeptical that sexual behavior in the workplace was a proper subject for the law. They thought sexual desire was just a law of nature, that the women workers were targeted because they were so luscious, not a protected category under the Civil Rights Act. After all, the bosses didn't solicit *all* the women in their office, just the desirable ones.

The resistance is understandable. Redefining even some workplace sex as illegal harassment was one of the most powerful social changes in the history of legal feminism. Foundational concepts of human identity—women as sexual temptresses, men as hardwired sexual predators, sexuality as incompatible with social equality—were at issue when the first administrative assistant sued her boss.

Hearing the stories, a student at Yale Law School, Catharine MacKinnon, began to develop a theory to address the emerging issue. As she saw it, the courts missed the civil rights implications of sexual harassment because there were no comparable male targets of the (straight) male bosses' desires. So the employers weren't discriminating on the grounds of gender, the judges said. What the judges missed, she thought, was that sexual harassment discriminated against working women regardless of the existence of comparable male victims, because it disparaged them. Just as racially segregated schools could never be equal because their goal was always to keep members of the subordinate group down.

Finally, in 1976, the D.C. Circuit issued the first ruling in favor of a female employee. Judge Spottswood Robinson, a legend of the racial civil rights movement, thought it was an easy case. The supervisor had solicited the plaintiff, Paulette Barnes, to have sex with him. So what if he didn't hit on all women? "But for her womanhood, from aught that appears, her participation in sexual activity would never have been solicited." When she refused, she was driven out of her job. Accordingly, it was sex discrimination under the Civil Rights Act. Deliciously, Catharine MacKinnon's father, the conservative Nixon appointee Judge George MacKinnon, was on the panel in that first case.

In hindsight, the Barnes case was an easy call. The court did not have to understand Catharine MacKinnon's theory of disparagement to find a simple case of disparate treatment. All it had to do was let go of the nonsensical notion that discrimination is only what is done to every woman in the picture (and no men). Being a woman was *necessary* to being treated badly, in the sex-harassment cases, even if it was not sufficient. Put another way, every woman was vulnerable to such treatment, even if they were not all "attractive" enough to be so lucky. Accordingly, the behavior qualifies as sex discrimination.

But even as the D.C. Circuit was deciding the first, easy case, the harder case was ineluctably making its way to the Court. Does sexed treatment of women in the workplace without any other harmful job action still violate the Civil Rights Act? For that case, MacKinnon's insight into the disparagement and subordination of women was essential.

HE'S GLAD TO SEE YOU *AND* IT'S A GUN IN HIS POCKET

When Mechelle Vinson, an aspiring young woman in the Baltimore ghetto, saw the little local bank in her neighborhood, it looked to her like a beacon of opportunity, a way out of her impoverished, dead-end life. As Vinson would later tell a court, during her probationary period as a trainee teller with the bank, her supervisor, the manager Sidney Taylor, "invited her out to dinner and, during the course of the meal, suggested that they go to a motel to have sexual relations. At first she refused, but her boss had a gun in his pocket: her job. Fearing losing her job, she eventually agreed.

"Taylor thereafter made repeated demands upon her for sexual favors, usually at the branch, both during and after business hours; she estimated that over the next several years she had intercourse with him some 40 or 50 times. In addition, respondent testified that Taylor fondled her in front of other employees, followed her into the women's restroom when she went there alone, exposed himself to her, and even forcibly raped her on several occasions." When Taylor fired Vinson, allegedly for unrelated reasons, she sued.

In February 1980 Vinson lost her case at trial. But then she got a huge break. Two weeks after the trial court decision, the EEOC recognized that sexual harassment of this sort was not just good fun: it was illegal job discrimination. Here's where MacKinnon's insight came in. Taylor's behavior wasn't just flattering or natural, it was discriminatory subordination and disparagement of his employee. The court of appeals sent the case back for a new trial under this new interpretation of the Civil Rights Act. The bank appealed the order, called a "remand," to the Supreme Court. Caught in the changing law, the bank was arguing that even if Vinson's version was true, she hadn't suffered in her work—by being fired or demoted—so she had no claim. In the alternative, the bank argued, she should not be suing the bank. Her real gripe was with Taylor. How was the bank to know about his alleged little sexual fiefdom in an obscure branch?

At oral argument, Justice O'Connor took the bank's lawyer, F. Robert Troll, Jr., in her jaws and shook him like a terrier shakes a rat:

SOC: "The trial court simply didn't handle the case as a . . . a sexual harassment . . . claim?"

Troll admitted the trial court had embraced a now-outdated understanding of the Civil Rights Act, which would not have recognized the wrong done to Vinson.

"Do you agree then," O'Connor pursued, "that today that could be a valid claim under Title VII?"

Troll asserted that the federal law protected people only against loss of tangible job benefits. Vinson's firing was unrelated to the abuse, he argued.

"I notice," she replied, that "the solicitor general suggests that there is a claim" for "the suffering that occurs in the hostile environment itself."

Troll begged to differ with the lawyer for the United States. He was on thin ice here, because it was settled law that racial harassment—Klan signs on peoples' lockers, the N word, et cetera—was actionable regardless of whether the black person got fired. The experience of harassment was enough.

This fact informed O'Connor's next question. Knowing the answer in advance, she asked, "Would you say that if it were a racially harmful environment claim that a tangible effect on employment is a necessary element?"

Troll admitted that "reasonable people could differ" about his position that Vinson had to suffer actual job penalties to have a claim. Congress had said nothing about people's psychological suffering, he ventured.

O'Connor did not blink: "Do you think the principles are similar in sex harassment as racial harassment?"

"Yes," Troll conceded, "we do."

Having basically admitted that Vinson had a claim, he argued that she had the wrong defendant. The bank still was not liable, because it had no idea what was going on.

O'Connor: "The lower court cases on racial harassment imputes the supervisor's knowledge to the company."

And it was the *supervisor* who was doing the harassing, she continued. Wasn't it the supervisor's job to care for the employees, O'Connor asked? He knew what he was doing. Wouldn't that be notice to the bank?

The listener can almost hear the bank's advocate panting on the recording of the oral argument by the time she finished with him.

When the time came, Justice O'Connor joined a unanimous court to hold that Vinson should have another chance to prove the harassment, which would be actionable, if proved, even if she didn't get fired because of it. Harassment that creates a hostile work environment, unheard of ten years before, was now ensconced firmly in the prohibitions of the Civil Rights Act. That was the easy part. What divided the Court was the question of whether the bank was strictly liable for its supervisor's harassment of the underling. Whether the big boss is liable in cases like this is usually what matters. If sexual harassment were ever going to stop, employers would have to stop it. If they were strictly liable, they'd do something to control sexual harassment in their workplace. Ambitious, frightened, vulnerable women could not police the workplace and the jerk at the branch office was unlikely to be able to pay meaningful damages.

Events followed a course drearily familiar to the liberals on the Burger Court. First, Chief Justice Burger switched his vote from supporting the bank at conference when he saw that only one of the other justices, Powell, agreed with him. Then, being in the majority, he got the right to assign the opinion. He assigned it to the justice in the majority least sympathetic to Vinson, William Rehnquist. On April 22, Rehnquist circulated a draft opinion so hostile to Vinson that even Justice Powell abandoned his dissent and agreed to sign on.

Although Vinson would get a chance to prove harassment, unlike employers in racial harassment cases, the bank would not be strictly liable. Vinson would have to prove the bank was liable under "ordinary principles of agency," a complex body of law about when employers are responsible for the acts of their agents, depending on what the employer knew or should have known about what the employee was doing. So in a case like Vinson's she would have to show the bank knew about Taylor's bizarre behavior, which would be almost impossible to prove. Or she could show that the bank had an obligation to monitor its employees in some way so that it would know when something so untoward was going on. Since sexual harassment was just being acknowledged as an offense, what the courts would say employers "should have known" was completely, well, unknown. Either way, her chance of winning would be much smaller than if the law just laid the burden of misbehavior strictly on the employer, the institution with the best chance to stop it.

Predictably, the four liberal justices—Brennan, Marshall, Blackmun, and Stevens—withdrew their support from Rehnquist's opinion. They thought the bank should be liable to its female employee if she was sexually harassed in the workplace, period. Justice Marshall wrote an opinion he characterized as concurring only in the actual judgment, as far from agreement as you can get while still supporting the Court's remanding Vinson's case for a new trial. Four to four: all eyes turned to Sandra Day O'Connor. Two weeks later she voted with Rehnquist, making five to limit sexual harassment claims against an employer. Vinson would have to prove not only that Taylor harassed her, but that the bank knew or should have known she was being harassed. Certainly the bank wasn't going to volunteer to help her out. As of 1986, seven years after Vinson sued, Sidney Taylor was still managing the branch.

O'Connor's clerk at the time, Stephen Gilles, speculates that she may have had a complicated and clever agenda in voting with the conservatives. "Maybe she thought that this case is so awful, even the conservatives are willing to buy into the theory of sexual harassment, but if I switch sides and vote with the liberals, they might write a few concurrences, and [it will be harder to] hold a coalition together." If the conservatives dissented, *Meritor Savings Bank v.*

Vinson would have been 5–4, rather than unanimous on the harassment matter. A 5–4 decision establishing sexual harassment as actionable would then be very vulnerable if any one of the liberal justices retired, just like *Roe* began to hang by a thread over the years. Better a unanimous Court for sexual harassment and let the liability thing play out over the future.

In the end, like so many of Justice O'Connor's tightfisted votes for equality, the decision *did* help women—in a tightfisted way. From the highest level of judicial authority, sexual harassment was now actionable, as racial harassment had been in the past, even if the offender just made the victim's daily life a misery rather than, say, firing her. The bank settled with Mechelle Vinson, and she used some of the money to go to nursing school and had a long good life. Years later, in 1988, Sidney Taylor was convicted of embezzlement from one of the bank's depositors, and, finally, the bank noticed him, and he lost his job. Burger was retiring, and Justice Rehnquist, who, gossip had it, did not want to be seen as defending sexist behavior just as he was up to replace Burger for the job of chief, got to be in the majority. But the lower courts struggled for years to figure out what an employee had to prove in order to hold an employer liable in a pure sexual harassment case under "principles of agency law." One case, heard by all eleven judges of the court of appeals in Chicago, generated eight different opinions! Please, Justice O'Connor, what should we be doing?

Right before Warren Burger retired, O'Connor's angel, John Driggs of the Lake Powell houseboat trip, came to D.C. with his wife to visit the O'Connors. As they were sitting at breakfast, Justice O'Connor was getting ready to go to work. Say, she said to her guests, would you like to go to the Court and see a session? Who would say *no*? As they sat in their seats in the justices' guest section, a messenger arrived with a note from the chief inviting them to come to his chambers after the session. When the Driggses arrived, Chief Justice Burger was waiting to crow over the great outcome of their houseboat trip all those years before. What an addition Justice O'Connor made to the court, he said. Why, he made it his business to use his powers as the chief to single her out to write the opinions in really important cases because he thought so highly of her. It was an extraordinary admission from Burger, who had long been accused of manipulating the assignment power, in violation of the unspoken norms of the institution he headed. Only thing is: it wasn't true. Even after five years on the tribunal, and numerous instances where the chief unexpectedly changed his position when he saw he would be on the losing side, Burger never assigned O'Connor to write the Court's opinion in any big cases. As one of her clerks said sarcastically, remembering those years, "Oh, boy, another tax case! Thanks, Justice Burger." In 1986, William Rehnquist took the retiring Warren Burger's place, and President Reagan filled the Supreme Court vacancy with the conservative appeals court judge Antonin Scalia.

FINESSING THE DIVIDE ON AFFIRMATIVE ACTION

Women were always bit players in the affirmative action drama. Affirmative action was the easiest target in the backlash against racial civil rights. By the time Sheriff Bull Connor's Birmingham dogs and fire hoses had consumed the evening news in the mid-'60s, it was hard to find a mainstream voice calling for a return to legal segregation. But social patterns outside the law—residential segregation, job seniority, a legacy of impoverishment dating back to slavery—ensured that most racial segregation survived without the lawman's help.

But when institutions such as state colleges started seeking to overcome that legacy with programs like affirmative action, a robust and self-righteous resistance arose almost overnight. Preference based on race? For shame! Affirmative action had everything a resistance movement could ask for. The programs, at places such as the University of California medical school, disadvantaged smart white men; the first plaintiff, Allan Bakke, looked just like the political and cultural opinion makers of the day. At the other end of the spectrum, the workplace programs disadvantaged white working-class males, the prime target of the Nixon political strategy, later the so-called Reagan Democrats. Think tanks to challenge affirmative action sprang up like mushrooms.

The first cases—and almost all of the cases for the next three decades—focused on race. Bakke challenged the University of California's consideration of race in higher education, and a steel-worker named Weber challenged a joint employer-union training program designed to put more black people in skilled craft jobs. The affirmative action cases badly splintered the Court, with Powell and Stewart swinging back and forth between supporting and opposing it. There was never a majority to embrace affirmative action wholeheartedly as a way of rectifying the past or reshaping the future. But neither was there a majority to condemn it whole-heartedly as a violation of white men's civil rights. The justices parsed the issues so finely—had the employer actually committed past violations; was the employer public or private; was the affirmative action in hiring or firing—that no case ever gave guidance for future decisions. The first affirmative action case, *Bakke*, did not command a majority for any one opinion. It was decided, technically, 4–1–4. What a mess.

Five years into O'Connor's tenure, the first women's affirmative action case, *Johnson v. Santa Clara Transportation Authority*, came before the Court. The Transportation Authority had adopted an affirmative action plan allowing sex to be considered as a factor in promotion; shortly thereafter, it promoted the first woman in its history to the position of head dispatcher, lowering the ratio of men to women in that job category from 238:0 to 237:1. Johnson, a man who had scored two points higher than the woman promoted on the graded interview, filed a lawsuit, claiming the affirmative action was actually reverse discrimination, in violation of the Civil Rights Act.

Affirmative action was always something of a problem for legal feminism. Ginsburg's great victories often challenged schemes that seemed to benefit women such as giving them preference for survivor's benefits or creating a tax break for widows. But Ginsburg was pretty clear that affirmative action, like all law governing women, had to be seen in context. Over history, all that good, beneficial stuff such as putting a cap on the maximum hours women could work and excusing them from jury service just kept women in a cage. When women were shut out from good jobs, including the job of citizenship, and expected to be caregivers, safe drivers, and worse, stereotyped as inferior, they were not benefiting from the so-called benefits. Her objective was to open the gates.

Where, however, the effect of affirmative action was not to seal women into old models of virtue and dependency, but to open new worlds, she was quite willing to contemplate its virtues. Especially if the affirmative action followed a long period when the employer, for example, engaged in practices that covertly excluded women. A particular bête noire of hers was the oral interview, exactly what kept the woman down in the Johnson case.

When the justices voted in *Johnson*, the liberal bloc of four—Brennan, Marshall, Blackmun, and Stevens—had attracted O'Connor and Powell to approve the affirmative action. Now that Rehnquist rather than Burger was chief, he voted honestly with the minority and therefore forfeited his power to assign the opinion. Brennan, the liberal senior justice in the majority, assigned it to himself.

O'Connor and Powell each mattered to Brennan. He very much wanted a robust six-vote majority in this hotly contested area and to avoid a raft of hair-splitting opinions again. Worst case, the two were often enough in agreement that if one split off, the other might endanger Brennan's majority.

Once Brennan circulated his draft opinion, it became clear that of the two, O'Connor was going to be his main concern. She wanted to allow employers to adopt affirmative action only as a remedy for past behavior so bad it amounted to a violation of the Civil Rights Act. In this case, she asked herself, before the Transportation Authority adopted affirmative action, could a woman have sued it on the grounds that only sex discrimination could account for the *total* absence of a single female among the 238 skilled workers? Indeed she could have, the justice thought, perhaps remembering the all-male law firms that had rejected her so robustly in the years before there was a Civil Rights Act on the books at all.

Brennan really did not want to require employers to confess to prior civil rights violations in order to defend a voluntary affirmative action program. What company would ever admit that? Brennan gave Powell the trivial changes he was demanding in the opinion and cut O'Connor loose. The majority simply required that the employer be trying to rectify a "manifest imbalance" in the workplace. O'Connor filed a separate opinion setting up her demanding standard for defending affirmative action: "the employer must have had a firm basis for believing that remedial action was required. An employer would have such a firm basis if it can point to a statistical disparity sufficient to support a *prima facie* claim under Title VII by the employee beneficiaries of the affirmative action plan of a pattern or practice claim of discrimination."

With Powell providing Brennan with his fifth vote, O'Connor's opinion in *Johnson* was technically a mere warning. Soon after the decision in *Johnson*, however, Powell left the Court. As most of the liberals left the Court in the ensuing years, the standard for affirmative action got harder and harder to meet, and O'Connor had a piece of tightening the noose. Although she provided the crucial fifth vote to keep affirmative action alive in her last years on the Court, she then retired.

She was not a robust voice for social change. The best outcome for women would have been if the Court had made decisions that incentivized private actors to help change the world, rather than women constantly having to sue them to enforce the equality norms the Court set out. Her concurring opinion on affirmative action, like her opinion on liability in the sexual harassment cases, excused employers from responsibility for making social change. Being forbidden to remedy the historically sex-segregated workplace with affirmative action unless the segregation was something illegal they had actively done, most employers would shun any affirmative efforts to bring women in lest they have to admit they had previously been violating the Civil Rights Act. Without strict liability for sexual harassment, employers would be little motivated to establish programs to train their workforce not to act out on the job.

In the sexual harassment arena, the Court eventually moved beyond O'Connor's tightfisted opinions, making it easier for women to tag the employer with liability for sexual harassment. But until that time, years later, women would have to keep fighting for every inch of progress, case by case, and with their bosses as their adversaries, in the trench warfare of social-change litigation.

As long as O'Connor held the swing, however, the justices never prohibited affirmative action outright. Even if the legal doctrine was incoherent, thousands if not millions of women and racial minorities got jobs and educations, which would never have happened if the Court had struck down affirmative action as reverse discrimination per se.

12

Queen Sandra's Court

꧁꧂

On June 26, 1987, Lewis Powell retired. President Reagan replaced him with the California federal appeals court judge Anthony Kennedy, who looked to be a lot more conservative than Powell was. The change altered the composition of the Court and O'Connor's role within it. Often, as in the recent affirmative action case, she and Powell and White made up the pool of potential votes for the liberal side. After Powell left, with Brennan, Marshall, Blackmun, and Stevens on her left and Rehnquist, Scalia, Kennedy, and White mostly to the right, a lot more of the courting from both sides focused on her alone.

She had by then established a very functional routine for running her little law firm of one justice and four clerks. As the cases came into the Court, she assigned one of the clerks to write a preliminary memo, called a "bench" memo, on how she should decide. But instead of handling each case with only the assigned helper, she had all the preliminary memos circulated to all the clerks. The Saturday before oral argument weeks, all the clerks would gather in chambers and talk about all the cases that were to be argued that week. Justice O'Connor brought one of her southwestern specialties for lunch, and they had a freewheeling discussion.

One of her clerks, the son of a working mother, thought the lunch business was weird. His mother rarely cooked. Why was the most important woman in the world making them lunch? Others responded with gratitude for her "maternal" acts of kindness. Writing a tribute after she retired, her 1985–86 clerk John Setear said they had by far the nicest, friendliest workplace in the entire

Supreme Court, a veritable matriarchy of courtesy and interest in the clerks' personal lives. Of course, there were always those who didn't like Mom's food. "Ugh, spicy chili," Setear remembers. "I'm a Midwesterner and I don't like spicy food."

Being an O'Connor clerk involved adopting a clutch of her cultural practices. Like many westerners, the O'Connors came to D.C. with a long tradition of amateur entertainment—themed parties, gag costume photographs on Christmas cards. The practice found a home in the hypercompetitive atmosphere of Supreme Court clerking. An innocent episode of a carved pumpkin in chambers one Halloween soon led to a contest for the most elaborate jack-o'-lantern, culminating in one clerk roping in an artist friend to set the curve. In 1986, the clerks put on a gag skit parodying the entire *Wizard of Oz*. The next year, they hijacked a copy of the video the Court showed to tourists and remade it for the reunion, replacing the serious presentation of the arrival of the mass of petitions for review with a version of the last scene from *Raiders of the Lost Ark*. Her female clerks soon learned that the early morning aerobics class was a command performance.

O'Connor had a well-established reputation for hiring clerks of diverse political views. When she was interviewing the liberal Joan Greco, her third clerk to come up from then–Judge Ginsburg's chambers in the D.C. Circuit, she asked Greco how she liked clerking for Ginsburg. "Oh, I love it," Greco gushed, lured into inattention by O'Connor's legendary skill at putting people at ease. "It's so great to work for someone whose opinions you always totally agree with." In the ensuing silence, Greco came to her senses. "Oh *no*," she reflected. "What have I just *said*?" "Well," Justice O'Connor responded, "how would you feel about working for someone whose positions you don't agree with?" "Why," Greco gushed, "that would be great, too." And O'Connor offered her the coveted job on the spot.

With Powell gone, O'Connor was ready to move into a position of serious influence. Life was good. Energetic and robust as always, she arranged athletic outings for her clerks, where she was often the toughest competitor among a crowd half her age.

A term after Powell retired, Guy Braibant, head of the highest administrative court in France, hosted a visit from American jurists in July. Justice O'Connor led the delegation, which included the appeals court judges Ginsburg, whom she had already met, and Stephen Breyer, from the First Circuit in Boston. It was clear who was top dog. During the trip, Justice O'Connor would describe the "general structure of [the American] court system," and Judge Ginsburg would comment on her remarks. True to form, on their first day in Paris, the energetic Justice O'Connor arranged a morning walk to the Picasso Museum for the group. In her travel diary, an adorable little volume with a picture of a hot air balloon on the cover, Ginsburg reports, "O'Connor read map, none too well, so it was an hour+, but very pleasant stroll as beautiful day." It must have been a merry trip; Ginsburg's diary records flower-filled hotel rooms, gifts of Hermès scarves and medals, champagne and meals ("mussels especially excellent"), including an "elegant lunch" at the Constitutional Court and a duck dinner at Versailles. After dinner at the legendary Paris restaurant Lapérouse, Ginsburg notes, "just say OUI!!"

UNTIL IT'S NOT

But sober news lay in store for O'Connor when she got back. In October 1988, the robust and energetic fifty-eight-year-old justice got the report so many women dread: breast cancer. When she first heard the news in a routine medical exam, she could not believe it. She was in the middle of a very busy term and told her doctors cancer would have to wait while she heard several more rounds of oral argument. The doctors dissented. So her first lesson was "everything had to stop." Worse, she had "so many decisions to make." She had always thought the doctors would just tell you what to do. And she did have on her team probably the premier cancer doctor in Washington, Mark Lippman, then the chairman of the department at Georgetown and an internationally renowned breast cancer researcher. Her disease had progressed too far to avoid mastectomy. Indeed, after the surgery, she had to undergo radiation and chemotherapy, the most aggressive treatments. The doctors did not agree on everything, which made it all the more difficult.

In 1994, six years after her diagnosis, she told her story to a breast cancer survivors' gathering, a speech sent out to the world on TV. Perhaps for the first time, this most decisive of women recalled, she had had trouble making decisions. She remembers even having trouble digesting the information. It was so emotional a time. So she did what she did at the Court. She did as much research as it was possible to do and then she made her decisions. "I don't look back and I don't say, 'Oh, what if I had done another thing?'" And she tried something new, too—relying on other people. "It helped me," she recalled, "to have a close friend who had been through it," not once but twice. Indeed, the justice found it "amazing how many people wrote letters" or came up to her to reassure her that they had had it too and that her life would go on. One day, after the surgery, it got so bad that she called her friend at home and asked her to come to the hospital, and "she dropped everything and came down and we shed a tear or two together and we talked about everything and somehow that helped."

"Depressing" and "traumatic," as she described it in a letter to Powell, even cancer did not turn the decisive no-nonsense O'Connor into a sensitive New Ager. When the support people at the hospital advised her to "visualize" her recovery, she recalled later, she balked. "I'm not a visual person. I'm a practical person." So she made a chart on her calendar with all the chemotherapy appointments, and checked them off: "first one, got through it. When does the hair start to fall," she asked herself. "Second one, check." She was surprised by how distressing her physical losses were. Again surprised by the kindness of relative strangers, her hairdresser "turned out" to be "one of the kindest most marvelous men" she ever met. And she just sucked it up. When she saw how her condition was distressing her family, she told herself she'd better shape up. "Put a better face on things," she resolved. "Don't distress other people." It's only cancer.

As she retold it later, the "best thing was" that she "had a job to go to." Tired and stressed out as she was, "I had a job that was important and was always there for me to do so I just went down to my office and kept working, I never missed a day at the court, I never missed a conference, and I wonder how people who don't have a job do."

In 2013, when Justice Ginsburg was asked to speak about her colleague, then long retired from the bench, she singled out O'Connor's 1994 cancer survivor speech as one of the most important legacies of her tenure. "Her account," Ginsburg noted, "gave women afflicted with that trying disease hope, the courage to continue, to do as she did." It is indeed impressive to see the video of Supreme Court justice O'Connor, this most dignified and self-sufficient woman, with a somber mien, her voice perceptibly shaking and eyes occasionally tearing up, telling her story to the survivors. When Marty had cancer all those years ago, legal work had given Justice Ginsburg some security, knowing she could support herself and her baby daughter. When Justice O'Connor was stricken herself, meaningful work gave her purpose, focus, and distraction.

A JOB TO DO

And so she continued to help women have access to that lifeline. On October 31, 1988, five days after she left the hospital, and despite press speculation to the contrary, she sat down to a full day of oral argument.

Ann Hopkins's challenge to her rejection for partnership at the accounting giant Price Waterhouse was the fourth and final matter of that long, hard first day back. Hopkins, a senior manager and the only female partnership candidate of the forty-plus people in line, had first been held over for a year for reconsideration and then rejected. No one disputed that she had been a very effective manager, landing a huge contract with the State Department in the run-up to her first partnership year. The crucial piece of evidence against Price Waterhouse in a warehouse full of damning admissions came from the man who bore responsibility for explaining to Hopkins the reasons for the decision. In order to improve her chances for partnership after the first delay, he advised, Hopkins should "walk more femininely, talk more femininely, dress more femininely, wear make-up, have her hair styled, and wear jewelry." It's hard to blame this gentleman entirely for the hilariously sexist advice, as he was looking at reports from partners that she was "macho," she "overcompensated for being a woman," she should take "a course at charm school," and she swore a lot. One of her supporters even wrote in a supposedly favorable evaluation that she "ha[d] matured from a tough-talking somewhat masculine hard-nosed mgr to an authoritative, formidable, but much more appealing lady ptr [partnership] candidate."

In previous years, other female candidates for partnership also had been evaluated in sex-based terms. As the trial record reflected, candidates at Price Waterhouse were viewed favorably if "partners believed they maintained their femin[in]ity while becoming effective professional managers." A partner who could not consider any woman seriously as a partnership candidate even had his vote recorded in the overall summary of the evaluations.

Price Waterhouse did what it could to ameliorate the damage. It contended that Hopkins was rejected because she could not get along with her coworkers. Maybe they said things that looked bad, the firm argued, but they had a completely independent reason for rejecting her, and that should be enough. Again, the Court was confronted with a major social policy matter masquerading as a procedural problem. Firing someone for having a bad attitude does not violate the Civil Rights Act. Firing her for not being feminine enough does. Such disputes are called "mixed motive" cases.

The lower courts had found for Hopkins, ruling that once Hopkins proved the existence of discrimination, the employer had to show "clear and convincing" evidence that it would have fired her anyway, a standard much higher than the normal preponderance of the evidence required for most proof. On appeal, even Hopkins's lawyer didn't defend his having required such a powerful showing from the employer. He was just hoping to eke out an opinion that, after the plaintiff showed the employer behaving badly, the employer had to do something to justify its conduct.

Price Waterhouse, of course, was seeking a ruling that the *plaintiff* had to prove not just discrimination but that the decision would have been different if the employer had not discriminated. It was a very important "procedural" decision. Employers almost always present some alternative reason for firing someone. So who has the burden of proving which motive actually generated the rejection is game, set, and match in discrimination litigation.

From where Hopkins sat, "Justice O'Connor's eyes stared through deep grey rings on a ghostly white, stoically expressionless face. In spite of a mastectomy ten days earlier, she was on the bench." Not only on the bench, but, three minutes into the accounting firm's argument, she was asking its lawyer, Kathryn Oberly, the crucial question. When there's evidence for both sides, who owns the tie? The employer's lawyer invoked a classic procedural answer: the person who brings the lawsuit always bears the burden of proving her case. At equipoise, the defendant wins. O'Connor jumped in immediately. If the rejected woman proves the employer did something bad, maybe that shifts the burden. Maybe the employer then has to prove *something*. No, the lawyer answers, it's the plaintiff's burden to "move the ball over the fifty yard line." No, says O'Connor, there is language in other cases that "it's enough to show that the discriminatory reason was a substantial factor." As Oberly resists her, she persists: "Are you saying the comments are irrelevant?" O'Connor asks incredulously. "It's discrimination in the air," Oberly answers. "But it did not touch the plaintiff."

The votes at conference revealed immediately that the Court recognized the pathology of airborne discrimination. Six of the justices agreed that once the employee showed some evidence of discrimination, the employer had to do something to defend itself. Although the majority decision ultimately favored Ann Hopkins, the vote in *Price Waterhouse* reflected the change in the Court: Kennedy now joined Rehnquist and Scalia in siding with the employer, period. Still, with both White and O'Connor voting to tag the employer with some responsibility, Brennan, senior liberal, had six votes to play with.

VITAL FOR THE COURT

If O'Connor had her way, the liberal bloc would not soon have that chance again. Brennan was manifestly ailing, and it seemed clear that the balance on the Court would turn on who won the upcoming election. The day after the argument in *Price Waterhouse* she wrote to her pal Barry Goldwater that after a "depressing and very traumatic three weeks" since the cancer diagnosis, "I am back at work and on the mend." It was, she noted, November 1, "a week until election day." In light of the possibility that people are so indifferent that "many will not vote," Justice O'Connor said to Goldwater, she "will be thankful if George B wins. It is vital for the Court and the nation that he does."

O'Connor's correspondence with her political godfather Goldwater provides a rare glimpse into the legendarily discreet justice's political life. Four years earlier, in 1984, then Congressman John McCain wrote to Senator Goldwater to solicit a federal judgeship for a black Democrat, Cecil Patterson, who had been enormously helpful to McCain in "bridg[ing] the gap that we Republicans have with the black community and . . . establishing an effective dialogue which transcends notions of party or race." In response, Goldwater wrote to John O'Connor. "I have a question to ask of both you and Sandra." What did both the O'Connors think "as to what might happen politically or legally or any other way if I appointed a black lawyer when only about three percent of our population is black?" There is no answer in the file, but the letter reveals that Goldwater felt free to introduce such a sensitive political subject to a sitting Supreme Court justice. Shortly after the senator sought their off-the-record advice, he had lunch with Justice O'Connor in Washington and presented her with a more overt political opportunity—the Arizona Young Republicans wished to have her receive their Barry Goldwater award (and, of course, speak at their event). "I could have told you," Goldwater reported to the youthful partisans after the lunch, "that her answer would be that the Court should not do this."

She was discreet. But she was not indifferent. In '86, Sandra joined the Court betting pool, Rehnquist, Stevens, and Powell, on the midterm elections. Paying up her losses afterward, she noted ruefully that her "optimism" cost her. She was too hopeful, it turned out, that the Republicans would win their races. Nonetheless, two years later, she told Goldwater that she remained hopeful for the Republican George H. W. Bush.

THE O'CONNOR COURT

Before the triumphant George H. W. Bush had a chance to prove his vitality to the Court, however, Brennan, frail but still sitting, wrote an ambitious draft in the Price Waterhouse case. The negotiation over the opinion in *Price Waterhouse* reveals graphically what a Court centered on Sandra Day O'Connor would do for women. O'Connor responded with a five-page single-spaced letter, suggesting he revise the opinion, making it easier on the employer in several ways. O'Connor's resistance always carried the threat that she would attract the lukewarm liberal White, leaving Brennan with only four votes. In the six exchanges that followed, the difference between the old liberal and her potentially crucial vote came down to whether the employee had to prove that the bad motive played a "substantial" role in the company's decision, as O'Connor insisted, or whether some lesser showing, per Brennan, would do. He resisted; she insisted, using the threat of a concurring opinion to press him into changing his language. Typically recognizing that "five is better than four," Brennan finally agreed to raise the employee's burden to showing the sexist beliefs "motivated" the adverse decision, not just played a part in it. She responded by saying she was going to write separately anyway.

And so she did, attracting the support of Justice White for her requirement that the plaintiff prove, by "direct evidence," that sexism was a "substantial" motive for the woman's bad treatment. Depriving Brennan of his majority, his opinion would speak for the four liberals only. Women, so often the victims of unconscious or covert sexism, had a terrible time proving that the sexism substantially motivated their lesser treatment. For women, as the later sexual harassment cases were to demonstrate, stray remarks around the watercooler were exactly what was keeping them down. Lower courts were left to struggle, with voluble displeasure, with what constituted "direct" evidence of a "substantial" role, often simply repeating what O'Connor said it was not—stray remarks around the watercooler. (In 1991, Congress amended the Civil Rights Act to incorporate Justice Brennan's standard and discard O'Connor's.)

O'Connor's importance soared. The clear center of the more conservative Court, she wielded her position like a seasoned politician. She cast ambiguous votes at conference or professed herself undecided until she saw the draft of the assigned author and then she dragged her feet about signing on to drafts that were circulating, all techniques designed to draw the authors of assigned opinions to her in order to ensure her support. Her most visible strategic tactic was the concurring opinion, agreeing with the outcome of her chosen majority but differing with the opinion of whoever was writing. Although she was not nearly the most prolific source of concurrences on the Court, her efforts were by far the most consequential, because she didn't just write to highlight a collateral issue or reveal a disagreement about doctrine.

When she was, as she often was, the critical fifth vote, O'Connor used the concurrence power to strip the majority opinion of its majority, setting out a different explanation for the outcome. Since she was the fifth vote in these cases, litigants and lower courts recognized that her position was the only one sure to attract the essential five supporters. Almost without exception she used the vehicle of the concurrence to make the conservative rulings more liberal and liberal opinions more conservative, usually by tying the outcome to the particular facts in the case. This pattern drove the lower courts to distraction from the lack of guidance on how to apply the decision in cases with similar issues but different facts.

13

No Queen's Peace in the Abortion Wars

Although her strategic behavior during the two decades from Powell's retirement in 1987 to her own leave-taking eighteen years later affected many areas of the law, O'Connor's new power had the biggest impact on women's equality in the hallmark women's issue: abortion. In 1992, two decades after the 7–2 decision in *Roe v. Wade*, she rewrote the rules on abortion. Her assault on the embattled 1973 consensus around *Roe* was eminently foreseeable. In *Akron v. Akron Center for Reproductive Health* in 1983, almost immediately after her appointment, she had registered her dissent from the six-man majority that reaffirmed *Roe*. She would have upheld a raft of local regulations discouraging abortions as not "unduly burdening" the right.

She was not alone in criticizing *Roe*. Ginsburg, now many years removed from advocacy by her appointment to the court of appeals, had been following O'Connor's pronouncements on women's issues closely from below. She used O'Connor's story about being offered a secretarial position in a speech right after O'Connor surfaced in public view and spoke admiringly about O'Connor's first discrimination opinion in the Mississippi women's college case in another speech in 1984.

Then Ginsburg surprised many followers by attacking *Roe v. Wade* in terms strikingly similar to O'Connor's 1983 dissent in the *Akron* case. Like O'Connor, Ginsburg strongly criticized Justice Blackmun's opinion in *Roe* for prescribing a time-based framework to govern all abortion matters. She would have struck the specific Texas law at issue in *Roe*, which made all abortions criminal.

Although Ginsburg did not specify which restrictions, if any, she would allow, she suggested the Court should have taken a passive posture, waiting to see what the states did. Had O'Connor had the votes, the Court would similarly have waited to see if the states did anything to unduly burden the right to abortion. So Ginsburg and O'Connor were in agreement on what the Court's procedures should be, if not on what would be allowed.

Unlike O'Connor, who, after *Hogan*, rarely articulated the social meaning of her decisions about women, Ginsburg strongly suggested that women's equality was the justification for protecting abortion rights. Women must control their reproduction in order to achieve legal and social equality. In Ginsburg's analysis, abortion rights would be securely anchored with the other women's rights she had achieved, in the equality language of the Fourteenth Amendment, not in some free-floating notion of privacy. Regardless of whether the state is interested in the fetus from the moment of conception, women's lives would be put on the other side of the scale. If women need abortion rights to achieve equality, it is difficult to envision what restrictions the state could legally impose, except those that serve the interests of women's health itself, such as requiring practitioners to be trained or licensed. Certainly the Court could not approve the restrictions O'Connor defended, such as making women listen to speeches and then wait for their abortions or making young women get permission from their parents. All those restrictions are designed to steer women away from abortions; under O'Connor's analysis anything short of making it impossible—driving women to coat hangers or foreign shores—is acceptable. Under Ginsburg's robust vision of women's lives, it is the unfettered right to make the decision that is central to a woman's equality. Telling her what to do is the core violation.

ABORTION BATTLES IN THE CULTURE WARS

In a devilish way, Ginsburg got her wish. Starting as early as the election of 1972, abortion was recognized as a skirmish in the battle over women's equality and, more broadly, as part of a war over competing concepts of American culture. The prescient antifeminist Phyllis Schlafly recognized the relationship early on and tarred abortion with the brush used on the Equal Rights Amendment—as a threat to the conventional family. The conservative revival picked up Schlafly's framing and her powerhouse alliance among Catholics, fundamentalist Protestants, and Orthodox Jews. They added abortion to the list of ominous cultural changes—gay rights, moral relativism, declining patriotism. When the New Right came into ascendancy in the Republican Party, formally with the election of Ronald Reagan in 1980, they inserted an explicit plank in the party platform to appoint judges "who respect traditional family values and the sanctity of innocent human life." After O'Connor, Reagan put the conservative, Catholic Antonin Scalia and Anthony Kennedy on the bench. O'Connor had already expressed her disaffection with *Roe v. Wade*, dissenting in the cases grouped together under *Akron v. Akron Center for Reproductive Health* in 1983.

Watching these developments, in 1986, the energetic Missouri Citizens for Life drafted the most ambitious legislation yet. The Missouri law included a preamble deeming life to begin at conception, an order that state laws must treat fetuses as having the rights of persons, a provision ordering doctors to test fetuses for viability, and a prohibition against use of public resources for abortions or even counseling abortions. The statute was so extreme, the Catholic Conference fretted that the Missouri attorney general would not be willing to defend the whole new law robustly, for fear of losing the case. The composition of the Court had changed enough to raise the possibility that it really would reverse *Roe* outright, and the Missouri activists wanted their AG to ask the Court to do so.

When the Missouri law came before the Court in *Webster v. Reproductive Health Services*, it did seem to leave it little room to escape the confrontation with *Roe*. As Bill Cox and his allies feared, the Missouri attorney general, perhaps suspecting that the Court might not be ready to overrule *Roe* directly, contended that the statute wasn't as bad as it looked. The life-begins-at-conception language was just bloviating advice in a preamble, the state's brief said (merely "precatory" and imposing no restrictions on anyone).

The state accepted that it could not forbid publicly funded doctors to tell female patients they needed an abortion. Doctors can
use their good judgment in administering the viability tests, the
state said. But the Court was interested enough in outright reversal to grant leave for the United States to intervene as friend of
the court to present the argument. George H. W. Bush's solicitor
general resubmitted the 1986 Reagan administration brief to the
newly altered tribunal, asking the Court to overrule *Roe*, and had
the unpleasant task of arguing for reversal to a tribunal that still
included its author, Harry Blackmun.

As usual, O'Connor's chambers included clerks of many diverse
views. The responsibility for the initial memo fell to a clerk who
came up from Ginsburg's chambers, Daniel Mandil. He came
down in favor of taking Missouri's olive branch. Just let them
minimize the severity of the restrictions, he counseled, and do the
judicial-restraint thing of not confronting a constitutional decision
until you must. If Mandil had his way, *Webster* would blow over
and, although women would be burdened with a list of restrictions
never before approved, *Roe* would remain the law as it was before
the clouds gathered.

O'Connor's other clerk Andrew McBride, fresh from the cham-
bers of the recently rejected conservative Supreme Court candidate
Judge Robert Bork of the D.C. Circuit, held down the right, while
Jane Stromseth, up from clerking for the liberal district judge Louis
Oberdorfer, occupied the opposite end of the political spectrum.
Even as Mandil undertook his assigned duties, Stromseth and
McBride both took the unusual step of preparing dueling memos.
McBride argued for reversing *Roe* and Stromseth suggested that
O'Connor find much of the statute to be an undue burden, a move
that would leave most of *Roe* intact. When the clerks walked into
O'Connor's chambers as usual the Saturday before oral argument,
no amount of chili was required for a hot discussion to ensue. The
justice gave no hint of where she was going.

At oral argument the next week, however, she signaled her
discomfort with allowing the states unlimited free rein over
women's reproduction. If the Court overruled *Roe v. Wade*, she

asked Solicitor General Fried, would the state have "a right to require the women to *have* abortions," say, if "we had a serious overpopulation problem?" When Fried denied this, she pressed him. If the woman had no liberty interest to protect her right to abortion, what would protect her against abortion? (This very unappealing scenario of the forced abortion was, of course, the case Ginsburg wanted to bring first to establish women's reproductive rights, all those years ago when the air force discharged her client Susan Struck for refusing to have an abortion. But the canny Solicitor General Erwin Griswold had settled with Struck, making the case moot.)

The oral argument in the Missouri case graphically illustrates the appeal of the equality strategy. Without a robust commitment to women's equality to control their destiny as the foundation for abortion rights, as Ginsburg advocated, abortion advocates were hampered in trying to rein in the states. With Justice Scalia in hot pursuit, the lawyer for the abortion providers was repeatedly forced back on the unconvincing argument that the laws should fall because reasonable people differed about when life began. Why isn't when life begins exactly the kind of dispute we leave to the states, Scalia wanted to know. If the state can decide life begins at conception, the question then is what is to stop the state from forcing women to carry the life to term? Ginsburg's answer would have been that women's equality is what stops the state. Women need to control their reproduction if they are going to participate as equals in American life. In the universe of perfect logic, unless women count, as Ginsburg cannily perceived, *Roe* falls, and the states can do whatever they want.

But the Court rarely operates in the universe of perfect logic. As Blackmun held his breath, the Court stepped back from the brink. After a majority of five voted at conference to uphold the Missouri law, Rehnquist circulated a draft proposing to abandon the trimester scheme of *Roe* in favor of something like O'Connor's original test of undue burden, but not to overrule *Roe* outright. It was hardly a white flag. He would then uphold everything Missouri did, including the section of Missouri law gagging doctors at public facilities, which the state had declined to appeal. If Missouri's requirement of tests for viability violated the bright line of viability set out in *Roe*, then that aspect of *Roe*, his draft suggested, was "not constitutionally relevant."

Rehnquist's analysis was totally lawless. The Court was still going to preserve the shell of *Roe*, that is, forbid the states to unduly burden women's access to abortions as an abstract matter, which is lawless enough. Then he went on to hold that nothing the state could dream up so far would actually fail the test. He was clearly testing to see what O'Connor would tolerate.

O'Connor immediately threatened to concur and even, if pushed, to dissent in part on the doctor gag order. The liberals, seeing an opening, offered to join O'Connor in dissent. Rehnquist backed down. He now knew that O'Connor was not going to overrule *Roe* outright. As long as she held the crucial swing vote, there was life in women's abortion rights, however faint the beat.

On the subject of the exact structure of *Roe*, she proposed that the Court just accept Missouri's concessions and act as if the Missouri law did not challenge the core of the opinion in *Roe*. "I see," she wrote, "no necessity to go further than that in this case." Rehnquist did not back down. As she had threatened to do, O'Connor duly filed a concurrence, depriving Rehnquist of his majority and formally preserving the trimester precedent of *Roe v. Wade*. She deliberately read the Missouri law to avoid a conflict and therefore, as she put it, to refuse "to accept the State's invitation to reexamine the constitutional validity of *Roe v. Wade*. . . . When the constitutional invalidity of a State's abortion statute actually turns on the constitutional validity of *Roe v. Wade*, there will be time enough to reexamine *Roe*. And to do so carefully."

Even *Roe*'s defenders, Blackmun and Stevens, said that pretending the Missouri law was compatible with *Roe* was "fraudulent" and "indecent." But O'Connor was not ready to jump off the abortion cliff. In the inevitable next term's abortion case, O'Connor actually made a five-justice majority with the liberals to strike down the law compelling a young woman to get both parents' approval for an abortion. It was the first time the right-to-life movement came up with any restriction on the women O'Connor didn't publicly vote for. O'Connor's opinion hardly amounted to a wholesale embrace of women's rights. With the other conservatives, she allowed the parental notification as long as it included an option to let the girl go to a judge for her abortion permission.

In 1990 Brennan left and was replaced by the Delphic David Souter, a man with no record on the subject of abortion at all. When Souter joined the conservatives to okay a doctor gag law in a 1991 case, the tension mounted. The next year, the conservative Clarence Thomas took Thurgood Marshall's place. Abortion inevitably surfaced again in 1992, in a Pennsylvania case, *Planned Parenthood v. Casey*, and it looked like there were six votes to reverse *Roe v. Wade* outright. Souter's one vote had been opposed to abortion rights, and the four from 1989—White, Rehnquist, Scalia, and Kennedy—plus the new conservative, Clarence Thomas, would act with or without Souter and certainly without their faithless ally Sandra Day O'Connor.

WWTFWOTSCD (WHAT WOULD THE FIRST WOMAN ON THE SUPREME COURT DO?)

Pennsylvania had imposed a lot of restrictions, such as strict parental notification and prescribing an elaborate presentation to the pregnant woman about the perils of abortion. But the real impact of the case was that two of the three judges on the Court of Appeals for the Third Circuit, which covers Pennsylvania, jumped the gun and ruled outright that *Roe* no longer commanded a majority of the Court. Instead, they would take their orders from the crucial swing vote, Sandra Day O'Connor. Having explicitly refused to follow *Roe v. Wade*, the circuit court then sustained almost the entire Pennsylvania scheme as an application of O'Connor's undue-burden standard. (Judge Samuel Alito of the Third Circuit even voted to uphold a requirement that pregnant women seeking abortion must notify their spouses, but he could not persuade either of the other two judges to join him on that point.) Still, the pro-choice activists were so scared of the Court that they actually debated not appealing from the Third Circuit. Pennsylvanians would just live with the draconian terms of the state's anti-abortion law.

But it was 1992. The lawyer in charge of the case, the ACLU's Kathryn Kolbert arguing for Planned Parenthood, made a political decision to provoke the Supreme Court into just overruling *Roe*. She would argue that there was no way to reconcile the Pennsylvania law with *Roe* and so the Court either had to strike down the law or overrule *Roe* at last. She wasn't happy to lose the foundation of women's abortion rights, but she was hoping women's furious reaction to the repeal of *Roe v. Wade* in the upcoming election would push George H. W. Bush right out of the White House. The next appointments would be made by a Democrat. In her mind anything would be better than having the lower courts start issuing a bunch of rogue opinions like the Pennsylvania court had just done. The ACLU petitioned for Supreme Court review, suggesting that the issue was whether the Supreme Court had overruled *Roe v. Wade*. For its part, Pennsylvania stepped right up and appealed the one issue it lost, asking the Court to approve of making women tell their husbands about their planned abortions. So no one was arguing for any more evasion.

For her political strategy to work, Kolbert had to get the case on the docket immediately, however. Any delay would put the issuance of the decision beyond the 1992 election, and it would be four long years before the next chance to test abortion rights at the ballot box. She filed her petition for review in record time three weeks later, on November 7, 1991. But she was no match for the chief justice, who controlled the calendar. For some gut-wrenching weeks, Rehnquist simply kept delaying consideration of *Casey*, a move called "relisting," of whether to review the abortion case. Finally, some combination of Justices Stevens and Blackmun got Rehnquist's attention by threatening to file an unprecedented public dissent from the decision to relist, and Rehnquist abandoned the tactic.

The Court voted to take the case, with plenty of time for a decision before the election. When the time came, only O'Connor and Rehnquist voted not to take it. Had they prevailed, the denial of review would, of course, have thwarted the abortion activists' plan to make abortion an issue in the election. Then Justice Souter, who had voted tentatively to take it, asked for more time! Alarms spread in the liberal chambers of justices such as Blackmun. After a scouting mission to Souter's chambers, Blackmun's clerk Stephanie Dangel assured him that Souter would not delay the case until after the presidential contest. "Unlike the Chief and SOC [Sandra O'Connor], Souter was not concerned about the election," Souter's clerk told Dangel.

As Blackmun's clerk reported, O'Connor *was* concerned about the election. Not until Senator Barry Goldwater's papers became available to the public many years after the clerks exchanged views on O'Connor's politics did her ongoing concern with the senior Bush's electoral fate emerge fully. Four years earlier, she had expressed to her Arizona colleague how critical Bush's election was "for the court and the nation." Now the abortion case threatened his retention in 1992. But other than voting against taking it, which she did, there was little she could do to stop it.

Kathryn Kolbert was particularly determined to use the appeal to dare the FWOTSC to overrule *Roe*. At oral argument, for seven long minutes, she extolled *Roe* and attacked Justice O'Connor's preservationist strategy from *Webster*. Kolbert was not grateful to O'Connor for barely preserving *Roe*. She thought *Roe* should be reaffirmed or rejected. Finally, beyond provocation, Justice O'Connor broke in, accusing Kolbert of not addressing the issues the Court had asked to review. Was the litigator ever going to address what the Court was interested in? Kolbert said she was, but indeed, she was not.

The leaks from the conference are laconic, but Justice Rehnquist apparently felt he had enough votes to affirm all of the Pennsylvania regulations, including the spousal notification, and so he again assigned the opinion to himself. It looked like *Roe* was done. Justice Souter was deeply troubled by the bald overruling of established precedent as a result of a simple change in the composition of the Court. But given the size of Rehnquist's majority, Justice Souter must have seemed unimportant at that moment.

Bad mistake. Suspecting, from her votes in *Webster* and the parental notification case, that Justice O'Connor was not on board with Rehnquist, Souter decided to see what she thought could be done. There was only one place for the two of them to go: to Justice Anthony Kennedy.

There is no evidence that it was Justice O'Connor who engineered the survival of formal abortion rights. Kennedy, the critical third vote, was a devout Catholic, he had been tight with the conservative Catholic Antonin Scalia since his appointment, and he was not particularly close to O'Connor. Indeed, O'Connor was not palling around with anyone that term. People on the scene believe it was Souter who approached Kennedy. Scalia's ideological rigidity and his over-the-top rhetoric had come to feel unseemly to the ethereal Anthony Kennedy, and, when Justice Souter approached him, he quickly abandoned the conservative ship. It did not hurt that Souter and Kennedy had worked together earlier that term to produce a centrist opinion in an important environmental case, again leaving the hard-core four conservatives without a majority, in that case, to gut the Endangered Species Act. They had a pathway to cooperation, and a common sense of themselves as occupying the center. They decided to cowrite an opinion, not a common practice in 1992. One month later, Kennedy wrote to Blackmun. "I want to tell you about some developments in Planned Parenthood v. Casey, and I think part of what I say should come as welcome news."

On the last day of the term, the three took their seats, to deliver, one after another, the single opinion they had crafted together. The constitutional right to an abortion would not be overturned.

Kennedy wrote a section of the joint opinion exalting the concept of liberty to include decisions involving the right to "define one's own concept of existence . . . and of the mystery of human life." A pregnant woman's suffering "is too intimate and personal for the state to insist on childbirth," he continued, teeing up the critical insight: out of "its own vision of the woman's role." No wonder Judge—later Justice—Ginsburg exulted over this opinion, otherwise a decidedly mixed bag for women. Getting the state out of the business of enforcing its vision of the woman's "concept of existence" was the work of her life. For his part, Souter is widely credited with the powerful argument against overturning a settled precedent that had governed people's sexual behavior and decisions for two decades in an act that would look like raw political power, not considered jurisprudence.

The third, workmanlike section of the opinion, dealing with the actual provisions of the Pennsylvania law, is attributed to O'Connor. In reviewing that effort and all future efforts to make abortion harder for women, O'Connor's concept of undue burden cemented the new order. In *Planned Parenthood v. Casey* and for the next twelve years, the Court has asked and answered her question: Did the state place an "undue burden" on a woman seeking to abort? Unlike Blackmun's injunction of no interference for three months, and nothing but the mother's health for the next three months, the undue-burden language provides no objective guidance for what might be allowed. For many years the Court was so closely divided that the question always wound up in the hands of the woman who was ultimately the crucial swing vote: What kinds of lives did she think women deserved? Of course, this phenomenon also meant the country would be asking the same question of whoever would succeed her when she retired.

All the litigation after *Casey*, then, started with her section of the opinion in *Casey*. O'Connor began answering that question by backing away from what she had allowed under her undue-burden test repeatedly and as recently as only three years before. I know, she admitted, I said the state has an interest in the fetus from conception that might outweigh the mother's interest, but I'm not saying that anymore: "we answer the question, left open in previous opinions discussing the undue burden formulation, whether a law designed to further the State's interest in fetal life which imposes an undue burden on the woman's decision before fetal viability could be constitutional. The answer is no." She then sustained every burdensome provision of the Pennsylvania law, all of which applied throughout pregnancy, except making women tell their husbands. Women were entitled to lives that did not automatically end in death in childbirth if the abortion were denied, and women were entitled to lives that did not involve their asking their husbands about their proposed abortions. That's it.

In 1983, when O'Connor had first suggested the states' campaigns against abortion rights be measured by whether they placed an "undue burden" on the woman's choice, she was not yet famous for her jurisprudence of good common sense. Over the ensuing years, she imposed similar open-ended standards on every crucial civil rights matter—freedom of religion, affirmative action, employment discrimination. The vague and general language she used means that each decision resolved no more than the case at hand, making the Supreme Court the Common Sense court of last resort. When did a Christmas crèche amount to the establishment of religion? When it was "excessive." When could a college prefer a black to a white applicant? Until such action was no longer "necessary." What would constitute actionable proof of sex discrimination? When it is "sufficiently severe or pervasive." Her decision in *Casey* follows suit.

Common sense—the practical wisdom of the common man—by definition requiring neither theory nor expertise, is an effective tool for allowing unexamined intuitions and prejudices into decision making. The abortion cases, then, create an insight into the much-debated issue of Justice O'Connor's lay intuition about women's lives. Of all the hurdles the states thought up to discourage women in the years from her first abortion decision in 1983 to *Casey*, in 1992—making doctors tell them abortion was dangerous or that there were people wanting to adopt their offspring, prohibiting public hospitals from involvement, making women endure waiting periods, getting parental consent or a judge's consent—O'Connor went along with them all. She dissented when the more liberal Court struck the state laws down in her early years, and she voted with the newly formed conservative majority when the Court eventually allowed the limitations on abortion. In all the cases before *Casey*, she had demanded only that a girl have an option to confide in a local judge instead of her parents. In *Casey* she gave her permission for the state to make providers tell women how dangerous abortion procedures could be to their health, make them wait twenty-four hours to digest the information, make young girls tell their parents in most cases.

The only provision that felt burdensome to her and her two colleagues was spousal notification. It grossed O'Connor out to think of the government making a married woman tell her husband, whom she would not otherwise inform of her plans, that she was about to have an abortion. Critics concluded that O'Connor could relate, from her life as a married bourgeois woman, to how onerous such a burden would be. As to the rest—poor women having to take days off from work to travel to where abortions were available, often hundreds of miles from their homes, and then listen to a lecture unrelated to their needs or health care—no problem.

Critics speculate that when she talked about common sense, she was unable to see outside the communally formed common sense of her community—white, middle class, married. This is a pretty serious criticism and one that an intuition-driven method like O'Connor's naturally evokes. But O'Connor's commonsense intuitions may be nothing more sinister than her telling the women to suck it up, travel to where abortions were offered, and listen to whatever they made you hear. Weaklings were not O'Connor's strong suit. She was even surprised at the outpouring of love and support for her when she needed help during her treatments for breast cancer.

Whatever the jurisprudence, the troika of Souter, Kennedy, and O'Connor at least ensured that women were granted some modicum of protection for their core decisions. And the center held. In 1992 a Democrat won the White House for the first time in sixteen years.

Part IV

Sisters in Law

The Supreme Court of the United States, 1993.

14

I'm Ruth, Not Sandra

꽃

When the Senate Judiciary Committee convened to consider the nomination of Circuit Judge Ruth Bader Ginsburg for appointment to the Supreme Court, the committee had two new members: Senator Dianne Feinstein of California and, from Illinois, Senator Carol Moseley Braun. Before Feinstein had her turn, the other members who had spoken had boasted of their long history of considering Supreme Court nominees. But, Feinstein noted, "for myself and Senator Moseley Braun, this is our first. And it is no coincidence that, as our first, it is someone such as yourself," she noted to the nominee. No coincidence indeed.

The year that swept Bill Clinton into the presidency, 1992, was called the Year of the Woman because a record number of women took office at every level across the nation. The Supreme Court had played an unexpected part in the women's year. When George H. W. Bush nominated Clarence Thomas to the Court in 1991, the Oklahoma law professor Anita Hill accused him of sexual harassment during the time they worked together. After widely televised hearings on the charges before the Senate Judiciary Committee, Thomas was confirmed, 52–48. Thomas's confirmation generated a loud outcry from people who believed Hill and felt that she—and the issue of sexual harassment—had been badly mishandled by an all-male Judiciary Committee. The political world looked very different after November 1992 than it had a few weeks before.

When Clinton, a former constitutional law professor with a keen eye on his legacy, got his first Supreme Court opening, merely three months after he took office, he was determined to make history. He recognized the impact of naming the second woman to the Supreme Court. Few women were more responsible for the changed universe that had put Dianne Feinstein and Carol Moseley Braun in the United States Senate than Clinton's nominee, Ruth Bader Ginsburg. It was a sweet moment.

WINDING UP TO THE PITCH

For someone about to nominate a brilliant, beautifully educated, experienced, and symbolic candidate, Clinton spent a long time considering. Partly this was not his fault. His first choice was the charming and charismatic Mario Cuomo, governor of New York. Likening Cuomo to another former governor turned justice, Earl Warren, Clinton thought Cuomo might persuade some members of the Republican-dominated bench into decisions more to his liking, rather than just being another liberal vote. The legendarily indecisive Cuomo kept the president dangling for months. At the White House, everyone seemed to have a different dream. Some dreamed of towering constitutional law scholars such as Harvard's Larry Tribe. Others thought it would be brilliant to appoint someone without a law degree (which is allowed, but unprecedented). Clinton was very enamored of his interior secretary, the smart and articulate Bruce Babbitt. The key Republican Senate Judiciary Committee member Orrin Hatch wanted his pal Ted Kennedy's former chief of staff, Stephen Breyer, then a judge on the First Circuit.

As Clinton dithered, Judge Ginsburg's posse was hard at work. Even her long-deceased mother, Celia Amster Bader, played a role. Bader's niece Cousin Beth, née Amster, was married to a good friend of Senator Daniel Patrick Moynihan of New York, one Stephen Hess. He and Moynihan had served together in the Nixon White House and Hess was then at a powerful centrist think tank in D.C., the Brookings Institution. Beth's husband sprang into action, reaching out to Senator Moynihan, who turned into Ruth's best advocate. Although they had never met, Moynihan, the brainy ex-Harvard professor, knew Ginsburg, the brainy ex-Columbia professor, from her writings and her advocacy. In some precincts, that's as good as long acquaintance, and so it was with Moynihan. It was her views on judicial respect for the legislature, he said in an interview, that attracted him to her. Of course, it didn't hurt that she was born in Brooklyn.

As the spring wore on, White House Counsel Bernard Nussbaum, who was a lead player in picking a nominee, received an unexpected phone call from one of his pals at NYU Law School. Would Nussbaum and his wife like to join him at a dinner for six at the posh Inn at Little Washington in the nearby Virginia countryside? The other couple would be . . . the caller's friends, Marty and Ruth Ginsburg. "Of course I knew exactly what people were doing," Nussbaum says. But the evening was delightful. "I really saw her close up. All these things have an impact. I was impressed on a personal basis."

Moynihan flew from Washington to New York City with the president on *Air Force One*, and he used the opportunity to lobby for his candidate. But Ginsburg was a bookish appeals court judge, just the kind of appointment Clinton said he did not want, a "footnote" type rather than a political type, who could sway the other justices his way. She was also sixty, and the White House staff was hoping for someone younger, who would outlast the youthful Clarence Thomas.

Then opposition to Ginsburg surfaced, and from an unanticipated place: the left. Ginsburg's entire approach was based on treating men and women as legally similar and equal. Since her feminist awakening in 1970, other players had arisen who challenged that strategy for helping women. Some said, for example, that women were different but still entitled to social initiatives that would empower them despite, or even because of, their differences.

It should not have been totally surprising; revolutions have been consuming their young since the Bastille. Feminism, heavily anchored in colleges and universities, was particularly susceptible to idealistic theorizing. In fact, just as Ruth was leaving the ACLU for the comfortable precincts of the life-tenured judiciary in the early 1980s, the two new difference-based movements, each of which profoundly challenged her life's work, gained real traction.

Both took aim at Ginsburg's organizing principle that men and women potentially aspire to the same avenues to human flourishing and so should be allowed the same options. Catharine MacKinnon, whose work played such an important role in the courts' recognizing an action for sexual harassment, asserted that men dominated women in ways unique to women. Ginsburg's equality argument was fueled by the denial that men and women could be assumed to be constitutively different, often called the "anti-stereotype principle." MacKinnon rejected this argument. Even when there was no similarly situated man, she contended, women should not be required to overcome the legacy of centuries of oppression and resemble men in order to claim the goods of society. The policies and practices that made women's lives worse—such as not supporting childbirth leave—were illegal. Starting in the late '80s, she attacked Ginsburg's decade of achievement of simple equality head-on. Most of what Ginsburg did, she argued, was to take away the few advantages women had—widow's preferences, for example. And she represented male plaintiffs! Women were different, MacKinnon asserted. The question should not be Ginsburg's question—are they treated differently from comparable men. The question is: Are they treated badly in ways that men, given their physiology, history, and social power, could or would never experience?

Women *are* different, the Harvard psychologist Carol Gilligan agreed in the second challenge to Ginsburg's work. They even think differently. When confronted with a moral problem like whether or not to have an abortion, women think about the effect of their actions on their web of relationships, not just on themselves. They reason, Gilligan concluded, not better or worse than men, but in a different voice. Although Gilligan—not a lawyer—never took on Ginsburg directly the way MacKinnon did, her arguments implied that women in decision-making positions might act quite differently from similarly situated men. If the different voice is still valuable, then Gilligan's claims, like MacKinnon's, are much more ambitious than Ginsburg's simple plea not to stereotype women in advance as different. Ginsburg's lifelong crusade—which came to be known as "equality feminism," so radical in its time, did not last ten years when it was challenged by the call to recognize women's differences without punishing women for them. "Difference feminism," as the new strands of thought were named, was more demanding than Ginsburg's theory. But it was also more dangerous. Whether the difference is in greater vulnerability or a divergent moral outlook, it is a slippery gradient from difference to discrimination.

Although Ginsburg was on the bench when much of this new thinking surfaced, she wasn't totally silenced politically. She was uncharacteristically open about her unhappiness with MacKinnon. After hearing MacKinnon speak on pornography at Columbia Law School in the late '70s, Ginsburg, who remained loyal to conventional liberal free speech, confided to a friend, "That woman has bad karma." In 1988 she even took MacKinnon on directly: "the ACLU Women's Rights Project was not so bold as to essay articulation of a complete theoretical world in which men did not define women's place." Her litigation, rather, was intended to "unsettle women's separate spheres." She was more annoyed by MacKinnon's ingratitude for her and the other pioneers' efforts than by the substance of MacKinnon's more ambitious claims to protection for women disadvantaged by history and culture. Next to MacKinnon's place on the program, she noted, "arrogant."

She was more circumspect with the different-voice theory. When confronted with such claims, she admitted in May 1991, "I abstain or fudge . . . [finding] no reliable indicator of distinctly male or female thinking." Coincidentally, by 1991, the sound of the different voice had even reached the ears of the less academically inclined Justice Sandra Day O'Connor. O'Connor was clearly nettled by the suggestion that her own decisions could be understood as an example of, as one benighted law professor essayed, "Judging in a Different Voice." O'Connor devoted a substantial portion of her 1991 Madison Lecture series at NYU to decrying these suggestions as a dangerous throwback to the era when women were judged as too delicate to participate in rough activities like practicing law and voting: "Ironically, the move to ask again the question whether women are different merely by virtue of being women recalls the old myths we have struggled to put behind us. Undaunted by the historical resonances, however, more and more writers have suggested that women practice law differently than men. One author has even concluded that my opinions differ in a peculiarly feminine way from those of my colleagues." A few months after O'Connor's lecture, Circuit judge Ruth Bader Ginsburg received a copy of O'Connor's remarks, faxed from the Supreme Court chambers.

The following year, Judge Ginsburg also chose the vehicle of the Madison Lecture to dissent from a feminist article of faith, the abortion decision, *Roe v. Wade*. Ginsburg repeated and amplified the critique she had first articulated in 1984. She was obviously very concerned about the political friction generated by the abortion issue, especially compared with the relatively smooth debut of the equality revolution she had orchestrated in the '70s. "A less encompassing *Roe*, one that merely struck down the extreme Texas law and went no further on that day," she asserted, "might have served to reduce rather than to fuel controversy." Abortion is not like school segregation, she asserts, because women are men's wives, daughters, and sisters. Politics could work better where people are intermingled. Once women saw the injustice of their inequality, they could educate their oppressors, literally, at "home." Maybe the men would not then have kept trying to oppress their wives, sisters, and daughters with criminal abortion laws. The racial minority, she argues, was, by contrast, hopelessly divided from the majority and could not bring about further change in any way but through the courts.

In retrospect, the best thinking is that Ginsburg was wrong about the backlash. Women, unlike racial minorities, were deeply divided on the subject of their rights. Their distribution in the households of their oppressors gave them a chance not only to educate but equally to sell out the movement. Religion would play a powerful role in women's thinking. The backlash against abortion rights was well under way when the Court decided *Roe v. Wade*.

And nothing the Court could have done would have staved off the resistance to abortion rights in particular or women's rights in general.

Right or wrong, however, the timing of her remarks could not have been worse. The week she unloaded on *Roe v. Wade* in the very public forum of the Madison Lecture, Justice Byron White announced his retirement, leaving President Clinton with a slot to fill. Ginsburg's name was on most of the long, early lists. White House temperature-takers learned, however, that there was resistance to her candidacy in "certain women's groups," the National Abortion Rights Action League's influential Kate Michelman among them. It's not that radical academic feminist theorizers are serious players in national political circles, but the competition for a Supreme Court seat is so tight that *any* opposition or problem at all is disproportionately threatening to the nominee. Soon Ginsburg stopped being the subject of speculative leaks. Other names took the fore.

Within weeks of the cooling on Ginsburg, Stanford Law Professor Barbara Babcock's phone went off at seven a.m. Martin Ginsburg was calling. "Those East Coasters," Babcock said. "They are up and it is way early here but what they want is so important to them, they call anyway." Babcock was one of a handful of prominent feminist law professors who could reassure the White House that Ruth was a legend in the women's movement. "He was absolutely sure I would go to bat for Ruth," Babcock recalls. "And, actually, he was right." Babcock reached out to her former student Cheryl Mills, deputy White House counsel, to speak for Ginsburg. Marty's minions ginned up so many letters, no one at the White House could read them all. The presidents of Stanford and Columbia wrote. The female Democratic governor of Texas, Ann Richards—a newly minted celebrity from her showstopping performance at the 1992 Democratic National Convention—wrote. That rare bird, the African-American Republican stalwart, and Gerald Ford's transportation secretary, William Coleman wrote. However, Clinton yearned for Cuomo and still leaned toward Stephen Breyer.

Then it emerged that the refined and aristocratic Judge Breyer (or his titled British wife, the Honourable Joanna Freda Hare Breyer or, technically, both) had failed to pay Social Security taxes for their household help, the same issue that had brought down two of Clinton's cabinet appointments. Although some in the White House thought Breyer was the perfect candidate to face down the "nanny tax" troops, in 1993, Clinton actually wasn't eager for another incident. (Ginsburg, who had many employees over her long working life, and her tax lawyer husband were squeaky clean.)

And so Ginsburg's name bobbed up again. Many observers credit Attorney General Janet Reno (who, one would think, Clinton might have consulted) with asking the president about Ginsburg. Nussbaum thought she would be a good selection because of her historic role at the ACLU. Somehow—sources credit Marty Ginsburg with digging out the quote—Clinton learned that Ginsburg's bête noire Dean Erwin Griswold of Harvard had called her the Thurgood Marshall of the women's movement. She sounded good, Clinton admitted to Bernie Nussbaum, but the president had heard she was a "cold fish." "Well," said Nussbaum, "did I mention that I had dinner with her three weeks ago? Her husband called, and I knew what they were doing, but I had dinner with her and she's actually very nice."

So, Nussbaum says, he called Ginsburg to come to the White House. "Oh, no," the judge said. "We're just back from Vermont, and I have informal clothes on." It was Sunday, after all. "Not to worry," Nussbaum assured her. "The president will be coming back from playing golf! I'm sure you don't have to worry." He went to the Watergate to pick her up. She had on perfectly respectable slacks, Nussbaum says, and some kind of a top. Just not what you'd ideally choose to go to the White House in.

When they arrived at the Residence in the White House, standing at the end of a long hallway, the president emerged, impeccably dressed in a navy blue suit, shirt and tie. That Sunday, Bill Clinton decided on church rather than golf. "Bernie, what have you done to me?" she asked. "Don't worry," he answered the famously impeccable dresser from the D.C. Circuit. "Everything is going to be fine."

An hour and a half later, the president called to tell Nussbaum they were finished talking and he could take Ginsburg back to the Watergate.

When Nussbaum circled back to the White House, Clinton said he'd made his choice. The two former law professors had talked mostly about her children and other kinds of personal things, nothing serious. "I'll call her after the basketball game," which was about to start, Clinton blithely announced. Nothing Nussbaum could say would get him to act sooner. But knowing that Ginsburg must be in purgatory, Nussbaum called her himself. He couldn't tell her she'd been chosen, but he said what he could. "Ruth," he said, "I don't know what time you go to bed normally, but don't turn in early tonight."

And he says he heard her begin to cry.

PLAY BALL

The next day the tall president and the judge who did not reach his shoulder appeared in the Rose Garden for the announcement. Ginsburg had on a natty blue coat dress with a big blue ribbon adorning her customary ponytail. She thanked many people. She thanked the women's movement and the racial movement from which it sprang. Finally, she remembered her mother and said she hoped she'd be all that her mother would have been had she lived in an age when women can aspire and achieve and daughters are cherished as much as sons.

Once nominated, "there was no chance, zero, that she would fail to be confirmed," says Clinton's advisor Joel Klein, who had the job of shepherding her through the process. She had racked up a relatively centrist record on the D.C. Circuit, with decisions tough on crime and sometimes in favor of business. Republicans had already greeted the appointment with praise. And, as usual, her calm and precise demeanor at the introduction was universally acclaimed. But Ruth Bader Ginsburg was obsessed. "She prepared for those hearings as if it was going to be 51–49," Klein recalls. She took to phoning him at all hours of the day or night. What if they ask this? What if they ask that?

Since the Supreme Court candidate Robert Bork told the Senate about his legal philosophy and went down in flames in 1987, all the players in the Supreme Court confirmation business have understood that the rule is to say nothing. Or at least give the smallest possible answers you can get away with. Judge Bork's experience gave rise to a verb, "borking," for killing a nominee by letting him expand upon his weirdly marginal beliefs. Ever since, administrations have instructed their nominees to plead the confirmation equivalent of the Fifth Amendment: I respectfully refuse to answer on the grounds that it might come up in a case that might come before me. "No one ever lost by saying nothing," Klein remembers.

Joel Klein tried, but she gave her minders fits. On July 14, the White House counsel Ron Klain wrote to Clinton's advisor David Gergen that he expected trouble in the hearings. "She has an instinct for defending some rather extreme liberal views" when asked about the ACLU, Klain said. "She also relishes defending the ACLU as an institution, and its importance in American society." And she takes forever to answer. And she nitpicks the questions. Don't tell her what we want her to do, though, Klain continued. She does not see her interests as the same as ours.

As it turned out, she was quite circumspect about her judicial views in the hearings themselves. But despite her unexpected compliance, her confirmation hearings actually tell a lot about her. For one thing, it quickly became clear—as a T-shirt given to her by the National Association of Women Judges would later say—"I'm Ruth, not Sandra." (The judges also gave O'Connor the companion T, "I'm Sandra, not Ruth.") The Second WOTSC sounded a lot more liberal than her sister in law. And on stuff that matters.

In the 1987 affirmative action case *Johnson v. Santa Clara County*, O'Connor had given Justice Brennan fits, insisting that an employer with an affirmative action plan must admit that it previously probably violated the Civil Rights Act. (Brennan had the votes, so O'Connor's was only a concurrence, but still.) When asked what she thought about that test for affirmative action, Ginsburg agreed with Brennan: "Sometimes it would be better for society if we didn't push people to the wall and make them say, yes, I was a discriminator," she testified. "In place of a knock-down-drag-out fight, it might be better to pursue voluntary action, always taking into account that there is a countervailing interest. . . ." Ginsburg shows a willingness to push private institutions such as employers to take up the burden of making the workplace better.

She also thought the harsh restrictions on women in the new abortion order since *Casey* were inconsistent with abortion rights laid down in the earlier cases: "So I must say yes, the . . . decisions are in tension, and I expect that the tension is going to be resolved sooner or later." In a less guarded moment in her Madison Lecture, she had already expressed her opinion of the plurality opinion that sustained the onerous restrictions upheld in *Casey*: "those Justices did not closely consider the plight of women without means to overcome the restrictions" when they accepted provisions of the Pennsylvania law that clearly violated *Roe v. Wade.*

While disagreeing with O'Connor on the substance of particular decisions, she also claimed O'Connor as a model on the big question of constitutional interpretation in general. Insofar as she had an overarching concept of the Constitution, O'Connor embraced a kind of moderate social analysis in deciding cases that made a claim for new rights. While not eager to overturn precedent, she was willing to consider whether the social concept of rights in a particular area had changed. She thought the Court had some obligation to honor people's expectations of how they would be able to live their lives. She signaled this open-mindedness early on when she cast the decisive fifth vote to integrate the all-female nursing program in *Hogan v. Mississippi.* Regardless of what the drafters had been thinking about sex discrimination in 1867, when they drafted the Fourteenth Amendment after the Civil War, by 1981, Justice O'Connor believed, people expected some restraints on arbitrary divisions by sex. This openness distinguished her from Justice Scalia, who would mostly stop the clock when the ink was dry on the Constitution.

In 1989, Justice Scalia had tried his hand at sneaking his rule of strict interpretation into a plurality decision. Traditional practices, he suggested, could not be undone by newly developed claims of right. Scalia's time travel would, needless to say, undo most of the jurisprudence of the prior six decades. But O'Connor and Kennedy had both called him on it, reducing his support for the footnote coup to a minority of two. In her hearings, Ginsburg embraces the O'Connor position on constitutional interpretation, a position that allows the Court a fair amount of latitude for bringing the Constitution out of the periwig age. Going up to the high court, the Second Woman agreed with the First that the Constitution needed to ride the train to the present world.

Still, their visions of the present world were very different. Not because they were living in different worlds; they were not. Their lives were actually so similar that a certain amount of Sandra/Ruth confusion might be understandable. They were only three years apart in age. By 1993, they were both rich and richly privileged. Ruth lived in the luxury Watergate apartment complex and Sandra in Chevy Chase. Children grown and husbands earning good money, they would often see each other at Washington National Opera performances or at a dinner for the Washington National Opera Lawyers' Committee. When not on the bench they traveled around, giving speeches and classes in nice places such as Florida and Salzburg.

In the confirmation process, it emerged that Ginsburg had long tried to see a world beyond her privileged surroundings. "One of the things that I have done every other year with my law clerks, more often, if they are so inclined," she testified, "is to visit the local jail and Lorton Penitentiary, which is the nearest penitentiary. We visited St. Elizabeth's, the facility for the criminally insane, when it was a Federal facility. . . . I do that to expose myself to those conditions, and also for my law clerks. Most of them will go on to practice in large law firms specializing in corporate business, and won't see the law as it affects most people. That is one of the things I do to stay in touch."

Even though the White House managed to control her inclination to extoll the ACLU in her hearings, Ginsburg's opponents from the right correctly figured out that the mild-mannered feminist with the history of occasional conservative votes on the appeals court would be bad for them. They were not happy with their inability to get any traction against her. In a heated exchange with the chairman of the Conservative Caucus, Howard Phillips, Senator Orrin Hatch made clear the congressional Republicans' position in those early days of the Clinton administration. They had lost the election of 1992 and they would not fight Ginsburg's nomination: "So don't try and change the Supreme Court in the sense of politicizing it and electing people who will be prolife," Hatch told Phillips. "We now have a President who believes this way and he has picked a person who believes this way, and he has a right to do so and that is the point."

The vote was 96 to 3.

AT HOME IN HER CHAMBERS

The new justice was novel to the Court in more ways than just her newness. Previous justices had always resigned themselves to the lousy chambers available to the newest member in order to be on the first floor, where all the other justices were. Not Ginsburg. She willingly paid the price of distance from her colleagues for much more gorgeous quarters on the isolated second floor. Then she broke with all existing Court decorating styles, with sheer curtains, a light-colored plain carpet, and the iconic mid-century modern Eero Saarinen Tulip Table beneath modern pictures borrowed from the National Gallery and from her own collection. Her office would be contemporary and luxurious, like her home.

And filled with family. To "Justice Ginsburg, the clerks were family," her first Supreme Court clerk, Margo Schlanger, says. After all, she picked them like family. First, like family, they had to resemble her, not physically, but in coming from somewhere in the vicinity of first in their class. Margo Schlanger was at Yale, which, famously, does not rank its students, but she was at the top of her class and did win the Vinson Prize for excellence in clinical casework and edit the *Law Journal*, a dead giveaway. Yalie David Schizer, also at the top of the class, edited the *Law Journal* too. Sean Donahue graduated with high honors from Chicago, and

David Post was summa at Georgetown. Exactly like Ruth, Alexandra Shapiro was first in her class at Columbia. But anyone who gets into the Supreme Court clerk pool is likely to have great paper. Ruth was looking for something much more basic. She wanted relatives. It was well known among the clerks that Ginsburg didn't, as the Chicago machine pol famously said, "want nobody nobody sent."

Yale Law Journal's Schlanger came from . . . her father Michael Schlanger, who grew up with Marty Ginsburg on Long Island. Their families belonged to the same golf club. And for years after they all grew up, Margo's father, a New York lawyer, and Martin Ginsburg, then a New York lawyer, would go out a couple times a year and play golf. Offspring of the handful of female students in Ruth's Class of '59 at Columbia Law School turned up with clerkships—whether it was David Goldberg in her Circuit Court days or David Schizer at the Supreme Court. All the clerks in 1991 knew Sean Donahue had an edge for Ginsburg's 1992 Circuit Court clerkship. He was a classmate of James Ginsburg at the University of Chicago Law School. (Even before she went up, her Circuit Court clerkships often led to a berth on the Supreme Court; Goldberg with Souter and Donahue with Stevens, for example.) Her strategy was to get clerks from people whose ties to *her* were deeper and more important than just regular reference writers. All the candidates were elite; she was just reproducing her trusted family circle.

Perhaps her favorite in those early years was David Post, who came back to her Supreme Court chambers after he had clerked for her on the lower court. Post's special appeal was that he, like Stephen Wiesenfeld, broke the sex-role-stereotype mold. When his first child was young, he took on the primary parenting role so his wife could work. "That was the best career move I could have made," Post says, because it made him so desirable for the first Ginsburg clerkship. When he went for the second round, he was already tending his second child, which he did throughout his clerkship. "She was the best boss you could have wished for," he says. "She did not care if you were there early or late or at all. As long as you got the work done."

On so many fronts, ties to Ruth Bader Ginsburg were ties that bind. In April 1993, she found out from Stephen Wiesenfeld that Baby Jason was applying to law school. Ruth advised him to send Jason to her daughter Jane at Columbia. When Wiesenfeld thought a letter from Ginsburg might motivate his son, she wrote to Jason directly: "Dear Jason, I have the good news from your father that you are applying to law school. My daughter, Jane, who now teaches at Columbia Law School, would be glad to talk to you." She corrected Jason's application essay. A year later, she called to congratulate Stephen on his son's acceptance. "Thank you for your phone call," Stephen wrote. "Jason was absolutely thrilled with his acceptance at Columbia." The stories are legion. One year she took all her clerks who had married or become engaged to each other to the fancy D.C. restaurant Asia Nora for dinner on Valentine's Day. After dinner they were presented with fortune cookies with love poems inside.

Nor did Ginsburg forget her tribe. The first Jewish justice in a generation, she was immediately approached by the clerk of the Court to help out with a Jewish question. Orthodox Jewish lawyers had been sporadically objecting to having the year on their certificates of admission described as "The Year of Our Lord." In typical Ginsburg fashion, she initiated a survey of the lower federal courts' practice. Learning that some had altered the certificate to avoid offending lawyers who didn't count the years from the birth of Jesus, she sent a letter to the chief, asking for a change in the practice. As she reports it, she caught some flak. "I was told by a colleague, 'Why are you making a fuss about this? It was good enough for Brandeis, it was good enough for Cardozo and Frankfurter.' I said, 'Stop. It's not good enough for Ginsburg.'" Although Ginsburg does not reveal the source of the resistance, one of her clerks thought Justice Rehnquist was less than pleased, and Justice Blackmun's papers include his note on the discussion to the effect that "we protest too much." Nonetheless the Court agreed to change its practice and offer people a choice in the wording of their ceremonial paper.

Unlike the tidal wave of attention that greeted the First

WOTSC, coming second, Justice Ginsburg's swearing-in was an intimate affair, with just "judicial colleagues, extended family, and closest friends" in the East Room of the White House. No phalanx of media, except the reporters drawn to the site by the awful coincidence of more scandal over the White House counsel Vince Foster's suicide. But it was a big day anyway. As Gloria Steinem's office wrote to Stephen Wiesenfeld, "now that Ruth Bader Ginsburg has been confirmed, we can rest assured that the Supreme Court now has a true feminist voice."

Ginsburg's Feminist Voice

＊ӂ＊

THE FEMINIST VOICE

As the October 1993 term opened, one of the first cases up was a sexual harassment suit, the notorious *Harris v. Forklift Systems.* Sexual conduct had been front and center in the culture wars since the courts began recognizing harassment at work, most notably in the 1986 Supreme Court decision in Mechelle Vinson's case against the bank. Nothing unbalances the balance of power between the sexes like the possibility that a woman can bring a costly and embarrassing lawsuit grounded in sex.

No one wanted to advocate for people like the noxious bank manager Sidney Taylor, so the discussion took cozier forms. Judge Alex Kozinski, a conservative intellectual beacon of the Ninth Circuit Court of Appeals, worried that people would hesitate to initiate "office romance." Without romance, the office would be a much less inviting place and who would want to work there? Harvard's media star Alan Dershowitz thought offensive sex talk in the workplace was protected free speech under the First Amendment. The well-respected conservative legal theorist Judge Richard Posner wondered if sexual harassment wasn't just usually a misunderstanding.

The pushback often focused on women's capacity to take a hit. Dershowitz called complaining women "crybabies." And that's exactly the issue the Court had to decide when it took up the matter again in *Harris.* How bad does it have to get before a woman can push back against sex in the workplace?

Harris was pretty raw: the company president, Charles Hardy, had called the manager Teresa Harris "a dumb-ass woman" in a company that "needed a man," he said. But while she was there, he asked her (and other female employees) to fish in his front pants pockets for coins, to pick up objects he threw on the ground, and to come down to the Holiday Inn to negotiate her raise. He was surprised, he said, that she was offended by this merriment and promised to stop. Instead, he interrupted her in conversation with a customer, asking her if she'd offered to "bugger him." (The Supreme Court opinion euphemistically translates Hardy's inquiry as did she "promise the guy some [sex] Saturday night?") Harris quit. Then she sued.

In the seven years since the Court's sexual-harassment decision in *Vinson v. Meritor Savings Bank* the lower courts had divided over how bad sexual harassment had to get before it violated the Civil Rights Act. *Meritor*, involving allegations of sexual extortion, rape, assault, and indecent exposure, hardly gave much guidance on how to handle lesser affronts. The law did not require the employee to have been fired or demoted before she could sue. However, some courts, like the lower courts in *Harris*, thought the employee had to have suffered somehow, and psychological injury was the next thing to suffering actual material damage. Other federal courts said no such injury was required. The Equal Employment Opportunity Commission had proposed guidelines rejecting the requirement of psychological injury and suggesting a looser standard still, which would require only that "the environment hampers her opportunity to succeed vis-à-vis her male peers or denies her credit for her achievements." The lower federal courts in Tennessee read the earlier decision to require severe psychological injury, and they did not think that Hardy's behavior was serious enough to cause Harris such harm. So they ruled against her.

At conference, everyone agreed that the lower courts should stop requiring plaintiffs to show severe psychological injury in sexual-harassment cases. Such a standard had the perverse result of rewarding the psychologically weak with a lawsuit for her suffering and penalizing the woman worker who can take the heat by requiring her to stay in the hot factory. The chief assigned O'Connor to write the opinion.

Her cautious first draft only marginally reduced the standard for proving sexual harassment, suggesting the workplace must be abusive before a victim could sue. O'Connor's effort immediately triggered a robust critique from Harry Blackmun. Even the Court's prior opinion, Blackmun reminded her, included redress for a "hostile" or "offensive" environment as well.

Ginsburg did not even try to negotiate the language of O'Connor's draft. Instead she joined immediately, always welcome when the writing justice is trying to assemble a majority, even when the vote at conference was unanimous. Ginsburg was, she said, merely appending a "brief concurring statement," just a tiny addition "on a point I wish to emphasize." Ginsburg's point, not remotely tiny, was that the standard for sexual harassment under the Civil Rights Act should be the same as the rule for race: Would the offending behavior make it harder for a reasonable person to do their job? At oral argument, she had leaned all over the lawyer for the obnoxious Mr. Hardy to admit this: "If it had been race-based or religion-based or national origin, would your analysis be any different?" she demanded. "It is the same statute, Title VII, what applies to race applies to gender, right?" And so in her modest addition, she asserted that the Court should apply the standard used to interpret the Civil Rights Act in racial harassment cases such as *Davis* v. *Monsanto Chemical Co.*

Under the racial standard, "it suffices to prove that a reasonable person subjected to the discriminatory conduct would find, as the plaintiff did, that the harassment so altered working conditions as to 'ma[k]e it more difficult to do the job.' . . . Title VII declares discriminatory practices based on race, gender, religion, or national origin equally unlawful." Ginsburg's "brief" addition, which closely tracks the EEOC's regulations, would have made it much easier to prove harassment and also emphasized the equality agenda always in the forefront of her analysis. Harassing a female worker made her unequal to her male colleague in the amount of effort she had to expend to do the same job.

Blackmun's clerk Sarah Cleveland thought Ginsburg had a capital idea. Her "brief" concurrence captured the inadequacy of O'Connor's draft and focused on an equality-oriented standard. Cleveland thought Justice Blackmun should join Ginsburg's concurring opinion. Instead he wrote to O'Connor again, suggesting using the *Davis* standard. But O'Connor was having none of it. "Perhaps," she wrote in her letter to him, with copies to everyone, "the *Davis* test will ultimately prove to be the right one, but now is not the time for us to decide this." And so, in the next round of drafts, she explicitly refused to chime in, opining, "We need not . . . specifically address the Equal Employment Opportunity Commission's new regulations on this subject."

Instead O'Connor invoked what the Court had said in the bank case seven years before. "When the workplace is permeated with discriminatory intimidation, ridicule, and insult," she held, "that is 'sufficiently severe or pervasive to alter the conditions of the victim's employment and create an abusive working environment.' . . . Title VII is violated."

Since the lower courts had been having a problem figuring out what in the world the Court had meant, she tried to clarify: "Conduct that is not severe or pervasive enough to create an objectively hostile or abusive work environment—an environment that a reasonable person would find hostile or abusive—is beyond Title VII's purview. Likewise, if the victim does not subjectively perceive the environment to be abusive, the conduct has not actually altered the conditions of the victim's employment, and there is no Title VII violation. But Title VII comes into play before the harassing conduct leads to a nervous breakdown."

Despite this explicit refusal to adopt her suggested standard, Ginsburg, who had received a copy of O'Connor's letter to Blackmun, apparently decided to "be a little deaf." In Ginsburg's concurring opinion pitching the standard in the race cases—exactly what O'Connor was not ready to embrace—she asserted that since O'Connor's majority opinion was "in harmony" with her beliefs, she would join in.

Ginsburg's right-hand man that first year, her former D.C.

Circuit clerk Hugh Baxter, calls these unfounded agreements Ginsburg's "happy face dissents, writing all the things that were good" about the majority decision. Her motivation to find "harmony," even in face of an explicit rejection, was partly strategic, he concluded, to save the day for another case by minimizing the harmful aspects of a loss. "Very smart," he thought. "After all, she was a cause lawyer and knows how to build things for the future."

DEFENSE AND OFFENSE ON THE SUPREME COURT

This exchange, from the very beginning of their twelve-year tenure together as justices, set O'Connor's and Ginsburg's respective roles in the cause of women's legal equality. Sandra Day O'Connor played defense; she would not permit the courts to roll the equality ball backward. O'Connor had already manifested that commitment when, most famously in *Casey*, she refused to overturn *Roe v. Wade.* In the sexual-harassment cases, she joined all her colleagues to deny that the employee must have "a nervous breakdown" to recover. But in the abortion cases, her rulings meant that women who wanted equality had to be willing to endure every burden short of criminal penalties and spousal notice in order to get their abortions. In the sexual-harassment arena, she would have them suck it up and survive harassment on the job until things got so bad the workplace was outright hostile or abusive. Channeling her father, Harry Day, plaintiffs would have to jump on the lug wrench and get the tire changed before the courts would come in to help them.

In hindsight, these opinions look ungenerous. But O'Connor's clerk Stephen Gilles and the ACLU's Aryeh Neier, an astute social observer, both credit her with laser judgment about what the Court—and the society—would digest at any particular moment. Certainly Anthony Kennedy, the crucial third vote in the opinion that saved abortion rights in *Casey*, repeatedly demonstrated his lack of sympathy for women's equality in the years after 1992. Had O'Connor used their brief agreement on abortion to strike down any more of the Pennsylvania law, he might well have walked.

Sometimes a courageous rearguard action is exactly what an army needs.

Ruth Bader Ginsburg, who had been presented to the solons of the Senate as a charming moderate, played offense. At the oral argument in *Harris* one month into her first term, she officially revealed how her life work for women's equality would infuse her judging on the Court. When Justice Stevens began a humorous colloquy with Harris's lawyer about an employer who might say "You're a man, what do you know" since, he admitted, Stevens's wife often says such things to him, she cut him off. She knew that "dumb broad" talk at work was the furthest thing from harmless sexual banter.

"Some of these are hard to transpose in that way," Ginsburg interrupted briskly. "'You're a woman, what do you know' means something different than 'you're a man, what do you know?'" The guys in the Supreme Court might be yucking it up about how their wives henpecked them, but Justice Ginsburg knew what the question meant to a woman trying to do her job in a world in which men held all the power. Consider, she continued, things that were once considered normal. "Why, even great professors had such things as Ladies' Day," she reminisced. And "What about the woman who doesn't see herself as a victim, but finds this terribly annoying." This was new territory for the old Supreme Court. In her Madison Lecture, Sandra Day O'Connor asserted that a wise old woman judge and a wise old man judge will reach the same conclusion. Ginsburg was not so sure. When she took her seat at the Supreme Court, she brought with her memories of outperforming in spite of Ladies' Day and the whole history of women's efforts to break into the workplace, experiences she called "a different medley of views." And it affected her judgment, as she thought it should.

Her concurrence in *Harris* was her first Supreme Court opinion. Asserting that women workers are made totally equal to male colleagues by operation of law, just as black Americans are equal to white ones, was a serious move. Although Ginsburg never got the Court to say that sex and race were equally suspect under the Fourteenth Amendment, she was trying to get the standards aligned in employment situations, under the equality provisions of the Civil Rights Act. The concurring opinion did not of course affect the outcome in a unanimous decision. She did not even deprive O'Connor of the votes of the other more liberal justices—Blackmun, Stevens, and Souter—but it laid down a marker.

Five years later, the Court moved beyond O'Connor's cautious formulation and explicitly adopted Ginsburg's standard as the law of the land. Ruling for the plaintiff in another harassment case, *Oncale v. Sundowner*, Justice Scalia invoked Ginsburg's concurring opinion verbatim when he wrote for a unanimous Court: "'The critical issue, Title VII's text indicates, is whether members of one sex are exposed to disadvantageous terms or conditions of employment to which members of the other sex are not exposed.' *Harris*, *supra*, at 25 (Ginsburg, J., concurring)."

O'Connor's slow-moving role in the development of sexual-harassment law also speaks to her larger role on the Court. For years during her period of dominance on the evenly divided court, commentators speculated about what Justice O'Connor was doing. Did she honestly believe the Supreme Court should decide cases like some state court, in the common-law tradition, just adding one incremental decision to the previous one? Was her hair-splitting a jurisprudence, like Scalia's originalism or Brennan's liberalism? She often asserted that centrism was a philosophy, although she never said what a philosophy of centrism would look like or why taking a position midway between competing substantive visions is itself a vision. Many believed that like the old legislative leader she had been, she just took the Court where the public was, regardless of what text or theory would have dictated.

The justice-as-legislator theory seems to be supported by the paper trail in *Harris*. Although Court watchers often scoured the archival material made available by justices who opened their papers to the public, it seems no one ever looked at the paper trail in *Harris*, a decision that mostly mattered to women. Yet in O'Connor's letter to Blackmun refusing to equate sex harassment with race, there was O'Connor saying outright that she thought the racial-harassment standard—that everyone in the workplace should have an equal chance to succeed—might be the right rule, but that she would wait, nonetheless, until "the time" for the Court to express the right outcome in a decision. The only thing that happened between O'Connor's decision to wait and the Court issuing the right opinion was that the lower courts wrestled unsuccessfully with what *Harris* actually required. Without comment, O'Connor joined the *Oncale* opinion. For reasons never expressed in opinion or in public, sometime between 1993 and 1998, O'Connor apparently decided the country was ready for the simple, equitable rule.

THE RELATIONSHIP WITH O'CONNOR WAS REALLY THE IMPORTANT ONE

Deliberately or coincidentally, the two women were more effective together than separately. Although Ginsburg pointed the way for the Court in *Harris*, she took great pains not to cross her predecessor. For a dozen years before she joined the Supreme Court, Ginsburg had followed O'Connor's career on the bench. Her files contain many articles about the FWOTSC. She had raved about O'Connor's opinion in the nursing school case, in which O'Connor ordered the Mississippi University for Women to admit men.

Hugh Baxter, back as Ginsburg's Supreme Court clerk after his first Ginsburg clerkship, quickly learned that O'Connor was a really important relationship to her. He never saw them going out together and it was not that the newer judge expected to influence O'Connor, but Ginsburg openly respected O'Connor as a fellow pioneer. Baxter thinks Ginsburg had a sense that, after she came, life was going to be different for O'Connor, and Ginsburg wanted it to be in a good way. Ginsburg was concerned about her relationship with the chief and with other justices, but, Baxter says, "It was really clear to me that the relationship with O'Connor was the most important one."

For her part, from 1981 on, O'Connor had taken more clerks from Ginsburg's chambers than from any other feeder judge on all the courts below. As one of them, Joan Greco, puts it, "I interviewed with Justice O'Connor for the position because Judge

Ginsburg recommended me to her. The reason there was this group of clerks that clerked for both of them is that Justice O'Connor put so much weight on Judge Ginsburg's recommendations." And when Ginsburg arrived at the Court that first summer, it was O'Connor who was her guide, just as Powell had been for O'Connor all those years before.

Justice Scalia would have been the obvious choice for Ginsburg to turn to—the Scalias and the Ginsburgs had been friends for years. Scalia was quoted, famously, in the run-up to Ginsburg's selection, as saying he'd pick her for his companion if consigned to a desert island. But O'Connor was "glad to have another woman on the Court." O'Connor's delight that her first companion was so skilled and competent was, for her, gushing. In one of her letters to Barry Goldwater that first two-woman term, O'Connor gratuitously drops into the otherwise completely social missive that "Justice Ginsburg is a very capable and knowledgeable Justice."

The Ginsburgs were not new to Washington, and Ginsburg was not new to judging federal questions. So she did not need the kind of heavy lifting that O'Connor got from Lewis Powell. But, when O'Connor paid the traditional call on the rookie, she told her to change the lighting in her chambers to a gentler glow. And from the beginning she did what she could to make sure Ginsburg succeeded. Ginsburg's first assignment was not the traditional "dog" case, where the Court is unanimous and the opinion uncomplicated. Instead, Chief Justice Rehnquist handed her a contentious 6–3 decision on one of the most complex federal statutes. "Sandra," Ginsburg asked her predecessor plaintively, "how can he do this to me?" O'Connor (who was on the other side in the decision) made her typical flat-tire response. "Just do it." Oh, and do it before he makes the next set of assignments, she advised. O'Connor knew—and it was one of the many unwritten rules of the institution that newbies must learn somewhere—that Chief Justice Rehnquist would not give Ginsburg another assignment until she had turned in the one she had. "Typical," Ginsburg remembered years later, of her predecessor's no-nonsense guidance. She called O'Connor "the most helpful big sister anyone could have." O'Connor welcomed her sister's delivery of her first opinion with a note: "This is your first opinion for the Court, it is a fine one, I look forward to many more."

A JUSTICE OF HER PEERS

Justice Ginsburg had reason to expect that she'd be writing one of those fine future opinions very soon. *J.E.B. v. Alabama*, a case challenging one of the few remaining instances of sex discrimination in jury service, came before the Court in her very first term.

Ginsburg's expectation of getting the assignment in *J.E.B.* was understandable. In the 1970s, she had been the architect of the legal strategy that got women equal access to jury service. On its face, the new jury case was just the latest in a long line of cases that applied the rules about racial exclusion to women. As part of the century-long battle over black jurors, prosecutors had been using their right to challenge jurors in any case for no reason at all to keep juries white. These attacks, called "peremptory challenges," have a long tradition of being the vehicle for a "lawyer's instinct" about who is likely to help or hurt their client. In 1985, the Court put a stop to this practice. In *J.E.B.*, the state used its peremptory challenges to keep the jury one sex. So *J.E.B.* was, on its face, just a mop-up operation to establish that the rules applying to race in jury service also applied to sex.

The state peremptorily struck the guys off the jury, because the case involved an order of paternity and child support for a baby the defendant had supposedly fathered. Predictably, the defendant struck as many women as he could, but the heavily female jury roster still produced a distaff gathering, and the all-female jury found J.E.B. to be the father and ordered child support. J.E.B. appealed, arguing that the state's use of peremptory challenges to eliminate one gender—in this case, men—from the jury was unconstitutional.

If it weren't for Ginsburg and her ilk, J.E.B., defendant in a paternity case, wouldn't have even had a problem with female jurors. Alabama didn't let the little darlings serve until women sued in

1966 in the original feminist campaign to integrate juries. The fact that the particular discrimination was leveled against male jurors in J.E.B.'s case did not matter. Whether feminists such as Catharine MacKinnon liked it or not, discrimination against men was now well accepted as a proxy for sex discrimination generally.

But sex is not always like race. The state asserted, and it presented some social-science research to support the claim, that the state had reason other than pure sex discrimination to strike all the guys. The state surmised that in a paternity case male jurors were a better bet for the defendant. It wasn't their sex per se that the state cared about; men's gender was a proxy for men being more likely to rule for the defendant. So the state knocked the men out of the jury.

Alabama may have had a good argument, but the justices voted 6–3 at conference to forbid the use of peremptory challenges to eliminate members of either sex. Since the chief was in the dissent, after conference, the decision about who should write the opinion fell to the senior in the liberal majority, Harry Blackmun. Giving the nod to Ginsburg, the author of the law of women's equality on juries, would have seemed the obvious move. But instead he kept it for himself.

Blackmun's tone deafness vis-à-vis his female colleagues was well known. Although he denied it at the time, the opening of his papers revealed that he resented Justice O'Connor from the get-go. After O'Connor was selected, he groused about her overnight fame and her energetic embrace of the Washington social scene. His clerks report that he did a wicked imitation of his female colleague's distinctive loud, nasal diction. Blackmun had actually never thought that much of Ginsburg either; when the legendary Supreme Court litigator first appeared, he gave her a C+ on her oral argument.

In fairness, Blackmun was not irrational to resist the love fest around O'Connor's appointment. He anticipated that the anti-abortion Reagan administration would appoint someone to undo *Roe v. Wade*. O'Connor's assertion during her confirmation process that she considered the procedure personally "abhorrent" did not reassure him. He knew his own beloved daughter would have had an abortion when confronted with an out-of-wedlock pregnancy before *Roe*, had the process been legal. That O'Connor adopted, whole cloth, the Reagan solicitor general's suggested cutback on *Roe* in the first abortion case of her tenure, *Akron v. Akron Center for Reproductive Health*, confirmed his worst fears.

It was one thing to take heat on abortion from O'Connor, an emissary from the Reagan Revolution, but how much more unjust was the same criticism coming from the lion of the women's movement, Ruth Bader Ginsburg! As Blackmun was well aware, Ginsburg began her criticism of his opinion and methodology in *Roe* in 1984 in a speech shortly after the *Akron* decision and then expanded on the theme in 1993 with great fanfare in her Madison Lecture. Although Ginsburg clearly supported the outcome in *Roe*, Blackmun was unhappy with her for the criticism. When she came on the Court, Ginsburg knew he was unhappy with her. In his papers he called her "pushy," which some people took as an unpleasant coded phrase.

Yet he actually produced a perfectly serviceable draft opinion in *J.E.B.* In a virtual recitation of Ginsburg's litigation career, he suggested that sex-based peremptory challenges are just as bad as the racial kind already struck down. The cost of excluding citizens from juries is high, the sexual stereotypes hoary. Blackmun emphasized the citizen's right *to be a juror*, which is the point Ginsburg was after all those years ago in her jury discrimination cases. He even included a footnote reminding the Court that it had reserved the question of whether sex discrimination is always the same as race, citing Ginsburg's concurrence in *Harris*. Within a day she wrote to tell him she would join his opinion and to thank him for the shout-out in the footnote. (The court reporter Linda Greenhouse called the footnote a "bouquet" to his new colleague.)

Ginsburg would have preferred power to the posies. She quite reasonably thought the *J.E.B.* opinion should have been hers. It must have been so galling, after finally crossing the bench to the other side, to still have to beg Harry Blackmun to get the opinion she wanted. But, Ginsburg is nothing if not disciplined. So, as she did with so many recalcitrant local lawyers at the ACLU all those years ago—she tried to write the thing for him. The exchanges that ensued give a delicious glimpse into the mano a mano that often engages the justices behind their exquisitely civilized trappings of robes, velvet curtains, ritual handshakes, and boring collective lunches on argument day.

In the sweetest possible way, Ginsburg wrote, she just had "a few suggestions for you to consider, take or leave." First, in listing the authority for not shaping juries by sex, why don't you cite *Duren v. Missouri*? Of course, she didn't say anything about *Duren* being her signature case. She instead reminded Blackmun that one of *his* former clerks worked on the brief for the petitioner, Duren. "Would it not be appropriate to cite the decision that administered the coup de grâce?" she asked. "Check the cite," Blackmun noted on his copy of the letter, as if the legendarily careful Ginsburg would miscite a case. Then, she asked, why are you citing *Schlesinger v. Ballard* for the proposition that laws can't rest on archaic generalizations about gender? *Schlesinger*, she reminds him, actually held that women could be excluded from the military, relying on an archaic generalization about gender. So although it has good language in it, why not cite—and here she appends a laundry list of cases that actually were decided in women's favor. Blackmun puts one of his signature exclamation points beside this suggestion, and then the number "6," probably reflecting his displeasure that Ginsburg offered him six better authorities for his statements. With her keen sense of history, she next suggested that he refer to the fact that Alabama had to get sued before it recognized women for its juries in 1966. Finally, she corrected his description of the holding in *Weinberger v. Wiesenfeld* as striking down part of the Social Security Act, which the decision decidedly did not do. Instead of calling him (or his clerk) on a technical error, she wrote, "It was critical to Stephen Wiesenfeld that the Court did not 'strike down' the provision. Because the provision survived, shorn of the sex classification, he was able to get child-in-care benefits."

Ginsburg was new, and Blackmun was famously thin-skinned.

Despite her best efforts, he was bound to see that she thought she would have been a vastly better choice to write the opinion in *J.E.B.* Blackmun's files do not include the first draft of his letter back to Ginsburg. But it must have been a doozy, because his clerk, Michelle Alexander, suggested that he might be "a bit more diplomatic." Why don't you say, Alexander advised, that Ginsburg's suggestions are primarily matters of style usually left to the author of the opinion. A week later, he wrote back to Ginsburg that he was disinclined to drop *Schlesinger v. Ballard*. After all, "the quotations are apt." As to the rest, he wrote, adopting Michelle Alexander's suggestion, such matters are usually a matter of authorial style. But, in a classic male-to-female move, Blackmun treated Ginsburg's letter as being an emotional event. Since Ginsburg "appear[s] to be *uncomfortable* [emphasis added] with some details" he had "tried to accommodate" her. And so he did, adding *Duren* and the Alabama litigation history and correcting the description of *Weinberger v. Wiesenfeld*.

Blackmun's *J.E.B.* opinion is a better opinion for Ginsburg's input, as is most written work she addresses. Her point in pressing Blackmun to include the sorry history of Alabama's treatment of women jurors was not just academic. She constantly argued from such history that arrangements that seemed to benefit women or acknowledge their difference actually harmed them. But her resentment at not getting the assignment is palpable. By the time she got to the Supreme Court of the United States, Ginsburg's earplugs may have worn a little thin.

O'Connor had a different agenda in writing a separate opinion in *J.E.B.* She wanted to reiterate a losing argument she had been making in the race-based jury cases—that the limits on peremptory challenges should apply only to the government. O'Connor had long argued that only the prosecutor acts for the state in these cases; criminal defendants are not the state. Since the Fourteenth Amendment applies only to the state and not to private citizens, O'Connor had been contending, defendants should still be able to shape the jury any way they want to.

Since she had consistently lost that battle, her opinion was unremarkable on this score. But the partial dissent matters, because, in the course of arguing about how seriously the Court was restricting defendants' rights, she made a much more radical argument about sex discrimination than Blackmun made. For years O'Connor had asserted that male and female judges would come to the same conclusions. Now she appears to recognize potential differences in jurors' decisions. The state presented actual social science on how male jurors go easier on accused rapists, she reminded the reader. As to the rest, "though there have been no similarly definitive studies regarding, for example, sexual harassment, child custody, or spousal or child abuse, one need not be a sexist to share the intuition that in certain cases a person's gender and resulting life experience will be relevant to his or her view of the case." (The social science on male jurors and rapists, though contested now, was in the record in *J.E.B.*)

Shockingly, the prim and proper Republican came within a hair of sounding exactly like the cutting-edge feminist theorists Carol Gilligan and Catharine MacKinnon. Women are different. Because women experience and know things differently, she asserted, the Court should do only what the Constitution absolutely demands when restricting litigants from shaping a jury through the traditional peremptory challenges.

While she used the cultural assumption of difference to argue for defendants' use of gendered challenges, she nonetheless concluded that the *state* cannot be allowed to base its peremptories on sex. That would be state action. It's not that gender makes no difference. When the state is acting, she argued, the state must affirmatively decide to ignore the differences in the interest of women's equality! Women, different as they may be in the jury box, deserve to be citizens, and therefore jurors, despite bringing all their differences with them into the jury room. It's radical. In his dissent in *J.E.B.*, Justice Scalia used O'Connor's flirtation with difference feminism as evidence of the willful blindness of the pro-equality side to the natural differences between the sexes. He lost in *J.E.B.*, but the concession to difference feminism is lying there in the precedent, like an unexploded grenade.

O'Connor's argument for a narrow reading of the Fourteenth Amendment in the jury selection cases was the rare example of an issue where she did not get her way. With the Court almost perfectly divided between its four conservative and four liberal justices, O'Connor was the avidly sought-after fifth vote in every close case. Historian Nancy Maveety titled her book about this period *The Queen's Court.* O'Connor also had something Ginsburg might never have: since the justices vote at conference with the chief first, and then by seniority, O'Connor was the fourth vote in conference. With only Rehnquist, Blackmun (who was soon to leave), and Stevens voting before her, she had a chance to make the argument for her position before there were five votes one way or the other and before the next-closest swing voters—Souter and Kennedy—had to declare themselves. In the very formal precincts of the Supreme Court, where the justices no longer walked the halls, as Brennan had, trolling for votes in advance, getting to make your pitch at conference had become much more important. The only other place a justice could be sure her brethren heard her analysis was through carefully positioned questions at oral argument.

By the time Justice Ginsburg voted in conference, by contrast, the die was usually cast. Ginsburg used oral argument with great skill, to be sure. (Blackmun churlishly kept track of how disproportionately Ginsburg asked questions in sexual-harassment cases.) However, when a case involving women's proper role in society was involved, it was O'Connor who got the chance to make the argument in conference while some of the other eight were still listening. O'Connor was by no means a committed strategist for women's rights. Her ungenerous opinions even in cases where she voted for the woman's side reflected her consensus-seeking, fact-bound style of decision making. Nonetheless, in these early years of Ginsburg's tenure, O'Connor was more likely to vote on the liberal side in women's cases than in any other area. Once she voted on the cases of women's equality, the remaining justices knew there would be at least five for the position. Ginsburg had no need to strive for attention to persuade her brethren to get the votes she needed: when O'Connor spoke, as the old E. F. Hutton ad had it, people listened.

HAND IN HAND

And so speculation about their "special relationship" arose. The large, blond, senior justice and her small junior liberal female colleague were spotted about the courthouse, one article reported, "clasping hands." This is not as meaningful as it sounded. Former State Senator O'Connor was renowned in Phoenix circles for her handholding. The small collection of pictures in Joan Biskupic's biography of O'Connor includes a classic photograph of her in a typical moment, clasping the hand of a dinner guest at "Sandra Day O'Connor Day" in 1981. When her former clerk Michelle Friedland was appointed to the federal court of appeals in California, O'Connor administered the oath of office, holding tightly to Friedland's left hand the entire time.

Except for O'Connor's habit of taking the hand of the person she was talking to, the first and second women on the Supreme Court did not in any overt way "hold hands." By all accounts they did not sneak out at lunch to go shoe shopping either, although Ginsburg's shopping excursions with others—Marty, her pal Nina Totenberg—are well documented. Their clerks did not tell tales of the phone ringing between the chambers even when critical cases about women's rights were coming up for decision.

But together they made paying attention to the distaff side a little more the norm. The Court finally added a women's bathroom in the judges' robing room. Within months of Ginsburg's arrival, she and her sister in law O'Connor were off to the investiture of another female Clinton appointee, Judith Rogers. Deliciously, Rogers was replacing Clarence Thomas on the D.C. Circuit Court of Appeals—another female empowered in part by Thomas's sexual-harassment scandal.

Six months later they spoke together at the installation of Connecticut Supreme Court's chief justice, Ellen Ash Peters, as the head of the National Center for State Courts. They again played their accustomed roles. Ginsburg chose to highlight the honoree's successful management of the quintessential female problem of competing claims of work and family. When Peters became the first female professor at Yale, "silencing the Doubting Thomases," Ginsburg noted, who thought women could not both reproduce and succeed in the workplace, "Ellen had one child as an assistant professor, one as an associate professor . . . and her third as a full professor." At the end of her remarks, the opera-loving feminist asked everyone to join her in "a resounding BRAVA."

When O'Connor's turn came, she said nothing about Peters's gender-bending career. She hailed Peters as a wonderful person, wife, mother, and friend. She highlighted their common good fortune in such nice husbands and asked Peters's husband—for the first time that evening—to stand up and be recognized. She spoke interestingly and at length about the role of the state courts in the federal system. O'Connor often said that the best thing a woman could do is be visible and do the job the men had kept to themselves. Her version of Justice Peters was completely gender neutral.

In time, the two justices hosted a lunch at the Supreme Court for the D.C. convention of the prestigious International Women's Forum, an invitation-only group of female movers and shakers from all over the world. In welcoming their guests to the Court, Ginsburg again invoked O'Connor's words, this time from a speech that predated O'Connor's tenure on any court: "As society sees what women can do, as women see what women can do, there will be more women out there doing things and we'll all be better off for it."

In 1997, when Ginsburg was asked to write about her singular subject, "Constitutional Adjudication and Equal Stature," for the *Hofstra Law Review*, she acknowledged that O'Connor had been on the Court but a year when in 1981 she was first called on to add a woman's voice. *Hogan v. Mississippi*, O'Connor's decision to admit men to the public Mississippi University for Women, Ginsburg noted, tipped the balance on the Court to a narrow 5–4 in favor of integration by sex.

Feminist speaker or not, different voice or no, Sandra Day

O'Connor became a regular character in Ginsburg's narrative—Ginsburg's "savvy, sympatique colleague and counselor." Ginsburg never told her own story of discrimination and discouragement without invoking O'Connor's treatment upon graduating from Stanford. She cited O'Connor as the source for her stories about the difference women make. Ginsburg usually followed her citation of Justice O'Connor on the similarity between a wise woman and a sage male jurist with a caveat: that women's experience would—and should—cause them to see the world differently. But she emphasized that it was O'Connor who called her attention to the singularity of a woman's voice, using the example of Helen Suzman, for years a lonely voice of opposition to apartheid in South Africa's parliament. And, Ginsburg adds, "the only woman in the legislative chamber." Thus Ginsburg veils her overtly feminist message with references to the more conservative sister justice. The reference to South Africa's Suzman is unambiguously an homage to O'Connor's courage when she, too, was the only woman in the room.

THIS SHOULD BE RUTH'S

Ginsburg was particularly respectful of O'Connor's casting the fifth vote in the sex-segregated-school case just months into her tenure as the first woman. But when the Court next confronted the issue of sex-segregated public schools head-on, this time in the government's suit to compel the Virginia Military Institute to admit women, Ginsburg was on the bench with O'Connor.

Many other things had changed between O'Connor's 1981 opinion ending sex segregation at the Mississippi University for Women in *Hogan* and 1995, when *United States v. Virginia* arrived at the Court. Most visibly, in 1981 Joe Hogan had to sue the university himself. Once *Hogan* was decided, the Civil Rights Division of the Justice Department began to take on the issue of sex discrimination in public colleges itself, deploying star attorney Judith Keith. When, in 1989, an anonymous female candidate decided her rejection from VMI was sex discrimination, Keith had just finished several years of hammering on the Massachusetts Maritime Academy to live up to its agreement to admit women on equal footing. Not surprisingly, the Justice Department concluded that Virginia's policy of excluding women from VMI violated the Fourteenth Amendment, which guarantees to all persons the equal protection of the laws. The United States would force Virginia to comply with the Constitution.

Not only had the Justice Department and the membership of the Supreme Court changed but so had the whole landscape of sex discrimination. When Ginsburg started her career at the ACLU, the issues usually involved formal discrimination, such as explicitly unequal pay or exclusion from jury service. But by 1989, when the case against VMI began, no law firm would have dared tell an aspiring associate that the best she could hope for was stenography. Instead, the feminist movement was increasingly confronting something squishier—cultural gender roles, or what Ginsburg always called stereotypes.

The society did not stand still while the movement lawyers cleared the decks of formal discrimination. As the legal action shifted to cases about women's nature, so, too, did the cultural debate. And it was a noisy debate. Carol Gilligan's "difference" argument, that women reasoned in a morally different voice, reflecting concern for others and the maintenance of communal ties, was echoed by sociobiologists, also called evolutionary psychologists. These scholars contended that evolutionary pressures made the sexes foundationally different—male hunters, naturally unfaithful and looks-oriented; women gatherers, monogamous and wallet-oriented.

Thus players with vastly different—indeed, opposite—political agendas converged on the issue of female difference. Feminist difference scholars were contending that public policy should respect women's moral claims and promote community and dialogue. The last thing Gilligan said she wanted was the creation of a leadership class with only male norms of moral behavior. She was outraged at the way her work was used. Evolutionary psychologists, often espousing conservative political agendas, were arguing that efforts to change exploitative male behaviors such as sexual harassment were futile and would require totalitarian governmental measures. As the VMI case was making its way to the Court, liberals with an interest in helping poor children succeed in urban public schools began agitating for sex-segregated schools. The initiative, while powerfully controversial, gave new respectability to the cause of single-sex schooling.

Ginsburg's strategy always aimed at changing beliefs about women's stereotyped roles by removing the symbol of formal state approval in the form of sexually discriminatory laws. To her credit, most of the battles for formal equality were won, so by the mid-1990s, there was little opportunity left in the law to challenge proper gender roles by challenging the laws that explicitly kept women down. But the case against the publicly funded all-male Virginia Military Institute was perfect climax to her campaign. VMI's whole argument rested on the cultural incompatibility of the sexes. VMI defenders said the methods they used to train and shape the male students could not work if there were women present in the moral world created at VMI. When reduced to defending the very different female leadership program VMI created elsewhere in response to the litigation, its lawyers relied heavily on Gilligan's research. Much to her dismay, they argued that women learned "in a different voice."

If the highest court in the land rejected that contention, the cultural consequences would be so much greater than the admission of a handful of girls to a parochial, financially strapped college. When the trial against VMI opened, there were so many reporters in the courtroom they had to sit in the jury box. The case got so much attention because the parties were fighting a culture war.

VMI called its culture "adversative." The institute isolated freshmen and put them through student-run ritualized hazing, imposed a heavy honor code, and stripped all the students of any privacy or refuge. There were not even doors on the toilets. Throughout the seven years of litigation, VMI's main defense was that the adversative method was uniquely suited to men. It was the ultimate cultural redoubt.

The famed "rat line," the hazing ritual for the entering

freshmen, was a perfect example. All year, the freshmen "rats" were reduced to serving the upperclassmen and enduring a variety of exercises—marching in painful poses, being hauled out of bed at all hours, being yelled at. In an eerie echo of classic torture practices, the victims were also assigned a protector, called a "daddy" or a "dyke," who provided the freshman with what passed for safe haven in that system.

On the first warm day in late winter, the rats competed to break out of the rat line. The town fire truck sprayed a hill with water to turn it into a mud field and the rats crawled on their bellies over a series of barriers, covering themselves with mud while the upperclassmen sat on them, pulled them back, and taunted them. Often, one study reported, the rats "lost their pants." Only after they climbed the last slope were they greeted, "tenderly embraced," "washed," and "wrapped in blankets." Then the young men raced to the barracks where their dykes hosed them down, "incorporating" them into the VMI body politic. They sang songs about impregnating the local women. (This was no New York public school trying to help poor black and Hispanic girls make it to graduation.)

And now some would-be female undergraduate (the name was never made public), aided by the female lawyer at the federal Department of Justice, wanted to force them to admit women to the club.

Although VMI, founded in 1839, no longer graduated America's soldiers as it had before the Civil War, that conflict was central to its mythos. Its graduates formed the very heart of the Confederate Army. Early on it was tagged "the West Point of the South." After most of the cadets enlisted following the Battle of Manassas, the school actually closed. General "Stonewall" Jackson is buried near there. So is his horse.

When the demands of the racial civil rights movement reached Virginia after *Brown*, VMI responded by requiring candidates with dubious qualifications to be recommended by three alumni, a guarantee of whiteness. When the Ford Foundation threatened to pull its support from the school, VMI told it to get lost. Only the specter of the Department of Health, Education and Welfare taking its federal funds away triggered the admission of five black cadets in 1968, fourteen years after *Brown*.

From the start of the case in 1989 until the Supreme Court ruled in 1996, the VMI community of alumni and friends was firmly committed to resisting the women. Although the state of Virginia ultimately resigned from defending its public university's exclusionary policy, VMI raised and spent $14 million defending itself against the United States.

Recognizing that they were in a culture war, VMI's lawyers did something very smart. When they received the letter from the Justice Department that usually precedes a suit, they raced to the courthouse and filed a preemptive action against the United States. Their alertness enabled them to choose which Virginia federal court would hear the action: they filed in the district nearest to VMI, in Roanoke. They thus drew a Reagan appointee, Judge Jackson Kiser, a local lawyer who was occasionally seen golfing with VMI's counsel. If anyone would understand the uniqueness and value of the VMI culture, it was Judge Jackson Kiser.

Although doomed, VMI's resistance was not completely crazy. The Court had never openly ruled that sex-segregated public education always violated the Constitution. In 1976, early in Ginsburg's tenure at the ACLU Women's Rights Project, Pennsylvania lawyers brought a challenge to Philadelphia's public boys' and girls' high schools. The case, badly argued and on an inadequate brief, divided the Court 4–4 (Rehnquist was away and could not vote). The split left in place the lower court decision approving the separate schools. Justice O'Connor's decision in *Hogan*, which disallowed the Mississippi women-only nurse's program, did prescribe a high standard for such schools to meet to justify the sex segregation. According to *Hogan*, VMI had to show an "exceedingly persuasive" reason for the division. But in *Hogan* there was little overt difference in educational goals separating the Mississippi University for Women nursing program from nursing taught at the rest of the state schools. It was just segregated. VMI invoked the new fashion for "difference feminism," trying to fit itself into a model of benign, separate but equal and functional education.

For VMI's strategy to succeed, they first had to convince the judges that women were unfit for an adversarial model of training for social leadership, and, therefore, women should be educated outside the norms of the VMI system. Then they had to argue that even if some women were okay with it, the girls' presence would ruin it for the boys, distracting them and diluting their solidarity. The case went to trial in the district court. Using experts such as the eighty-two-year-old sociologist David Riesman and the work of Carol Gilligan, VMI made its case for the uniqueness of the VMI method, women's unsuitability for the method, and the centrality of sex exclusion to its success.

Judge Kiser found for VMI on all counts. VMI both promoted difference, he found, in its special approach, which would be badly hurt by admitting women, and yet was not discriminatory, in that women could take the same kinds of courses at another nearby school without ruinous access to what made VMI special. Kiser's opinion, as well as VMI's forum-shopping strategy of seeking a sympathetic local Republican-appointed jurist, interestingly reveals how women's equality had become less a matter of law and more a matter of deep beliefs about human nature and society.

Even the conservative Court of Appeals for the Fourth Circuit could not gag down Kiser's first opinion. The panel, consisting of judges appointed by Presidents Nixon, George H. W. Bush, and Carter, reversed unanimously: VMI could not simply limit its programs to men. The panel did not, however, compel VMI to integrate. Instead, they suggested that the state extend the excellent advantages of VMI to women without diluting it by establishing a separate program for them.

VMI, in response, proposed to start a parallel program at the nearby Mary Baldwin College to offer "substantively comparable" leadership opportunities for women in a nonadversative environment. On remand, Judge Kiser agreed again. In his opinion upholding the male-only military institute, Judge Kiser likened VMI to the "beat of a drum," while Mary Baldwin was the "melody of a fife." On a second appeal, the court agreed that VMI had done enough. The separate program was less prestigious and less well funded and espoused a different learning philosophy, but, to satisfy the equal-protection demands of the law, the court ruled, the women's option had only to be "substantively comparable" to the segregated one. "Substantive comparability" was a new concept for the Fourteenth Amendment and generated a powerful dissent from the Democratic appointee on the panel. The VMI case came within a single vote of getting a rehearing en banc from the full circuit court. Falling shy, however, the United States appealed to the Supreme Court.

And so the VMI case appeared before the high court, trailing a patently groundless interpretation of equal-protection law, and built around a totally inferior program, which, in its exclusionary origins and nod to the military, even many Mary Baldwin faculty didn't like.

VMI's prospects were bleak. Justice Thomas had a son at VMI and so would probably recuse himself, but the four liberals could likely count on O'Connor. And that made five. There was a lot of talk in the air about the virtues of sex-segregated education, but any reasonable defense of it would have had to *prove* that, unlike racial segregation, sex-segregated education was superior to integrated education. Or that the single-sex programs were established and maintained as compensation for past wrongs, like affirmative action, rather than as a desperate last-ditch effort to save an imperiled old men-only establishment. VMI looked more like a weird leftover from another era than an experiment in catering to the morally different voices of males and females.

Assisted, in 1995, by a sympathetic Justice Department led by Solicitor General Drew Days, the government asked the Court, once and for all, to make the standard for sex discrimination the same as for race. The Court should apply strict scrutiny to arrangements like VMI's. This would have required it to show that the VMI experience was a compelling state interest that only a segregated institution could achieve, a test almost no arrangement has ever passed. A raft of women's groups filed friend of the court briefs to the same effect.

The line to get into the oral argument wound around the block.

It soon became clear that VMI was going to go down. It was just too raw: Virginia had a long history of excluding women from its most prestigious public universities, and the actual military academies such as West Point had filed numerous amicus briefs telling the Court that coeducational schools can train people to be soldiers. At oral argument, Ginsburg skated very close to calling out the sexist assumptions embedded in the VMI method, asking VMI's lawyer whether training for future leadership didn't include the ability to coexist with—indeed, take orders from—female citizens or citizen-soldiers.

Representing VMI, Theodore Olson, the legendary Supreme Court advocate who was later the victor in *Bush v. Gore*, was forced to rely on the assertion that the VMI method worked really well for the students it attracted. So what, asked Justice Breyer, cutting to the chase immediately. Why is helping males who need an all-male adversative system important to the public? Breyer was invoking the standard for discriminatory plans: a compelling public interest. What if there were a segment of the public that did better in racially exclusionary schools? That would not mean the Court should reverse *Brown*! Didn't Virginia need to show why we, the people, benefited so heavily from satisfying a few male individuals' needs that the benefit outweighed our suspicion of segregated schools, Breyer asked? Why is the adversative method so important to the society at large?

Olson had no answer, because there was no answer. The boys-only rat-line world assumed that women were constitutively unfit for some avenues to citizenship. More important, as Justice Breyer's devilishly clever question teased out, VMI had to persuade the Court that the world needed men like their specially trained male-bonded graduates to run things in the society. By 1996, the Court had created more than two decades of precedents rejecting these arguments. Even the military said it didn't need men like the alumni of the VMI rat line. Under those past decisions, the odds were great that an assumption about women's nature would be regarded as a product of a discriminatory past and could not be dressed up as helping women. Some boys' need for a boys' club would be treated as simply not socially meaningful enough to out-weigh the damage to women from the discrimination.

Why had the case even gone so far? Because even after three decades of modern feminism, many Americans still believed that women were different. VMI also represented the belief that women were unsuited for some valuable parts of life. The conservative lo-cal federal judge believed it. And so did two of the three appeals court judges on the very conservative Fourth Circuit and a major-ity of the whole circuit, who voted not to hear it en banc. Everyone who thought about the case understood that an important cultural debate was going to be recast when the Supreme Court weighed in. Public faith in the Court as an institution was still very high, over 60 percent. That's why the line for oral argument was around the block.

When the Court gathered at conference, the line to support old cultural beliefs was substantially shorter. Only the chief and Jus-tice Scalia supported VMI. Six justices voted to compel the school to admit women. Justice Stevens, being the senior in the majority, would normally have had the right to assign the opinion. Since Chief Justice Rehnquist eventually switched his vote to join the majority in compelling VMI to integrate, Stevens thinks Rehn-quist had the assigning honors. Regardless of which man it was, either Stevens or Rehnquist assigned it to O'Connor. And savvy, sympatique O'Connor turned it down. This should be Ruth's, she said.

Ginsburg started the opinion-drafting process with six votes. She had some wiggle room, so she had a decision to make. Would she use this six-vote majority to try to get the Court to equate sex discrimination with race at last, fulfilling the work she began at the Women's Rights Project of the ACLU, where equating sex with race had been her goal? Had she succeeded, any legal distinction between men and women would have been almost impossible to defend, just as official governmental discrimination against black people is.

Ginsburg would not take the risk. She feared losing Ken-nedy and O'Connor, the weak links among her six votes. At oral

argument, O'Connor had snapped at the Justice Department lawyer for claiming the standard in sex-discrimination cases was still
an open question (as Blackmun had said it was just a year before in
the jury case, *J.E.B.*). Was the standard still on the table? "Not exactly," O'Connor said. "The Court has decided a number of cases
applying a sort of intermediate scrutiny." A plurality opinion of
four for strict scrutiny would be no better than Justice Brennan
had achieved two decades before in *Frontiero*. Ginsburg wanted
the broadest majority for women's equality she could get, and
O'Connor's agreement on this landmark sex case was disproportionately important to her. And so she invoked the well-established
standard that O'Connor described in her opinion in *Hogan*. The
state lost because it failed to provide an "exceedingly persuasive justification" for the distinction between the sexes at VMI.

But Ginsburg was never one to waste an opportunity. She
would use her big majority in the VMI case to "blur" the difference between the lower standard of review for sex discrimination
she had had to accept all these years and the high standard the
Court accorded to race. Cherry-picking the decades of decisions
inching toward women's legal equality since she started her work
a generation before, she wove together the most favorable language
from O'Connor's *Hogan* opinion and Kennedy's concurrence in
J.E.B. and concluded that the Court was now engaged in "skeptical scrutiny of official actions denying rights or opportunities based
on sex."

And so it should be skeptical of VMI's position, too, she affirms,
given the sorry history of sex discrimination woven throughout
the nation's history. And in Virginia. Wielding Virginia's long
and public record of resistance to educational equality for women,
the opinion dismisses out of hand VMI's newfound interest in the
virtues of single-sex education for all, as manifest in its litigation-
driven support for the program at Mary Baldwin College. Although Ginsburg sweetens the demanding sound of skeptical
scrutiny with a coquettish reference to "celebrate" the "inherent
differences between the sexes," the concession is just that—an
empty, flirtatious smile. Almost no discriminatory scheme can

escape the burden of history she lays upon it. Here, in the midst of the scary cultural revival of arguments for the natural moral uniqueness of women—for good or ill—the Supreme Court justice comes full circle to the work of the liberal philosopher John Stuart Mill, her earliest inspiration and the father of women's equality. Maybe someday women should be treated differently from men as opposed to being treated the same, Mill said in his landmark essay "The Subjection of Women" a century before Ginsburg set out on her quest, but first we must try equality. "Experience cannot possibly have decided between two courses, so long as there has only been experience of one."

Skeptical scrutiny raised the standard. Had it been scrupulously followed, Ginsburg's refusal to allow women to be lumped together and then treated as a group should have doomed essentially all gender-based discrimination. VMI had defended itself with the argument that most women did not want anything remotely resembling what VMI offered. The Court rejected the argument out of hand: "the question is whether the commonwealth can constitutionally deny to women who have the will and capacity, the training and attendant opportunities that VMI uniquely affords." If even one woman was ready, willing, and able to attend VMI, the policy of exclusion must fall. Ginsburg's antistereotyping dogma was written into law.

Dissenting, Justice Scalia asserted that scrutiny of sex-based classifications now required a perfect fit. If even one woman was suited for the all-male undertaking, the line between the sexes would not hold. He accused his good friend and former D.C. Circuit colleague of enacting strict scrutiny for women without admitting it. Despite the traditional back and forth of opinion and dissent, Ginsburg's opinion never challenges the accusation. And despite her comment at oral argument, O'Connor did not file a separate opinion and said not a word about preserving "a sort of intermediate scrutiny."

The next year a handful of young women appeared on the VMI campus, hair cropped and sporting hilariously ill-fitting uniform skirts. When the time came, they scrambled up the muddy hill and made it to the top. Although there were real challenges at the beginning, there are females at VMI to this day.

Ginsburg liked being on the Supreme Court (she called it "the good job").

Although she held her predecessor there in high esteem, she did not adopt her routine. Ginsburg had the temerity to eschew the morning aerobics classes. In typical Ginsburg fashion, she didn't *criticize* O'Connor's female ritual of early aerobics, she just said the class met too early. And she did not spend anything like the time and energy O'Connor did giving speeches in often obscure places, cheerleading for the American rule of law. It wasn't easy being second to the lively westerner. Ginsburg constantly received requests for appearances or publications from places announcing that O'Connor had already been there or done that. Her secretaries speculated O'Connor had a secret twin sister covering some of the gigs.

But Ginsburg certainly enjoyed the travel that her job enabled her to do. She participated fully in the grand opportunities the justices had to teach and confer abroad, especially during the summers. Wherever they go they are treated like American royalty. Ginsburg's files are full of references to trips to places with good opera companies. In 1998, for instance, she went to the Salzburg seminar on a trip that started with a Mercedes waiting at the airport to take her and Marty to the Imperial Hotel in Vienna and then shuttle them to a private opera performance at the Schonbrun Palace. Good job indeed.

It wasn't all palaces and Imperial Hotels. In 1998, she flew to Coral Gables, Florida, and used the authority vested in her to perform the wedding ceremony for Jason Wiesenfeld, her favorite client's son, who had started the litigation so long ago. Unlike most royalty, when she noticed a $78 error in the tiny hotel bill, she immediately wrote to the bride's father to alert him to the discrepancy. Three months later she was comforting the family as Jason came down with cancer in his twenties. Ginsburg reassured them that it would eventually pass and shared how she and Marty had gotten through the dark days of his disease themselves. Stephen has a beautiful handwritten card from Ginsburg's chambers with her mother-in-law's advice: "This too shall pass. And butterflies will follow."

It was a happy time. Jason Wiesenfeld did recover. And Marty began cooking for the Court's spouses' dinners.

The Importance of Being O'Connor and Ginsburg

꙳

In the years after *VMI*, the sisters in law heard almost twenty cases about women. Most involved relatively uncontroversial fine-tuning of the big decisions of sexual harassment and discrimination that had characterized the prior decade. The cases rarely divided the Court closely; most decisions claimed six or more votes for the majority position. It was clear that the Court was moving in the direction of increasing the protection for female plaintiffs in these two important areas of civil rights law.

SWINGING IN THE SCHOOL YARD

A short-lived and rare split appeared between the two female justices in 1998 when, in *Gebser v. Lago Vista Independent School District*, the Court confronted a new issue. Did the civil rights laws prohibit sexual harassment of *students*?

Students were sort of the stepchildren of legal feminism, a movement that began with Betty Friedan's 1963 clarion call to women to get to work. The 1964 Civil Rights Act, which included the revolutionary word "sex" in its protections, was mostly about employment. Early in the game, however, Bernice ("Bunny") Sandler, a humble lecturer at the University of Maryland, figured out that President Lyndon Johnson's 1968 executive order prohibiting race—and sex—discrimination should apply to schools receiving federal money. The government started investigating Harvard for its almost entirely male faculty. Columbia Law School noticed that it had no women on board and hired the young Ruth Bader Ginsburg. One of the few female members of Congress, Rep. Edith Green, put Sandler on the staff of the committee updating the Civil Rights Act. Four years later, the protections from the executive order were written into federal law, in a provision called Title IX. Sandler became, as *The New York Times* had it, "the godmother of Title IX." When Congress was considering Title IX, education lobbyists were so busy worrying about whether schools would have to use female football players they didn't notice there was a sexual revolution in the making. Okay, maybe Harvard Law School would eventually have to hire a Ruth Bader Ginsburg type. But in 1972, when President Nixon signed Title IX, sexual harassment didn't even have a name. Who ever dreamed that dreamy teachers couldn't hit on their worshipful female students? A million academic novels would have to be rewritten.

But as Tocqueville says, sooner or later every social issue in American life winds up in the courts. In this case, it arose in a plot straight out of one of those academic novels. The teenage plaintiff, Alida Star Gebser, had been engaged in a long sexual relationship with her high school social studies teacher. Although other students had complained about the teacher's inappropriate remarks and the like, Gebser and her teacher went to great lengths to conceal their behavior. When they were caught having sex in a parked car, the school threw the teacher out and the state pulled his license. Then Gebser's family sued the school. O'Connor sided with the four conservatives to deny that a school district was responsible when a teacher harassed a student. Unlike in the employment arena, the protections for students under the federal education law, Title IX, were not nearly as clear and robust as the prohibition against workplace harassment in the Civil Rights Act, she said. So the only way the Court would tag the school was if the school actually knew what was going on and ignored it. Stevens, Souter, Breyer, and Ginsburg dissented.

A year later, in *Davis v. Monroe County Board of Education*, O'Connor switched sides. Unlike Gebser, Davis was an "attractive" plaintiff, as O'Connor often used the term. The youngster had been the blameless victim of relentless unwanted sexual harassment by a fifth-grade schoolmate; while her teachers and principal ignored her countless complaints, her grades tanked, and she contemplated suicide. Granting her fifth vote to the liberals to hold a school district responsible when it ignored complaints of student-on-student abuse, O'Connor authored the second opinion with Ginsburg firmly in agreement.

Although most of the employment and harassment cases were not close, the *Gebser/Davis* sequence was a reminder of how crucial O'Connor's vote was to any novel or contestable issue of women's rights.

WOMEN MAY BE EQUAL BUT MOTHERS ARE SPECIAL

While women workers and students were faring pretty well in the Court, the cause of women's equality ran into trouble, predictably, where the cases challenged women's traditional role as child bearers. Abortion having been pretty quiet since *Casey*, in 1998, the issue of how the law tied women to childbirth came up in a novel way: immigration. During the Vietnam War from 1964 to 1974, the United States sent hundreds of thousands of people, mostly men, to Asia. A lot of them fathered children with foreign women. American citizenship law gave the fathers eighteen years to claim their offspring, in order to confer citizenship on them. American mothers of children born abroad to foreign fathers had no such duty. Their children's citizenship was assumed. The law discriminated. While the offspring of the Vietnam War were growing up, the Supreme Court had told the country it was skeptical of arbitrary distinctions between men and women. By the 1990s the door was closing on these children. And so the issue of parenthood arrived again at the Supreme Court.

Like many American soldiers stationed in Asia, Charles Miller fathered a child out of wedlock with a foreigner, in this case a Filipino woman, and did not claim her within the statutory time allowed. Twenty years later the daughter tried to become an American citizen.

The case, *Miller v. Albright*, is muddied, and Justice O'Connor concurred on the outcome for procedural reasons unrelated to the sex discrimination in the law. However, the rhetoric of the opinions made it clear that as of 1998 a majority of the Court was still not ready to demand equal treatment of men and women when the issue turned on their different roles in childbearing. Women, Justice Stevens suggested in his majority opinion, must be rewarded for the work of childbirth: "If the citizen is the unmarried female, she must first choose to carry the pregnancy to term and reject the alternative of abortion—an alternative that is available by law to many, and in reality to most, women around the world. She must then actually give birth to the child. [The citizenship law] rewards that choice and that labor by conferring citizenship on her child." And not just bearing children. The law also favors women because it expects them to do the rearing: "their initial custody will at least give them the opportunity to develop a caring relationship with the child." The law that a child born out of wedlock to an alien mother and American father must be legitimated before age eighteen "is therefore supported by the undisputed assumption that fathers are less likely than mothers to have the *opportunity* to develop relationships."

In her dissent, Ginsburg first tries to put her standard smiley face on the decision. Maybe it's just a run-of-the-mill case about whether the daughter can raise the father's discrimination claim.

But she's worried:

"Even if one accepts at face value the Government's current rationale, it is surely based on generalizations (stereotypes) about the way women (or men) are. These generalizations pervade the opinion of Justice Stevens, which constantly relates and relies on what 'typically,' or 'normally,' or 'probably' happens 'often.'

"We have repeatedly cautioned, however, that when the Government controls 'gates to opportunity,' it may not exclude qualified individuals based on 'fixed notions concerning the roles and abilities of males and females.'"

Ginsburg's opinion draws on just a small sample of the decades of rhetoric from the Court, disclaiming any intent to close the gates of opportunity based on fixed notions. But even with the sturdy foundation she had built, as advocate and jurist, childbearing is never far from the scene in any discussion about women. *Miller*, the immigration case, seemed to approve the government's policy of rewarding women by giving them automatic citizenship for their children.

As the Supreme Court approved rewarding women for child-bearing, a raft of state laws were passed to drive them to it, by outlawing a common form of late-term abortion, dilation and ex-traction ("D&X"). A self-described "feminist," the mental health advocate Jenny Westberg, says she started the new anti-abortion initiative in 1992 by getting hold of a copy of a medical paper describing the procedure for abortion providers. Westberg was a pretty good cartoonist, and she created a series of illustrations for the anti-abortion *Life Advocate* magazine. Aides to a Republican Florida congressman renamed D&X with the catchy phrase "par-tial birth abortion." And the abortion wars flared up again. By the mid-'90s, the Republicans in Congress and states across the coun-try began passing laws to prohibit D&X. (President Clinton vetoed the federal laws.)

Despite Justice O'Connor's profound desire to put the abortion matter behind her, some of the new anti-abortion laws could be read to apply even before the fetus was viable outside the womb and expressly refused to make an exception for women's health, even if the forbidden procedure were better for the woman's health. Ac-cordingly, a lower federal court found the Nebraska "partial birth abortion" law unconstitutional under the Supreme Court ruling in *Casey*, reaffirming the right to abortion and seeming to pre-serve the basic protection for abortions. In 2000, the Court agreed to review the case. Would the *Casey* troika—O'Connor, Souter, Kennedy—hold?

When the conference met, there were five votes to overturn the Nebraska law, but Kennedy had jumped ship. In *Casey*, Ken-nedy was widely credited with holding that abortion rights were the manifestation of a fundamental American concept of liberty: "At the heart of liberty is the right to define one's own concept of existence, of meaning, of the universe, and of the mystery of human life."

His dissent in the new case revealed how little protection he thought *Casey* afforded women. In his view, states should be able to regulate abortion, even just to protect the moral health of the society: "States . . . have an interest in forbidding medical procedures which, in the State's reasonable determination, might cause the medical profession or society as a whole to become insensitive, even disdainful, to life, including life in the human fetus. Abortion, *Casey* held, has consequences beyond the woman and her fetus. *Casey* recognized," he continued, "that abortion is fraught with consequences for . . . the persons who perform and assist in the procedure [and for] society which must confront the knowledge that these procedures exist, procedures some deem nothing short of an act of violence against innocent human life. A State may take measures to ensure the medical profession and its members are viewed as healers, sustained by a compassionate and rigorous ethic and cognizant of the dignity and value of human life, even life which cannot survive without the assistance of others."

O'Connor, although voting in the liberal majority, concurred to speculate that some prohibition might survive if it were drafted to avoid procedures used before viability and contained an exception for the health of the mother. O'Connor's opinion thus reduces the liberal majority to a plurality of four. More important, her endless dalliance with allowing ever more intrusive restrictions helped give moral legitimacy to the anti-choice campaign. O'Connor's opinion is of a piece with her abortion jurisprudence since 1983. She would never provide the crucial fifth vote to send women back to 1972. But she would not let them move beyond the backlash that erupted after 1973 either. With the tantalizing possibility that some intrusion might hit the sweet spot of O'Connor's burden test, the abortion battles would continue unabated. Two years after the decision in *Stenberg v. Carhart*, Congress passed a bill banning the procedure used in late abortions.

The lawyer for the Thomas More Center had worked closely with the senators to craft a bill that would meet O'Connor's undue-burden test. President George W. Bush signed the bill, and the law slowly began to make its way to the Court. It contained no exception for the mother's health.

Miller, the citizenship case, was muddy, and *Stenberg*, the partial birth abortion case, was a victory for women. But for anyone watching carefully, the warning signs for women's equality were manifest. In the crude, vote-counting sense, any retirement among the pro-woman five—Stevens, O'Connor, Souter, Ginsburg, Breyer—would split the court 4–4. Stevens's defection in *Miller* was an oddity. He was not going to be a swing vote in most women's cases. A liberal retirement under a Republican president would put Anthony Kennedy in the swing seat. WWKD? What Would Kennedy Do?

Kennedy's vote in *Miller* and his dissenting opinion in *Stenberg* were ominous. When Kennedy was being considered in 1987, movement conservatives in the Justice Department opposed his selection, because they believed he was in the O'Connor mold and open to a modern approach to the Constitution. After his decisions in *Casey* and in some environmental cases, conservatives had an orgy of I told you so, framing him as someone who cared more about pleasing the establishment than in conservative constitutionalism. Kennedy was "drifting left in response to elite opinion," as one prominent critic put it. This should have suited Ginsburg perfectly, as one of Ginsburg's primary strategies was slowly to embed formal equality for women deeply in establishment thinking, using the law to categorize stereotyped treatment of women an "idea whose time has gone." If Kennedy, the bellwether of elite opinion, felt free to rule or opine as he did on women's issues after *Casey*, her whole strategy of making women's equality the conventional wisdom was in trouble.

Almost as bad as his votes were the opinions he expressed. Like Ginsburg's only defeat—the Florida widow's tax case, *Kahn v. Shevin*, all those years ago in 1974—the opinions in *Miller* and *Stenberg* undermined her core strategy of protection for women's equality. Since 1971 she had been steadily advancing the case for women by building a structure of precedent that ruled out every element of Kennedy's analysis. From *Reed v. Reed* in 1971 to *United States v. Virginia* in 1996, the Court moved to treat women as individuals, not members of a class reduced to the average behavior of the group. Even if it were administratively convenient, as the state argued in *Reed*, the Court forbade it. Specifically, women could not be lumped together and presumed to be dependent while men were typecast as self-sufficient. All the Social Security decisions, starting with Stephen Wiesenfeld's landmark case, denied the government the easy path of stereotyping women as dependent hausfraus who must be cared for when their husbands die. The jury cases shut the state out from the defense that it was merely seeing to the moral well-being of such fragile creatures and from coarsening society, by protecting women from the rough-and-tumble of the courthouse. The jury cases and the Social Security cases also stripped the state of the argument that women must be treated differently because they needed to stay home and tend the children. Women couldn't escape jury service because they were the presumptive caregivers and they wouldn't automatically get better Social Security benefits if left behind either.

After all that effort, suddenly, in the citizenship case in 1998 and scarily in Kennedy's dissent in *Stenberg*, Ginsburg found herself confronting the zombie invasion of sex-role stereotypes she had thought buried long ago. If Kennedy were the deciding vote, women would be treated as a class, based on their behavior, especially as childbearers and caregivers. Giving birth would be rewarded for the good of the nation. Refusing to give birth would be heavily penalized to defend the moral health of the society.

FRAGILE MAJORITY

Things got worse. Teaching in Crete the summer of 1999, Ginsburg started feeling unwell. Doctors, thinking she had diverticulitis, found colon cancer. In September, she had surgery—"9-1/2 hours" of it, she later reported to Stephen Wiesenfeld. Sister in law O'Connor was the first one to phone her after surgery. Here's the deal with cancer, O'Connor advised. Have your chemotherapy on

Friday so you have the weekend to recover before the Court's session on Monday.

It was good advice. After her surgery, Ginsburg endured eight months of chemotherapy and radiation. Court records contain no announcement of her missing any meetings, even the ones before the term opened that fall, although she ruefully admitted she was "trying to say no to any 'extras.'" (A year later, the aftermath of the surgery and radiation was still causing her what she euphemistically called "shut downs." The best remedy, she confided to Wiesenfeld, was to "tough it out.") She was there for the argument in the partial birth abortion case and to cast the critical fifth vote at conference. In August 2000, her one-year checkup revealed no further signs of colon cancer. Come back in three years, the doctors said. "Great words to hear," she crowed.

Still one Supreme Court appointment was all that stood between American women and the tender ministrations of Justice Kennedy. The election of 2000 loomed.

17

Justice O'Connor's Self-Inflicted Wound

⋆⋇⋆

On election night 2000, Justice O'Connor and John O'Connor were at an election party at the home of Mary Ann Stoessel, doyenne of the Washington establishment and widow of the legendary diplomat Walter Stoessel. Shortly before 8 p.m. NBC called Florida, and thus the election, for the Democrat, Al Gore. "This is terrible," the justice said. "That means it's over." She rose from her chair in front of the TV with an air of disgust. John O'Connor volunteered an explanation of her abrupt behavior. She wanted to retire, he told them, so that they could go back to Phoenix. She would not, however, hand her seat over to a Democratic president. So if Gore won Florida, they were doomed to at least four more years in Washington, D.C.

In the ensuing years it emerged that she had good reason to be concerned about their future: John O'Connor was suffering from early onset Alzheimer's disease. Indeed, that may explain his uncharacteristically imprudent remarks about the justice's political allegiance. Sooner or later he would have to be institutionalized, and most of their children, who might help her with the burden of caring for him, lived in Arizona. Her upset, it soon emerged, may have been premature. Within hours the networks declared Florida—and the election—too close to call. Both sides embarked upon a frantic five-week campaign to pull the outcome in their direction, the Democrats to re-count the votes and the Republicans to defend the Republican secretary of state's assignment of victory to Bush.

Five weeks later, O'Connor cast the decisive fifth vote in *Bush v.*

Gore, stopping the election contest with Bush as the declared winner in Florida and thus the nation. The most extreme conservatives on the Court—Rehnquist, Scalia, Thomas—wanted to rule that the Florida state court had no business telling its state how to handle an election dispute. Election disputes are for the state legislatures, they contended. Their position was problematical, because if courts can't review state law, even state election law, much of the last two centuries of constitutional law, including the Supreme Court's authority to review acts of Congress, was cast into doubt.

Anthony Kennedy wanted to rule that the Florida re-count would violate the equal-protection clause of the Fourteenth Amendment because it didn't re-count the ballots from the whole state. The equal-protection argument had obvious problems of its own, because the Court could simply have ordered Florida to conduct a uniform and universal re-count. Worse, since balloting all over the country is wildly variable, the implications for future elections were catastrophic. Kennedy solved the problem by adding a line that the decision applied only in the exact facts of the Florida re-count in *Bush v. Gore*. His words, he said, carried no precedential value for any other case. Joined by O'Connor, Kennedy's opinion for the court (Rehnquist, Scalia, and Thomas concurred on their separate theory) put George Bush in the White House.

How could she? The woman who helped outlaw sexual harassment and saved abortion rights, turning the power to shape the Court over to a Republican president from Texas. "It will be impossible to look at O'Connor, Kennedy, Scalia, Rehnquist, and Thomas in the same light again," declared the *New Republic* legal commentator Jeffrey Rosen. Instead of "carefully thought out positions," as the *Los Angeles Times* described her work in 1993, after *Bush v. Gore*, her minimalist jurisprudence suddenly looked "addled and uncertain."

That the decision was so transparently devoid of any legal foundation left only a search for a political explanation. Perhaps she didn't know, commentators speculated, that the gun—pointed squarely at women's rights—was loaded. After all, George W. Bush came from such a fine family. Maybe, she thought, he would have governed in the mode of his father, who, as O'Connor wrote to Goldwater in 1988, was so "vital for the Court and for the nation." Given O'Connor's robust history as an avid observer of electoral politics, the ignorance explanation is almost impossible to credit. As the electoral website *On the Issues* reported at the time, Bush the candidate had said he supported a constitutional amendment outlawing abortion except in cases of rape or incest or to protect the life of a mother. He was "disappointed" by the Court's decision, with O'Connor providing the crucial swing vote, to strike down the Nebraska "partial birth abortion" law. He "believed in strict constructionists," and in one strict constructionist in particular: "I have great respect for Justice Scalia, for the strength of his mind, the consistency of his convictions, and the judicial philosophy he defends." For fourteen years, Justice Scalia had been the most consistent vote on the Court to defeat women's claims. He even voted in favor of VMI.

The reporter Jeffrey Toobin, who had written many positive reports about the FWOTSC, tried to explain her vote in *Bush v. Gore* as driven by her loyalty to the Republican Party: "She loved politics and more to the point the Republican Party." Not only, as he reports, did she refer to the Republicans as "we" and "us" when discussing Rehnquist's betting pools on the elections, she also explained her poor performance in the wagering of 1986 as the result of her "optimism" that the Republicans would win more races than they did. As recently available material reveals, fretting with Barry Goldwater that George H. W. Bush might not win the election of 1988, she had described Bush as vital to the nation—and to the Court.

At a tony D.C. dinner party right in the middle of *Bush v. Gore*, she loudly assured her fellow guests that she knew terrible things about the Gore campaign's behavior in Florida: " 'You just don't know what those Gore people have been doing,' she said. 'They went into a nursing home and registered people that they shouldn't have. It was just outrageous' " As Toobin points out, there is no obvious explanation for why the Supreme Court justice was broadcasting a baseless canard from some right-wing website. But the remark is telling. To establishment Republicans like Sandra Day O'Connor, the Democrats would always carry a faint whiff of Tammany Hall bosses, voting the cemetery (or the nursing homes) and stealing elections.

Not only were the Democrats supposedly voted for by ineligible nursing home patients, the voters they did have didn't seem to know what they were doing. In the Florida contest, the Gore side argued that old Democratic voters didn't know how to cast their ballots when the form of the ballot changed in Palm Beach County. O'Connor was legendarily impatient with people who couldn't handle the business of everyday life; she was always telling people how to drive and giving them directions to places whether they wanted them or not. The Democratic-dominated Florida Supreme Court came down with a very heavy-handed opinion in Gore's favor, in what looked like a transparently partisan effort. Like the Democratic Party and its inept voters, Florida was a "mess" by O'Connor's tidy standards. By contrast, the Republican Party represented her old friend Barbara Bush's son George, a "compassionate conservative" and the certified winner under Florida's designated certifier, Secretary of State Katherine Harris.

One fact unites O'Connor's decisions: from her choice of the lightweight, errant Harry Rathbun as her mentor in 1951 to her vote in *Bush v. Gore* a half century later, O'Connor was impervious to political theory. Rathbun promoted the making of a better world without any stable vision of what that better world would look like. O'Connor cast her vote on everything from freedom of religion to freedom to abort with a similar absence of vision. When she retired, she devoted herself to causes such as civic education and the merit selection of judges, good-government initiatives, similarly empty of political goals.

But picking that president changed the country irretrievably. The Republican Party of 2000 had a clear theory of how America should be governed and a scorched earth commitment to the outcome. She might have thought she was picking the more attractive litigant or tidying up a messy situation, but, when the old-fashioned good-government Girl of the Golden West met the ideologues of the twenty-first-century Republican Party in *Bush v. Gore*, they took her lunch. Five years later, John's illness having become totally unmanageable, she retired. In her place, George W. Bush nominated Samuel Alito, the judge from Pennsylvania who had thought married women should have to go to their husbands if they needed an abortion.

INDIAN SUMMER

To be clear, the Supreme Court's decision may not have changed history. The re-count might very well have confirmed Bush's election, or the other institutions the Constitution entrusted with election disputes—the Florida legislature, the House of Representatives— might have installed him in the Oval Office. What the Court did, by stopping the re-count, was to terminate any chance of another outcome to the election of 2000. On January 20, 2001, George W. Bush was inaugurated as the forty-third president of the United States. Two days later, he reinstated the prohibition, suspended by Bill Clinton, against giving foreign aid to any organization that performed or "promoted" abortion. Planned Parenthood International's budget went down by 20 percent.

When the new crop of clerks arrived in 2001, after the *Bush v. Gore* term, they had the clear sense that something wrenching had happened in the Court. Not just disagreement, which was normal, but a fundamental violation of institutional norms. In O'Connor's chambers, the clerks were focused on getting along and working with the other clerks across all the chambers. Sometimes all nine clerks assigned to a case would get together to work on the memos they were writing, and often all the clerks on one side would meet. The justices meanwhile retreated to exchanging views in the most "democratic" manner—sending formal memos to the entire conference, exchanging views on paper accessible to all.

Perhaps it was buyer's remorse, but, after *Bush v. Gore*, Justice O'Connor embarked upon a five-year stretch of voting with the liberals in the big cases of civil rights and equality. She voted— and wrote two important decisions—on behalf of women in every case after *Bush v. Gore.* She reversed decades of her prior decisions and voted to allow a state to make a district that would support a black representative and struck down, after many years of resistance on the issue, a death penalty law that allowed execution of the retarded. In 2003, she voted to declare the criminal sodomy laws unconstitutional. O'Connor was the only justice of the five who had upheld the criminal sodomy laws in 1986 to change her vote. Chief Justice Rehnquist remained in favor of criminalization. The other three justices who voted with Rehnquist in 1986 had all left the Court. Unwilling to say she had been wrong before, she came up with a novel equal-protection argument for striking down the law, and filed a solitary concurring opinion. (Apparently the justice's decision to swing to the majority on gay sex caused a flap among her clerks, one of whom was a committed member of the conservative lawyers' organization the Federalist Society, and later a counselor to George W. Bush.) And finally, O'Connor wrote the opinion that saved, for a time, affirmative action in college admissions.

Even Justice Kennedy moved more toward the liberal bloc, supporting limits on partisan redistricting, protecting the government's right of eminent domain, and reining in the death penalty. He won the task of writing the opinion striking the last of the laws making sodomy criminal; Kennedy's obviously heartfelt paean to the respect owed to gay men and lesbian women is rightly seen as a high point in his time on the bench.

JUSTICE KENNEDY'S MADONNAS AND WHORES

But Kennedy never again weighed in on the side of women.

A couple of the women's rights cases involved fine-tuning the now sturdy structure of equality in public institutions and in the workplace that was topped off with the decision in *U.S. v. Virginia*, the VMI case. But most of the disputes still circled back to the perennially unsettled issue: their role in producing and bringing up baby. When it came to women, Justice Kennedy seemed almost to be doing penance for having saved *Roe v. Wade.*

The most glaring example of Justice Kennedy's abandonment of the cause of women's equality had to be his concurring opinion in 2001 in *Ferguson v. Charleston*, a suit by ten black pregnant women against the hospital run by the Medical University of South Carolina. The trouble at the hospital started when Shirley Brown, a white nurse at the overwhelmingly black public facility in Charleston, heard on the radio that the local police were arresting pregnant drug users for child abuse. Nurse Brown decided that any of her patients taking drugs while pregnant should be prosecuted as criminals. After all, under South Carolina law, viable fetuses were persons. She and the hospital lawyer got in touch with the city lawyer to set up a program to identify pregnant offenders. If the hospital suspected a pregnant women of using cocaine, the hospital would test the urine samples they took from her for medical purposes and, if they tested positive, turn the patient in to the police. According to the Court papers, scenes of harrowing abuse ensued. Pregnant women went to jail to await childbirth. Women were arrested within days and sometimes even hours of giving birth, handcuffed, shackled, torn from their babies, and taken off to jail. (Later the new mothers were given "amnesty" if they agreed to go into drug treatment.)

Lawyers for the Center for Reproductive Law and Policy in New York sued, arguing that the involuntary use of patients' medical urine samples for drug arrests was unconstitutional search and seizure. The somewhat startling record at trial included testimony that Nurse Brown had been heard suggesting that black women should have their tubes tied and that birth control should be put in the water in black communities. Center lawyers also sued the hospital for race discrimination. A local jury found for the hospital, and the court of appeals affirmed.

The hospital contended that the program fell under an exception to constitutional protections against unlawful search, called "special needs." The catch was that, under the Court's prior precedents, a special need had to be special, serving some interest other than the social well-being that undergirds any provision of criminal law. In this case, the special reason justifying the search was the physical well-being of the mother and the fetus. Since all antidrug law enforcement was driven by the harm to the drug-taking adult, the fetus was the only novel factor in the case. Indeed, the hospital itself admitted that it had been motivated in part by the unprecedented media attention to a so-called epidemic of "crack babies." Justice Stevens assigned the case to himself and wrote an opinion treating the issue as a straightforward search-and-seizure matter with no distinction between the mother and the fetus. The public hospital, he ruled, did not have a special-enough need to take urine samples as if for routine health care and then, without a warrant or the patient's consent, hand it over to the police for prosecution.

Justice Kennedy filed a concurring opinion, formally casting his vote to stop Nurse Brown and her minions from this action. Technically this was a vote for the female plaintiffs. But rather than just stopping there, he spent most of his opinion on the special status of the fetus and how the government was justified in using criminal law to compel women to take care of their "unborn." "The beginning point," Justice Kennedy writes, "ought to be to acknowledge the legitimacy of the State's interest in fetal life. . . . There should be no doubt that South Carolina can impose punishment upon an expectant mother who has so little regard for her own unborn that she risks causing him or her lifelong damage and suffering." Although the hospital cannot collect urine from a patient under the guise of health, once the urine is in the jar, he suggests, the police should get a warrant to collect the evidence from the hospital. And then punish the women who have transgressed.

The entire essay is completely unnecessary to the decision on a search-and-seizure point. But Justice Kennedy always seemed to perceive women as saints or whores. Seeing that devilish dichotomy appear again at the hands of one of the key votes on the Supreme Court had to scare the dickens out of his female colleagues.

Kennedy got another chance to reward the blessed mothers when the discriminatory immigration law issue surfaced again, this time in a procedurally clean case. Justice Ginsburg calls the cases of American men fathering children with Asian women the "Madame Butterfly" cases, reflecting both her rhetorical gift and love of opera. In the second case, *Nguyen v. INS*, Nguyen's father, like Lt. Pinkerton in that saddest of operas, brought his young son home from Vietnam and raised him in America. When Nguyen got in trouble with the law years later, it emerged that his father had failed to do the paperwork to claim him in time, and the United States proposed to deport the young man, who had lived in America since he was six. If Nguyen had been fathered by a Vietnamese tea planter and born to a philandering American woman in Vietnam, he would have been an American citizen automatically. Nguyen was a clear case of sex discrimination, but Justice Kennedy was having no part of sexual equality. With the rare and unlikely fifth vote of Justice Stevens, he wrote the opinion denying fathers the automatic transmittal of citizenship that American women abroad exercised at childbirth.

The immigration law may grant citizenship at birth to the foreign-born, out-of-wedlock children of American women, but not of American men, Kennedy wrote. "There is nothing irrational or improper in the recognition that at the moment of birth—a critical event in the statutory scheme and in the whole tradition of citizenship law—the mother's knowledge of the child and the fact of parenthood have been established in a way not guaranteed in the case of the unwed father. This is not a stereotype."

The discrimination against the out-of-wedlock offspring of American men abroad may seem trivial against the Court's now long and impressive record of establishing women's equality. Thanks in large part to Ginsburg's work as a lawyer, the Court had opened up the possibilities for acceptable female behavior in the years since Sally Reed sued to administer her son's estate in 1971.

And that accomplishment is just where Justice Kennedy's blow fell in *Nguyen*. His opinion for the majority, stereotyping women as natural parents, strikes at the core of the house Ginsburg had built. The devilish thing about stereotyping is that it often rests on how the majority of people act. Unlike Stephen Wiesenfeld, most men do not need Social Security to raise their motherless children. Even when they were allowed, female college applicants didn't flood into the Virginia Military Institute. The old norms persist. Many—even most—people behave in the ways their history and culture hands down. Ginsburg's project from the beginning was to remove that formal legal support for the old behaviors as a means to make room for new ways of acting. The law should not enshrine social distinctions that seemed like common sense to people like Anthony Kennedy.

With Stevens unexpectedly in the conservative bloc, O'Connor was the most senior justice in dissent. She assigned to herself the task of answering Kennedy. "[T]he majority," she explained, moving directly to the heart of the backlash in Kennedy's opinion, "articulates a misshapen notion of 'stereotype' and its significance in our equal protection jurisprudence. The majority asserts that a 'stereotype' is 'defined as a frame of mind resulting from irrational or uncritical analysis.' This Court has long recognized, however, that an impermissible stereotype may enjoy empirical support and thus be in a sense 'rational.'"

Under the guidance of the equal-protection clause, O'Connor set out, we as a society have agreed to ignore the evidence, because of the harm such sweeping assumptions do to the people trying to live differently. She reminded her brethren that since *Reed v. Reed*, they had repeatedly ruled to this effect. In a Girlz Rule string of citations, she reiterated to the Court: "We have made abundantly clear in past cases that gender classifications that rest on impermissible stereotypes violate the Equal Protection Clause, even when some statistical support can be conjured up for the generalization." Her authorities ranged from her own dissent in the jury case and Ginsburg's most potent victories—*Craig v. Boren*, the teenage boys, beer, and driving case, and Stephen Wiesenfeld's distinctly untypical claim for child support.

And the majority can't just hide the stereotype by asserting it's not a stereotype if it's not nasty. It's not that you're hurting my feelings, she added. She didn't care if Kennedy thought of mothers as the Blessed Mother. It's still a stereotype. And it's still harmful. It was a great dissent. But it was still a dissent. The prospects for women's equality dimmed.

The downside of Justice Kennedy's worshipful assignment of the maternal role to women became apparent almost immediately in the next sex case. In *Nevada v. Hibbs*, a male caregiver, William Hibbs, sued his employer, the state of Nevada, for money damages for denying him leave provided by the federal family-leave law. In the American constitutional system, suits against the states are not favored. Nonetheless, with Stevens back in the liberal camp and even Justice Rehnquist on the side of family leave, six justices voted that Hibbs could sue Nevada for damages for violating the federal law. Rehnquist assigned the opinion to himself. Remedying discrimination between the sexes and making leave available for everyone is an important-enough justification for allowing employees to sue their employers for damages in federal court, Rehnquist concluded, even when the employer happened to be a sovereign state like Nevada.

For all his earlier prose about family values, Justice Kennedy dissented. The talk about sex-role stereotypes and the history of discrimination against women in the workplace was unpersuasive to him. "All would agree that women historically have been subjected to conditions in which their employment opportunities are more limited than those available to men. As the Court acknowledges, however, Congress responded to this problem by allowing people to sue their states for money if the states violated the Civil Rights Act of 1964," he concluded with satisfaction. Now they're making a fuss about family leave being offered on a sex-neutral basis so they won't be stigmatized as caregivers. What next?

Whatever it was, they weren't going to get it from Anthony Kennedy.

THE LAST CASE

Justice O'Connor thwarted Justice Kennedy in one last sex case before she left. She provided the critical fifth vote—and wrote the opinion—in *Jackson v. Birmingham Board of Education*, a surprisingly close decision for a relatively unremarkable case. Federal law, called Title IX, had long prohibited sex discrimination in schools that got federal funds. When a longtime physical education teacher, Roderick Jackson, got assigned to a new school and discovered his girls' basketball team was getting the short end of the court, he complained. His evaluations suddenly went south, and he was eventually fired.

Earlier cases had established that students could sue to enforce the prohibition against sex discrimination in schools. *Jackson v. Birmingham* merely confirmed that Title IX, prohibiting sex discrimination, also prohibited retaliating against a whistle-blower who complained about sex discrimination. Justice Kennedy joined in Justice Thomas's dissenting opinion for the four conservatives, arguing that discrimination against someone for complaining about sex discrimination wasn't sex discrimination. O'Connor made relatively short work of the argument. "[R]etaliation is discrimination 'on the basis of sex,'" she ruled, "because it is an intentional response to the nature of the complaint: an allegation of sex discrimination."

O'Connor had her finger in the dike. Kennedy's entire track record, after *Casey*, unambiguously showed that there would be little hope for women if O'Connor left. The only question left was how boldly Anthony Kennedy was going to move to reverse what the sisters in law had achieved.

YOU THINK, "OH, DEAR."

The Supreme Court reporter Jeffrey Toobin always listened at oral argument for Justice O'Connor to interject one of her ladylike exclamations: Oh, dear! Well, goodness! Then you knew, he had figured out, that she was really serious about what she was saying and how she might rule. In a symposium at William and Mary Law School in 2010, five years after she stepped down, she admitted that she was disappointed in the Court's decisions undoing some of her rulings. "If you think you've been helpful, and then it's dismantled, you think, 'Oh, dear.'" Applying Toobin's rule, this is as close as the self-described cowgirl gets to admitting she's very upset. "But," she continued in her usual suck-it-up-and-change-the-tire fashion, "life goes on. It's not always positive."

The fate of her legacy as the FWOTSC was clear long before she left. George W. Bush was running a movement conservative White House, and Anthony Kennedy didn't like women's rights. But she was, as she saw it, trapped. Her husband John, diagnosed with Alzheimer's disease fifteen years earlier, while still young, was deteriorating rapidly. Sometime before the 2002 term he had gone to work at the law firm in D.C. where he was still titularly employed and got lost coming home. By 2003, the justice had stopped having her famous Saturday morning chili fests with her clerks; she could not leave her husband alone. She began bringing him to chambers with her and watching him constantly when the two of them went out.

According to the Supreme Court reporter Jan Crawford Greenburg, it was actually Chief Justice William Rehnquist who drove O'Connor to retire when she did. In June 2005, she met with him for a frank conversation about the future of the institution they both loved. He had thyroid cancer; nine months earlier the doctors had given him a year, and she thought he would tell her he was about to step down. Not wanting to burden the Court with two vacancies at once, she planned to stay another year and then go back to Phoenix with John. Instead, Rehnquist surprised her with the news that he would stay on for another year. If she didn't leave now, she would have to wait two years to allow him to retire first or cause the dreaded dual vacancies. Just like that, O'Connor agreed she'd be the one to go.

O'Connor wrote her letter of resignation, timed for delivery the same day the mail versions would reach her sons out west. "I'll retire as soon as my replacement is confirmed," she wrote to President Bush. "You make your decision and you live with it," she told Greenburg. Hours after the letters arrived, she got on a plane for Phoenix.

That abrupt decision cost her a year on the Court and possibly altered the course of history. In July 2005, President Bush nominated John Roberts, a shoo-in, to replace Justice O'Connor. Wonderful choice, she pronounced to the press. "Except," she added, "he's not a woman." Knowing full well what it was like to be the only woman, she did not embrace the prospect of leaving Justice Ginsburg home alone.

By the time Roberts began his confirmation hearings, however, he was not succeeding the first female justice. On September 4, in the middle of the process of replacing Justice O'Connor, Chief Justice Rehnquist died. Bush promoted Roberts to be the candidate for the next chief, necessitating another pick for O'Connor's seat. Less than a month later, Roberts was confirmed. Had O'Connor simply waited a couple of months before sending her letter, she could have had another term to decide what to do. Instead, she was out, and eventually was replaced by Judge Samuel Alito of the Third Circuit.

Alito's conservative politics and jurisprudence were public information. He was the only Third Circuit judge on the abortion case panel who thought women should have to tell their husbands about their plans to abort. But Supreme Court confirmation hearings are, in the modern era, mostly political theater. Soft-spoken "Sam" Alito, with the humble life story and emotional wife who cried in the hearing room when she thought he was getting a raw deal, came across as Jimmy Stewart. He was confirmed 58 to 42. In January 2006, Sandra Day O'Connor stepped away from the closing doors.

LEFT BEHIND

By the time the 2003 federal "partial birth abortion" law reached the Supreme Court in 2007 in *Gonzales v. Carhart*, it no longer mattered what retired Justice Sandra Day O'Connor thought was burdensome. Although the law was drafted to avoid impinging on procedures used before viability, it contained no exception for protecting women's health and was otherwise indistinguishable from the Nebraska law the Court had struck down in 2000. But Sandra Day O'Connor had been replaced by Samuel Alito, and the four conservatives became a majority of five. The "partial birth abortion" law would now stand.

Dissenting, Justice Ginsburg made no bones about the real political explanation for the decision: "Though today's opinion does not go so far as to discard *Roe* or *Casey*, the Court, *differently composed than it was when we last considered a restrictive abortion regulation,* is hardly faithful to our earlier invocations of 'the rule of law' and the 'principles of *stare decisis.*'"

Ginsburg, dissenting, points up the core problem with the case. As bad as it was for the few women affected (most abortions are in the early months), the loss was the Court's symbolic framing of women's status. Since 1971, Justice Ginsburg's real enterprise had been not just the achievement of formal legal equality, but the re-construction of what it meant to be an authentic and honorable female person. Having the Court recognize women's equal legal rights was a huge achievement, but legal rights were a means to a larger cultural and moral goal. The change in women's prospects also explains some of the impact O'Connor had simply by being such an effective and respected female justice despite her decidedly lukewarm pronouncements on the subject of abortion.

Just shy of forty years after Ginsburg's first victory, Justice Kennedy put Ginsburg's and O'Connor's female beneficiaries in their place. Whether they be administrators of estates, air force officers, grade school teachers, bank tellers, management consultants, law firm partners, or military school cadets, in Kennedy's mind all women's roles pale beside their role as mothers. Indeed, all of human behavior is but the inadequate expression of "[r]espect for human life," which, he opined, "finds an ultimate expression in the bond of love the mother has for her child." There is no evidence for Justice Kennedy's concept of how women should feel about their role in the expression of respect for human life, but he believes it nonetheless: "Whether to have an abortion requires a difficult and painful moral decision. . . . While we find no reliable data to measure the phenomenon, it seems unexceptionable to conclude some women come to regret their choice to abort the infant life they once created and sustained."

Ginsburg was irate: "This way of thinking reflects ancient notions about women's place in the family and under the Constitution—ideas that have long since been discredited." She unloaded the biggest guns she had, citing the *Dred Scott* of the women's movement, *Bradwell v. State*, which allowed the government to bar women from practicing law in 1873: "Man is, or should be," she recites from the old case, "woman's protector and defender. The natural and proper timidity and delicacy which belongs to the female sex evidently unfits it for many of the occupations of civil life. . . . The paramount destiny and mission of woman are to fulfill the noble and benign offices of wife and mother." Compare that, Ginsburg says, with our landmark decision in the VMI case: The State may not rely on "overbroad generalizations" about the "talents, capacities, or preferences" of women; "[s]uch judgments have . . . impeded . . . women's progress toward full citizenship stature throughout our Nation's history." Such judicial pronouncements about women's place were, she concludes, "long since discredited."

Worse, under Kennedy's formulation, even if no one can prove that women regret breaking their life-defining bond, Congress gets to decide that they do: "The Act recognizes this reality," Kennedy opines. But Ginsburg thinks women ought to make up their own minds about the reality of . . . their own minds. "Though today's majority may regard women's feelings on the matter as 'self-evident' . . . this Court has repeatedly confirmed that '[t]he destiny of the woman must be shaped . . . on her own conception of her spiritual imperatives and her place in society.'"

What a difference one retirement makes. "The word I would use to describe my position on the bench is 'lonely,'" Ginsburg, seventy-three, said in an interview a year after O'Connor left. "This is how it was for Sandra's first twelve years. Neither of us ever thought this would happen again."

Now that their time together was over, the remaining female justice summed up the sisterhood perfectly. The men might have seen O'Connor as indistinguishable from themselves (and cherished her for that), but Ginsburg saw a world of difference between the two women and their seven male brethren. She and Justice O'Connor "have very different backgrounds," she admitted. "We divide on a lot of important questions, but we have had the experience of growing up women and we have certain sensitivities that our male colleagues lack."

"I didn't realize how much I would miss her until she was gone."

Part V

Absolute Legacy

Sandra Day O'Connor and Ruth Bader Ginsburg
at the U.S. Capitol, March 28, 2001.

18

The Great Dissenter

Ginsburg's clerks did not see her as a lonely outlier in the years immediately following O'Connor's departure. They saw her as a living legend. Cozily ensconced with her "family" of four law clerks, two secretaries, and a messenger, Ginsburg's chambers busily, as one clerk described it, "drank champagne from a fire hydrant" as they addressed a stream of cases of the highest order of interest and significance. Pausing only to celebrate every single birthday of anyone in the family with a wonderful cake from master chef Martin Ginsburg and presents for all, the young lawyers finished their year of service with a dramatic presentation parodying their august employers.

But Ginsburg, the "Thurgood Marshall of the woman's movement," found herself in the position not of Thurgood Marshall but of John Marshall Harlan, Oliver Wendell Holmes, Jr., and Louis D. Brandeis, the Supreme Court's "great dissenters." In disagreeing with their colleagues at the time they served among them, these legendary jurists anticipated every core development of twentieth-century constitutional law: the dismantling of Jim Crow segregation, the protection of free speech, and the allowance of economic regulation. The renowned Supreme Court decision in *Brown v. Board of Education* effectively adopted Justice Harlan's scathing dissent from *Plessy v. Ferguson*, the decision upholding segregation in 1896. (Years before she became the dissenter in chief, Ginsburg had sponsored a book about Harlan's wife, Malvina, who encouraged him to resist the other justices' shameful concession to the Jim Crow south.)

Dissenting was not her role of choice: she would have preferred to be writing the opinion for the winning majority. When she won—or others, after her, won cases that invoked Stephen Wiesenfeld's long-ago case—she would write a crowing letter to her favorite client. From *Reed v. Reed* in 1971 to *U.S. v. Virginia* twenty-five years later—"woo hoo," as she gleefully put it to Wiesenfeld—Ginsburg loved a victory.

FROM WOO HOO TO BOO HOO

Her long string of victories was not to last. A year after O'Connor left, Ginsburg uncharacteristically read two dissents from the bench in one term. Justices dissent all the time, but they rarely read the opinions aloud. As Ginsburg puts it, "It signals that, in the dissenters' view, the Court's opinion is not just wrong, but grievously misguided." Prior to 2006, Ginsburg had read a dissent only once every couple of years. When a member of the Court takes advantage of the chance to speak their disagreement out loud, they are choosing to draw the whole country's eyes to the seriousness of the Court's decision.

Such a delivery is treated as an act of legal performance art. For years, the Court has made and released audio recordings of its public deliberations, including Ginsburg's dramatically worded dissents. In addition, at least since Bob Woodward's blockbuster tell-all book *The Brethren*, the Court has been the subject of intense scrutiny by the media. Dozens of reporters have the high court as their regular beat. When the tiny justice clears her throat and unfolds a sheaf of papers on announcement day, reporters on the Supreme Court beat sit up. It would be a good story.

DISSENTING TO CONGRESS

Both of Ginsburg's performed dissents in 2007 came in cases involving grievous losses to the rights of women. One was *Gonzales*, Justice Kennedy's decision for five upholding the restraints on abortion. The other was *Lilly Ledbetter v. Goodyear Tire and*

Rubber, cutting off a sex-discrimination claim because the woman didn't sue fast enough.

Lilly Ledbetter had been discriminated against in the 1970s; afterward many discriminatory performance evaluations kept pushing her pay down. Starting from such a low base, every successive paycheck until the day she retired was lower than it would have been if she had been fairly treated in the early years. In 1998 she finally sued. Sorry, said the Court, Goodyear didn't evaluate you unfairly within six months of the time you sued, and that's the limitations period under the Civil Rights Act. That your lower paychecks rested on the past discrimination does you no good.

Not only did Ginsburg read her dissent aloud, she used the moment to point squarely at her new colleague, opening with the phrase "Justice Alito announced." By contrast, her written dissent starts in the much more conventional fashion with the facts of the case: "Lilly Ledbetter was a supervisor at Goodyear Tire and Rubber's plant in Gadsden, Alabama." Being now the only one on the Court with the experience of growing up being a woman, she felt obliged to speak her truth: "Pay disparities often occur, as they did in Ledbetter's case, in small increments; only over time is there strong cause to suspect that discrimination is at work," she wrote. And, Ginsburg continued, "An employee like Ledbetter, trying to succeed in a male-dominated workplace, in a job filled only by men before she was hired, understandably may be anxious to avoid making waves."

Justice Ginsburg had a very different audience than Samuel Alito in mind. The old movement activist looked at Lilly Ledbetter—silver-haired Alabama wife and mother, only female supervisor at her southern rubber plant, and victim of decades of discrimination—and she saw an irresistible political opportunity. Ginsburg aimed her dissent directly at Congress: "This is not the first time the Court has ordered a cramped interpretation of Title VII, incompatible with the statute's broad remedial purpose," she wrote. "Once again, the ball is in Congress's court. As in 1991, the Legislature may act to correct this Court's parsimonious reading of Title VII." A year later in 2008, Lilly Ledbetter addressed the

Democratic National Convention, asking for a change in the law for the benefit of other women and minorities to come. Each lower paycheck should violate the Civil Rights Act anew. On January 29, 2009, President Obama signed his first bill, the Lilly Ledbetter Fair Pay Act, into law.

HER COLLEAGUES JUST DON'T GET IT

But it was lonely. Reporters at oral argument that spring in *Safford School District v. Redding* noticed a distinct waspishness in the solitary female's questioning. Ginsburg's attention was powerfully drawn to the plaintiff in that case, thirteen-year-old honor student Savanna Redding. Redding was in court because, when talk of illicit ibuprofen use came to the attention of the school authorities, they ordered her to take off her clothes and pull the pants and bra away from her body and shake out any errant painkillers. Finding nothing, the principal sat her in the hall outside his office for hours until she finally was allowed to call her mother. The mother, predictably, sued. The case made its way to the Supreme Court on the issue of whether the school acted unreasonably in searching Savanna Redding in this fashion.

The oral argument was inexplicably merry to Ginsburg's way of thinking. While the ever-boyish Justice Breyer relished a walk down memory lane to happy naked days in the locker room, and the justices had good fun about what he kept in his underwear, Ginsburg angrily tried to get her brethren to understand how a young girl would react to being told to pull out her panties and shake. "It wasn't just that they were stripped to their underwear!" she interrupted. "They were asked to shake their bra out, to stretch the top of their pants and shake that out!" After the argument, she took the unusual step of giving an interview to *USA Today* complaining that her colleagues didn't get what such a demand would mean to a sensitive thirteen-year-old.

After all their insensitive shenanigans, the Court *did* rule 8–1 that the search was unconstitutional (although they ultimately found the school administrators to be immune from suit because the law had not been clear). And that summer Ginsburg got a nice surprise. Although she must have been sad to see Justice Souter— whom she had liked and called her "date" when he accompanied her to Court functions—step down, President Obama selected another woman to replace him. When Judge Sonia Sotomayor of the Second Circuit was confirmed in August 2009, Ginsburg was no longer alone. "It is good," she wrote to Wiesenfeld a few months later, "to have her company."

LOVE LOST, WORK LEFT

Even with her victories in Congress and in the Redding case, 2009 was a tough year. A month after Obama signed the Ledbetter Act, a routine CT scan seemed to indicate cancer in her pancreas. On February 5, 2009, the Court announced, she was in surgery. Although the surgery did turn up a tiny malignancy, the doctors pronounced themselves satisfied with her prospects in this most deadly cancer, caught early and by chance. Thirteen days later, she wrote to Wiesenfeld to assure him she was "mending steadily" and that she was planning to be back at the Court for its next sitting, February 23. And so it was that she was there for Savanna Redding that spring when her male colleagues were having so much fun with the brassiere-and-panties discussion.

As 2009 drew to a close, though, there was another crisis. This time Marty was having "health problems." Some problems: he had a tumor at the base of his spine and was in pain, or as the legendarily understated jurist put it, "considerable discomfort." As of March of the new year, they were still hoping. Marty saw a pain doctor for his "discomfort," and their daughter, Jane, came for a visit to raise his spirits. On June 27, 2010, just after their fifty-sixth wedding anniversary, he died.

Twenty-four hours later, Ginsburg was on the bench. She was okay, she believed, thanks to "the good job Marty helped" her get. "I had a life partner who thought my work was as important as his," she described their relationship, "and I think that made all the difference for me." The year he died, she listed their assets on the required forms as ranging up to $45 million, surely enough for some modest shoe shopping. He even occasionally went shopping with her. And he made sure that the shoes they bought sometimes touched the ground, teasing her mercilessly for her legendary eccentricities and calling her "Her Royal Highness." At one of the dinner parties they held every year for the clerks, he took on her poky eating habits and demanded that they "let these kids go home. If they wait for you to finish eating your dinner," Marty told the justice, "they will be here all night!"

Indeed, he had always been her not-so-secret weapon. From 1976 until the day she was appointed to the Supreme Court in 1993, movers and shakers in every Democratic administration received an unending stream of letters about her virtues, and visits from Marty, his law partners, and his many devoted friends, to promote her career. He moved to Washington the minute she got her first judgeship.

Even Ginsburg's former Columbia colleague Professor Henry Monaghan, a curmudgeonly dead ringer for the fictional Professor Kingsfield from *The Paper Chase*, melted in the warmth of the Ginsburgs' bond. "Talk about a love affair," he remembers of a dinner with the couple in Paris. "It was so clear they had a certain routine, it was a very moving experience. In their gestures, you just got a feeling, you could just see it, it's like the ballet is music made visible as if you were brought into another dimension!"

GIRLS DON'T RULE

The summer after Marty died, Ginsburg's old friend the former dean of Harvard Law School, Solicitor General Elena Kagan, joined the Court in another history-making development: three of the nine justices were now women. "No one," Kagan later reported, ever mixed her up with either her senior colleague or her immediate predecessor, Sonia Sotomayor. Justice Ginsburg pronounced herself officially thrilled.

After Sotomayor and Kagan, liberal commentators began

making noises about Ginsburg—and her younger liberal colleague, Stephen Breyer—retiring to make room for more good, young Obama appointees. Ginsburg was not pleased, making her signature move to push back by granting a series of interviews with reporters emphasizing how mentally and physically fit she was. The only standard must be, she told journalist Joan Biskupic: "Am I equipped to do the job?"

Regardless of her fitness, the calls for her to step down reflected that, as Justice Brennan put it a half century before, even with a bench full of women, size matters. Specifically the number five. Ginsburg had to know that. With O'Connor gone, the decision almost always came down to one guy: Justice Anthony Kennedy. In the 2010 and 2011 terms, which ended in June 2012, he agreed with the liberals in nine and with the conservatives in ten close cases. In the last two terms—2012 and 2013, ending June 2014—he was more often on the conservative side.

Every time Kennedy swung the Court to a conservative outcome, Ginsburg disagreed. With Stevens gone, she had inherited the power to assign the dissent. On most of the cases—and on the cases Ginsburg chose to emphasize during those terms—her two female colleagues and Stephen Breyer were all in agreement. She knew exactly how powerful a dissent could be. No surprise, then, that she kept many of the most important ones for herself.

SPEAKING TRUTH ABOUT POWER

On June 27, 2011, she told the public two stories: one about a man exonerated mere weeks from the electric chair, and one about the man whose fingers were cut off by a malfunctioning scrap metal machine. The two dissents are a graphic reminder that Justice Ginsburg is not just an advocate for women; her judicial philosophy is rooted in a commitment to equal access to justice that goes all the way back to her years at Cornell with her mentor Robert Cushman.

Neither of her 2011 spoken dissents involved her usual focus on equality of sex or even, overtly, race. Indeed, she is often criticized by progressives for her narrow and reluctant extension of rights against police misconduct. Lawyer's lawyer that she was, however, when it came to unequal access to justice, it was the court system that attracted her most passionate concern.

In the first story, the government had actually planned to kill the plaintiff. In May 1985, Louisiana convicted New Orleans resident John Thompson of murder. He did not testify on his own behalf, because, a few weeks earlier, he had been tried and convicted of armed robbery, and if he testified, the jury would learn about the prior conviction. Unknown to him, he actually had had a good defense to the robbery charge, because the state had found a garment from the robbery victim that was stained with the blood of the robber, type B. Although prosecutors have a constitutional obligation to disclose to a criminal defendant evidence that might clear him if they find it, the team of prosecutors said nothing, so Thompson never had his blood tested. Instead, right before Thompson's trial, one of the prosecutors removed the fabric from the lab and never returned it. Years later, the absconding lawyer, facing terminal cancer, confessed to one of his colleagues, another ex-prosecutor, about hiding the evidence that would have exonerated Thompson.

Afraid to testify in his murder trial, Thompson was convicted of murder. Despite Thompson's pending execution, the second prosecutor also remained silent about the blood test. As Thompson was facing certain death, a private investigator employed by his pro bono lawyer discovered the lab report. Thompson was tested and turned out to be Type O. The state vacated the robbery conviction. Thirty minutes after a new trial, Thompson was also acquitted of the murder.

The lawyer who framed Thompson being dead by then, Thompson sued the prosecutor's office for violating his civil rights by failing to train its people to follow the constitutional mandate to share exculpatory evidence with the defense. In an opinion by Justice Thomas, the five conservatives on the Supreme Court ruled that the prosecutor was not liable for damages to the man his office almost killed. After all, it was only one violation. You could not sue a whole prosecutor's office for the act of one "rogue" attorney, the Court said.

Ginsburg dissented, in a stunning condemnation drawn largely from the uncontested record of the civil rights trial. The New Orleans prosecutor acknowledged that he did not understand what the Constitution required, she reported. His training manual misrepresented the duty to disclose, he had no idea whether his green assistant prosecutors understood either, and he certainly hadn't studied anything since he was elected a decade before this case. Anyway, he testified, compliance would make his job so much harder. And now the Court was going to let him get away with it. So powerful was her attack on Thomas's opinion that Justice Scalia, in the majority, felt compelled to file a separate concurring opinion to try to rebut it. The media went wild: "not possible for the Court to sink any lower"; "Justice Thomas's meanest opinion."

In the second case, Ginsburg opened the substance of her dissent in good storytelling fashion: "On October 11, 2001, a three-ton metal shearing machine severed four fingers on Robert Nicastro's right hand." The case hinged on whether New Jersey, where the accident took place, had sufficient ties to the manufacturer of the machine, based in Great Britain, to allow Nicastro to sue in the state. In its opinion, the Court's five conservatives, joined by the normally liberal Justice Breyer, said no. The question of when a sovereign state has jurisdiction to haul a foreign company into court has been a—perhaps the—staple of law school procedure classes for over a hundred years. Ginsburg, herself a former procedure teacher, and a well-respected scholar in the area, doubtless took an outsized interest in the case.

But the decision to read the two dissents in court demonstrates Ginsburg's deepest commitments. Both men were harmed, terribly and irreparably, by large forces well beyond their control. In both cases, Ginsburg's dissents direct her audience's attention to the lack of equality between the plaintiff and the large social institutions. John Thompson, an African American accused of a capital crime by the prosecutors of Orleans Parish, and Robert Nicastro, a worker in the perilous fields of scrap metal cutting plants in New Jersey, had only the law to make them whole when the blunt forces of these institutions bore down on them. When Ginsburg spoke her dissents aloud in her soft, unemotional voice in 2011, she was calling the conservative majority on its decision to give the powerful a pass. The two landmark dissents of the 2011 term gave the world a glimpse of the fundamental liberalism of Ginsburg's thought. Her vision of equal access to justice extended well beyond the cases that had made her famous.

RACE AND SEX

By 2011, her first year of widowhood was coming to an end. Her "good job" had gotten her through the hard first year. But even that year was not without its consolations. She was standing on the podium receiving an honorary degree from Harvard in the spring, when her fellow honoree Placido Domingo turned to her and burst into song: the greatest living tenor serenading her with a rendition of the Verdi aria "Celeste Aida." "One of life's great moments," she said. Although she did not lecture abroad as she normally did in the summer, she did go, as usual, to the opera festival at Glimmerglass in Cooperstown, New York, and to Santa Fe with her family. Autumn found her celebrating her daughter and son-in-law's thirtieth anniversary in New York. She also had the gratification of seeing the tribute cookbook to Marty, *Chef Supreme*, published by the Supreme Court Historical Society.

But mostly she was working harder than ever, and mostly fighting a rearguard action for women.

Unlike the "partial birth abortion" and sexual-harassment cases from a few years before, none of the battles were new. With its new majority now in place, the Court was just returning to recent disputes and rolling back the feminist legal revolution. In March 2012, Justice Kennedy, armed with a new conservative Court, took another swipe at the Family and Medical Leave Act, which had survived his negative vote in *Nevada v. Hibbs* a mere nine years before. The 2012 case, *Coleman v. Court of Appeals of Maryland*, looks to the layperson exactly like the earlier case. The only difference between them was that Hibbs needed leave to care for his family, while Coleman needed leave because he was sick himself. Like Nevada had in the Hibbs case, Maryland said no. This time Kennedy and the four other conservatives ruled for the state. Ginsburg read her dissent aloud. As Ginsburg pointed out, the entire law—maternity leave, family leave, self-care sick leave—was enacted in an effort to neutralize all caregiving away from the assumption that it was always the women who did the caring. Where women were stereotyped as caregivers, even for their own care when pregnant, they were routinely undervalued as workers. The Constitution prohibits sex discrimination and the Leave Act enforces that prohibition. Therefore, when the state violates the federal law, people should be able to sue the state.

Scariest of all to Ginsburg was Kennedy's willful refusal to recognize the impact of social programs such as health leave on women's equality at work and thus on the equality mandated by the Fourteenth Amendment. Getting the Court to treat sex discrimination as a serious violation of the Fourteenth Amendment had been Ginsburg's life work. Kennedy didn't go as far as Scalia, who concurred specially to remind the reader that he never thought the Fourteenth Amendment treated sex like race. Scalia's position would have led the Court to invalidate the act altogether. Kennedy's opinion, however, was just a kinder, gentler version of Scalia's call to undo women's legal equality under the Constitution.

Coleman was also a warning that conservatives on the Court were affirmatively going to go after *progressive* legislation such as the Leave Act, help that women had achieved when there was a Democratic Congress and a sympathetic president. Scholars and Court watchers were starting to talk about a return to the days when the Court invoked the Constitution and struck down the laws that created Franklin Roosevelt's New Deal.

DISSENTING WOMAN

A year later, as the Court entered the always fraught last week of the term, the reliably collegial Justice Ginsburg actually broke a record for oral disagreement in one day. All three of the opinions delivered on Dissenting Monday, June 24, 2013, were about equal rights. Two of the cases made it vastly harder for women and minorities to use the Civil Rights Act to make the workplace more inclusive. The third made it harder for well-meaning institutions such as the University of Texas to take affirmative action to become more inclusive, particularly of race.

The two employment-discrimination cases were obvious targets for Ginsburg's ire. In one, *Vance v. Ball State*, the Court read the Civil Rights Act to cut back heavily on who could be considered a supervisor at work. Since supervisors can make the employing company liable for their sexist acts, the effect of the decision was to make it harder for wronged employees to reach the deep pockets of the employer. Being less exposed, companies had less reason to guard against, say, having their employees invite female subordinates to fish coins from their pants.

The second dissent, *University of Texas Southwestern Hospital v. Nassar*, was a response to an exceptionally bold move by Justice Kennedy to reverse another of his defeats at the hands of Justice O'Connor a mere nine years before. The hospital, Dr. Nassar charged, fired him because he had complained about discrimination. With a bare majority, O'Connor had ruled in the girls' basketball coach case, *Jackson v. Birmingham Board of Education*, that retaliation against someone who complained of discrimination was itself an illegal act of discrimination. Kennedy had dissented in that earlier case. The obvious route to toss Nassar's claims would have been for Kennedy to use his majority to overrule *Jackson v. Birmingham* with no better explanation than a change of court personnel. Rather than indulge in such an obvious political move, he achieved the same end by holding that, while retaliation might constitute discrimination, the *standard* for proving retaliation would be much harder than the standard for proving straight discrimination. The hospital had offered another reason for canning Nassar, which made his a mixed-motive case. Even if the employer is trying to punish a complainer, Justice Kennedy said, if it can come up with any other reason to fire the guy, the employer gets off.

Kennedy's opinion is particularly egregious. Twenty years before the *Nassar* case, O'Connor had suggested a very modest shift in the standard for a plaintiff in a mixed-motive case, Ann Hopkins's suit against Price Waterhouse. Kennedy dissented in *Price Waterhouse*; even O'Connor's modest change in the law to favor the female plaintiff was too generous for him. But thereafter, in response to the tightfistedness of her opinion, Congress changed the Civil Rights Act to adopt a superliberal standard for discrimination cases where the employer had mixed motives. So when the conference met to decide *Nassar*, in 2013, the law was that 1) retaliation was just like discrimination and 2) an employee wins if he proves that discrimination was a motivating factor, even if the employer had other reasons too. Nonetheless, in *Nassar*, five justices voted that in a retaliation case, any other good reason for firing the complaining employee would exonerate the employer. After all, Kennedy reasoned, retaliation was the subject of a different *section* of the Civil Rights Act than the one Congress had changed to make it easier on plaintiffs.

Ginsburg was not polite. In her dissent she repeatedly reminded Kennedy that he was the *dissenter* in *Price Waterhouse*, the mixed-motive case, in 1989. Again, without overtly overruling the two decisions where he had lost the earlier battle, he made the law as hostile as possible to civil rights plaintiffs.

The same day, the Court issued its 7–1 decision in *Fisher v. University of Texas*, the latest racial affirmative action case. (Only eight justices sat, because Kagan had been disqualified from participating by her earlier involvement while solicitor general.) Although racial affirmative action had long been subject to the hardest constitutional standard—strict scrutiny—O'Connor's fifth vote had saved it in 2005. Her majority opinion held that the University of Michigan's consideration of race served a compelling state interest in diversity and did not "unduly harm" nonminority applicants. Now that she was gone, Court watchers had speculated that the conservatives were going to forbid consideration of race—a common practice at almost all institutions of higher learning—altogether. Instead the justices sent the University of Texas program for giving some weight to racial diversity back to the lower court to review for themselves whether the consideration of race in Texas's plan was small enough to meet the high standard of strict scrutiny. The decision was so unprincipled and so unexpected that commentators speculated either Justice Kennedy or Chief Justice Roberts had gotten "cold feet" about saying that the Civil War amendments actually prohibited helping African Americans.

Despite the narrow escape, Ginsburg had had it. When, in 2013, her fellow liberals breathed an audible sigh of relief that the Court did not, once and for all, rule that affirmative action was unconstitutional per se, she was the only dissenter. The lopsided vote may have given her license. Had the Court split 4–4 in *Fisher*, she would have disciplined herself to save something of affirmative action. But, protected by the majority vote of seven to remand the case, she was free to speak to the ages, reading her dissent from the bench.

She was particularly exercised about the pretense that the lower courts should ensure that schools did not put too much weight on race in their efforts to achieve a racially diverse student body. The Court's opinion—and, indeed, the jurisprudence around affirmative action going back decades—is ridiculous, Ginsburg wrote. You cannot have programs aimed at racial diversity that are not about race. Affirmative action remedies are racially motivated. Anything else anyone says is a lie: "I have said before and reiterate here that only an ostrich could regard the supposedly neutral alternatives as race unconscious. As Justice Souter observed [in the earlier affirmative action case *Gratz v. Bollinger*], the vaunted alternatives suffer from 'the disadvantage of deliberate obfuscation.' As I said in my dissent to the last round of this nonsense, 'If universities cannot explicitly include race as a factor, many may "resort to camouflage" to "maintain their minority enrollment."'"

Pretending to believe lies, Ginsburg says, is the shame of the legal profession: "Or as a legendary critic of lawyers put it, 'If you think that you can think about a thing inextricably attached to something else without thinking of the thing which it is attached to, then you have a legal mind . . .' Only that kind of legal mind could conclude that an admissions plan specifically designed to produce racial diversity is not race conscious."

As she had said repeatedly (were they never going to learn?), there is no need to obfuscate, because affirmative action is not unconstitutional: "I have several times explained why government actors, including state universities, need not be blind to the lingering effects of 'an overtly discriminatory past,' the legacy of 'centuries of law-sanctioned inequality.'"

There is a certain irony in Justice Ginsburg being the speaker for the constitutionality of affirmative action. On a superficial level, laws that helped women, such as bigger Social Security benefits, which she had challenged in the '70s, might also be framed as affirmative action. The difference was that the laws she challenged in her litigation years, such as excusing women from jury service, often concealed their repressive effect with a seductive guise of beneficence. As she always said, it took some hard looking to distinguish the cage of being stereotyped as dependent from the gilt of more benefits.

By contrast, she early recognized that affirmative action had a proper place in realizing the equality principle, not "to confer favors" but to "ensure that women with the capacity to do the job are set on a par with men of a similar capacity." Above all, she was clear that unlike the protective laws for women, programs that looked like they benefited black people, such as giving them extra consideration in college admissions, usually actually benefited them rather than being designed to keep them in a place created by rabid historical injustice. The legacy of history was always prominent in Ginsburg's analysis.

The vote for obfuscation, professional misbehavior, and constitutional error in *Fisher* was 7–1. But she was not talking to her brethren. She was talking to the future.

The next day she got up and did it again.   •

On Tuesday, June 25, Chief Justice Roberts announced that the section of the Voting Rights Act of 1965 requiring states such as Alabama to check with the Justice Department when tinkering with their election laws—a process called "preclearance"—was unconstitutional. After all, look at how many African Americans are voting in Alabama now, he crowed. Surely it was no longer rational—and therefore unconstitutional—for Congress to refuse to release those southern states long targeted by the feds.

Ginsburg dissented. After a long and harrowing recitation of the endlessly resourceful campaigns to keep black people from voting, the most recent example being from Alabama in 2010, she concluded: "Throwing out preclearance when it has worked and is continuing to work to stop discriminatory changes is like throwing away your umbrella in a rainstorm because you are not getting wet."

It was June 2013. She put her dissent in a bottle and floated it to an unknown Court to come.

19

Notorious R.B.G.

✴

A second-year law student at NYU, Shana Knizhnik, thought the author of the dissent in *Shelby County v. Holder* deserved something a little more up to date than a headline in *The New York Times*. Starting with her sarcastic throwaway line during the oral argument in the gay marriage case ("there's full marriage and then there's sort of skim milk marriage?") earlier that spring, Justice Ginsburg was becoming, well, notorious, for her take-no-prisoners rhetoric on behalf of the marginalized and excluded. Sort of like the late rap singer Christopher George LaTore Wallace, a tall, heavy guy who performed under the name of Notorious B.I.G. Like RBG, B.I.G., too, was born in Brooklyn and was an outstanding student before he became Notorious.

Knizhnik had seen the Web phenomenon *Texts from Hillary* transform the sixty-something diplomat with the pastel pantsuits into a shades-and-smart-phone boss lady with thousands of followers. The day Ginsburg delivered her dissent in *Holder*, Knizhnik opened a page on the Internet blogging site Tumblr: *Notorious R.B.G.*

Her first post was the umbrella line from the dissent in *Holder*. But of course, once she got going the hits just kept on coming: ostriches from the dissent in *Fisher v. University of Texas*; her colleagues' self-fulfilling prophecy that re-counts wouldn't work from the dissent in *Bush v. Gore*; the YouTube video from Ginsburg's appearance with Diane Sawyer, where she suggested that nine would be a nice number for female justices. Before the day was out the first T-shirt appeared, a conventional image of the justice

in her robe with the frilly collar. Twenty-four hours later, a Notorious T. Then a picture of her with the BIG crown and sparkly
stars. The day after that, *New York* magazine's "The Cut" reported
that Ginsburg had joined Beyoncé and Hillary as an Internet phenom. Before a week was out, the trend spotter BuzzFeed was on
it: "19 Reasons Ruth Bader Ginsburg Is Your Favorite Supreme
Court Justice—R.B.G. is a complete and total boss. Plain and simple." Bluewater Comics published a Ginsburg volume in its comic
book series *Female Force.*

And so the year went by. There was an entry for every holiday.
The annual Halloween contest in the gossipy website *Above the
Law* displayed R Baby Ginsburg in its crib with a white lace collar
around a black robe, a tiny pair of round glasses, and a gavel where
the rattle would normally be.

And Christmas witnessed the birth of Ruth Slayder Ginsburg,
superhero with a judicial robe cape and a white jabot. You violated
the Fifth Amendment, the RBG Valentine proclaimed in February, when you took my heart without due process.

Justice Ginsburg knew right away that she was Notorious. Her
clerk Josh Johnson's wife saw the Tumblr page as soon as it went
up and the clerks took it to the justice. Once her law clerks explained who Notorious had been, she was all over it.

When an old Ginsburg friend, Janet Benshoof, heard about it
over at the women's rights organization Global Justice Center, she
told her interns they should make a rap video, and she would send
it to the justice. They decided to use Notorious B.I.G.'s insurgent
song "Juicy" as their model. The brainy girls Kelly Cosby and Elizabeth Gavin set about learning everything they could about the
justice, including some fairly obscure stuff such as her encounter
with Dean Erwin Griswold and her wardrobe of symbolic collars.
Gavin had a friend who did sound recording and knew a guy who
actually made and edited music videos. The kids closed the Global
Justice Center for a day, and everyone pitched in.

Where Notorious B.I.G. had dedicated his work "to all the
teachers that told me I'd never amount to nothin'," "RBGuicy,"
performed by two tea-sipping brunettes, Kelly Cosby and Beth

Gavin, in RBG T-shirts, sunglasses, and jeweled collars, is dedicated

> to all the judges that told me I'd never amount to nothin'
> because of my gender, to all the people that lived in their
> ivory towers that I was hustlin' in front of,
> that tried to buy me off by putting Susan B. Anthony on
>   the dollar,
> and all the women in the struggle, you know what I'm
>   sayin'?

Ginsburg loved the attention. In the reception area for the New
York City Bar Association's annual Ruth Bader Ginsburg Distinguished Lecture on Women and the Law, where she was going to
introduce the speaker, Justice Kagan, the rap song was playing on
a giant video screen. Ginsburg admitted to Janet Benshoof that she
watches it when she's feeling down.

NO TRUTH WITHOUT RUTH

Many justices dissented. But Justice Ginsburg was the only dissenter in history who had a rap song. The RBGuicy raps, "Now
I'm in the limelight cuz I decide right." The law students who
turned her into a cultural icon were not just enamored of her lace
gloves. They put her in the limelight, as the rap song went, cuz
they thought she decided right. At a moment when the Court was
firmly in the grip of a conservative majority, the eruption of support for the tiny old rich grandmother with the radical principles
was a political act, even though in 2013 she was losing on almost
every issue she cared about.

Changing the culture on subjects such as affirmative action, defendants' rights, and employment discrimination is an agonizingly
long process. That process depends in turn on the election of a
president and a Senate inclined to seek appointments of a different
mind-set. Before that can happen, the minds of people likely to
seek office and the voters who elect them must change. But it's no

wonder that sixty years elapsed after Justice Harlan warned his brethren that separate could never be equal before the Court ordered desegregation in 1954.

Dissents are the seeds of that process. The dissent is made for the Internet: it is inherently confrontational. Armed with life tenure and disinclined by nature to try to patch together a centrist compromise, Justice Ginsburg repeatedly produced radically confrontational rhetoric directed at her retrograde male colleagues. Listening to her flay them with her logic made the viewer feel genuinely empowered. In the demographics of the Supreme Court even the visuals—the three women and their male ally, Justice Breyer, on one side and five male conservatives on the other—work perfectly.

In any story of power in the twenty-first century, the power of the Internet to make social change is the wild card. The creator of the Notorious R.B.G. phenomenon is gay as well as liberal. (The individuals behind *Texts from Hillary* are also gay.) And no social movement in America has made better use of social media than the gay revolution. Ruth Bader Ginsburg's emergence as a cultural icon actually started in the spring of 2013 with her indignant interrogation of the lawyer for the Republican Congress defending the antigay Defense of Marriage Act about real marriage and skim milk marriage. That summer she became the first Supreme Court justice to perform a same-sex marriage ceremony. And she was well aware of the message her decision conveyed. "She wasn't saying there was a constitutional right to marriage," her clerk Josh Johnson says. "Washington, D.C., had already made that decision. They were entitled to be married. But she was clear on how her actions would play in the public realm."

THE DISSENT AS ARIA

A year after she went viral on the Web, Ginsburg issued her most potent dissent, disagreeing with the stunningly antiwoman decision allowing employers to exclude birth control from their health insurance, *Burwell v. Hobby Lobby*. Ginsburg's dissent in *Hobby*

Lobby is a veritable "Se vuol ballare," the incendiary aria that Mozart penned for the upstart servant Figaro in his opera *The Marriage of Figaro* just before the French Revolution. Like Figaro, Ginsburg reminds the men in power, the majority, that they may now hold the power, but, as Figaro says, in time: "If you want to dance, my dear little Count, / It is I who will call the tune, / If you'll come to my school, / I'll teach you how to caper!"

The majority had ruled that the billion-dollar Hobby Lobby craft store chain did not have to cover contraception for its female employees under the federal health-care law. Some contraception, such as the widely used IUD, struck the owners as somewhat like an early abortion and thus violated their sincerely held religious beliefs. Despite its grounding in disputes about religious freedom, *Hobby Lobby* was not a First Amendment case. Rather, the Court held, it was applying the Religious Freedom Restoration Act, a 1993 federal law, which mandates that "government shall not substantially burden a person's exercise of religion even if the burden results from a rule of general applicability." To exempt Hobby Lobby from the health-care law, the Court had to take some pretty bold steps. First, it found that profit-making corporations, just like real human beings, could be "persons" who had religion. Then it found that although women's health, including their contraceptive needs, might be a serious-enough matter to warrant restricting religion, the United States had not shown that the health-care law was the least restrictive means to protect that interest. Maybe the insurance companies Hobby Lobby used could just pay for the women's IUDs, Justice Alito suggested. Or the government itself, if it was so interested in women. Maybe in the form of a tax credit. Some of these oblique approaches were already being used by churches, which had gotten an opt out.

Ginsburg dissented. The Hobby Lobby owners' sincerely held religious beliefs were too attenuated from the use of contraception to be harmed by the health-care law's requirements. After all, "the decisions whether to claim benefits under the plans are made not by Hobby Lobby . . . but by the covered employees. . . . Should an employee . . . share the religious beliefs of the [owners], she is of course under no compulsion to use the contraceptives in question." Even if the Hobby Lobby folks were properly upset, she continues, there is no viable less restrictive scheme. Hobby Lobby and the other health-care resisters refused to concede that they'd be satisfied with letting their insurers cover the dreaded birth control methods indirectly, the deal Congress gave to churches. Resistance to that accommodation for the churches was, at the time, already making its way to the Supreme Court. With nothing left but letting the government pay for Hobby Lobby's belief system, she concludes, the health-care law was not set up to dump the uninsured employees of religious hobby store chains onto the public fisc. It's cumbersome, expensive, and not fair to other employers.

But none of this was the real point of Ginsburg's pointed dissent. She was fighting the latest battle of her lifetime war to have women treated the same as any other social group. Although both Justice Alito, for the Court, and Kennedy, concurring, *say* they recognize women's health as a compelling government interest, in fact, Hobby Lobby carves out a special exemption from the health-care law for those who object to benefits for women. And nothing else. Ginsburg calls the majority on it in graphic terms: "Where is the stopping point to the 'let the government pay' alternative? Suppose an employer's sincerely held religious belief is offended by health coverage of vaccines, or paying the minimum wage," she asks, citing the cases where exactly those arguments were made (and rejected). Why, a religious organization even tried to use its beliefs to get out of according women equal pay for substantially similar work.

"Would the exemption," she asks, that the Court extends to "employers with religiously grounded objections to the use of certain contraceptives extend to employers with religiously grounded objections to blood transfusions (Jehovah's Witnesses); antidepressants (Scientologists); medications derived from pigs, including anesthesia, intravenous fluids, and pills coated with gelatin (certain Muslims, Jews, and Hindus); and vaccinations (Christian Scientists, among others)?"

On these issues which do not harm women exclusively, she

notes, "The Court . . . sees nothing to worry about." The Court expressly said that its "decision should not be understood to hold that an insurance-coverage mandate must necessarily fall if it conflicts with an employer's religious beliefs. Other coverage requirements, such as immunizations, may be supported by different interests (for example, the need to combat the spread of infectious diseases) and may involve different arguments about the least restrictive means of providing them." What is this, the reader can hear her saying, a one-off that allows the Court just to punish women?

Jonathan Mann, the Internet song-a-day guy, promptly turned the opera-loving feminist's great dissent into a song, uploaded it to the *Notorious* site, and broadcast it over YouTube.

GINSBURG AND KENNEDY

The long confrontation between Ginsburg and Kennedy over the emancipation of women is always on the table. In *Hobby Lobby*, the majority said it took women's health as a compelling interest. Kennedy, making the crucial fifth vote, was at pains to describe the government's compelling interest in providing insurance coverage for birth control on the grounds that "There are many medical conditions for which pregnancy is contraindicated." Ginsburg's dissent makes clear the universe of difference between Kennedy's concern for women with, for example, severe heart disease and the real reason contraception matters to women: "The ability of women to participate equally in the economic and social life of the Nation has been facilitated by their ability to control their reproductive lives," she wrote, quoting Kennedy's own opinion in *Planned Parenthood of Southeastern Pa. v. Casey*. "Congress acted on that understanding when, as part of a nationwide insurance program intended to be comprehensive, it called for coverage of preventive care responsive to women's needs."

Six weeks after the decision, in August 2014, Justice Ginsburg gave an interview to Katie Couric. She decried the inability of most of her male colleagues to understand the lives of women well enough to see the importance of contraception. She hoped they would evolve, under the benign influence of their "wives and daughters."

A few short weeks later, Ginsburg took the opportunity to reiterate her profound disagreement with Justice Kennedy on the subject of women: "What concerned me [in *Gonzales v. Carhart*, the "partial birth abortion" case] about the Court's attitude, they were looking at the woman as not really an adult individual," she told Couric. "The opinion said that the woman would live to regret her choice. That was not anything this Court should have thought or said. Adult women are able to make decisions about their own lives' course no less than men are. So, yes, I thought in *Carhart* the Court was *way* out of line. It was a new form of 'Big Brother must protect the woman against her own weakness and immature misjudgment.'" The author of the opinion in *Carhart* was none other than Justice Anthony Kennedy.

After her raft of public appearances in the summer of 2014, pundits speculated that she was trying to use public shaming on Justice Kennedy, who is notoriously conscious of his public image. And it may work.

The Internet troubadour Jonathan Mann sings it:

> Chorus: OH the Court I FEAR has ventured into a
> minefield
> Of slut-shaming geezers and religious extremism.

Ginsburg would never call them geezers, but at the end of the day, you can hear her warbling along with Mann's last line:

> Oh, but one thing's CLEAR this fight isn't over we gotta
> stand together for what we know is ri-i-ight.

What is right? In the summer of 2014, as the calls for her to step down intensified in face of the imminent Republican takeover of the Senate, she abandoned her stance of political neutrality on the subject of retirement. Even before the midterm election, she asked in her interview with *Elle* magazine, "Who do you think

President Obama could appoint at this very day, given the boundaries that we have?" she asked. "If I resign any time this year, he could not successfully appoint anyone I would like to see in the court. [The Senate Democrats] took off the filibuster for lower federal court appointments, but it remains for this court. So anybody who thinks that if I step down, Obama could appoint someone like me, they're misguided." Any Republican might have been enough for the pragmatic Sandra Day O'Connor, when she contemplated retirement on election night in 2000, but the theorist Ruth Bader Ginsburg wouldn't give up her seat even for any Democrat. She was waiting for someone just like her.

On November 4, 2014, the Republicans captured the Senate.

On November 25, 2014, Ginsburg began experiencing chest pains during her workout with her personal trainer. Doctors implanted a stent in her artery the next day; four days later, she took her customary seat on the bench for oral argument.

20

Our Heroines

⁂

And so the story of Justices Ginsburg and O'Connor comes full circle. In most versions of the story, Sandra Day O'Connor is the icon and the cultural engine of change. A WASPy country club Republican with a passion for low taxes and states' rights, she was the only kind of woman who could have carried Ronald Reagan's rash promise of a female justice all the way to the high court. When push came to shove, she was loyal to the Republicans who put her in her high place. With her stiff-upper-lip rendition of the model minority, she was the perfect First.

She certainly made it easier for her sister in law, Justice Ginsburg. O'Connor was determined not to be the last, she said. After her arrival in what Justice Stevens described as their "trouble"-free integration, when President Clinton nominated Ginsburg, no one on the Supreme Court would have dared to utter a peep.

When Ginsburg first hit the public scene, she, the brainy Jew from Brooklyn with the ACLU card, was not an obvious candidate for the symbol of digestible social change. Her contribution was more in the arena of razor-sharp legal analysis and a farsighted strategy that would bring about social change, as Thurgood Marshall did, step by step. Until the Court had gone too far to turn back the clock.

As O'Connor had made it easier for her, she had made it easier for Elena Kagan, the first female dean at Harvard Law School, the first woman to serve as solicitor general, and the fourth WOTSC. Appointed in 2011 and now the youngest woman on the Supreme Court, she credits Ginsburg, her oldest colleague, with making her career possible: "As a litigator and then as a judge she changed the face of American antidiscrimination law." The barriers lifted, and Kagan rose just as traditional liberal feminism would have predicted.

Then something unexpected happened. With the gift of the new media, Ginsburg herself became an icon. A half century after she took the helm at the ACLU, Ginsburg, with her minuscule frame, her classical taste in music, her subtly expensive outfits, her long, happy marriage, her children and grandchildren, seemed the embodiment of conventionality—until she opened her mouth. To the generation of young women hungry for reassurance about the normalcy of female power, as the Court increasingly began turning back the clock, such an unlikely ally was a gift from heaven. "That she was still so radical!" Knizhnik crows. "After all these years."

Less visibly, the story took a final turn. As the Court began to roll the clock backward, the long-retired Justice O'Connor, whose uninspiring prose and uninformative analysis made her seem like the furthest thing from a big legal thinker, began to seem, in retrospect, like a gift from the gods of jurisprudence. Sounding so conservative and framing her mildly pro-woman decisions time after time as protective of authority—employers, school administrators—she represented the farthest women could hope to go in light of the irresistible conservative resurgence of the late twentieth and early twenty-first centuries. From the first women's rights case of her tenure to the last case she decided in 2006, she made the law for women more liberal or at least preserved the gains of the past. Public colleges are not segregated by sex, nowhere in the United States is abortion automatically criminal, and the Civil Rights Act prohibits employers from asking their employees to come down to the motel and negotiate their raise.

By now, both sisters in law are icons and both are beacons of feminist jurisprudence.

MAKING ALL THE DIFFERENCE

Are women justices different? Are women different? Society has been debating this issue probably since the apes fell from the trees.

The modern feminist movement started by attacking the difference, which had been used to keep women from serving on juries or owning their own bars, practicing law in firms, making equal pay, and serving their country. But as the formal barriers began to fall, the debate revived almost immediately with claims that women's voices were different, but just as good, because of the experience of subordination.

Ginsburg always "fudged" the question, she admitted. Her basic liberal principles were sufficient for most of the decisions she made. But from the editors of the *Harvard Law Review* equal-protection issue circa 1969 to the hilarity at oral argument in Savanna Redding's school search case decades later, when even liberal men seemed blind to women's lives, she was there to represent their existence.

O'Connor was explicit in her displeasure with the suggestion that she judged in a different voice. But she did. The law is not different for men and for women, and Justice O'Connor was not morally different from her peers. But she had her life experience as a woman. She worked for no salary in order to get a law job at all at the outset of her career. In ordering the integration of Mississippi's nursing school, right after she ascended the bench, she noted that the almost all-female nursing profession didn't claim such great wages. A fancy law firm offered her a secretarial job. Years later, she voted to take the case of a young woman turned down by King & Spalding right away rather than wait for a split in the courts below. With the richness of her experiences as a woman lawyer coming up when society was arrayed against her, O'Connor's record on women's issues is by far the most liberal of all the bodies of law she created in her long career and much more liberal than the other Reagan appointees, Scalia and Kennedy.

A WISE LATINA WOMAN

Sooner or later, someone was going to admit the obvious. It turned out to be then Circuit Judge Sonia Sotomayor, daughter of immigrants from Puerto Rico. "I would hope," she said in a speech in

2001, "that a wise Latina woman with the richness of her experiences, would more often than not reach a better conclusion than a white male who hasn't lived that life." Her critics made that statement into a rope to hang her with during her confirmation hearings, until, at last, she repudiated her own words, calling it "a rhetorical flourish that fell flat."

Although she took the statement back, Justice Sotomayor quickly turned out to be the change she was seeking. Four years after she took her seat on the Supreme Court, Sotomayor wrote the story of her experience, specifically of growing up as a poor Puerto Rican immigrant child in the Bronx. The book was a bestseller, and Sotomayor became a genuine celebrity. In 2014 she wrote a long and impassioned dissent from her white male colleague John Roberts's opinion allowing a state to ban the use of affirmative action. A wise Latina judge, she explained how she would rule differently than that white man: "Race matters to a young woman's sense of self when she states her hometown, and then is pressed, 'No, where are you really from?' regardless of how many generations her family has been in the country," she wrote. "Race matters to a young person addressed by a stranger in a foreign language, which he does not understand because only English was spoken at home."

When, during the flap over Sotomayor's confirmation, an interviewer asked Ginsburg if the results might be different in discrimination cases if more women sat on the Supreme Court, Ginsburg gave this answer: "I think for the most part, yes. I would suspect that, because the women will relate to their own experiences."

Acknowledgments

David Kuhn: you saved my life. Thanks to Becky Sweren, Jessie Borkan, and all the good people at Kuhn Projects. Thanks again to best editor and dearest friend Gail Winston at HarperCollins and to all the good people there—Jonathan Burnham, Emily Cunningham. And to Sarah Blustain, the mother of it all. Stephen Wagley again did yeoman service on the citation front. I had research help from Jessica Anne Gresko and Robert Wyatt. No one writes about women and judging without a big boost from the incomparable Lynn Hecht Schafran, and the University of Chicago's Geoffrey Stone provided stimulation as well as information. Thanks to all the clerks who chatted, overtly and covertly. I never had such a smart set of interview subjects. Walking pals Loretta McCarthy, Jill Faber, and Gloria Feldt listened patiently and helped every way they could. Phoenix pal Paul Eckstein knew everyone. Washington and Lee's Ann and Kent Massie put me up and put up with me. Powell papers' John Jacobs was incredibly helpful. I get by with a little help from my friends. My daughter, Sarah Shapiro, herself a lawyer, reminded me that a new generation of women had come to the Court, and gave me an ending.

Notes

✤

Note: Final bound volumes for the U.S. Supreme Court's United States Reports exist only through volume 557, covering cases decided on or before October 2, 2009. Cases decided after that date are published without a page number.

INTRODUCTION: RUFFLED COLLARS

xi somber black robe: William Peacock, "Friday Frills: The Jabot (or Neck Doily)," *Findlaw Supreme Court*, February 7, 2014, http://blogs.findlaw.com/supreme_court/2014/02/friday-frills-the-jabot-or-neck-doily.html.

xi *United States v. Virginia*: 518 U.S. 515 (1996), http://www.oyez.org/cases/1990-1999/1995/1995_94_1941.

xii "This should be Ruth's," she said: Nina Totenberg, interview with the author, September 6, 2013. Nina Totenberg, Introduction to *The Legacy of Ruth Bader Ginsburg*, edited by Scott Dodson (New York: Cambridge University Press, 2015), p. 18 of draft; Totenberg apparently means Justice Stevens, who would have been the assigning justice if Rehnquist had voted for VMI. Stevens has no memory of the conversation (Justice John Paul Stevens, interview with author, July 21, 2014). Rehnquist ultimately concurred with the majority, so it may have been Justice Rehnquist whom O'Connor approached.

xiii and nodded: Linda Greenhouse, "From the High Court, a Voice Quite Distinctly a Woman's," *New York Times*, May 26, 1999; Lyle Denniston, "Justice's Crusade: 'We the People' Includes Women—Ginsburg Led Military-School Ruling," *Seattle Times*, June 27, 1996, http://community.seattletimes.nwsource.com/archive/?date=19960627&slug=2336534.

xiii "everything changes": Gail Collins's excellent history of the modern women's movement is *When Everything Changed: The Amazing Journey of American Women from 1960 to the Present* (Boston: Little, Brown, 2009).

xv Girl of the Golden West: Aryeh Neier, interview with the author, July 8, 2013.

xv know who she was: Mike Sacks, "Women Supreme Court Justices Celebrate 30 Years Since Court's First Female," *Huffington Post*, April 11, 2012, http://www.huffingtonpost.com/2012/04/11/supreme-court-women-justices_n_1419183.html.

xv   "she never held us up": Justice John Paul Stevens, interview with the author, July 21, 2014.

xvi   Associations of Women Judges: "Sandra Day O'Connor—Member," *Iraq Study Group Report*, Future of the Book, http://www.futureofthebook.org/iraqreport/sandra-day-oconnor/index.html; "O'Connor is a member of the American Bar Association, the State Bar of Arizona, the State Bar of California, the Maricopa County Bar Association, the Arizona Judges' Association, the *National Association of Women Judges*, and the Arizona Women Lawyers' Association."

xvi   "into a judicial question": Alexis de Tocqueville, *Democracy in America*, chapter 16, "Causes Which Mitigate the Tyranny of the Majority in the United States," http://xroads.virginia.edu/~Hyper/DETOC/1_ch16.htm.

xvii   whole web of discriminatory laws at once: Roberta W. Francis, "The History Behind the Equal Rights Amendment," *Equal Rights Amendment* (website), http://www.equalrightsamendment.org/history.htm.

xviii   "bra and her wedding ring": Joan Biskupic, *Sandra Day O'Connor: How the First Woman on the Supreme Court Became Its Most Influential Justice* (New York: Harper Perennial, 2006), 4 and prologue 9.

xviii   believing it: Harriet Rabb, interview with the author, October 15, 2013.

xix   firstborn child: Biskupic, *Sandra Day O'Connor*, 21.

xix   when she graduated in 1957: Sheldon M. Novick, "What Makes a Great Judge, His Reasoning or His Vision?" *Los Angeles Times*, April 22, 1994, http://articles.latimes.com/1994-05-22/books/bk-60553_1_learned-hand/2.

xix   most fun talk she'd ever delivered: Brian Baxter, "Justice O'Connor Dings Gibson Dunn on Letterman Show," *Am Law Daily* (blog), June 24, 2009, http://amlawdaily.typepad.com/amlawdaily/2009/06/oconnor-on-letterman.html.

xix   it had been a *joke*: Ira E. Stoll, "Ginsburg Blasts Harvard Law; Past, Present Deans Defend School," *Harvard Crimson*, July 23, 1993, http://www.thecrimson.com/article/1993/7/23/ginsburg-blasts-harvard-law-pin-testimony/.

xx   demands of the Junior League: Biskupic, *Sandra Day O'Connor*, 34.

xxi   first year on the Court in 1981: Ibid., 119.

xxi   "worst mistake I ever made": Totenberg interview, September 6, 2013.

xxi   to save him: Mel Wulf, interview with the author, June 20, 2013.

xxii   men in power have always done: Ginsburg, letter to Philip Kurland, March 20, 1975, Ginsburg Archive, Library of Congress, Box 16.

xxii   should be spanked: Michael Murphy, "Conservative Pioneer Became an Outcast," *Arizona Republic*, May 31, 1998, http://archive.azcentral.com/specials/special25/articles/0531goldwater2.html.

xxii   viewed generically: Catherine Ho, "Justice Ginsburg Happy to No Longer Be Confused with Sandra Day O'Connor," *Washington Post*, December 17, 2013, http://www.washingtonpost.com/business/capitalbusiness/justice-ginsburg-happy-to-no-longer-be-confused-with-sandra-day-oconnor/2013/12/17/d8ba9c5c-6731-11e3-a0b9-249bbb34602c_story.html.

xxii wrong name: Lawrence S. Wrightsman, *Oral Arguments Before the Supreme Court: An Empirical Approach* (New York: Oxford University Press, 2008), 45.

xxiii "than mouse": Jeffrey Rosen, "The Book of Ruth," *The New Republic*, August 2, 1993, http://www.newrepublic.com/article/politics/the-book-ruth.

CHAPTER I: COUNTRY GIRL, CITY KID

3 Growing up on a ranch: The story of O'Connor's early years was beautifully remembered in her memoir with her brother, Sandra Day O'Connor and Alan Day, *Lazy B: Growing Up on a Cattle Ranch in the American Southwest* (New York: Random House, 2002), and in Joan Biskupic's invaluable biography, *Sandra Day O'Connor*, esp. 7–21.

3 always "a lady": "Sandra Day O'Connor," biography.com, http://www .biography.com/people/sandra-day-oconnor-9426834?page=1#early-life-and-career.

4 "head down the path together": Biskupic, *Sandra Day O'Connor*, 21.

4 free-market variety: Ibid., 13–14.

4 "we survived": C-Span, Influential Women of the West, January 14, 2015, http://www.c-span.org/video/?323615-1/discussion-influential-women-west.

4 flat tire: The story appears, essentially exactly like this, in *Lazy B*, 240–41.

5 "gorgeous clothes": Biskupic, *Sandra Day O'Connor*, 23.

5 "We were blown away": Ibid., 23.

5 for only one year: Harriet Haskell, interview with Phoenix History Project, January 31, 1980.

5 calls herself a "cowgirl": "Sandra Day O'Connor Pt. 2," *The Daily Show*, March 3, 2009, http://thedailyshow.cc.com/video-playlists/rldluj/daily-show-14030/8twc80.

6 read to her: Ruth Bader Ginsburg, interview, Academy of Achievement, August 17, 2010, http://www.achievement.org/autodoc/page/ginoint-3.

6 distinguishing herself: Assistant Principal Rita Menkes, interview with the author, October 2013.

6 doing her homework: Phil Schatz, "Judicial Profile: Hon. Ruth Bader Ginsburg," *Federal Lawyer*, May 2010, available at http://www.wandslaw.com/ phils-book-reviews/90-judicial-profile-hon-ruth-bader-ginsberg.html.

7 "as much as sons": Malvina Halberstam, "Ruth Bader Ginsburg," *Encyclopedia*, Jewish Women's Archive, http://jwa.org/encyclopedia/article/ginsburg-ruth-bader; "Ginsburg Supreme Court Nomination," C-SPAN, June 14, 1993, http://www.c-spanvideo.org/program/42908-1.

7 scholarship help: Nichola D. Gutgold, *The Rhetoric of Supreme Court Women: From Obstacles to Options* (Lanham, Md.: Lexington Books, 2012), 48.

7 little knotted scarf: Richard H. Penner, *Cornell University* (Charleston, S.C.: Arcadia Publishing, 2013).

7 of human life: "The Reality of Ideas," *Stanford Review*, May 29, 2009, http:// stanfordreview.org/article/reality-ideas/.

7 "What is my destination?": Harry J. Rathbun, audio recording, 1955, Stanford Digital Repository, http://purl.stanford.edu/qq737wt2311.

7 was mesmerized: Charles Lane, "Courting O'Connor: Why the Chief Justice Isn't the Chief Justice," *Washington Post*, July 4, 2004, http://www.washingtonpost.com/wp-dyn/articles/A16332-2004Jun29_3.html.

8 bright and curious youngster: Biskupic, *Sandra Day O'Connor*, 23–24.

8 an unknown world: Rathbun.

8 "nature of reality": Ibid.

8 "new religion": Steven M. Gelber and Martin L. Cook, *Saving the Earth: The History of a Middle-Class Millenarian Movement* (Berkeley: University of California Press, 1990).

8 "it would blow away": Steven M. Gelber, interview with the author, April 2013.

9 "philosophy of life": Adam Gorlick, "Former Justice Reflects on How Law Professor Helped Shape Her Life Philosophy," *Stanford Report*, April 23, 2008, http://news.stanford.edu/news/2008/april30/sandra-043008.html.

9 public lawn (allowed): Angie A. Welborn, *The Law of Church and State: Selected Opinions of Justice O'Connor*, Congressional Research Service, Report for Congress, July 20, 2005, http://congressionalresearch.com/RS22201/document.php?study=The+Law+of+Church+and+State+Selected+Opinions+of+Justice+OConnor.

9 "ineffable gift": Aryeh Neier, interview with the author, July 11, 2013.

10 "Civil Liberty After the War": Robert Cushman, "Civil Liberty After the War," *American Political Science Review* 38 (February 1944): 12–13.

10 "in government and in private life": Guenter Lewy, *The Cause That Failed: Communism in American Political Life* (New York: Oxford University Press, 1990), 99.

11 "a little better for others": Ruth Bader Ginsburg, interview, Academy of Achievement, August 17, 2010, http://www.achievement.org/autodoc/printmember/ginoint-1.

11 a cutting-edge legal thinker: Geoffrey Stone, interview with the author, September 12, 2013.

12 participation in national life: *The Nomination of Ruth Bader Ginsburg, to Be Associate Justice of the Supreme Court of the United States: Hearings Before the S. Comm. on the Judiciary*, 103d Cong. 127 (1993), Statement of Ruth Bader Ginsburg, http://www.loc.gov/law/find/nominations/ginsburg/hearing.pdf.

12 to study law: Biskupic, *Sandra Day O'Connor*, 24. Rathbun considered law as the expression of an orderly society: Harry J. Rathbun, audio recording, 1955, Stanford Digital Repository, http://purl.stanford.edu/qq737wt2311.

12 respectable, but not outstanding: Henry Monaghan, interview with the author, October 14, 2013.

12 Carl Spaeth: Biskupic, *Sandra Day O'Connor*, 24–25.

12 right to privacy: Samuel D. Warren and Louis D. Brandeis, "The Right to Privacy," *Harvard Law Review* 4 (December 15, 1890): 193–220, http://

www.english.illinois.edu/-people-/faculty/debaron/582/582%20readings/
right%20to%20privacy.pdf.

12 rule of law itself: Oliver Wendell Holmes, Jr., "The Path of the Law," *Harvard Law Review* 10 (1897): 457, http://www.gutenberg.org/ebooks/2373.

12 secretary of state: Warren Christopher, *Chances of a Lifetime: A Memoir* (New York: Simon and Schuster, 2001), 19–20.

13 Everybody loved Sandra: A titillating factoid is that apparently Sandra spent a few evenings with Bill Rehnquist, a fellow student just out of the army, and destined as well for higher things. McFeatters, *Sandra Day O'Connor*, 43.

13 never dated anyone else: Biskupic, *Sandra Day O'Connor*, 26, n. 18.

13 to phone around: Ann McFeatters, *Sandra Day O'Connor: Justice in the Balance* (Albuquerque: University of New Mexico Press, 2005), 45; David Gergen, "A Candid Conversation with Sandra Day O'Connor: 'I Can Still Make a Difference,'" *Parade*, September 30, 2012, http://www.civicmissionofschools.org/news/2012-10-parade-magazine-a-candid-conversation-with-sandra-da.

14 had a brain: Marlo Thomas, *The Right Words at the Right Time* (New York: Atria, 2002), 115.

14 a similar fate: Seymour Brody, "Ruth Bader Ginsburg," *Jewish Heroes and Heroines of America: 150 True Stories of Jewish Heroism* (Hollywood, Fla.: Lifetime Books, 1996), http://www.jewishvirtuallibrary.org/jsource/biography/Ginsburg.html

15 two classroom buildings: Bradley Blackburn, "Justices Ruth Bader Ginsburg and Sandra Day O'Connor on Life and the Supreme Court," *ABC News*, October 26, 2010, http://abcnews.go.com/WN/diane-sawyer-interviews-maria-shriver-sandra-day-oconnor/story?id=11977195.

15 1954 desegregation decision: Herbert Wechsler, "Toward Neutral Principles of Constitutional Law," *Harvard Law Review* 73 (1959): 1.

16 "their husband's work": Ira E. Stoll, "Ginsburg Blasts Harvard Law; Past, Present Deans Defend School," *Harvard Crimson*, July 23, 1993, http://www.thecrimson.com/article/1993/7/23/ginsburg-blasts-harvard-law-pin-testimony/.

16 with a Harvard degree: Martin D. Ginsburg, "Spousal Transfers: In '58, It Was Different," *Harvard Law Record*, May 6, 1977, 11.

16 "or had been a male": Ginsburg Archive, Library of Congress, Box 19, F Bio 1976–78.

17 lymph nodes: Ginsburg, letter to Stephen Wiesenfeld, December 22, 1998.

17 died of the disease: Testicular Cancer Resource Center, "Testicular Cancer Treatments: Chemotherapy," http://tcrc.acor.org/chemo.html.

17 she says flatly: Debra Bruno, "Justice Ginsburg Remembers Her First Steps in the Law," *Legal Times*, November 13, 2007, www.law.com/jsp/article.jsp?id=1194861838591 and http://www.law.com/jsp/article.jsp?id=900005558448&Justice_Ginsburg_Remembers_Her_First_Steps_in_the_Law&slreturn=20130313123922.

17 of radiation: Ginsburg, letter to Stephen Wiesenfeld, December 22, 1998.

17 "a set of notes": Ibid.

17 the only woman: "Ruth Bader Ginsburg," *Miriam's Cup* (website), http://www.miriamscup.com/GinsburgBiog.htm.

17 no further evidence of cancer: Ginsburg, letter to Stephen Wiesenfeld, December 22, 1998.

17 "couldn't cope with": Bruno, "Justice Ginsburg Remembers."

17 no more children: Ginsburg, letter to Stephen Wiesenfeld, December 22, 1998.

18 "would not give it up": Stephanie Frances Ward, "Family Ties," *ABA Journal*, October 1, 2010, http://www.abajournal.com/magazine/article/family_ties1/.

18 applied to him: Biskupic, *Sandra Day O'Connor*, 28.

19 "run out of money": taped interview with Sandra O'Connor, Phoenix Oral History Project, 1980, Arizona Historical Society.

19 old, tired, and corrupt: Paul Eckstein, interview with the author, April 16, 2013; Zachary Smith, *Politics and Public Policy in Arizona* (Westport, Conn.: Praeger, 1996).

19 took over the state media: "The Arizona Republic: An Overview," azcentral .com, http://www.azcentral.com/help/articles/about2.html.

19 up-and-coming Young Republicans: Dennis Abrams, *Sandra Day O'Connor* (New York: Chelsea House, 2009), 42.

20 county vice chairman: "Justice Sandra Day O'Connor Talks about Her Life on Valley Girl," AOL.com, July 12, 2012, http://on.aol.com/video/justice-sandra-day-oconnor-talks-about-her-life-on-the-valley-girl-517415204.

20 voluntary organization: Phoenix Oral History Project, taped interview with Sandra Day O'Connor, 1980, Arizona Historical Society.

20 365 nights: Ibid.

20 gave a party: John Driggs, interview with the author, January 25, 2014.

21 "I'm not hiring a woman": Ruth Bader Ginsburg, interview, Academy of Achievement, August 17, 2010, http://www.achievement.org/autodoc/page/ginoint-4.

21 salty style of speech: "A Conversation with Justice Ruth Bader Ginsburg," C-SPAN, September 15, 2009, http://www.c-span.org/video/?288900-1/conversation-justice-ruth-bader-ginsburg.

21 as harshly as race: Seth Stern and Stephen Wermiel, *Justice Brennan: Liberal Champion* (Boston: Houghton Mifflin Harcourt, 2010), 400. In 1973, a former Brennan clerk, then teaching at Berkeley, baldly pressured his former justice to hire his first woman clerk, Marsha Berzon. The *Harvard Law Review* had just done a study of the paucity of female clerks, the male ex-clerk warned Brennan, and it was just a matter of time before the spotlight on him grew more intense.

21 "as if I wasn't there": "A Conversation with Justice Ruth Bader Ginsburg," C-SPAN, September 15, 2009, http://www.c-span.org/video/?288900-1/conversation-justice-ruth-bader-ginsburg.

21 rest of the year: Sandra Grayson, interview with the author, November 8, 2013.

21 Eva Moberg: Moberg's article, "Kvinnans villkorliga frigivning," appeared in an anthology, *Unga Liberaler: nio inlägg i idédebatten* (Stockholm: Bonnier, 1961). Ginsburg's Swedish roots are the subject of a pathbreaking revisionist

history of her jurisprudence by the young legal scholar Cary C. Franklin, "The Anti-Stereotyping Principle in Constitutional Sex Discrimination Law," *NYU Law Review* 85 (2010), electronic copy available at http://ssrn .com/abstract=1589754. Much of this section of *Sisters in Law* is indebted to Franklin's research, as well as my own findings in the Ginsburg archives.

22 sex-role stereotyping: Franklin, "The Anti-Stereotyping Principle," 119.

22 "The Emancipation of Man": Olof Palme, "The Emancipation of Man," Address Before the Women's National Democratic Club (June 8, 1970), http:// www.olofpalme.org/wp-content/dokument/700608_emancipation_of_ man".pdf. Kenneth M. Davidson, Ruth B. Ginsburg, and Herma H. Kay, *Sex-Based Discrimination: Text, Cases and Materials* (Saint Paul, Minn.: West Publishing, 1974), 938, 944.

22 "her personal talents": Palme, "The Emancipation of Man."

22 reproducing on the job: Malvina Halberstam, "Ruth Bader Ginsburg," *Encyclopedia*, Jewish Women's Archive, http://jwa.org/encyclopedia/article/ ginsburg-ruth-bader.

22 she crowed: Ginsburg, letter to Stephen Wiesenfeld, December 22, 1998.

23 "bra and panties": Frank Askin, interview with the author, June 18, 2013.

23 his unforthcoming spouse: Monagahn interview; Askin interview.

23 pictures her children had drawn: Paul Rosenblatt, interview with the author, February 7, 2014.

23 "we were so busy": Ibid.

24 *any State on account of sex*: The text of the amendment is available at http:// en.wikipedia.org/wiki/Equal_Rights_Amendment.

24 "I never had a further problem": Phoenix Oral History Project, transcript of taped interview with Sandra Day O'Connor, 1980, Arizona Historical Society, 10.

25 "child care as a result": Biskupic, *Sandra Day O'Connor*, 31.

25 did the people's business: "Sandra Day O'Connor House," Tempe Preservation on Flickr, http://www.tempe.gov/city-hall/community-development/historic-preservation/tempe-historic-property-register/sandra-day-o-connor-house.

25 discriminatory hiring hall: *Kaplowitz v. University of Chicago*, 387 F.Supp. 42 (1974), http://www.leagle.com/decision/1974429387FSupp42_1422.xml/ KAPLOWITZ%20v.%20UNIVERSITY%20OF%20CHICAGO.

25 influence of the feminist revolution: Frank Askin, interview with author, June 18, 2013.

25 there was so little written: Fred Strebeigh, *Equal: Women Reshape American Law* (New York: W. W. Norton, 2009), 19.

25 "putting up with them?": David Margolick, "Trial by Adversity Shapes Jurist's Outlook," *New York Times*, June 25, 1993, http://www.nytimes .com/1993/06/25/us/trial-by-adversity-shapes-jurist-s-outlook.html?page-wanted=all&src=pm.

26 in support of the Equal Rights Amendment: Ginsburg Archive, Library of Congress, Box 20, folder 1970–71, ERA correspondence, contains various letters to each of the members of the Senate and House Judiciary Committees.

26 "Realizing the Equality Principle": Ginsburg Archive, Library of Congress, Box 12.

26 stay-at-home dad during law school: David G. Post, interview with the author, June 3, 2014.

26 down the pipeline: Ginsburg Archive, Library of Congress, Box 11, folder speeches 70–71 includes the first of many speeches to the National Conference of Law Women. Ruth Bader Ginsburg, "Sex and Unequal Protection: Men and Women as Victims," keynote address, Southern Regional Conference of the National Conference of Law Women, Duke University, October 1, 1971, published in *Journal of Family Law* 11 (1971): 347 (hereafter Duke Speech).

27 feminist heroine's consciousness-raising: Ginsburg Archive, Library of Congress, Box 46, F. Sex Equality, 1970.

27 "advantaged treatment today": Duke Speech.

27 "extra work during the week": Alix Kates Shulman, "A Marriage Agreement," *Up from Under* (August/September 1970); reprinted in *A Marriage Agreement and Other Essays: Four Decades of Feminist Writing* (New York: Open Road Integrated Media, 2012), available at http://jwa.org/sites/jwa .org/files/mediaobjects/a_marriage_agreement_alix_kates_shulman.jpg.

28 Shulman's little essay: Arlie Russell Hochschild, *The Second Shift* (New York: Avon, 1990).

28 She collected: Ginsburg Archive, Library of Congress, Box 46, F. Sex Equality, 1972–73.

28 impoverishes women and enriches men: Lenore J. Weitzman, "The Economics of Divorce: Social and Economic Consequences of Property, Alimony and Child Support Awards," *UCLA Law Review* 28 (1980–81): 1181.

28 "within the meaning of the Constitution": Ruth Bader Ginsburg, "*Muller v. Oregon*: One Hundred Years Later," *Willamette Law Review* 45 (2009): 359–80 (see 370), http://www.willamette.edu/wucl/resources/journals/review/ pdf/Volume%2045/WLR45-3_Justice_Ginsburg.pdf.

28 "take their feet off our necks": Duke Speech.

29 discuss life and law: Jan Goodman, interview with the author, July 31, 2013.

29 at Duke University: Duke Speech.

30 students in her seminar: Ginsburg Archive, Library of Congress, Box 20, folder ERA Correspondence, 1970–71.

30 appearances in the Supreme Court: Amy Davidson, "Ruth Bader Ginsburg's Retirement Dissent," *The New Yorker,* September 24, 2014, http://www .newyorker.com/news/amy-davidson.

30 she was now undertaking: Ginsburg, letter to Stephen Wiesenfeld, November 8, 1978.

CHAPTER 2: THE LAWSUIT OF RUTH'S DREAMS

32 tax advance sheet: The story is by now *vieux jeu*, but this version comes from Fred Strebeigh, *Equal: Women Reshape American Law* (New York: W. W.

Norton, 2009), 23, which he credits to an interview with MG and a letter from him.

32 lifelong bachelor: From opinion of the Tenth Circuit in *Moritz v. Commissioner of IRS*, 469 F.2d 466 (1972), http://law.justia.com/cases/federal/appellate-courts/F2/469/466/79852/.

33 thought might be interested: Strebeigh, *Equal*, 24.

33 "absolutely brilliant piece of work": Norman Dorsen, interview with the author, June 18, 2013.

34 "from obscurity": Strebeigh, *Equal*, 25.

35 on behalf of women's rights: Ibid., 27.

36 Those were laws that discriminate on race: *United States v. Carolene Products Company*, 304 U.S. 144 (1938).

37 Ginsburg was counting on: "Developments in the Law—Equal Protection," note, *Harvard Law Review* 82 (1969): 1065.

37 to be his law clerk: Seth Stern and Stephen Wermiel, *Justice Brennan: Liberal Champion* (Boston: Houghton Mifflin Harcourt, 2010), 388.

37 "related to performance": "Developments in the Law—Equal Protection," note, *Harvard Law Review* 82 (1969): 1068, n. 61. The authors give a passing nod to the 1964 Civil Rights Act, which forbids discrimination based on sex, without further commentary.

37 91 percent was male: Susan M. Hartmann, *The Other Feminists: Activists in the Liberal Establishment* (New Haven, Conn.: Yale University Press, 1998), 80.

37 Dorsen (New York, Harvard J.D.): "Aryeh Neier," ACLU ProCon.org, June 27, 2012, http://aclu.procon.org/view.source.php?sourceID=002205; "Melvin Wulf, LLB," ACLU ProCon.org, June 12, 2008, http://aclu.procon.org/view.source.php?sourceID=002223.

38 could wait until "tomorrow": Hartmann, *The Other Feminists*, 72–73.

38 apply only to race: See Kurland discussion below.

38 starting to have "tantrums": Hartmann, *The Other Feminists*, 74.

38 racial civil rights movement: Suzy Post, KY Civil Rights Hall of Fame, oral history project, http://nunncenter.org/civilrights/category/interviewees/suzy-post/.

38 Suzy Post went to the next level: Hartmann, *The Other Feminists*, 81.

39 civil liberties frame around it: Samuel Walker, *In Defense of American Liberties: A History of the ACLU* (New York: Oxford University Press, 1990; 2nd edition, Carbondale: Southern Illinois University Press, 1999), 299.

39 their network a little harder: Fred Strebeigh, *Equal: Women Reshape American Law* (New York: W. W. Norton, 2009), 27, note citing copy of Dorsen letter from Ginsburg files.

39 who had just graduated: Ibid., 34.

39 attending Yale Law School: Ann Freedman, interview with the author, October 29, 2013.

40 "always a lawyer's lawyer": Ibid.

41 not in a good way: Fighting the Ginsburgs in *Moritz*, the solicitor general of the United States had produced a great gift to the project of women's

equality—a comprehensive list of all the U.S. laws and regulations that distinguished between the sexes; see http://www.supremecourt.gov/publicinfo/speeches/viewspeeches.aspx?Filename=sp_02-10-06.html.

41 known how to use it: Nina Totenberg, interview with the author, September 6, 2013.

42 "the task at hand": Ann Freedman, interview with the author, October 29, 2013.

43 original *Moritz* appeal: Ruth always said that *Moritz* was really the grandmother brief, because that's the case she worked on first and that's where she found *Royster Guano*. Elizabeth Vrato, *The Counselors: Conversations with 18 Courageous Women Who Have Changed the World* (Philadelphia: Running Press, 2002).

44 "history of the Republic": Geoffrey Stone, interview with the author, September 12, 2013.

CHAPTER 3: GOLDWATER GIRL AND CARD-CARRYING MEMBER OF THE ACLU

45 like Ginsburg's: O'Connor legislator's papers, Arizona History and Archives, Box 1:1.

45 new feminists of Los Angeles: "Los Angeles' New Feminists," June 1970, O'Connor papers, Arizona History and Archives, Box 1:1.

45 filthy Greenwich Village walk-ups: O'Connor papers, Box 1:1.

45 cosmopolitan *Atlantic Monthly*: O'Connor papers, Box 1:1, contains the whole issue; see also http://www.theatlantic.com/magazine/archive/1970/03/women-and-the-law/304923/.

45 got an earful: Elizabeth Pantazelos, "Women at Work: Articles from the '70s, '80s, and '90s Address the Ongoing Obstacles that Career Women Face," *The Atlantic*, May 2006, http://www.theatlantic.com/magazine/archive/2006/05/women-at-work/304944/.

46 "part time or occasional nature": Remarks, May 7, 1970, O'Connor papers, Arizona History and Archives, Box 1:1.

46 "elected to high public office": Ibid.

47 "been a splendid choice": Letter to President Nixon, October 1, 1971, O'Connor files, Arizona History and Archives, Box 1:1.

47 polluted the Court with a woman: Nixon tapes, cited in Joan Biskupic, *Sandra Day O'Connor: How the First Woman on the Supreme Court Became Its Most Influential Justice* (New York: Harper Perennial, 2006), 41, n. 11.

47 treated women differently: Diane Schulder, "Women and the Laws," *Atlantic Monthly*, March 1970; clipping in O'Connor papers, Arizona History and Archives, Box 1:1.

47 by only a single vote: Biskupic, *Sandra Day O'Connor*, 60.

47 "in a meaningful way": Remarks, May 7, 1970, O'Connor papers, Arizona History and Archives, Box 1:1.

48 run for public office: Biskupic, *Sandra Day O'Connor*, 36, n. 57.

48 it was a done deal: "Irene Rasmussen on the Equal Rights Amendment," Arizona Memory Project, Arizona State Archives, http://azmemory.azlibrary .gov/cdm/ref/collection/archpriv/id/1794

49 defend the amendment: Sarah Slavin, ed., *U.S. Women's Interest Groups: Institutional Profiles* (Westport, Conn.: Greenwood Press, 1995), 578.

49 "making men and women identical": Biskupic, *Sandra Day O'Connor*, 59.

49 "questions have been raised," she wrote: "Form letter from Senator Sandra Day O'Connor, February 18, 1984, re: Equal Rights Amendment," Arizona Memory Project, Arizona State Archives, http://azmemory.azlibrary.gov/ cdm/ref/collection/archgov/id/481.

50 justices' dining room: "Irene Rasmussen on the Equal Rights Amendment."

51 "be sure his sox match": Duke Speech.

51 a *lesbian*, of all things: Doris L. Sassower, "Women's Rights Ignored," *ABA Journal* (October 1971), 950.

51 one at a time: Ruth Bader Ginsburg, "The Need for the Equal Rights Amendment," *ABA Journal* 59 (1973): 1013.

51 "women or bridges": Duke Speech.

52 "Some Problems of Construction": Philip B. Kurland, "The Equal Rights Amendment: Some Problems of Construction," *Harvard Civil Rights–Civil Liberties Law Review* 6 (1970–71): 243.

52 decisions of the Warren Court: Philip B. Kurland, Foreword, "Equal in Origin and Equal in Title to the Legislative and Executive Branches of the Government," *Harvard Law Review* 78 (1964): 143, 145 (referring to "the absence of workmanlike product, the absence of right quality . . . disingenuousness and misrepresentation" in the landmark racial decision). Philip B. Kurland, " '*Brown v. Board of Education* Was the Beginning': The School Desegregation Cases in the United States Supreme Court, 1954–1979," *Washington University Law Quarterly* (1979): 309, 313, 316.

52 upset the Lord's order: Donald G. Mathews and Jane S. De Hart, *Sex, Gender, and the Politics of ERA: A State and the Nation* (New York: Oxford University Press, 1990), 37.

52 opponent of racial civil rights: Karl E. Campbell, *Senator Sam Ervin, Last of the Founding Fathers* (Chapel Hill: University of North Carolina Press, 2007), 124.

53 school desegregation decision: Kurland, "*Brown v. Board of Education* Was the Beginning."

53 men's prisons and toilets: American Civil Liberties Union Records, Princeton University Library, Box 23, Minutes of Meeting Board of Directors, November 26, 1970.

53 heat of battle: Ginsburg Archive, Library of Congress, Box 20, Folder ERA Correspondence, 1974.

53 "making relevant connections": Ruth Bader Ginsburg, "Women at the Bar—A Generation of Change," *University of Puget Sound Law Review*

2 (1978): 1, http://digitalcommons.law.seattleu.edu/cgi/viewcontent.cgi ?article=1081&context=sulr

54 the ERA went down: Amy Leigh Campbell, *Raising the Bar: Ruth Bader Ginsburg and the ACLU Women's Rights Project* (Bloomington, Ind.: Xlibris, 2004), 40, citing Ginsburg's internal memorandum on *Reed*, Ginsburg Archive, Library of Congress, Box 6.

54 "facts and cool reason": Ruth Bader Ginsburg, letter to Joan Krauskopf, Ginsburg Archive, Library of Congress, Box 20, Folder ERA Correspondence, 1974.

54 opinion page at *The New York Times*: clippings reflect that she got picked by the *NYT* to do the op-ed in favor of the ERA, Ginsburg Archive, Library of Congress, Box 16, F1975.

54 League of Women Voters: Ginsburg Archives, Library of Congress, Box 20, Folder ERA Correspondence, 1975.

54 predicted the world would end: Ibid.

54 "Three Minutes on the ERA" on NPR: Ginsburg Archives, Library of Congress, Box 14, folder April 1978.

55 cover of the brief: "Tribute: The Legacy of Ruth Bader Ginsburg and WRP Staff," ACLU.org (website), March 7, 2006, http://www.aclu.org/womensrights/tribute-legacy-ruth-bader-ginsburg-and-wrp-staff.

55 pursued full throttle: ACLU Biennial Conference, Equality Committee report, November 1970, American Civil Liberties Union Records, Princeton University Library, Box 24, folder 4.

55 equality broadly defined: American Civil Liberties Union Records, Princeton University Library, Box 23, Board minutes of January 18, 1971.

56 to a similar action: "The Trailblazers," *Rutgers Magazine*, Winter 2013, http://magazine.rutgers.edu/features/winter-2013/the-trailblazers.

56 *"no longer be acceptable"*: Memo from "The Office" to "Board of Directors," November 20, 1970, American Civil Liberties Union Records, Princeton University Library, Box 24, folder 4.

56 women's rights as a new priority: Minutes of the Board of Directors, October 2–3, 1971, American Civil Liberties Union Records, Princeton University Library, Box 24, folder 6.

56 a women's rights project: Minutes of the Board of Directors, December 4–5, 1971, American Civil Liberties Union Records, Princeton University Library, Box 24, folder 6.

56 "Harvard University law professor": Ibid.

57 answerable directly to him: Aryeh Neier, interview with the author, July 11, 2013.

57 overriding and lifelong message: Ibid.

57 "'making *Ruth* the head of that?'": Ann Freedman, interview with the author, October 29, 2013.

58 would be the director: Minutes of the Board of Directors, February 1972, American Civil Liberties Union Records, Princeton University Library, Box 25, folder 5.

58 "supporting memorandum": Supporting memorandum, September 29, 1971, American Civil Liberties Union Records, Princeton University Library, Box 26, folder 2.

58 national and local ACLU boardrooms: Susan M. Hartmann, *The Other Feminists: Activists in the Liberal Establishment* (New Haven, Conn.: Yale University Press, 1998), 80.

59 a legendary fund-raiser: Marilyn Haft, interview with the author, June 19, 2013.

59 reproductive control: Draft Prospectus for a Women's Rights Project, October 1972, Ginsburg Archive, Library of Congress.

59 complaints arrived with alarming speed: ACLU archives, Box 3113.

60 male-only draft: Ruth B. Cowan, "Womens Rights through Litigation: An Examination of the American Civil Liberties Union Women's Rights Project, 1971–1976," *Columbia Human Rights Law Review* 8 (1977): 373–89.

60 petition Congress to stop the practice: Biskupic, *Sandra Day O'Connor*, 58.

60 when the time came: Ibid., 97.

61 abortion rights for women: Aryeh Neier, interview with the author, July 11, 2013.

61 sterilize criminals: *Skinner v. Oklahoma* ex rel. Williamson 316 U.S. 535 (1942).

63 Playboy Foundation: Aryeh Neier, interview with the author, July 11, 2013.

63 "so confident about it": Susan Berresford, interview with the author, November 5, 2013.

63 "sensitivity meetings": Hartmann, *The Other Feminists*, 156, citing FFA transcripts.

63 growing structure of favorable decisions: Cowan, "Women's Rights through Litigation," page 381–82.

63 reinventing the wheel: Ginsburg Archive, Library of Congress, Box 20, Folder Conference of Equal Rights Advocates, April 1973.

65 Amendment to the state constitution: *Baehr v. Lewin*, 74 Haw. 530, 852 P.2d 44 (1993), reconsideration and clarification granted in part, 74 Haw. 645, 852 P.2d 74 (1993).

65 always her priority: Janice Goodman, interview with the author, July 31, 2013.

66 "that quiet voice": Nina Totenberg, interview with author, September 6, 2013.

66 more women on the faculty: Ginsburg, letter to William McGill, 1972, Ginsburg Archive, Library of Congress, Box 18, F71–73.

66 women in bar functions: Ginsburg, letter to New York City Bar Association, Ginsburg Archive, Library of Congress, Box 12, folder June/November 1972.

66 Century Club was in the '70s: Ginsburg Archive, Library of Congress, Box 12, SALT speech; Harvey Goldschmid, interview with the author, November 4, 2013, re: her whispering in Herbert Wechsler's ear.

66 big-enough room at its meeting: Ginsburg Archive, Library of Congress,

Box 13, folder August '76, correspondence with the ABA bicentennial celebration programmers.

CHAPTER 4: ACT ONE: BUILDING WOMEN'S EQUALITY

69 she would throw it up: Fred Strebeigh, *Equal: Women Reshape American Law* (New York: W. W. Norton, 2009), 52, citing Elinor Porter Swiger, *Women Lawyers at Work* (New York: Messner, 1978), 52.

71 give it to Ruth to argue: Strebeigh, *Equal*, 50–51.

71 Ginsburg had won in *Reed v. Reed*: Serena Mayeri, "'When the Trouble Started': The Story of *Frontiero v. Richardson*," in *Women and the Law Stories*, edited by Elizabeth M. Schneider and Stephanie M. Wildman (New York: Foundation Press, 2011), http://lsr.nellco.org/cgi/viewcontent.cgi?article=1321&context=upenn_wps.

72 manage the Nixon Court: Michael J. Klarman, "Social Reform Litigation and Its Challenges: An Essay in Honor of Justice Ruth Bader Ginsburg," *Harvard Journal of Law & Gender* 32 (2009): 251–302, citing a letter from Charles F. Abernathy to Brenda Fasteau, October 19, 1972 (on file with the Harvard Law School Library), http://www.law.harvard.edu/students/orgs/jlg/vol322/251-302.pdf.

72 her suggestions on anything: Charles F. Abernathy, Southern Poverty Law Center, letter to Brenda Fasteau, American Civil Liberties Union, October 19, 1972, Ginsburg Archive, Library of Congress, Box 3, Folder *Frontiero v. Richardson*, 1972.

72 was important, she asserted: Ginsburg, letter to Joseph Levin, Southern Poverty Law Center, October 24, 1972, Ginsburg Archive, Library of Congress, Box 3, Folder *Frontiero v. Richardson*, 1972.

73 oral argument purposes: Joseph Levin, Southern Poverty Law Center, letter to Ginsburg, October 27, 1972, Ginsburg Archive, Library of Congress, Box 3, Folder *Frontiero v. Richardson*, 1972.

74 "when Ruth starts to perform": Nina Totenberg, interview with the author, September 6, 2013.

75 for the bold move: Geoffrey Stone, interview with the author, September 12, 2013; Seth Stern and Stephen Wermiel, *Justice Brennan: Liberal Champion* (Boston: Houghton Mifflin Harcourt, 2010).

76 "emotional discussion about women's rights": Linda Greenhouse, *Becoming Justice Blackmun: Harry Blackmun's Supreme Court Journey* (New York: Times Books, 2005), 210.

76 "mute the outrage of Women's Lib": Lewis Powell, letter to William Brennan, May 8, 1973, Lewis F. Powell, Jr., Archive, 1921–1998: Washington and Lee University School of Law, 001, *Frontiero v. Richardson*.

76 various lawyers' performances: Blackmun papers, cited in Greenhouse, *Becoming Justice Blackmun*, 215.

76 very conventional Virginia gentleman: Penny Clark, interview with the author, December 27, 2013.

77 he reminds himself: Lewis Powell, notes to self, Lewis F. Powell, Jr., Archive, Washington and Lee University School of Law, 001, *Frontiero v. Richardson*, document labeled "argued 1/17/73."

77 he wrote to Brennan: Lewis F. Powell to William Brennan, March 2, 1973, in Thurgood Marshall Papers, Library of Congress; Strebeigh, *Equal*, 59.

CHAPTER 5: INTERMISSION: ABORTION

78 "emancipation of American women": Tinsley E. Yarbrough, *Harry A. Blackmun: The Outsider Justice* (New York: Oxford University Press, 2008), 230.

78 "right of the physician": Linda Greenhouse and Reva Siegel, eds., *Before* Roe v. Wade: *Voices that Shaped the Abortion Debate before the Supreme Court's Ruling* (New York: Kaplan, 2010), 248.

78 feminists, radical or mainstream: Leslie J. Reagan, *When Abortion Was a Crime: Women, Medicine, and Law in the United States, 1867–1973* (Berkeley: University of California Press, 1997), 217.

79 health of the pregnant woman: "Abortion—Twentieth-Century Abortion Law Reform," law.jrank (website), http://law.jrank.org/pages/447/Abortion-Twentieth-century-abortion-law-reform.html.

79 missing arms or legs: Greenhouse and Siegel, *Before* Roe v. Wade, 11; "Sherri Finkbine's Abortion: Its Meaning 50 Years Later," Planned Parenthood Advocates of Arizona (blog), http://blog.advocatesaz.org/2012/08/15/sherri-finkbines-abortion-its-meaning-50-years-later/.

79 feminist movement in 1963: Greenhouse and Siegel, *Before* Roe v. Wade, 14–16; Reagan, *When Abortion Was a Crime*, 231–34.

80 state of their mental health: Reagan, *When Abortion Was a Crime*, 231–34.

80 had been presented to the Court: Greenhouse and Siegel, *Before* Roe v. Wade; see, for example, "Brief *Amicus Curiae* on Behalf of New Women Lawyers, Women's Health and Abortion Project, Inc., National Abortion Action Coalition (1971)," in *Public Women, Public Words: A Documentary History of American Feminism*, vol. 3, *1960 to the Present*, edited by Dawn Keetley and John Pettegrew (Oxford and Lanham, Md.: Rowman and Littlefield, 2002), 215.

80 Women's Rights Project: Strictly speaking, *Roe* came through Sarah Weddington's group of young lawyers and graduate students out of the University of Texas at Austin, but the ACLU was the show runner of the companion case, *Doe v. Bolton*. The two are, for purposes of the ACLU involvement, as one.

82 Center for Constitutional Rights: Greenhouse and Siegel, *Before* Roe v. Wade, 333.

82 "self-fulfillment potential": Ginsburg Archive, Library of Congress, Box 13, folder November 75.

83 "the basic unit of society": Phyllis Schlafly, "Women's Libbers do NOT Speak for Us," *Phyllis Schlafly Report*, February 1972, reprinted in Siegel and Greenhouse, *Before* Roe v. Wade, 218–19.

CHAPTER 6: ACT TWO: EQUALITY IN PERIL

84 "appointed to the Supreme Court": Ruth Bader Ginsburg, "U.S. Supreme Court Justice Nomination Acceptance Address," American Rhetoric Online Speech Bank, June 14, 1993, http://www.americanrhetoric.com/speeches/ruthbaderginsburgusscnominationspeech.htm.

84 almost no women on any court: In 1971, women were fewer than 5 percent of all judges. "Before there was Sotomayor, before even Ginsburg and O'Connor . . . there was Mildred Lillie," *Peter Jennings Project*, August 3, 2009, http://peterjenningsproject.blogspot.com/2009/08/before-there-was-sotomayor-before-even.html.

84 highest court in New York: Ginsburg Archive, Library of Congress, Box 18, F73.

85 When the Equal Rights Amendment: https://www.aclu.org/tribute-legacy-ruth-bader-ginsburg-and-wrp-staff.

86 struggled mightily to survive: Fred Strebeigh, *Equal: Women Reshape American Law* (New York: W. W. Norton, 2009), 63.

86 *Frontiero* to two: *Kahn v. Shevin*, 416 U.S. 351 (1974).

87 Ginsburg was alarmed: Ginsburg, letter to Stephen Wiesenfeld, May 3, 1974.

88 "unconstitutional and simply wrong": Seth Stern and Stephen Wermiel, *Justice Brennan: Liberal Champion* (Boston: Houghton Mifflin Harcourt, 2010), 400.

88 his daughter rebooted her career: Ibid., 402.

88 Clark knew her customer: Penny Clark, interview with the author, December 27, 2013.

88 "play in this controversial area": Penny Clark, memo to Lewis F. Powell, Lewis F. Powell, Jr. Archives, Washington and Lee University School of Law, 001, Taylor file.

89 need affirmative action too: Ginsburg Archive, Library of Congress, Box 14; speech to ABA: Affirmative Action, the Impact of Bakke, 1978.

92 "affirmed in her case": Hearings before the Committee on the Judiciary of the United States Senate . . . on the Nomination of Ruth Bader Ginsburg, July 20–23, 1993, http://www.loc.gov/law/find/nominations/ginsburg/hearing.pdf.

92 "the liberal Warren Court": Ibid.

92 judged by—their peers: Ruth Bader Ginsburg, "Sex and Unequal Protection: Men and Women as Victims," keynote address, Southern Regional Conference of the National Conference of Law Women, Duke University, October 1, 1971, published in *Journal of Family Law* 11 (1971): 347;

"Realizing the Equality Principle," Ginsburg Archive, Library of Congress, Box 12.

CHAPTER 7: ACT THREE: THE STAY-AT-HOME DAD TO THE RESCUE

94 "can't get any better than that!": Strebeigh, *Equal*, 67, quoting interview with M. E. Freeman.

94 "part of equality for all": Stephen Wiesenfeld, letter to Ginsburg, August 8, 1993.

95 "when I wrote the letter": Ibid.

95 "what the procedures would be": Stephen Wiesenfeld, interview with the author, October 14, 2013.

96 air force spouse case: O'Neill is an interesting bit player. When he clerked for William Rehnquist in 1974, he was a veteran of the war in Vietnam and had served time on a Swift Boat there. Decades later, he wrote a hotly controversial book about John Kerry, *Unfit for Command*, and in 2004 he was the mastermind of the Swift Boat Veterans for Truth, widely credited with destabilizing John Kerry's campaign for the presidency by attacking his version of his war record.

96 *Kahn v. Shevin*: Lewis F. Powell, Jr. Archives, Washington and Lee University School of Law, 001, Wiesenfeld case file, Preliminary Memo.

98 "in view of *Kahn*": Lewis F. Powell, Jr. Archives, Washington and Lee University School of Law, 001, Weinberger case file notes from conference.

98 *Kahn* should carry the day: Linda Greenhouse, *Becoming Justice Blackmun: Harry Blackmun's Supreme Court Journey* (New York: Times Books, 2005), 217.

99 key to the outcome: Strebeigh, *Equal*, Wiesenfeld 75.

99 worried letter from Wiesenfeld: Ginsburg to Stephen Wiesenfeld, May 3, 1974.

99 tie for Wiesenfeld: Stephen Wiesenfeld, interview with the author, October 14, 2013.

100 "This accords with statutory intent": Powell's notes on conference, Lewis F. Powell, Jr. Archives, Washington and Lee University School of Law, 001, Wiesenfeld case file.

100 "countervailing interest, protection": *Weinberger v. Wiesenfeld*, 420 U.S. 636 (1975).

101 "mothers may make this choice": Ibid., 655.

101 "child of a contributing worker": Rehnquist concurrence in *Weinberger v. Wiesenfeld*, Ibid.

102 "not thrust upon them 'willy-nilly'": Ginsburg Archive, Library of Congress, Box 12, February–March 1973.

102 on this year's docket: Kurland letter, March 1975, from Ginsburg Archive, Library of Congress, Box 16.

102 told Stephen in a phone call: Stephen Wiesenfeld, interview with the author, October 14, 2013.

102 Wiesenfeld's phone rang again: Ibid.

102 Penny Clark remembers: Penny Clark, interview with the author, December 27, 2013.

103 began a lifelong correspondence: Ginsburg, letter to Stephen Wiesenfeld, May 1, 1975.

104 "[*Weinberger v.*] *Wiesenfeld* and *Frontiero*": Notes on Conference, October 8, 1976, Lewis F. Powell, Jr. Archives, Washington and Lee University School of Law, Goldfarb case.

104 Stevens voted for Ginsburg: John Paul Stevens to William Brennan, October 21, 1976, Lewis F. Powell, Jr. Archives, Washington and Lee University School of Law, Goldfarb case.

104 [in Ginsburg's favor]: Notes on Conference, October 8, 1976, Lewis F. Powell, Jr. Archives, Washington and Lee University School of Law, Goldfarb case.

CHAPTER 8: FINALE: BOYS AND GIRLS TOGETHER

105 "economic discrimination against women": Clark Memorandum, October 1, 1974, Lewis F. Powell, Jr. Archives, Washington and Lee University School of Law.

105 held the Utah law unconstitutional: *Stanton v. Stanton* 421 U.S. 7 (1975).

106 law was "ridiculous": Brief for ACLU as Amicus Curiae, *Craig v. Boren*, 429 U.S. 190 (1976) (No. 75-628), 21.

106 thought the case was "silly": notes on Preliminary Memo, January 9, 1976, Conference, Lewis F. Powell, Jr. Archives, Washington and Lee University School of Law, *Craig v. Boren* file.

106 oral argument at the high court: Fred Gilbert correspondence, Ginsburg Archive, Library of Congress, ACLU file, Box 2.

106 October 5, 1976: Ginsburg to Fred Gilbert, August 13, 1976, Ginsburg Archive, Library of Congress, ACLU File, Box 2. The story about Ginsburg's people arranging the order of argument with the Supreme Court clerk is in Amy Leigh Campbell, *Raising the Bar: Ruth Bader Ginsburg and the ACLU Women's Rights Project* (Bloomington, Ind.: Xlibris, 2004), 162 n. 521, citing bcc of August letter to Jill Hoffman.

107 "achievement of those objectives": *Craig v. Boren*, 429 U.S. 190 (1976), http://www.law.cornell.edu/supremecourt/text/429/190.

107 Baker noted in a memo: Baker memorandum to Powell, November 2, 1976, Lewis F. Powell, Jr. Archives, Washington and Lee University School of Law, *Craig v. Boren* file.

108 "never have achieved this success": Ginsburg, letter to Stephen Wiesenfeld, March 2, 1977.

108 death penalty, Anthony Amsterdam: "The Law: Ten Teachers Who Shape the Future," *Time*, March 14, 1977, http://content.time.com/time/magazine/article/0,9171,947277,00.html.

108 all-powerful *Harvard Law Review*: Ginsburg, letter to Stephen Wiesenfeld, November 8, 1978.

108 "a rare thing these days," she thought: Ginsburg, letter to Stephen Wiesenfeld, May 31, 1979.

109 "romantic attachment to her": Aryeh Neier, interview with the author, July 11, 2013.

109 So they were colleagues: Ginsburg, letter to Stephen Wiesenfeld, August 31, 1979.

109 women's expectations went way up: Nancy Scherer, "Diversifying the Federal Bench: Is Universal Legitimacy for the U.S. Justice System Possible?" *Northwestern University Law Review* 105 (2011): 587; see also Scherer, "Why Has the Lower Court Appointment Process Become So Politicized and What We Can Do about It?" *Jurist* (online journal of the University of Pittsburgh Law School), 2004, http://www.jurist.law.pitt.edu/forum/symposium-jc/scherer .php.

109 not a hotbed of diversity: Sally Jane Kenney, *Gender and Justice: Why Women in the Judiciary Really Matter* (New York: Routledge, 2013), 72.

109 list of likely nominees: Ginsburg Archive, Library of Congress, Box 19, Folder Bio 1976.

110 letter-writing campaign: Ginsburg Archive, Library of Congress, Box 18, letters.

110 "complained of each others' snoring": Ginsburg, letter to Stephen Wiesenfeld, May 31, 1979.

110 Lawrence Walsh: Jon O. Newman, "Probing and Allegations in the Confirmation of Federal Judges," *Journal of Civil Rights and Economic Development* 7 (1991): 15, http://scholarship.law.stjohns.edu/cgi/viewcontent.cgi?article =1520&context=jcred.

111 women lawyers in the country: Susan Ness, "A Sexist Selection Process Keeps Qualified Women off the Bench," *Washington Post*, March 26, 1978; Susan Ness, "The Bench: Where Are All the Women?" *Los Angeles Times*, April 4, 1979; Susan Ness and Fredrica Wechsler, "Women Judges—Why So Few?" *Graduate Woman*, November/December 10–12, 1979, 46–49.

111 "expectations were unrealistic": Ginsburg to Spann, Ginsburg Archive, Library of Congress, Box 16, December 1978.

111 deafened herself to ignore: American Trial Lawyers Association speech, Ginsburg Archive, Library of Congress, Box 13, 1977.

111 earlier in her campaign: *Duren v. Missouri*, 439 U.S. 357 (1979).

112 "explicit sex lines in the law": Ginsburg, letter to Stephen Wiesenfeld, May 31, 1979.

112 standing in her office: Marilyn Haft, interview with the author, June 19, 2013.

113 "anyone changes his mind": Sarah Weddington, interview with the author, December 5, 2012.

113 "U.S. Court of Appeals Here": Laura Kiernan, "Feminist Picked for U.S. Court of Appeals Here," *Washington Post*, December 16, 1979.

113 a long, anxious wait: Ginsburg, letter to Stephen Wiesenfeld, February 15, 1980.

113 even setting a hearing: Lynn Hecht Schafran, letter to the author, October 9, 2014.

113 "ground of my 'militant feminism'": Ginsburg to Lynn Hecht Schafran, Ginsburg Archive, Library of Congress, Box 19, Folder Century 1980.

113 law partner Ira Millstein: Ginsburg confirmation hearings, http://www.gpo.gov/fdsys/pkg/GPO-CHRG-GINSBURG/pdf/GPO-CHRG-GINSBURG-4-28-1.pdf.

113 cases involving his companies: Gardiner Harris, "M. D. Ginsburg, 78, Dies, Lawyer and Tax Expert," *New York Times*, June 27, 2010.

CHAPTER 9: SANDRA O'CONNOR RAISES ARIZONA

117 great time to add a woman: O'Connor papers, Arizona History and Archive, Box 1:1, letter to President Nixon, October 1, 1971.

117 school desegregation in *Brown*: William H. Rehnquist, "A Random Thought on the Segregation Cases," 1952, http://www.gpo.gov/fdsys/pkg/GPO-CHRG-REHNQUIST/pdf/GPO-CHRG-REHNQUIST-4-16-6.pdf.

118 told the city council: O'Connor papers, Arizona History and Archives, 3:9.

119 "how do you think I got here?": "10 Things You Didn't Know about Antonin Scalia," *US News and World Report*, October 2, 2007, http://www.usnews.com/news/national/articles/2007/10/02/10-things-you-didnt-know-about-justice-antonin-scalia.

120 Booze, Beefsteaks, and Blondes: David R. Berman, *Arizona Politics and Government* (Lincoln: University of Nebraska Press, 1998), 50.

120 useful economic growth: Ibid., 51–52.

120 redistricted to favor Republicans: Joan Biskupic, *Sandra Day O'Connor: How the First Woman on the Supreme Court Became Its Most Influential Justice* (New York: Harper Perennial, 2006), 37.

120 would do the same: *Arizona Republic* editorial, October 24, 1971, cited in Biskupic, *Sandra Day O'Connor*, 352.

120 better governors: Letter from O'Connor with calculation of election predictions, undated, Lewis F. Powell, Jr. Archives, Washington and Lee University School of Law; O'Connor, letter to Barry M. Goldwater, November 1, 1988, Personal and Political Papers of Senator Barry M. Goldwater, Arizona State University Libraries Arizona Collection; Jeffrey Toobin, *Too Close to Call: The Thirty-Six-Day Battle to Decide the 2000 Election* (New York: Random House, 2001), 248.

120 to contact their senators: O'Connor papers, Arizona History and Archives, 3:8.

121 "not come out": O'Connor to William H. Rehnquist, October 29, 1971, O'Connor papers, Arizona History and Archives, 3:10.

121 "he was hanged": William H. Rehnquist, "A Cat Looks at Five Kings," O'Connor papers, Arizona History and Archives, 3:10. Rehnquist's admiration for

Judge Parker surfaced at some point years later when it could no longer do harm. William H. Rehnquist, "Isaac Parker, Bill Sykes and the Rule of Law," *University of Arkansas Little Rock Law Journal* 6 (1983): 485 (defending Parker against contemporary criticisms of his administration of justice).

121 "future of the Court": O'Connor, letters to supporters, O'Connor papers, Arizona History and Archives, 3:10.

121 almost without exception voted no: The exception was *Weinberger v. Wiesenfeld*, where he voted for Baby Jason.

122 1972 election effort: Biskupic, *Sandra Day O'Connor*, 53.

122 identity groups within the campaign: O'Connor papers, Arizona History and Archives, 2:3.

122 boys in school, she said: Interview with Thomas Reed, head of regional Committee to Re-elect the President, reported in Biskupic, *Sandra Day O'Connor*, 56.

122 "I wanted enacted": Phoenix Oral History Project, taped interview with Sandra Day O'Connor, 1980, Arizona Historical Society.

122 approach to welfare: Nancy Maveety, *Justice Sandra Day O'Connor, Strategist on the Supreme Court* (Lanham, Md.: Rowman and Littlefield, 1996), 15, citing Edward V. Heck and Paula C. Arledge, "Justice O'Connor and the First Amendment, 1981–84," *Pepperdine Law Review* 13 (1986): 993–1019, and Howard Kohn, "Front and Center: Sandra Day O'Connor," *Los Angeles Times Magazine*, April 18, 1993.

123 ancient divisions survived: "Uniform Disposition of Community Property Rights at Death Act," National Conference of Commissioners on Uniform State Laws, August 21–28, 1971, http://www.uniformlaws.org/shared/docs/disposition%20of%20community%20property%20rights/udcprda%201971.pdf.

123 injury of a child: Schafran testimony at confirmation hearings, http://www.gpo.gov/fdsys/pkg/GPO-CHRG-OCONNOR/pdf/GPO-CHRG-OCONNOR-4-24-2.pdf and statutes cited at Schafran notes 2 and 3. The *Arizona Republic* specifically credits O'Connor with fighting efforts to water down the equalizing initiative, May 4, 1973, http://www.newspapers.com/image/8349961/.

123 total personal income of the state: O'Connor papers, Arizona History and Archives, 5:1, 5:8.

123 "similar action in other states": Personal and Political Papers of Senator Barry M. Goldwater, Arizona State University Libraries Arizona Collection, correspondence, O'Connor file.

123 Majority Leader Burton Barr: "Arizona's Expenditure and Tax Limitation Proposal: An Analysis of Proposition 106," Arizona State University Papers in Public Administration, 1974, O'Connor papers, Arizona History and Archives, 5:2.

123 Trunk 'n Tusk Club: Ibid.

124 "Miller Time": "Justice Sandra Day O'Connor Announces Retirement after 24 Years," *Metropolitan News-Enterprise,* July 5, 2005, http://www.metnews.com/articles/2005/ocon070505.htm.

124 legislature too long: Interview, O'Connor, Arizona History Project, January 31, 1980.

124 responded, "you could": Biskupic, *Sandra Day O'Connor*, 52.

124 "never one of the boys": Ibid., 63, citing Kohn, "Front and Center."

124 ordinary criminal trials: Ibid., 64–65.

124 human emotions and experiences: Ibid., 65.

125 "Ogg/judicial Miller Time": Rosenblatt interview, February 7, 2014.

CHAPTER 10: WELCOME JUSTICE O'CONNOR

126 married "wealthily": Shakespeare, *The Taming of the Shrew*, Act I, scene 2, "Wive it wealthily," technically.

126 advisor to Richard Nixon: Joe Holley, "Leading Texas Republican Anne Armstrong," *Washington Post*, July 31, 2008, http://www.washingtonpost .com/wp-dyn/content/article/2008/07/30/AR2008073002605.html.

126 it was Armstrong he asked: Biskupic, *Sandra Day O'Connor*, 56.

126 special assistant for women: Ann Wood, "Pat Lindh Says She 'Nags a Lot' as Special Assistant to President," *Toledo Blade*, November 17, 1975, http://news.google.com/newspapers?nid=1350&dat=19751117&id= BQ9PAAAAIBAJ&sjid=QgIEAAAAIBAJ&pg=7176,4753121.

127 William O. Douglas in 1975: Janet M. Martin, *The Presidency and Women: Promise, Performance, and Illusion* (College Station: Texas A&M University Press, 2003).

127 spice up his social life: The story of the whole trip is from John and Gail Driggs, interview with the author, January 25, 2014.

129 his Republican opponent: Paul Rosenblatt, interview with the author, February 7, 2014. Babbitt apparently denies this; see Biskupic, *Sandra Day O'Connor*, 68.

130 "these things were making": Penny Clark, interview with the author, December 27, 2013.

130 men the Republican: Biskupic, *Sandra Day O'Connor*, 70. Biskupic tells the story of O'Connor's nomination and confirmation in painstaking detail in chapter 5.

130 yields social change: In 1992, Bill Clinton casually tossed off a commitment to stop the United States driving gay soldiers out of the military. Linda Hirshman, *Victory: The Triumphant Gay Revolution* (New York: Harper-Collins, 2012), 22.

130 campaign advisor Stuart Spencer: "Interview with Stuart Spencer," 2005, Ronald Reagan Oral History, Miller Center, University of Virginia, http:// millercenter.org/president/reagan/oralhistory/stuart-spencer.

131 getting her on the list: Ann Carey McFeatters, *Sandra Day O'Connor: Justice in the Balance* (Albuquerque: University of New Mexico Press, 2005), 11–12.

131 right-to-life activists in Arizona: Goldwater to "each of the family," Goldwater correspondence, May 14, 1980, Personal and Political Papers of Senator

Barry M. Goldwater, Arizona State University Libraries Arizona Collection; Biskupic, *Sandra Day O'Connor*, 85.

131 Reagan's own hand: Biskupic, *Sandra Day O'Connor*, 77–78.

132 foot in the door: "The only problem I ever had," she told an interviewer in 1980, "was in obtaining employment initially," from transcript of the Arizona historical society interview, 10.

132 O'Connor's house: McFeatters, *Sandra Day O'Connor*, 12–13.

132 he told his team: Biskupic, *Sandra Day O'Connor*, 77.

132 never heard of the nominee: Mike Sacks, "Women Supreme Court Justices Celebrate 30 Years since Court's First Female," *Huffington Post*, April 11, 2012, http://www.huffingtonpost.com/2012/04/11/supreme-court-women-justices_n_1419183.html.

133 prepare her for her hearings: Ruth McGregor, interview with the author, January 23, 2013.

133 John Driggs got a call: John and Gail Driggs, interview with the author, January 25, 2014.

133 her short-term memory: Biskupic, *Sandra Day O'Connor*, 91.

134 advocacy of the Equal Rights Amendment: Ibid., 86–96.

134 when there clearly was: Ibid., 84.

134 steadfast silence: Ibid., 96–97.

134 women and the judiciary: Lynn Hecht Schafran, "Sandra O'Connor and the Supremes," *Ms.*, October 1981.

134 experience of discrimination: Virginia Kerr, "Supreme Court Justice O'Connor: The Woman Whose Word Is Law," *Ms.*, December 1982, 52; Margaret A. Miller, "Justice Sandra Day O'Connor: Token or Triumph from a Feminist Perspective," *Golden Gate University Law Review* 15 (2010): 493–525, http://digitalcommons.law.ggu.edu/cgi/viewcontent.cgi?article=1373&context=ggulrev.

135 "good many problems": Burger Memorandum to the Conference, September 22, 1981, Lewis F. Powell, Jr. Archives, Washington and Lee University School of Law.

135 the new nominee: O'Connor, family letter, October 8, 1981.

135 attend her ascension: Paul Rosenblatt, interview with the author, February 7, 2014.

135 "I did not want to be the last": "Justice Sandra Day O'Connor Visits Duke Law," *Duke Law News* (website), http://law.duke.edu/features/news_oconnor/ (accessed November 18, 2014).

136 O'Connor hates mess: Dahleen Glanton, "O'Connor Questions Court's Decision to Take On *Bush v. Gore*," *Chicago Tribune*, April 27, 2013, http://articles.chicagotribune.com/2013-04-27/news/ct-met-sandra-day-oconnor-edit-board-20130427_1_o-connor-bush-v-high-court.

136 "watch over Sandra": Mary-Audrey Weicker Mellor to Powell, July 8, 1981, Lewis F. Powell, Jr. Archives, Washington and Lee University School of Law, correspondence.

136 apartment in the Watergate: "A Tribute to Lewis F. Powell, Jr," *Washington*

and Lee Law Review 56 (1999): 6, http://scholarlycommons.law.wlu.edu/cgi/viewcontent.cgi?article=1532&context=wlulr.

136 find her place in her notes: Ruth McGregor, interview with the author, January 23, 2013.

136 "partly through your eyes": O'Connor to Powell, November 15, 1982, Lewis F. Powell, Jr. Archives, Washington and Lee University School of Law.

137 "Pebble Beach Corp and Aspen Corp.": O'Connor to Powell, May 25, 1984, Lewis F. Powell, Jr. Archives, Washington and Lee University School of Law.

137 would not have women as members: Lynn Hecht Schafran, testimony at the confirmation hearing, http://www.gpo.gov/fdsys/pkg/GPO-CHRG-OCONNOR/pdf/GPO-CHRG-OCONNOR-4-24-2.pdf.

137 behavior of the PVCC: "Paradise Valley Country Club," *A People's Guide to Maricopa County* (website), May 2, 2011, http://peoplesguidetomaricopa.blogspot.com/2011/05/paradise-valley-country-club.html.

138 could not be reached for comment: "Senators Decry 'Racism' of Exclusive Country Club," *Prescott Courier* (Associated Press), April 3, 1990, http://news.google.com/newspapers?nid=886&dat=19900803&id=bQtTAAAAIBAJ&sjid=woEDAAAAIBAJ&pg=4272,278272.

138 And the Ginsburgs left: "Ginsburgs Say Clubs Scored Poorly in Conscience," *Orlando Sentinal* (*Washington Post*), June 20, 1993, http://articles.orlandosentinel.com/1993-06-20/news/9306200267_1_martin-ginsburg-harvard-club-country-club.

138 or hurt them: Ruth McGregor, Preliminary Memorandum, October 30, 1981, Lewis F. Powell, Jr. Archives, Washington and Lee University School of Law, *Hogan* case file.

139 male-only draft registration: *Rostker v. Goldberg*, 453 U.S. 57 (1981); *Michael M. v. Superior Court of Sonoma County*, 450 U.S. 464 (1981).

139 never had trouble making decisions: Stephen Gilles, interview with the author, March 28, 2014.

140 Mississippi schools: "School Desegregation," *West's Encyclopedia of American Law* (2005), http://www.encyclopedia.com/topic/School_integration.aspx.

140 working skills such as farming: Jill Elaine Hasday, "The Principle and Practice of Women's 'Full Citizenship': A Case Study of Sex-Segregated Public Education," University of Chicago Public Law and Legal Theory Working Paper no. 35 (2002), http://chicagounbound.uchicago.edu/cgi/viewcontent.cgi?article=1333&context=public_law_and_legal_theory.

140 "drawing, painting, designing, and engraving": Ibid.

140 weapon against racial integration: Ibid.

140 living room window: Birney Imes, "Joe Hogan's Legacy," *The Dispatch*, March 14, 2009, http://www.cdispatch.com/opinions/article.asp?aid=678&TRID=1&TID=.

140 away from black men: Hasday, "Principle and Practice."

140 the Mississippi establishment: Wilbur Colom, e-mail to the author, November 11, 2014.

140 "the traditional fear": Ibid.

141 "'procedures in social situations'": John Wiley to Powell, Lewis F. Powell, Jr. Archives, Washington and Lee University School of Law, *Hogan* folder.

141 "benefit of unisex schools": Powell notes on conference votes, Lewis F. Powell, Jr. Archives, Washington and Lee University School of Law, *Hogan* folder.

144 is just fashion: Powell memo to file, Lewis F. Powell Jr. Archive, Washington and Lee University School of Law, *Hogan* folder.

144 "proud and respected reputation": Powell memo to Wiley, Lewis F. Powell, Jr. Archives, Washington and Lee University School of Law, *Hogan* folder.

145 one or two lynchings: Avis Thomas-Lester, "A History Scarred by Lynchings," *Washington Post*, July 7, 2005, http://www.washingtonpost.com/wp-dyn/content/article/2005/07/06/AR2005070600637.html.

145 "every other school or department": Burger to Powell and Powell to Burger, June 22, 1982, Lewis F. Powell Jr. Archive, Washington and Lee University School of Law, *Hogan* folder.

145 "the entire university": Powell, revised draft dissent, June 25, 1982, Lewis F. Powell, Jr. Archives, Washington and Lee University School of Law, *Hogan* folder.

146 get his degree: Wilbur Colom, e-mails to the author, November 11, 2014.

146 "if the college were coed": Ibid.

147 the Supreme Court steps: "Supreme Court Justice Sandra Day O'Connor and Chief Justice Warren Burger on Steps of Supreme Court, Washington DC," image by Ron Bennett Photography, http://ronbennett.photoshelter.com/image/I0000Del5UB91v3M.

147 criticism and comment: Mary Schroeder, interview with the author, February 27, 2014.

147 determined not to fail: Darragh Johnson, "Sandra Day O'Connor: Well Judged," *Washington Post*, March 7, 2006, http://www.washingtonpost.com/wp-dyn/content/article/2006/03/07/AR2006030700008_2.html.

147 "highest court in the land": "Hoops at the Supreme Court, Literally," *Baller-in-Chief* (blog), March 31, 2009, http://baller-in-chief.com/articles/hoops-at-the-supreme-court-literally/.

147 a decade later: David Goldberg, interview with the author, November 24, 2014.

147 two prominent judges' associations: Biskupic, *Sandra Day O'Connor*, 142; Barbara Babcock, interview with the author, March 9, 2014; Alexis K. Hill, *Keeping the Promise of Justice: Celebrating 25 Years of the National Association of Women Judges* (Paducah, Ky.: Turner, 2003), 22.

148 where they were: Biskupic, *Sandra Day O'Connor*, 142; Babcock interview.

148 always a fast learner: Stephen Gilles, interview with the author, March 28, 2014.

148 "Improve the Courts": O'Connor, "What Individuals Can Do to Improve the Courts" (remarks at Commencement Address at Stanford University), June 21, 1982, *Los Angeles Daily Journal*, 4.

148 "Social Responsibility": O'Connor, "Professional Competence and Social Responsibility: Fulfilling the Vanderbilt Vision," *Vanderbilt Law Review* 36 (1983): 1.

149 "being admitted to practice": O'Connor, "Foreword," *New England Law Review* 18 (1982–83): ix.

149 "give remarks today": O'Connor, "Legal Education and Social Responsibility," *Fordham Law Review* 53 (1985).

150 abortion laws since the 1960s: Linda Greenhouse and Reva Siegel, eds., *Before* Roe v. Wade: *Voices that Shaped the Abortion Debate before the Supreme Court's Ruling* (New York: Kaplan, 2010), 282.

150 what the Court had done: for the full story of the Missouri setup, see Mike Hoey, "A Short History of the Missouri Catholic Conference 1967–2007," http://www.mocatholic.org/wp-content/uploads/2012/10/MCC-Short-History-1.pdf.

150 attract Catholic Democrats: Greenhouse and Siegel, *Before* Roe v. Wade, 291–92.

151 "Mr. Justice" salutation: Linda Greenhouse, *Becoming Justice Blackmun: Harry Blackmun's Supreme Court Journey* (New York: Times Books, 2005), 142.

151 who proposed the change: Justice John Paul Stevens, interview with the author, July 21, 2014.

151 too much to take: Biskupic, *Sandra Day O'Connor*, 140–41.

152 *Roe* emerged unscathed: *Akron v. Akron Center for Reproductive Health, Inc.* 462 U.S. 416 (1983), http://www.law.cornell.edu/supremecourt/text/462/416.

153 her dissenting opinion: Biskupic, *Sandra Day O'Connor*, 152.

154 overrule *Roe v. Wade* altogether: U.S. amicus curiae brief, *Akron v. Akron Center for Reproductive Health*, http://searchjustice.usdoj.gov/search?q=cache:GWtsK44B-J4J:www.justice.gov/osg/briefs/1982/sg820172.txt+repeal+roe+v.+wade&output=xml_no_dtd&ie=iso-8859-1&client=default_frontend&proxystylesheet=default_frontend&site=default_collection&access=p&oe=ISO-8859-1. The Reagan and Bush I solicitor general's office were much criticized for their escalating attack on *Roe*, culminating, in 1992, with Solicitor General Charles Fried's argument to overturn it; Lincoln Caplan, *The Tenth Justice: The Solicitor General and the Rule of Law* (New York: Knopf, 1987), 143–45.

154 first female champion: Biskupic, *Sandra Day O'Connor*, 151–52.

154 George Washington Law School: David Von Drehle, "Ruth Bader Ginsburg: Her Life and Her Law," *Washington Post*, July 18–20, 1993, Ginsburg Archive, Library of Congress, Box 46 (picture of Ginsburg and O'Connor at the 1983 conference).

155 casebooks on the subject: Pat Cain, interview with the author, March 21, 2014.

CHAPTER 11: WOMEN WORK FOR JUSTICE O'CONNOR

156 female law students to the steno pool: Fred Strebeigh, *Equal: Women Reshape American Law* (New York: W. W. Norton, 2009), 146.

157 Out of seventy-five partners: Ibid., 199.

157 a few years earlier: David Margolick, "Sex Bias Suit Perils Law Firms' Methods of Picking Partners," *New York Times*, April 23, 1983, http://www.nytimes.com/1983/04/23/us/sex-bias-suit-perils-law-firms-methods-of-picking-partners.html.

158 over the moon: Nina Burleigh and Stephanie B. Goldberg, "Breaking the Silence: Sexual Harassment in Law Firms," *ABA Journal*, August 1989, http://books.google.com/books?id=_EhWudQgJpoC&pg=PA46&dq=king+and+spalding+wet+t+shirt+wall+street+journal&hl=en&sa=X&ei=AxZhVJKtKLLdsAT8k4CoAg&ved=0CCgQ6AEwAA#v=onepage&q=king%20and%20spalding%20wet%20t%20shirt%20wall%20street%20journal&f=false.

158 "have said so?": *Hishon v. King & Spalding*, 467 U.S. 69 (1984), oral argument, http://www.oyez.org/cases/1980-1989/1983/1983_82_940.

159 hidden from view: Lewis F. Powell, Jr. Archives, Washington and Lee University School of Law, *Hishon* file.

159 steal his majority: Bob Woodward and Scott Armstrong, *The Brethren: Inside the Supreme Court* (New York: Simon and Schuster, 1979), 75. At least one of Burger's colleagues, Potter Stewart, blew the whistle on him with the reporters here; see J. Anthony Lukas, "Playboy Interview: Bob Woodward," *Playboy* (February 1, 1989), 51.

160 "modern law firm": Powell, memo to self, October 27, 1983, Lewis F. Powell, Jr. Archives, Washington and Lee University School of Law, *Hishon* file.

160 Women in the Profession: Lynn Hecht Schafran, interview with the author, March 22, 2014.

161 changed by females: Barbara Harris, *Beyond Her Sphere: Women and the Professions in American History* (Westport, Conn.: Greenwood Press, 1978), 110.

161 women in the legal profession: O'Connor, "Introduction: Achievements of Women in the Legal Profession," *New York State Bar Journal* 57 (1985): 8.

162 '70s consciousness-raising: Strebeigh, *Equal*, 218–26.

162 proper subject for the law: Ibid. Strebeigh tells this story thoroughly and well.

163 administrative assistant sued her boss: Julie Berebitsky, *Sex and the Office: A History of Gender, Power, and Desire* (New Haven, Conn.: Yale University Press, 2012).

163 "never have been solicited": *Barnes v. Costle*, 561 F.2d 983 (1977).

164 dead-end life: Strebeigh, *Equal*, 209.

164 "raped her on several occasions": *Meritor Savings Bank v. Vinson*, 477 U.S. 57, 60 (1986).

166 liberals on the Burger Court: Powell's papers trace the developments on the Court; Lewis F. Powell, Jr. Archives, Washington and Lee University School of Law, *Meritor v. Vinson*.

167 turned to Sandra Day O'Connor: Strebeigh, *Equal*, 303.

167 voting with the conservatives: Stephen Gilles, interview with the author, March 28, 2014.

168 had a long good life: Strebeigh, *Equal*, 305.

168 he lost his job: Ibid.

168 eight different opinions!: *Ellereth v. Burlington Industries*, 123 F.3d 490 (1997) (United States Court of Appeals, Seventh Circuit).

169 in any big cases: Beverly B. Cook, "Sandra Day O'Connor," in *The Burger Court: Political and Judicial Profiles*, edited by Charles M. Lamb and Stephen C. Halpern (Urbana: University of Illinois Press, 1991), 272.

171 willing to contemplate its virtues: Ruth Bader Ginsburg, "Gender and the Constitution," *University of Cincinnati Law Review* 44 (1975): 1–42, 75.

171 the Johnson case: Ginsburg, speech, New York Historical Society, October 28, 2014.

171 she asked herself: Powell, notes on conference, Lewis F. Powell, Jr. Archives, Washington and Lee University School of Law, *Johnson* file.

172 "claim of discrimination":*Johnson v. Transportation Agency*, 480 U.S. 616 (1987), at 647, http://www.law.cornell.edu/supremecourt/text/480/616#writing-USSC_CR_0480_0616_ZC1.

172 tightening the noose: *Adarand Construction v. Pena*, 515 U.S. 200 (1995), http://www.law.cornell.edu/supremecourt/text/515/200.

CHAPTER 12: QUEEN SANDRA'S COURT

174 "maternal" acts of kindness: John Setear, interview with the author, April 1, 2014.

175 *Raiders of the Lost Ark*: Joan Greco, interview with the author, April 4, 2014.

175 she liked clerking for Ginsburg: Ibid.

175 a crowd half her age: Ibid.

176 she had already met: Ginsburg, letter to O'Connor, April 25, 1988, Ginsburg Archive, Library of Congress, Box 39.

176 comment on her remarks: Ibid.

176 In her travel diary: Ginsburg Archive, Library of Congress, Box 39.

176 breast cancer: She did not speak of it for six years, until she gave a graphically revealing speech to a convention of breast cancer survivors. O'Connor, "Surviving Cancer," C-SPAN, November 3, 1994, http://www.c-span.org/video/?61342-1/surviving-cancer.

176 Mark Lippman: Ibid.

177 "Depressing" and "traumatic": O'Connor, letter to Powell, Lewis F. Powell, Jr. Archives, Washington and Lee University School of Law, Octobrer 28, 1988, and letter to Goldwater, Personal and Political Papers of Senator Barry M. Goldwater, Arizona State University Libraries Arizona Collection, November 1, 1988.

178 legacies of her tenure: Ginsburg, "A Woman's Voice May Do Some Good," *Politico*, September 25, 2013, http://www.politico.com/story/2013/09/women-oconnor-ginsburg-supreme-court-97313.html.

178 accounting giant Price Waterhouse: *Price Waterhouse v. Hopkins*, 490 U.S. 228 (1989).

179 "hair styled, and wear jewelry": 618 F.Supp. at 1117.

179 "appealing lady ptr [partnership] candidate": *Price Waterhouse v. Hopkins*, at 237.

180 "she was on the bench": Ann Hopkins, *"Price Waterhouse v. Hopkins*: A Personal Account of a Sexual Discrimination Plaintiff," *Hofstra Labor & Employment Law Journal* 22 (2005): 357, http://law.hofstra.edu/pdf/academics/journals/laborandemploymentlawjournal/labor_hopkins_vol22no2.pdf.

181 Brennan was manifestly ailing: Biskupic, *Sandra Day O'Connor*, 195.

181 "the nation that he does": O'Connor to Barry Goldwater, November 1, 1988, Personal and Political Papers of Senator Barry M. Goldwater, Arizona State University Libraries Arizona Collection.

181 "notions of party or race": John McCain to Goldwater, November 26, 1984, Personal and Political Papers of Senator Barry M. Goldwater, Arizona State University Libraries Arizona Collection, O'Connor file.

181 "our population is black?": Goldwater to John O'Connor, December 3, 1984, Personal and Political Papers of Senator Barry M. Goldwater, Arizona State University Libraries Arizona Collection, O'Connor file.

182 Republicans would win their races: O'Connor, letter with calculation of election predictions, undated, Lewis F. Powell, Jr. Archives, Washington and Lee University School of Law.

182 going to write separately anyway: Byron R. White Papers, Library of Congress, *Hopkins* case file.

183 with voluble displeasure: Robert A. Kearny, "The High Price of *Price Waterhouse*: Dealing with Direct Evidence of Discrimination," *University of Pennsylvania Journal of Labor and Employment Law* 5 (2003): 303–33, at 305, and cases cited in footnotes therein, https://www.law.upenn.edu/journals/jbl/articles/volume5/issue2/Kearney5U.Pa.J.Lab.&Emp.L.303(2003).pdf.

183 ensure her support: Maveety, *Justice Sandra Day O'Connor, Strategist on the Supreme Court* (Lanham, Md.: Rowman and Littlefield, 1996), 51 (from the Marshall papers).

183 opinion of whoever was writing: ibid., 61; Robert W. Van Sickel, *Not a Particularly Different Voice: The Jurisprudence of Sandra Day O'Connor* (New York: P. Lang, 1998), 49, citing Susan Behuniak-Long, "Justice Sandra Day O'Connor and the Power of Maternal Legal Thinking," *Review of Politics* 54 (1992): 428.

CHAPTER 13: NO QUEEN'S PEACE IN THE ABORTION WARS

184 attacking *Roe v. Wade*: The lecture, which was delivered on April 6, 1984, was later published as Ruth Bader Ginsburg, "Some Thoughts on Autonomy and Equality in Relation to *Roe v. Wade*," *North Carolina Law Review* 63 (1985): 375–86.

186 "sanctity of innocent human life": Linda Greenhouse and Reva Siegel, eds., *Before* Roe v. Wade: *Voices that Shaped the Abortion Debate before the Supreme Court's Ruling* (New York: Kaplan, 2010), 260.

186 ask the Court to do so: Mike Hoey, "A Short History of the Missouri Catholic Conference 1967–2007," http://www.mocatholic.org/wp-content/uploads/2012/10/MCC-Short-History-1.pdf.

186 escape the confrontation with *Roe*: *Webster v. Reproductive Health Services*, 492 U.S. 490 (1989), http://www.oyez.org/cases/1980-1989/1988/1988_88_605.

186 wasn't as bad as it looked: Ibid., oral argument.

187 from Ginsburg's chambers, Daniel Mandil: Edward Lazarus, *Closed Chambers: The First Eyewitness Account of the Epic Struggles Inside the Supreme Court* (New York: Times Books, 1998). A lot of the inside information on *Webster* comes from Lazarus, who explicitly cites Mandil as his source.

187 Judge Robert Bork: The clerks' political commitments can often be verified by a quick check of their political contributions; see, for example, "Andrew McBride: Political Campaign Contributions, 2010 Election Cycle," CampaignMoney.com, http://www.campaignmoney.com/political/contributions/andrew-mcbride.asp?cycle=10 (accessed November 17, 2014).

187 opposite end of the political spectrum: "Jane Stromseth Contributions," FindTheBest.com, http://individual-contributions.findthedata.org/l/1010743/Jane-Stromseth (accessed November 17, 2014).

189 doctor gag order: O'Connor, memorandum, May 23, 1989, Byron R. White Papers, Library of Congress.

189 "And to do so carefully": *Webster v. Reproductive Health Services*, 492 U.S. 490 (1989), at 526, http://supreme.justia.com/cases/federal/us/492/490/case.html.

189 "fraudulent" and "indecent": Linda Greenhouse, *Becoming Justice Blackmun: Harry Blackmun's Supreme Court Journey* (New York: Times Books, 2005), 193.

191 Pennsylvania court had just done: Ibid., 201–3, for the story on Kolbert's strategy and the Court's scheduling of the appeal. The memo on O'Connor's concerns about the election comes from Blackmun's papers; see David Garrow "The Brains Behind Blackmun," *Legal Affairs*, May–June 2005, http://www.legalaffairs.org/issues/May-June-2005/feature_garrow_mayjun05.msp; David Garrow, "A Landmark Decision—*Planned Parenthood of Southeastern Pennsylvania v. Casey*," *Dissent* 39 (Fall 1992): 427–29, n. 4; Harry A. Blackmun Papers, Library of Congress, Box 601.

191 review the abortion case: Jeffrey Toobin, *The Nine: Inside the Secret World of the Supreme Court* (New York: Doubleday, 2007), 49–50; Lazarus, *Closed Chambers*, 463.

191 Justices Stevens and Blackmun: different leakers have different versions.

191 Rehnquist abandoned the tactic: Toobin, *The Nine*, 50, on Stevens; Lazarus, *Closed Chambers*, 463, on Blackmun and Stevens.

192 Souter's clerk told Dangel: Greenhouse, *Becoming Justice Blackmun*, 201.

192 FWOTSC to overrule *Roe*: Tom Zemaitis, interview with the author, April 17, 2014.

192 assigned the opinion to himself: Lazarus, *Closed Chambers*, 466–70, for the story; also Dennis J. Hutchinson, *The Man Who Once Was Whizzer White: A Portrait of Justice Byron R. White* (New York: Free Press, 1998), 428–29.

193 Endangered Species Act: *Lujan v. Defenders of Wildlife,* 504 U.S. 555 (1992), http://www.law.cornell.edu/supremecourt/text/504/555.

193 "come as welcome news": Harry A. Blackmun Papers, Library of Congress, 1992.

193 "vision of the woman's role": *Planned Parenthood v. Casey,* 505 U.S. 833 (1992), troika opinion, http://supreme.justia.com/cases/federal/us/505/833/case.html.

193 exulted over this opinion: Ginsberg delivered the Madison Lecture at New York University School of Law in 1992; Ruth Bader Ginsburg, "Speaking in a Judicial Voice," *New York University Law Review* 67 (1992): 1185, 1199, http://www.law.nyu.edu/sites/default/files/ECM_PRO_059254.pdf.

196 Critics concluded: There are many examples. One of the best summaries is Judith Olans Brown, Wendy E. Parmet, and Mary E. O'Connell, "The Rugged Feminism of Sandra Day O'Connor," *Indiana Law Review* 32 (1999): 1219–46, Northeastern University School of Law Research Paper, http://ssrn.com/abstract=1984862 or http://dx.doi.org/10.2139/ssrn.1984862.

196 white, middle class, married: Ibid., 1227.

CHAPTER 14: I'M RUTH, NOT SANDRA

199 determined to make history: Richard Davis, *Electing Justice: Fixing the Supreme Court Nomination Process* (New York: Oxford University Press, 2005), http://www.thedivineconspiracy.org/Z5252I.pdf.

200 another liberal vote: David Alistair Yalof, *Pursuit of Justices: Presidential Politics and the Selection of Supreme Court Nominees* (Chicago: University of Chicago Press, 1999).

200 dangling for months: George Stephanopoulos, *All Too Human: A Political Education* (Boston: Little, Brown, 1999), 165–70.

200 posse was hard at work: Stephen Labaton, "Senators See Easy Approval for Nominee," *New York Times,* June 16, 1993, http://www.nytimes.com/1993/06/16/us/senators-see-easy-approval-for-nominee.html.

201 "impressed on a personal basis": Bernard Nussbaum, interview with the author, June 2, 2014.

201 "footnote" type: Jeffrey Toobin, *The Nine,* 75.

202 "anti-stereotype principle": Cary Franklin, "The Anti-Stereotyping Principle in Constitutional Sex Discrimination Law," *New York University Law Review* 85, no. 1 (2010).

202 would never experience?: Catharine MacKinnon, *Sexual Harassment of Working Women* (New Haven, Conn.: Yale University Press 1979), Introduction, 1–8; Fred Strebeigh, *Equal: Women Reshape American Law* (New York: W. W. Norton, 2009), 240–41; Jeffrey Rosen, "The Book of Ruth," *The New Republic,* August 2, 1993, http://www.newrepublic.com/article/politics/the-book-ruth and http://www.holysmoke.org/sdhok/femo2.htm.

202 in a different voice: Carol Gilligan, *In a Different Voice: Psychological Theory*

and Women's Development (Cambridge, Mass.: Harvard University Press, 1982).

203 "That woman has bad karma": Rosen, "The Book of Ruth."

203 "unsettle women's separate spheres": Ginsburg Archive, Library of Congress, Box 15, F 1988.

203 disadvantaged by history and culture: Rosen, "The Book of Ruth"; http://www.newrepublic.com/article/politics/the-book-ruth.

203 she noted, "arrogant": Ginsburg Archive, Library of Congress, Box 15, F 1988.

203 "distinctly male or female thinking": Ginsburg Archive, Library of Congress, Box 15, F May 1991, Amherst speech.

203 "Judging in a Different Voice": Suzanna Sherry, "Civic Virtue and the Feminine Voice in Constitutional Adjudication," *Virginia Law Review* 72 (1986): 543; see O'Connor's comments in the Madison Lecture, delivered at New York University School of Law in 1991, Sandra Day O'Connor, "Portia's Progress," *New York University Law Review* 66 (1991): 1546.

204 "those of my colleagues": Portia's Progress, http://midcoastseniorcollege.org/wp-content/uploads/2014/03/Sandra-Day-OConnor-Portias-Progress.pdf, citing Sherry, "Civic Virtue."

204 faxed from the Supreme Court chambers: Ginsburg Archive, Library of Congress, Box 30, December 1991 folder.

204 abortion decision, *Roe v. Wade*: Ruth Bader Ginsburg, "Speaking in a Judicial Voice," *New York University Law Review* 67 (1992), http://www.law.nyu.edu/sites/default/files/ECM_PRO_059254.pdf.

205 Kate Michelman among them: Tom Brokaw and Lisa Myers, "Reaction to Nomination of Ruth Bader Ginsburg to Supreme Court," *NBC Nightly News*, June 14, 1993, https://highered.nbclearn.com/portal/site/HigherEd/flatview?cuecard=3734.

205 subject of speculative leaks: Anthony Lewis, "Abroad at Home: How Not to Choose," *New York Times*, May 10, 1993, http://news.google.com/newspapers?nid=1755&dat=19930512&id=qQocAAAAIBAJ&sjid=q3sEAAAAIBAJ&pg=6654,2594453.

205 William Coleman wrote: Stephen Labaton, "Senators See Easy Approval for Nominee," *New York Times*, June 16, 1993, http://www.nytimes.com/1993/06/16/us/senators-see-easy-approval-for-nominee.html.

206 were squeaky clean: Gardiner Harris, "M. D. Ginsburg, 78, Dies, Lawyer and Tax Expert," *New York Times*, June 27, 2010.

206 Many observers credit: Jeffrey Toobin, *The Nine: Inside the Secret World of the Supreme Court* (New York: Doubleday, 2007), 81.

207 Rose Garden for the announcement: "Ginsburg Supreme Court Nomination," C-SPAN, June 14, 1993, http://www.c-span.org/video/?42908-1/ginsburg-supreme-court-nomination.

207 through the process: Joel Klein, interview with the author, May 21, 2014.

208 she gave her minders fits: Marcia Coyle, Tony Mauro, and Todd Ruger, "Clinton Docs Reveal Concerns About Court Nominees," *LegalTimes*, July 18,

2014, http://www.nationallawjournal.com/legaltimes/id=1202663790913/Clinton-Docs-Reveal-Concerns-About-Court-Nominees#ixzz3IsohEp8v.

209 "countervailing interest": *The Nomination of Ruth Bader Ginsburg, to Be Associate Justice of the Supreme Court of the United States: Hearings Before the S. Comm. on the Judiciary,* 103d Cong. 127 (1993), http://www.loc.gov/law/find/nominations/ginsburg/hearing.pdf.

210 minority of three: *Michael H. v. Gerald D.,* 491 U.S. 110 (1989).

210 Sandra in Chevy Chase: Ann Carey McFeatters, *Sandra Day O'Connor: Justice in the Balance* (Albuquerque: University of New Mexico Press, 2005).

210 National Opera Lawyers' Committee: Ginsburg Archive, Library of Congress, Box 154, Supreme Court general, copy of O'Connor speech to Opera Lawyers' dinner.

210 Florida and Salzburg: Ginsburg to Stephen Wiesenfeld, correspondence 1982–83; Joan Biskupic, *Sandra Day O'Connor: How the First Woman on the Supreme Court Became Its Most Influential Justice* (New York: Harper Perennial, 2006), 244.

211 "that is the point": *The Nomination of Ruth Bader Ginsburg,* http://www.loc.gov/law/find/nominations/ginsburg/hearing.pdf.

211 the National Gallery: Ruth Bader Ginsburg, televised interview with Brian Lamb, C-SPAN, July 1, 2009, http://supremecourt.c-span.org/assets/pdf/RBGinsburg.pdf; photograph of Ginsburg in her chambers, August 2013, http://www.msnbc.com/sites/msnbc/files/2013/08/ap800767019711.jpg.

211 dead giveaway: Margo Schlanger, University of Michigan Law School faculty website, http://www.law.umich.edu/FacultyBio/Pages/FacultyBio.aspx?FacID=mschlan (accessed November 18, 2014).

211 edited the *Law Journal* too: David M. Schizer, Columbia Law School faculty website, http://www.law.columbia.edu/fac/David_Schizer (accessed November 18, 2014).

212 David Post: David G. Post, Beasley School of Law, Temple University faculty website, http://www.law.temple.edu/pages/faculty/n_faculty_post_main.aspx (accessed November 18, 2014).

212 first in her class at Columbia: Alexandra A. E. Shapiro, Shapiro Arato & Isserles biography, http://www.shapiroarato.com/person/alexandra-shapiro/ (accessed November 18, 2014).

212 David Schizer: David Goldberg, interview with the author, November 24, 2014.

212 University of Chicago Law School: Ibid.

212 reference writers: Margo Schlanger, interview with the author, May 28, 2014.

212 "got the work done": David G. Post, interview with the author, June 3, 2014.

213 Jane at Columbia: Ginsburg, letter to Stephen Wiesenfeld, April 30, 1993.

213 "glad to talk to you": Ginsburg, letter to Jason Wiesenfeld, May 27, 1993.

213 corrected Jason's application essay: Ginsburg to William Brennan, copy in Wiesenfeld collection, November 8, 1993.

213 "acceptance at Columbia": Stephen Wiesenfeld, letter to Ginsburg, May 9, 1994.

213 change in the practice: Ruth Bader Ginsburg to William H. Rehnquist, November 30, 1993, Blackmun Papers, Box 1420, folder 12.

213 "not good enough for Ginsburg": Ruth Bader Ginsburg, oral history page, *Jewish Washington*, May 27, 2005, http://www.jhsgw.org/exhibitions/online/jewishwashington/oral-histories/ruth-bader-ginsburg.

213 "protest too much": Blackmun Papers, Box 1420, folder 12.

213 ceremonial paper: Tony Mauro, "Lifting the Veil: Justice Blackmun's Papers and the Public Perception of the Supreme Court," *Missouri Law Review* 70 (2005): 1037–47, http://scholarship.law.missouri.edu/cgi/viewcontent.cgi?article=3674&context=mlr.

214 "extended family, and closest friends": Ginsburg to Joel D. Lowinger, copy in Wiesenfeld Collection, November 11, 1993.

214 "true feminist voice": Amy Richards, Steinem assistant, to Wiesenfeld, November 11, 1993.

CHAPTER 15: GINSBURG'S FEMINIST VOICE

215 *Harris v. Forklift Systems*: 510 U.S. 17 (1993), http://supreme.justia.com/cases/federal/us/510/17/case.html.

215 who would want to work there?: Alex Kozinski, Foreword to Barara Lindemann and David D. Kadue, *Sexual Harassment in Employment Law* (Washington, D.C.: Bureau of National Affairs, 1992), 5, vii.

215 free speech under the First Amendment: Alan Dershowitz, "Putting a Gender Bias on Free Speech," *Buffalo News*, July 27, 1993, B3.

215 usually a misunderstanding: Richard A. Posner, *Sex and Reason* (Cambridge, Mass.: Harvard University Press, 1992), 391–92.

216 "bugger him": The trial court was not so dainty; *Harris v. Forklift Systems,* 60 Empl. Prac. Dec. (CCH) 74,245, 74,247 (M.D. Tenn. 1990) (the District Court opinion was unpublished).

216 "credit for her achievements": Equal Employment Opportunity Commission, brief in Barbara Harris, *Beyond Her Sphere: Women and the Professions in American History* (Westport, Conn.: Greenwood Press, 1978), 25.

218 equality-oriented standard: Sarah Cleveland to Blackmun, Blackmun Papers, Library of Congress, October 26, 1993.

218 "for us to decide this": O'Connor, letter to Harry Blackmun, October 25, 1993, Blackmun Papers, Library of Congress, Harris folder, Box 635, folder 1.

219 "build things for the future": Hugh Baxter, interview with the author, June 24, 2014.

220 what an army needs: Plato, *Symposium*, 220d–221c, describing Socrates's calm courage in retreating to a more defensible stronghold after the Battle of Delium.

220 her judging on the Court: oral argument, *Harris v. Forklift Systems,* http://www.oyez.org/cases/1990-1999/1993/1993_92_1168.

220 will reach the same conclusion: Sandra Day O'Connor, "Portia's Progress," Madison Lecture, 1991, *New York University Law Review* 66 (1991): 1546, 1558, quoting Justice Jeanne Coyne.

220 thought it should: Golden Slipper Club Humanitarian Award 1995, Ginsburg Archive, Library of Congress, Box 146.

221 Ginsburg, J., concurring: *Oncale v. Sundowner Offshore Services*, 523 U.S. 75 (1998), http://supreme.justia.com/cases/federal/us/523/75/case.html.

222 Mississippi University for Women to admit men: Ginsburg Archive, Library of Congress, Box 37, F February 14.

222 "most important one": Hugh Baxter, interview with the author, June 24, 2014.

223 "Judge Ginsburg's recommendations": Joan Greco, interview with the author, April 4, 2014.

223 consigned to a desert island: *The Nomination of Ruth Bader Ginsburg*, 227.

223 a gentler glow: Hugh Baxter, interview with the author, June 24, 2014.

223 "how can he do this to me?": Joan Biskupic, *Sandra Day O'Connor: How the First Woman on the Supreme Court Became Its Most Influential Justice* (New York: Harper Perennial, 2006), 261.

223 the one she had: Jeffrey Toobin, *The Nine: Inside the Secret World of the Supreme Court* (New York: Doubleday, 2007), 35.

223 "big sister anyone could have": Biskupic, *Sandra Day O'Connor*, 260; Joan Biskupic, "Female Justices Attest to Fraternity on Bench; O'Connor and Ginsburg, in Separate Speeches, Discuss Personal Aspects of Supreme Court Life," *Washington Post*, August 21, 1994.

224 "I look forward to many more": Ruth Bader Ginsburg, "A Woman's Voice May Do Some Good," *Politico*, September 25, 2013, http://www.politico.com/story/2013/09/women-oconnor-ginsburg-supreme-court-97313.html#ixzz32wJiBxtP.

225 feminist campaign to integrate juries: *Black v. Wilson*, 198 So.2d 286 (1967), http://law.justia.com/cases/alabama/supreme-court/1967/198-so-2d-286-1.html.

225 from the get-go: Biskupic, *Sandra Day O'Connor*, 140.

225 loud, nasal diction: Ibid., 175.

226 had the process been legal: Cynthia L. Cooper, "Daughter of Justice Blackmun Goes Public about Roe," *The Nation*, February 29, 2004, http://womensenews.org/story/the-nation/040229/daughter-justice-blackmun-goes-public-about-roe#.U6GvXsYQhG4.

226 unhappy with her: Hugh Baxter, interview with the author, June 24, 2014.

226 unpleasant coded phrase: Ibid.

226 shout out in the footnote: Blackmun Papers, Library of Congress, Box 636, folder 6.

226 "bouquet" to his new colleague: Linda Greenhouse, "The Evolution of a Justice," *New York Times Magazine*, April 10, 2005, http://www.nytimes.com/2005/04/10/magazine/10BLACKMUN.html.

226 should have been hers: Philippa Strum, *Women in the Barracks: The VMI*

Case and Equal Rights (Lawrence: University of Kansas Press, 2002), 81, n. 86, cites Wilson, May 19, 1995, in Federal Judicial Center, "Diversifying the Judiciary: An Oral History of Women Federal Judges" (on file with the Federal Judicial Center's History Office).

227 The exchanges that ensued: Ginsburg, letter to Blackmun, January 20, 1994, with his annotations, Blackmun Papers, Library of Congress, Box 36, folder 6.

229 easier on accused rapists: this social science was and is heavily disputed. Hubert S. Feild, "Juror Background Characteristics and Attitudes Toward Rape: Correlates of Jurors' Decisions in Rape Trials," *Law and Human Behavior* 2 (1978): 73–93, http://www.socio-legal.sjtu.edu.cn/uploads/papers /2012/qtl120203050423823.pdf.

230 in every close case: Jeffrey Toobin, *The Nine: Inside the Secret World of the Supreme Court* (New York: Doubleday, 2007), 112 ("if she thought a law was unconstitutional, it was; if not, it wasn't").

230 *Queen's Court*: Nancy Maveety, *The Queen's Court: Judicial Power in the Rehnquist Era* (Lawrence: University of Kansas Press, 2008), http://www .kansaspress.ku.edu/mavque.html.

230 much more important: Tom Goldstein, "Oral Argument as a Bridge Between the Briefs and the Court's Opinion," in *The Legacy of Ruth Bader Ginsburg*, edited by Scott Dodson (New York: Cambridge University Press, 2015).

230 questions in sexual-harassment cases: Blackmun Papers, Library of Congress, Case 636, F6.

231 "clasping hands": Biskupic, "Female Justices Attest to Fraternity on Bench."

231 her handholding: Loretta McCarthy, interview with the author, June 1, 2014.

231 "Sandra Day O'Connor Day" in 1981: Joan Biskupic, *Sandra Day O'Connor: How the First Woman on the Supreme Court Became Its Most Influential Justice* (New York: Harper Perennial, 2006), image section after 276.

231 left hand the entire time: "Investiture of Judge Friedland," United States Court of Appeals for the Ninth Circuit, YouTube, June 30, 2014, https:// www.youtube.com/watch?v=7D-8OhPjKHY.

231 are well documented: Travel diary from Paris ("chaussures"), Ginsburg Archive, Library of Congress, Box 39, and Nina Totenberg, interview with the author, September 6, 2013.

231 judges' robing room: Linda Myers, "Justice Ruth Bader Ginsburg Weighs In on Women's Progress in the Law Profession—and What Kept Them Out for So Long," *Cornell Chronicle*, July 1, 2004, http://www.news.cornell.edu/ stories/2004/07/justice-ruth-bader-ginsburg-womens-progress-law.

231 Clinton appointee, Judith Rogers: Ginsburg Archive, Library of Congress, Box 155, folder Women 1994.

231 National Center for State Courts: Ibid.

232 "a resounding BRAVA": "Chief Justice Peters Dinner," C-SPAN, October 17, 1994, http://www.c-span.org/video/?60896-1/chief-justice-peters-dinner.

232 "better off for it": Ginsburg, Remarks for Women's Forum Lunch, Ginsburg Archive, Library of Congress, Box 147, April 8, 1999.

232 "Constitutional Adjudication and Equal Stature": Ginsburg Archive, Library of Congress, Box 148, 1997; Ginsburg, "Consitutional Adjudication in the United States as a Means of Advancing the Equal Stature of Men and Women under the Law," *Hofstra Law Review* 26 (1997): 263.

233 "savvy, sympatique colleague and counselor": "Remarks on Women's Progress in the Legal Profession in the United States," speech at July Institute on World Legal Problems in Innsbruck, Ginsburg Archive, Library of Congress, Box 151, F Seminars 1995; *Fordham Law Review* 64 (1995): 288; Ginsburg Archive, Library of Congress, Ginsburg Archive, Library of Congress, Box 148, 1995.

233 graduating from Stanford: "Remarks on Women's Progress in the Legal Profession in the United States," speech at July Institute on World Legal Problems in Innsbruck, Ginsburg Archive, Library of Congress, Box 151, F Seminars 1995.

233 difference women make: Oklahoma Bar Association Women in Law Conference Banquet Address, 1997, Ginsburg Archive, Library of Congress, Box 146.

233 South Africa's parliament: Ibid.

233 The Virginia Military Institute: Much of the description of the VMI scene comes from Strum's excellent history of the VMI case, Strum, *Women in the Barracks,* 85–86.

234 monogamous and wallet-oriented: Zuleyma Tang-Martinez, "The Curious Courtship of Sociobiology and Feminism: A Case of Irreconcilable Differences," in *Feminism and Evolutionary Biology: Boundaries, Intersections, and Frontiers,* edited by Patricia Gowaty (New York: Chapman and Hall, 1997), 126.

234 the way her work was used: Philippa Strum, "Do Women Belong in Military Academies?" *Historic U.S. Court Cases: An Encyclopedia,* 2nd ed., edited by John W. Johnson (New York: Routledge, 2001), vol. 2, 781.

235 agitating for sex-segregated schools: Rosemary C. Salamone, *Same, Different, Equal: Rethinking Single-Sex Schooling* (New Haven, Conn.: Yale University Press, 2003), 135–37.

235 sit in the jury box: Strum, *Women in the Barracks,* 140.

236 "daddy" or a "dyke": supposedly a perversion of the pronunciation of "deck," as in "all decked out." The rats help the dykes to dress. Abigail E. Adams, "The Military Academy Metaphors of Family for Pedagogy and Public Life," *Wives and Warriors: Women and the Military in the United States and Canada,* edited by Laurie Lee Weinstein and Christie C. White (Westport, Conn.: Bergin & Garvey, 1997).

236 impregnating the local women: Ibid., 68–69.

236 school actually closed: Strum, *Women in the Barracks,* 20.

236 guarantee of whiteness: Ibid., 29.

237 resisting the women: Ibid., 88.

237 against the United States: Katherine T. Bartlett, "Unconstitutionally Male?: The Story of United States v. Virginia," Duke Law Scholarship Repository, Working Papers (2010), http://scholarship.law.duke.edu/cgi/viewcontent .cgi?article=2936&context=faculty_scholarship; published in *Women and the Law Stories*, edited by Elizabeth M. Schneider and Stephanie M. Wildman (New York: Thomson Reuters/Foundation Press, 2011).

237 boys' and girls' high schools: *Vorchheimer v. School District of Philadelphia*, 430 U.S. 703 (1977).

238 Kiser's opinion: *United States v. Virginia*, 766 F. Supp. 1407 (W.D. Va. 1991).

239 faculty didn't like: Strum, *Women in the Barracks*, 206–9.

240 the students it attracted: *United States v. Virginia*, oral argument, http:// www.oyez.org/cases/1990-1999/1995/1995_94_1941.

241 assigning honors: John Paul Stevens, interview with the author, July 21, 2014.

242 "sort of intermediate scrutiny": Strum, *Women in the Barracks*, 270, citing the oral argument tape.

242 accorded to race: Strum, *Women in the Barracks*, 267, citing Jeffrey Rosen, "The New Look of Liberalism on the Court," *New York Times Magazine*, October 5, 1997, http://www.nytimes.com/1997/10/05/magazine/the-new- look-of-liberalism-on-the-court.html?module=Search&mabReward=relbi as%3As%2C{%221%22%3A%22RI%3A10%22}, who quotes a Ginsburg speech to students in 1997 that there is no practical difference between what has evolved and the ERA.

242 "opportunities based on sex": *United States v. Virginia et al.*, at 531.

242 Mary Baldwin College: Ibid., at 537.

242 "inherent differences between the sexes": Ibid., at 533.

243 John Stuart Mill: Ruth Bader Ginsburg, "Sex and Unequal Protection: Men and Women as Victims," keynote address, Southern Regional Conference of the National Conference of Law Women, Duke University, October 1, 1971, published in *Journal of Family Law* 11 (1971): 347 (hereafter Duke Speech).

243 "only been experience of one": John Stuart Mill, "The Subjection of Women" (1869), chapter 1, http://www.constitution.org/jsm/women.htm.

243 Dissenting: *United States v. Virginia et al.*, at 566.

244 "the good job": Ginsburg, letter to Stephen Wiesenfeld, June 13, 2011.

244 class met too early: Adam Liptak, "Honoring O'Connor's Legacy at the Su- preme Court," *New York Times,* April 12, 2012, http://thecaucus.blogs.nytimes .com/2012/04/12/honoring-oconnors-legacy-at-the-supreme-court/?_r=0.

244 covering some of the gigs: Ruth Bader Ginsburg, "A Woman's Voice May Do Some Good," *Politico*, September 25, 2013, http://www.politico.com/ story/2013/09/women-oconnor-ginsburg-supreme-court-97313.html.

244 Schonbrun Palace: Ginsburg Archive, Library of Congress, Box 153, Semi- nar 1998 summer Salzburg.

244 litigation so long ago: Ginsburg, letter to Stephen Wiesenfeld, September 8, 1998.

245 dark days of his disease: Ginsburg, letters to Stephen Wiesenfeld, December 7 and 22, 1998.

245 "butterflies will follow": Ginsburg, letter to Stephen Wiesenfeld, undated but 1998 series.

CHAPTER 16: THE IMPORTANCE OF BEING O'CONNOR AND GINSBURG

246 *Gebser v. Lago Vista Independent School District*: 524 U.S. 274 (1998).

247 "the godmother of Title IX": "All about Bernice Sandler," http://www.bernicesandler.com/id2.htm.

247 sexual revolution in the making: Iram Valentin, "Title IX: A Brief History," Womens Equity Action League, Equity Resource Center, August 1997, http://www2.edc.org/WomensEquity/pdffiles/t9digest.pdf.

247 *Davis v. Monroe County Board of Education*: 526 U.S. 629 (1999).

248 arrived again at the Supreme Court: *Miller v. Albright* 523 U.S. 420 (1998).

249 "conferring citizenship on her child": *Miller v. Albright*, 434.

249 "*opportunity* to develop relationships": Stevens opinion for the Court, *Miller v. Albright*, at 444.

249 "Even if one accepts": Ginsburg, J., dissenting, *Miller v. Albright*, at 469.

250 procedure for abortion providers: Jenny Westberg, "D&X: Grim Technology for Abortion's Older Victims," LifeAdvocate.org, 1997, http://lifeadvocate.org/arc/dx.htm. Toobin describes the genesis of the movement as coming from an anonymous tip to Douglas Johnson, a lobbyist for the National Right to Life Committee; Jeffrey Toobin, *The Nine: Inside the Secret World of the Supreme Court* (New York: Doubleday, 2007), 155.

250 "partial birth abortion": Gloria Feldt, *The War on Choice: The Right-Wing Attack on Women's Rights and How to Fight Back* (New York: Bantam Books, 2004), 174.

250 flared up again: Drew Halfmann and Michael P. Young, "War Pictures: The Grotesque as a Mobilizing Tactic," *Mobilization* 15 (2010): 1–24, http://sociology.ucdavis.edu/people/halfmann/grotesque.

250 Clinton vetoed the federal laws: "Bill Clinton on Abortion," OnTheIssues.org, http://www.ontheissues.org/celeb/Bill_Clinton_Abortion.htm (accessed November 18, 2014).

250 agreed to review the case: *Stenberg v. Carhart*, 530 U.S. 914 (2000).

251 *Casey* afforded women: *Stenberg v. Carhart*, Kennedy dissenting, http://www.law.cornell.edu/supct/html/99-830.ZD2.html.

251 health of the mother: *Stenberg v. Carhart*, O'Connor concurring, http://www.law.cornell.edu/supct/html/99-830.ZC1.html.

252 undue-burden test: "Defending the Innocent," *Washington Times*, November 8, 2003, http://www.washingtontimes.com/news/2003/nov/8/20031108-111532-9290r/.

252 modern approach to the Constitution: Jan Crawford Greenburg, *Supreme Conflict: The Inside Story of the Struggle for Control of the United States Supreme Court* (New York: Penguin, 2007), location 830 of 5283 in Kindle edition.

252 one prominent critic put it: Jason DeParle, "In Battle to Pick Next Justice, Right Says, Avoid a Kennedy," *New York Times*, June 27, 2005, http://www .nytimes.com/2005/06/27/politics/27kennedy.html?pagewanted=all&_r=0.

253 found colon cancer: Sheryl Gay Stolberg, "Ginsburg Leaves Hospital; Prognosis on Cancer Is Good," *New York Times*, September 29, 1999, http:// www.nytimes.com/1999/09/29/us/ginsburg-leaves-hospital-prognosis-on-cancer-is-good.html.

254 Court's session on Monday: Jon Craig, "Ruth Bader Ginsburg Reminisces About Her Time on the Hill," *Cornell Chronicle*, September 22 and November 16, 2014, http://www.news.cornell.edu/stories/2014/09/ruth-bader-ginsburg-reminisces-about-her-time-hill.

254 "say no to any 'extras'": Ginsburg, letter to Stephen Wiesenfeld, December 6 1999.

254 "shut downs": Ginsburg, letter to Stephen Wiesenfeld, February 27, 2001.

254 "tough it out": Ginsburg, letter to Stephen Wiesenfeld, September 24, 2001.

254 the doctors said: Ginsburg, letter to Stephen Wiesenfeld, September 22, 2000.

CHAPTER 17: JUSTICE O'CONNOR'S SELF-INFLICTED WOUND

255 legendary diplomat Walter Stoessel: The story was apparently first reported by Christopher Hitchens, "Now There Is No Referee Left," *Evening Standard* (London), December 13, 2000, 13, but gained widespread currency when it appeared in Evan Thomas and Michael Isikoff, "The Truth Behind the Pillars," *Newsweek*, December 25, 2000, 46.

255 *Bush v. Gore*: 531 U.S. 98 (2000).

256 cast into doubt: Jeffrey Toobin, *The Nine: Inside the Secret World of the Supreme Court* (New York: Doubleday, 2007), 187.

256 George Bush in the White House: Ibid., 200.

256 legal commentator Jeffrey Rosen: Jeffrey Rosen, "Disgrace," *The New Republic*, December 24, 2000, http://www.newrepublic.com/article/politics/ disgrace.

256 described her work in 1993: David M. O'Brien, "Holding the Center: As Thomas and Scalia Stake Out the Far Right, O'Connor Takes the Moral High Ground," *Los Angeles Times*, March 8, 1992, http://articles.latimes .com/1992-03-08/opinion/op-5987_1_justice-clarence-thomas; David O. Stewart, "Holding the Center—Sandra O'Connor Evolves into Major Force on Supreme Court," *ABA Journal* 79 (1993): 48, http://heinonline.org/HOL/ LandingPage?handle=hein.journals/abaj79&div=61&id=&page=.

256 "addled and uncertain": Rosen, "Disgrace."

256 women's rights—was loaded: Toobin, *The Nine*, 166.

256 such a fine family: David Margolick, "Meet the Supremes," *New York Times*, September 23, 2007.

257 "good for the Court and for the nation": O'Connor, letter to Barry Goldwater,

1988, Personal and Political Papers of Senator Barry M. Goldwater, Arizona State University Libraries Arizona Collection.

257 avid observer of electoral politics: Lewis F. Powell, Jr. Archives, Washington and Lee University School of Law, letter from O'Connor with calculation of election predictions, undated; O'Connor, letter to Goldwater, November 1, 1988, Personal and Political Papers of Senator Barry M. Goldwater, Arizona State University Libraries Arizona Collection; Jeffrey Toobin, *Too Close to Call: The Thirty-Six-Day Battle to Decide the 2000 Election* (New York: Random House, 2001), 248.

257 protect the life of a mother: "George W. Bush on Abortion" and "George W. Bush on the Constitution," *OnTheIssues*, http://www.ontheissues.org/Celeb/George_W__Bush_Abortion.htm#Supreme_Court_+_Constitution (accessed November 18, 2014).

257 "partial birth abortion" law: Ibid., citing Sandra Sobieraj, AP article in *Washington Post*, June 28, 2000.

257 "judicial philosophy he defends": Fred Barnes, "Bush Scalia," *Weekly Standard* July 5, 1999, http://www.weeklystandard.com/Content/Protected/Articles/000/000/010/268gdffq.asp.

257 "more to the point the Republican Party": Toobin, *The Nine*, 165.

257 betting pools on the elections: Ibid., 165.

257 and to the Court: O'Connor, letter to Barry Goldwater, 1988.

257 "It was just outrageous": Toobin, *Too Close to Call*, 248.

258 O'Connor's tidy standards: Dahleen Glanton, "O'Connor Questions Court's Decision to Take On *Bush v. Gore*," *Chicago Tribune*, April 27, 2013, http://articles.chicagotribune.com/2013-04-27/news/ct-met-sandra-day-oconnor-edit-board-20130427_1_0-connor-bush-v-high-court.

259 performed or "promoted" abortion: "George W. Bush on Abortion" and "George W. Bush on the Constitution," *OnTheIssues*, http://www.ontheissues.org/Celeb/George_W__Bush_Abortion.htm#Supreme_Court_+_Constitution (accessed November 18, 2014).

259 budget went down by 20 percent: Alison Motluk, "US Abortion Policy: A Healthy Strategy for Whom?" *New Scientist*, October 6, 2004 (retrieved September 29, 2007).

259 across all the chambers: Michelle Friedland, interview with the author, June 20, 2014.

260 support a black representative: *Easley v. Cromartie*, 532 U.S. 234 (2001), http://www.oyez.org/cases/2000-2009/2000/2000_99_1864.

260 execution of the retarded: *Atkins v. Virginia*, 536 U.S. 304 (2002), http://www.oyez.org/cases/2000-2009/2001/2001_00_8452/.

260 sodomy laws unconstitutional: *Lawrence v. Texas*, 539 U.S. 558 (2003).

260 affirmative action in college admissions: *Grutter v. Bollinger*, 539 U.S. 306 (2003), http://www.oyez.org/cases/2000-2009/2002/2002_02_241/.

260 toward the liberal bloc: David Cole, "The Liberal Legacy of *Bush v. Gore*," *Georgetown Law Journal* 94 (2006): 1427, 1443, http://www.scotusblog.com/archives/bushvgore-cole.pdf.

260 partisan redistricting: *Vieth v. Jubelirer*, 541 U.S. 267 (2004).

260 right of eminent domain: *Kelo v. City of New London*, 125 S. Ct. 2655 (2005).

260 reining in the death penalty: *Atkins v. Virginia*, 536 U.S. 304, 321 (2002); *Ring v. Arizona*, 536 U.S. 584, 609 (2002).

261 *Ferguson v. Charleston*: 532 U.S. 67 (2001).

261 called special needs: Ibid., at 70.

261 drug users for child abuse: Philip J. Hilts, "Hospital Sought Out Prenatal Drug Abuse," *New York Times*, January 21, 1994, http://www.nytimes .com/1994/01/21/us/hospital-sought-out-prenatal-drug-abuse.html.

261 hospital for race discrimination: Dorothy E. Roberts, *Killing the Black Body: Race, Reproduction, and the Meaning of Liberty* (New York: Vintage, 1998), 174–75, citing the plaintiffs' filings in the trial court.

263 *Nguyen v. INS*: *Tuan Anh Nguyen v. INS*, 533 U.S. 53 (2001), http://supreme .justia.com/cases/federal/us/533/53/case.html.

264 the task of answering Kennedy: Ibid., at 74.

265 federal family-leave law: This was very contentious, four—Stevens, Souter, Breyer, Ginsburg—didn't agree with the premise, but all agreed that FMLA abrogated the immunity. For our purposes, Rehnquist/Kennedy is the interesting view. *Nevada Department of Human Resources v. Hibbs*, 538 U.S. 721 (2003).

265 *Jackson v. Birmingham Board of Education*: *Jackson v. Birmingham Board of Education*, 544 U.S. 167 (2005), http://www.law.cornell.edu/supct/pdf/02-1672P.ZO.

266 Well, goodness!: Toobin, *The Nine*, 198. O'Connor was asking Gore's lawyer David Boies why the Florida court didn't set a uniform standard for whether a ballot should be included in the count. "For goodness' sake!" she exclaimed impatiently.

266 "It's not always positive": Rebecca Lowe, "Supremely Confident: The Legacy of Sandra Day O'Connor," Guardian Legal Network, August 30, 2011, http://www.theguardian.com/law/2011/aug/30/us-supreme-court-george-bush.

267 as she saw it, trapped: Jan Crawford Greenburg, *Supreme Conflict: The Inside Story of the Struggle for Control of the United States Supreme Court* (New York: Penguin, 2007), location 300 of 5283 in Kindle version.

267 two of them went out: Joan Biskupic, *Sandra Day O'Connor: How the First Woman on the Supreme Court Became Its Most Influential Justice* (New York: Harper Perennial, 2006), 324–25.

267 drove O'Connor to retirement: Greenburg, *Supreme Conflict*, location 302 of 5283 in Kindle version.

267 "he's not a woman": Elisabeth Bumiller, "An Interview by, Not with, the President," *New York Times*, July 21, 2005, http://www.nytimes.com/2005/07/21/ politics/21bush.html?pagewanted=all.

268 "Sam" Alito: Greenburg calls him "Sam," *Supreme Conflict*, location 724.

268 law would now stand: *Gonzales v. Carhart*, 550 U.S. 124 (2007), http://www .law.cornell.edu/supct/html/05-380.ZO.html.

269 "principles of *stare decisis*": Ibid., emphasis added.

269 "once created and sustained": Ibid., at page 29 of the draft.

270 "long since discredited": Ibid., Ginsburg dissenting, at page 18 of the dissent draft.

270 "this would happen again": Joan Biskupic, "Ginsburg 'Lonely' without O'Connor," *USA Today,* January 25, 2007, http://usatoday30.usatoday.com/news/washington/2007-01-25-ginsburg-court_x.htm.

270 "our male colleagues lack": "Ginsburg Feels Isolated on Court," *Washington Post* (Associated Press), January 28, 2007, http://www.washingtonpost.com/wp-dyn/content/article/2007/01/27/AR2007012701065.html.

270 "until she was gone": Biskupic, "Ginsburg 'Lonely' without O'Connor."

CHAPTER 18: THE GREAT DISSENTER

273 a living legend: Michael Li-Ming Wong, interview with the author, July 17, 2014.

273 Louis D. Brandeis: Richard A. Primus, "Canon, Anti-Canon, and Judicial Dissent," *Duke Law Journal* 48 (1998): 243, http://scholarship.law.duke.edu/cgi/viewcontent.cgi?article=1040&context=dlj.

273 Jim Crow south: Linda Greenhouse, "A Justice Champions a Witness to History," *New York Times,* August 5, 2001, http://www.nytimes.com/2001/08/05/us/a-justice-champions-a-witness-to-history.html.

274 gleefully put it to Wiesenfeld: Ginsburg, letter to Stephen Wiesenfeld, March 2, 1977.

274 "grievously misguided": Ruth Bader Ginsburg, "The Role of Dissenting Opinions," *Minnesota Law Review* 95 (2010): 1, http://www.minnesotalawreview.org/wp-content/uploads/2011/07/Ginsburg_MLR.pdf.

274 *Goodyear Tire and Rubber*: Lilly Ledbetter v. Goodyear Tire and Rubber, 550 U.S. 618 (2007).

275 "Gadsden, Alabama": Jill Duffy and Elizabeth Lambert, "Dissents from the Bench: A Compilation of Oral Dissents by U.S. Supreme Court Justices," *Law Library Journal* 102 (2010): 1, note 6, http://www.aallnet.org/main-menu/Publications/llj/LLJ-Archives/Vol-102/pub_llj_v102no1/2010-01.pdf.

276 Fair Pay Act, into law: "Ruth's Greatest Hit's [*sic*]: Ledbetter v. Goodyear," Ruth Bader GinsBlog, August 15, 2012, http://ruthbaderginsblog.blogspot.com/2012/08/ruths-greatest-hits-ledbetter-v_15.html.

276 solitary female's questioning: Dahlia Lithwick, "Search Me," *Slate,* April 21, 2009, http://www.slate.com/articles/news_and_politics/supreme_court_dispatches/2009/04/search_me.html.

276 sensitive thirteen-year-old: Joan Biskupic, "Ginsburg: Court Needs Another Woman," *USAToday,* October 5, 2009, http://usatoday30.usatoday.com/news/washington/judicial/2009-05-05-ruthginsburg_N.htm.

277 "to have her company": Ginsburg, letter to Stephen Wiesenfeld, December 9, 2009.

277 she wrote to Wiesenfeld: Ginsburg, letter to Stephen Wiesenfeld, February 18, 2009.

277 "health problems": Ginsburg, letter to Stephen Wiesenfeld, December 29, 2009.

277 raise his spirits: Ginsburg, letter to Stephen Wiesenfeld, March 9, 2010.

277 "the good job Marty helped" her get: Ginsburg, letter to Stephen Wiesenfeld, June 13, 2011.

277 "all the difference for me": Elahe Izadi, "Ruth Bader Ginsburg's Advice on Love and Leaning In," *Washington Post*, July 31, 2014, http://www.washingtonpost .com/news/post-nation/wp/2014/07/31/ruth-bader-ginsburgs-advice-on-love-and-leaning-in/.

278 ranging up to $45 million: "Supreme Court Runs Financial Gamut," *New York Times*, June 11, 2010, http://www.nytimes.com/2010/06/12/us/12scotus .html?_r=0.

278 went shopping with her: travel diary from 1988 trip to Paris, Ginsburg Archive, Library of Congress, Box 39.

278 "they will be here all night!": Michael Li-Ming Wong, interview with the author, July 17, 2014.

278 a curmudgeonly: "Symposium Honors and Roasts Professor Monaghan," *Columbia Law School Magazine*, Winter 2010, http://www.law.columbia .edu/magazine/153298/symposium-honors-and-roasts-professor-monaghan.

278 "brought into another dimension!": Henry Paul Monaghan, interview with the author, October 14, 2013.

279 more good, young Obama appointees: Randall Kennedy, "The Case for Early Retirement," *New Republic*, April 28, 2011, http://www.newrepublic .com/article/politics/87543/ginsburg-breyer-resign-supereme-court.

279 "equipped to do the job?": Joan Biskupic, "Ruth Bader Ginsburg Resists Retirement Pressure," Reuters, July 4, 2013.

279 ten close cases: Veronika Polakova, "Predicting Anthony Kennedy," *The Monkey Cage*, American Enterprise Institute blog, July 13, 2012, http://www .aei.org/article/politics-and-public-opinion/judicial/predicting-anthony-kennedy/.

279 from the electric chair: *Connick v. Thompson*, 131 S.Ct. 1350, 563 (2011), http://scholar.google.com/scholar_case?case=16887528200611439212&hl =en&as_sdt=6&as_vis=1&oi=scholar.

279 scrap metal machine: *J. Mcintyre Machinery v. Robert Nicastro*, 131 S.Ct. 2780, 564 (2011).

280 against police misconduct: Lisa Kern Griffin, "Barriers to Entry and Justice Ginsburg's Criminal Procedure Jurisprudence," in *The Legacy of Ruth Bader Ginsburg*, edited by Scott Dodson (New York: Cambridge University Press, 2015).

280 her most passionate concern: Ibid.

281 civil rights trial: *Connick v. Thompson*, at 1370.

281 "sink any lower": Mike Appleton, "Connick v. Thompson and Prosecutorial Impunity," Jonathan Turley (blog), April 10, 2011, http://jonathanturley .org/2011/04/10/connick-v-thompson-and-prosecutorial-impunity/.

281 "Justice Thomas's meanest opinion": Dahlia Lithwick, "Cruel but Not

Unusual: Clarence Thomas Writes One of the Meanest Supreme Court Decisions Ever," *Slate*, April 1, 2011, http://www.slate.com/articles/news_ and_politics/jurisprudence/2011/04/cruel_but_not_unusual.html.

282 not without its consolations: Ginsburg, letter to Stephen Wiesenfeld, June 13, 2011.

282 Supreme Court Historical Society: *Martin Ginsburg: Chef Supreme* (Washington, D.C.: Supreme Court Historical Society, 2011), http://supremecourt gifts.org/chefsupreme.aspx.

282 *Coleman v. Maryland Court of Appeals*: 566 U.S. 12 (2012).

283 Franklin Roosevelt's New Deal: Laurence Tribe, "The Roberts Court: New Frontiers in Constitutional Doctrine," *Washington Post*, June 6, 2014, http://www.washingtonpost.com/news/volokh-conspiracy/wp/2014/06/06/ by-prof-laurence-tribe-the-roberts-court-new-frontiers-in-constitutional-doctrine/.

284 record for oral disagreement: Stephen Wermiel, "Dissenting from the Bench," *SCOTUS for Law Students*, SCOTUSblog, July 2, 2013, http://www .scotusblog.com/2013/07/scotus-for-law-students-sponsored-by-bloomberg-law-dissenting-from-the-bench/.

284 *Vance v. Ball State*: 133 S. Ct. 2434 (2013).

284 *University of Texas Southwestern Hospital v. Nassar*: 570 (2012), http://www. supremecourt.gov/opinions/12pdf/12-484_0759.pdf

285 *Fisher v. University of Texas*: 133 S.Ct. 2411, 570 (2013).

286 "cold feet": Paul M. Barrett, "A Fascinating Supreme Court Punt on Affirmative Action," *BloombergBusinessWeek*, June 24, 2013, http://www .businessweek.com/articles/2013-06-24/a-fascinating-supreme-court-punt-on-affirmative-action.

287 "'law-sanctioned inequality'": "Realizing the Equality Principle," at note 123 in present draft, Ginsburg Archive, Library of Congress, Box 12.

287 "preclearance"—was unconstitutional: *Shelby County Alabama v. Holder*, 133 S.Ct. 2612 (2013).

CHAPTER 19: NOTORIOUS R.B.G.

289 marginalized and excluded: Shana Knizhnik, interview with the author, August 11, 2014.

289 he became Notorious: "The Notorious B.I.G.," Wikipedia, http://en .wikipedia.org/wiki/The_Notorious_B.I.G. (accessed November 19, 2014).

289 thousands of followers: *Texts from Hillary*, April 11, 2012, http://textsfrom hillaryclinton.tumblr.com.

289 *Notorious R.B.G.*: *Notorious R.B.G.: Justice Ruth Bader Ginsburg in All Her Glory* (blog), http://notoriousrbg.tumblr.com (accessed November 19, 2014).

290 an Internet phenom: Allison P. Davis, "NYU Law Student Is Making Ruth Bader Ginsburg a Meme," *New York*, June 27, 2013,http://nymag.com/ thecut/2013/06/nyu-law-student-is-making-bader-ginsburg-a-meme.html.

290 "Plain and simple": Jamison Doran, "19 Reasons Ruth Bader Ginsburg Is Your Favorite Supreme Court Justice: R.B.G. is a complete and total boss. Plain and simple," BuzzFeed Community, July 30, 2013, http://www.buzzfeed.com/jamisond/19-reasons-why-ruth-bader-ginsburg-is-your-favorit-7fxd.

290 *Female Force*: Bill Mulligan and Tsubasa Yozora, *Preview: Female Force: Ruth Bader Ginsburg #1*, Blue Water Comics, June 24, 2013, http://www.comicbookresources.com/?page=preview&id=17037.

290 clerks took it to the Justice: Josh Johnson, interview with the author, August 11, 2014.

290 send it to the justice: Akila Radhakrishnan, interview with the author, August 13, 2014.

290 made and edited music videos: Elizabeth Gavin, e-mail to the author, October 31, 2014.

290 "RBGuicy": http://rap.genius.com/Notorious-rbg-rbguicy-lyrics.

292 are also gay: Andy Towle, "Gay 'Texts from Hillary' Creators Get Invite to State Department Meeting with Hillary," *Towleroad* (blog), April 10, 2012, http://www.towleroad.com/2012/04/gay-texts-from-hillary-creators-get-invite-to-state-department-meeting-with-hillary.html.

292 "play in the public realm": Josh Johnson, interview with the author, August 11, 2014.

292 *Burwell v. Hobby Lobby*: 573 (2014), http://www.law.cornell.edu/supremecourt/text/13-354#writing-13-354_OPINION_3.

293 "Se vuol ballare": Wikipedia, http://simple.wikipedia.org/wiki/Se_vuol_ballare (accessed November 19, 2014); translation by Jane Bishop, Aria Database, http://www.aria-database.com/translations/nozze03_sevuol.txt (accessed November 19, 2014).

293 "how to caper": Lorenzo da Ponte, libretto to Wolfgang Amadeus Mozart, *The Marriage of Figaro*, Recording Booklet, at 121, Chandos Music, https://www.chandos.net/pdf/CHAN%203113.pdf.

293 sincerely held religious beliefs: *Burwell v Hobby Lobby Stores*, 573 (2014), http://www.law.cornell.edu/supremecourt/text/13-354#writing-13-354_OPINION_3.

295 broadcast it over YouTube: "Ginsburg's Hobby Lobby Dissent, Song a Day #2007," YouTube, June 30, 2014, https://www.youtube.com/watch?v=GYiTJ8JazkQ.

295 severe heart disease: Sahar Naderi and Russell Raymond, "Pregnancy and Heart Disease," Center for Continuing Education, Cleveland Clinic, February 2014, http://www.clevelandclinicmeded.com/medicalpubs/diseasemanagement/cardiology/pregnancy-and-heart-disease/.

296 "immature misjudgment": Jeffrey Rosen, "Ruth Bader Ginsburg Is an American Hero," *The New Republic*, September 28, 2014, http://www.newrepublic.com/article/119578/ruth-bader-ginsburg-interview-retirement-feminists-jazzercise.

297 "they're misguided": Jessica Weisberg, "Supreme Court Justice Ruth Bader

Ginsburg: I'm Not Going Anywhere," *Elle*, October 2014, http://www.elle.com/life-love/society-career/supreme-court-justice-ruth-bader-ginsburg.

297 stent in her artery the next day: Richard Wolf, "Justice Ginsburg Has Stent Implanted in Heart Procedure," *USA Today*, November 26, 2014.

CHAPTER 20: OUR HEROINES

299 "the face of American antidiscrimination law": Adam Liptak, "Kagan Says Her Path to Supreme Court Was Made Smoother by Ginsburg's," *New York Times*, February 10, 2014, http://www.nytimes.com/2014/02/11/us/kagan-says-her-path-to-supreme-court-was-made-smoother-by-ginsburg.html.

301 "hasn't lived that life": Sonia Sotomayor, "A Latina Judge's Voice" (2001), *New York Times*, May 14, 2009, http://www.nytimes.com/2009/05/15/us/politics/15judge.text.html?pagewanted=all&_r=0.

301 "a rhetorical flourish that fell flat": Robert Barnes and Paul Kane, "Sotomayor Repudiates 'Wise Latina' Comment," *Washington Post*, July 15, 2009, http://www.boston.com/news/nation/washington/articles/2009/07/15/sotomayor_backs_off_wise_latina_quote/.

301 "only English was spoken at home": Adam Liptak, "Sotomayor Finds Her Voice Among Justices," *New York Times*, May 6, 2014, http://www.nytimes.com/2014/05/07/us/politics/sotomayor-finds-her-voice-among-the-justices.html?smid=pl-share&_r=0.

301 "relate to their own experiences": Debra Cassens Weiss, "Ginsburg Defends Sotomayor, Calls 'Wise Latina' Flap Ridiculous," *ABA Journal*, July 9, 2009, http://www.abajournal.com/news/article/ginsburg_defends_sotomayor_calls_wise_latina_flap_ridiculous.

Bibliography and Sources

✦

BOOKS

Abrams, Dennis. *Sandra Day O'Connor.* New York: Chelsea House, 2009.

Berebitsky, Julie. *Sex and the Office: A History of Gender, Power, and Desire.* New Haven, Conn.: Yale University Press, 2012.

Berman, David R. *Arizona Politics and Government.* Lincoln: University of Nebraska Press, 1998.

Biskupic, Joan. *Sandra Day O'Connor: How the First Woman on the Supreme Court Became Its Most Influential Justice.* New York: Harper Perennial, 2006.

Campbell, Amy Leigh. *Raising the Bar: Ruth Bader Ginsburg and the ACLU Women's Rights Project.* Bloomington, Ind.: Xlibris, 2004.

Campbell, Karl E. *Senator Sam Ervin, Last of the Founding Fathers.* Chapel Hill: University of North Carolina Press, 2007.

Caplan, Lincoln. *The Tenth Justice: The Solicitor General and the Rule of Law.* New York: Knopf, 1987.

Collins, Gail. *When Everything Changed: The Amazing Journey of American Women from 1960 to the Present.* Boston: Little, Brown, 2009.

Christopher, Warren. *Chances of a Lifetime: A Memoir.* New York: Simon and Schuster, 2001.

Davidson, Kenneth M., Ruth B. Ginsburg, and Herma H. Kay. *Sex-Based Discrimination: Text, Cases and Materials.* Saint Paul, Minn.: West Publishing, 1974.

Davis, Richard. *Electing Justice: Fixing the Supreme Court Nomination Process.* New York: Oxford University Press, 2005.

Feldt, Gloria. *The War on Choice: The Right-Wing Attack on Women's Rights and How to Fight Back.* New York: Bantam Books, 2004.

Gelber, Steven M., and Martin L. Cook. *Saving the Earth: The History of a Middle-Class Millenarian Movement.* Berkeley: University of California Press, 1990.

Gilligan, Carol. *In a Different Voice: Psychological Theory and Women's Development.* Cambridge, Mass.: Harvard University Press, 1982.

Greenburg, Jan Crawford. *Supreme Conflict: The Inside Story of the Struggle for Control of the United States Supreme Court.* New York: Penguin, 2007. Kindle edition.

Greenhouse, Linda. *Becoming Justice Blackmun: Harry Blackmun's Supreme Court Journey.* New York: Times Books, 2005.

Greenhouse, Linda, and Reva Siegel, eds. *Before* Roe v. Wade: *Voices that Shaped the Abortion Debate before the Supreme Court's Ruling.* New York: Kaplan, 2010.

Gutgold, Nichola D. *The Rhetoric of Supreme Court Women: From Obstacles to Options.* Lanham, Md.: Lexington Books, 2012.

Harris, Barbara. *Beyond Her Sphere: Women and the Professions in American History.* Westport, Conn.: Greenwood Press, 1978.

Hartmann, Susan M. *The Other Feminists: Activists in the Liberal Establishment.* New Haven, Conn.: Yale University Press, 1998.

Hill, Alexis K. *Keeping the Promise of Justice: Celebrating 25 Years of the National Association of Women Judges.* Paducah, Ky.: Turner, 2003.

Hirshman, Linda. *Victory: The Triumphant Gay Revolution.* New York: Harper-Collins, 2012.

Hochschild, Arlie Russell. *The Second Shift.* New York: Avon, 1990.

Hutchinson, Dennis J. *The Man Who Once Was Whizzer White: A Portrait of Justice Byron R. White.* New York: Free Press, 1998.

Keetley, Dawn, and John Pettegrew, eds. *Public Women, Public Words: A Documentary History of American Feminism,* vol. 3, *1960 to the Present.* Lanham, Md.: Rowman and Littlefield, 2002.

Kenney, Sally Jane. *Gender and Justice: Why Women in the Judiciary Really Matter.* New York: Routledge, 2013.

Lamb, Charles M., and Stephen C. Halpern, eds., *The Burger Court: Political and Judicial Profiles.* Urbana: University of Illinois Press, 1991.

Lazarus, Edward. *Closed Chambers: The First Eyewitness Account of the Epic Struggles Inside the Supreme Court.* New York: Times Books, 1998.

Lewy, Guenter. *The Cause That Failed: Communism in American Political Life.* New York: Oxford University Press, 1990.

Lindemann, Barbara, and David D. Kadue. *Sexual Harassment in Employment Law.* Washington, D.C.: Bureau of National Affairs, 1992.

McFeatters, Ann Carey. *Sandra Day O'Connor: Justice in the Balance.* Albuquerque: University of New Mexico Press, 2005.

MacKinnon, Catharine. *Sexual Harassment of Working Women.* New Haven, Conn.: Yale University Press, 1979.

Martin, Janet M. *The Presidency and Women: Promise, Performance, and Illusion.* College Station: Texas A&M University Press, 2003.

Martin Ginsburg: Chef Supreme. Washington, D.C.: Supreme Court Historical Society, 2011. http://supremecourtgifts.org/chefsupreme.aspx.

Mathews, Donald G., and Jane S. De Hart. *Sex, Gender, and the Politics of ERA: A State and the Nation.* New York: Oxford University Press, 1990.

Maveety, Nancy. *Justice Sandra Day O'Connor, Strategist on the Supreme Court.* Lanham, Md.: Rowman and Littlefield, 1996.

Maveety, Nancy. *Queen's Court: Judicial Power in the Rehnquist Era.* Lawrence: University of Kansas Press, 2008.

Mill, John Stuart. "The Subjection of Women." 1869.

Mulligan, Bill, and Tsubasa Yozora. *Female Force*: *Ruth Bader Ginsburg*. Vancouver: Blue Water Prod., 2013.

O'Connor, Sandra Day, and Alan Day. *Lazy B: Growing Up on a Cattle Ranch in the American Southwest*. New York: Random House, 2002.

Penner, Richard H. *Cornell University*. Charleston, S.C.: Arcadia Publishing, 2013.

Posner, Richard A. *Sex and Reason*. Cambridge, Mass.: Harvard University Press, 1992.

Reagan, Leslie J. *When Abortion Was a Crime: Women, Medicine, and Law in the United States, 1867–1973*. Berkeley: University of California Press, 1997.

Roberts, Dorothy E. *Killing the Black Body: Race, Reproduction, and the Meaning of Liberty*. New York: Vintage, 1998.

Salamone, Rosemary C. *Same, Different, Equal: Rethinking Single-Sex Schooling*. New Haven, Conn.: Yale University Press, 2003.

Smith, Zachary. *Politics and Public Policy in Arizona*. Westport, Conn.: Praeger, 1996.

Stephanopoulos, George. *All Too Human: A Political Education*. Boston: Little, Brown, 1999.

Stern, Seth, and Stephen Wermiel. *Justice Brennan: Liberal Champion*. Boston: Houghton Mifflin Harcourt, 2010.

Strebeigh, Fred. *Equal: Women Reshape American Law*. New York: W. W. Norton, 2009.

Strum, Philippa. *Women in the Barracks: The VMI Case and Equal Rights*. Lawrence: University of Kansas Press, 2002.

Swiger, Elinor Porter. *Women Lawyers at Work*. New York: Messner, 1978.

Tocqueville, Alexis de. *Democracy in America*.

Thomas, Marlo. *The Right Words at the Right Time*. New York: Atria, 2002.

Toobin, Jeffrey. *The Nine: Inside the Secret World of the Supreme Court*. New York: Doubleday, 2007.

———. *Too Close to Call: The Thirty-Six-Day Battle to Decide the 2000 Election*. New York: Random House, 2001.

Van Sickel, Robert W. *Not a Particularly Different Voice: The Jurisprudence of Sandra Day O'Connor*. New York: P. Lang, 1998.

Vrato, Elizabeth. *The Counselors: Conversations with 18 Courageous Women Who Have Changed the World*. Philadelphia: Running Press, 2002.

Walker, Samuel. *In Defense of American Liberties: A History of the ACLU*. New York: Oxford University Press, 1990; 2nd ed., Carbondale: Southern Illinois University Press, 1999.

Woodward, Bob, and Scott Armstrong. *The Brethren: Inside the Supreme Court*. New York: Simon and Schuster, 1979.

Wrightsman, Lawrence S. *Oral Arguments Before the Supreme Court: An Empirical Approach*. New York: Oxford University Press, 2008.

Yalof, David Alistair. *Pursuit of Justices: Presidential Politics and the Selection of Supreme Court Nominees*. Chicago: University of Chicago Press, 1999.

Yarbrough, Tinsley E. *Harry A. Blackmun: The Outsider Justice*. New York: Oxford University Press, 2008.

PERIODICAL AND JOURNAL ARTICLES
AND CHAPTERS IN COLLECTIONS

Adams, Abigail E. "The Military Academy Metaphors of Family for Pedagogy and Public Life." In *Wives and Warriors: Women and the Military in the United States and Canada*, edited by Laurie Lee Weinstein and Christie C. White (Westport, Conn.: Bergin & Garvey, 1997).

Barnes, Fred. "Bush Scalia." *Weekly Standard*, July 5, 1999. http://www.weekly-standard.com/Content/Protected/Articles/000/000/010/268gdffq.asp.

Barnes, Robert, and Paul Kane. "Sotomayor Repudiates 'Wise Latina' Comment." *Washington Post*, July 15, 2009, http://www.boston.com/news/nation/washington/articles/2009/07/15/sotomayor_backs_off_wise_latina_quote/.

Barrett, Paul M. "A Fascinating Supreme Court Punt on Affirmative Action." *BloombergBusinessWeek*, June 24, 2013, http://www.businessweek.com/articles/2013-06-24/a-fascinating-supreme-court-punt-on-affirmative-action.

Katherine T. Bartlett. "Unconstitutionally Male?: The Story of United States v. Virginia." Duke Law Scholarship Repository, Working Papers (2010), http://scholarship.law.duke.edu/cgi/viewcontent.cgi?article=2936&context=faculty_scholarship Published in *Women and the Law Stories*, edited by Elizabeth M. Schneider and Stephanie M. Wildman (New York: Thomson Reuters/Foundation Press, 2011).

Behuniak-Long, Susan. "Justice Sandra Day O'Connor and the Power of Maternal Legal Thinking." *Review of Politics* 54 (1992): 417–44.

Biskupic, Joan. "Female Justices Attest to Fraternity on Bench; O'Connor and Ginsburg, in Separate Speeches, Discuss Personal Aspects of Supreme Court Life." *Washington Post*, August 21, 1994.

———. "Ginsburg: Court Needs Another Woman." *USAToday*, October 5, 2009, http://usatoday30.usatoday.com/news/washington/judicial/2009-05-05-ruthginsburg_N.htm.

Brody, Seymour. "Ruth Bader Ginsburg." In *Jewish Heroes and Heroines of America: 150 True Stories of Jewish Heroism* (Hollywood, Fla.: Lifetime Books, 1996), http://www.jewishvirtuallibrary.org/jsource/biography/Ginsburg.html.

Brown, Judith Olans, Wendy E. Parmet, and Mary E. O'Connell. "The Rugged Feminism of Sandra Day O'Connor." *Indiana Law Review* 32 (1999): 1219–46; Northeastern University School of Law Research Paper, http://ssrn.com/abstract=1984862 or http://dx.doi.org/10.2139/ssrn.1984862.

Bruno, Debra. "Justice Ginsburg Remembers Her First Steps in the Law." *Legal Times* (November 13, 2007), http://www.law.com/jsp/article.jsp?id=1194861838591.

Bumiller, Elisabeth. "An Interview by, Not with, the President." *New York Times*, July 21, 2005, http://www.nytimes.com/2005/07/21/politics/21bush.html?pagewanted=all.

Burleigh, Nina, and Stephanie B. Goldberg. "Breaking the Silence: Sexual Harassment in Law Firms." *ABA Journal*, August 1989, http://books.google.com.

Cole, David. "The Liberal Legacy of *Bush v. Gore*." *Georgetown Law Journal* 94 (2006): 1427–74, http://www.scotusblog.com/archives/bushvgore-cole.pdf.

Cook, Beverly B. "Sandra Day O'Connor." In *The Burger Court: Political and Judicial Profiles*, edited by Charles M. Lamb and Stephen C. Halpern (Urbana: University of Illinois Press, 1991).

Cooper, Cynthia L. "Daughter of Justice Blackmun Goes Public about Roe." *The Nation*, February 29, 2004, http://womensenews.org/story/the-nation/040229/daughter-justice-blackmun-goes-public-about-roe#.

Cowan, Ruth B. "Women's Rights through Litigation: An Examination of the American Civil Liberties Union Women's Rights Project, 1971–1976." *Columbia Human Rights Law Review* 8 (1977): 373.

Craig, Jon. "Ruth Bader Ginsburg Reminisces about Her Time on the Hill." *Cornell Chronicle*, September 22 and November 16, 2014, http://www.news.cornell.edu/stories/2014/09/ruth-bader-ginsburg-reminisces-about-her-time-hill.

Cushman, Robert. "Civil Liberty after the War." *American Political Science Review* 38 (February 1944): 12–13.

Davidson, Amy. "Ruth Bader Ginsburg's Retirement Dissent." *The New Yorker*, September 24, 2014, http://www.newyorker.com/news/amy-davidson.

Davis, Allison P. "NYU Law Student Is Making Ruth Bader Ginsburg a Meme." *New York*, June 27, 2013, http://nymag.com/thecut/2013/06/nyu-law-student-is-making-bader-ginsburg-a-meme.html.

"Defending the Innocent," *Washington Times*, November 8, 2003, http://www.washingtontimes.com/news/2003/nov/8/20031108-111532-9290r/.

Denniston, Lyle. "Justice's Crusade: 'We the People' Includes Women—Ginsburg Led Military-School Ruling." *Seattle Times*, June 27, 1996, http://community.seattletimes.nwsource.com/archive/?date=19960627&slug=2336534.

DeParle, Jason. "In Battle to Pick Next Justice, Right Says, Avoid a Kennedy." *New York Times*, June 27, 2005, http://www.nytimes.com/2005/06/27/politics/27kennedy.html?pagewanted=all&_r=0.

Dershowitz, Alan. "Putting a Gender Bias on Free Speech." *Buffalo News*, July 27, 1993.

"Developments in the Law—Equal Protection," note, *Harvard Law Review* 82 (1969): 1065.

Duffy, Jill, and Elizabeth Lambert. "Dissents from the Bench: A Compilation of Oral Dissents by U.S. Supreme Court Justices." *Law Library Journal* 102 (2010): 1, http://www.aallnet.org/main-menu/Publications/llj/LLJ-Archives/Vol-102/pub_llj_v102no1/2010-01.pdf.

Feild, Hubert S. "Juror Background Characteristics and Attitudes Toward Rape: Correlates of Jurors' Decisions in Rape Trials." *Law and Human Behavior* 2 (1978): 73–93, http://www.socio-legal.sjtu.edu.cn/uploads/papers/2012/qtl120203050423823.pdf.

Franklin, Cary. "The Anti-Stereotyping Principle in Constitutional Sex Discrimination Law." *New York University Law Review* 85, no. 1 (2010), electronic copy available at http://ssrn.com/abstract=1589754.

Garrow, David. "A Landmark Decision—*Planned Parenthood of Southeastern Pennsylvania* v. *Casey*." *Dissent* 39 (Fall 1992): 427–29.

Gergen, David. "A Candid Conversation with Sandra Day O'Connor: 'I Can Still Make a Difference.' " *Parade* magazine, September 30, 2012, http://www.civic-missionofschools.org/news/2012-10-parade-magazine-a-candid-conversation-with-sandra-da.

Ginsburg, Martin D. "Spousal Transfers: In '58, It Was Different." *Harvard Law Record*, May 6, 1977.

Ginsburg, Ruth Bader. "Consitutional Adjudication in the United States as a Means of Advancing the Equal Stature of Men and Women under the Law." *Hofstra Law Review* 26 (1997): 263.

———. "Gender and the Constitution." *University of Cincinnati Law Review* 44 (1975): 1–42, 75.

———. "*Muller v. Oregon*: One Hundred Years Later." *Willamette Law Review* 45 (2009): 359–80, http://www.willamette.edu/wucl/resources/journals/review/pdf/Volume%2045/WLR45-3_Justice_Ginsburg.pdf.

———. "The Need for the Equal Rights Amendment." *American Bar Association Journal* 59 (1973): 1013.

———. "The Role of Dissenting Opinions." *Minnesota Law Review* 95 (2010): 1, http://www.minnesotalawreview.org/wp-content/uploads/2011/07/Ginsburg_MLR.pdf.

———. "Some Thoughts on Autonomy and Equality in Relation to *Roe v. Wade*." *North Carolina Law Review* 63 (1985): 375–86.

———. "Speaking in a Judicial Voice," Madison Lecture, 1992. *New York University Law Review* 67 (1992): 1185–1209.

———. "Women at the Bar—A Generation of Change." *University of Puget Sound Law Review* 2 (1978): 1, http://digitalcommons.law.seattleu.edu/cgi/viewcontent.cgi?article=1081&context=sulr.

"Ginsburg Feels Isolated on Court." *Washington Post* (Associated Press), January 28, 2007, http://www.washingtonpost.com/wp-dyn/content/article/2007/01/27/AR2007012701065.html.

"Ginsburgs Say Clubs Scored Poorly in Conscience." *Orlando Sentinel* (*Washington Post*), June 20, 1993, http://articles.orlandosentinel.com/1993-06-20/news/9306200267_1_martin-ginsburg-harvard-club-country-club.

Glanton, Dahleen. "O'Connor Questions Court's Decision to Take On *Bush v. Gore*." *Chicago Tribune*, April 27, 2013, http://articles.chicagotribune.com/2013-04-27/news/ct-met-sandra-day-oconnor-edit-board-20130427_1_0-connor-bush-v-high-court.

Goldstein, Tom. "Oral Argument as a Bridge between the Briefs and the Court's Opinion." In *The Legacy of Ruth Bader Ginsburg*, edited by Scott Dodson (New York: Cambridge University Press, 2015).

Greenhouse, Linda. "The Evolution of a Justice." *New York Times Magazine*, April 10, 2005, http://www.nytimes.com/2005/04/10/magazine/10BLACKMUN.html.

———. "From the High Court, a Voice Quite Distinctly a Woman's." *New York Times*, May 26, 1999.

———. "A Justice Champions a Witness to History." *New York Times*, August 5, 2001, http://www.nytimes.com/2001/08/05/us/a-justice-champions-a-witness-to-history.html.

Griffin, Lisa Kern. "Barriers to Entry and Justice Ginsburg's Criminal Procedure Jurisprudence." In *The Legacy of Ruth Bader Ginsburg*, edited by Scott Dodson (New York: Cambridge University Press, 2015).

Halberstam, Malvina. "Ruth Bader Ginsburg." In *Encyclopedia*, Jewish Women's Archive, http://jwa.org/encyclopedia/article/ginsburg-ruth-bader.

Halfmann, Drew, and Michael P. Young. "War Pictures: The Grotesque as a Mobilizing Tactic." *Mobilization* 15 (2010): 1–24, http://sociology.ucdavis.edu/people/halfmann/grotesque.

Harris, Gardiner. "M. D. Ginsburg, 78, Dies, Lawyer and Tax Expert." *New York Times*, June 27, 2010.

Heck, Edward V., and Paula C. Arledge. "Justice O'Connor and the First Amendment, 1981–84." *Pepperdine Law Review* 13 (1986): 993–1019.

Hilts, Philip J. "Hospital Sought Out Prenatal Drug Abuse." *New York Times*, January 21, 1994, http://www.nytimes.com/1994/01/21/us/hospital-sought-out-prenatal-drug-abuse.html.

Hitchens, Christopher. "Now There Is No Referee Left." *Evening Standard* (London), December 13, 2000.

Ho, Catherine. "Justice Ginsburg Happy to No Longer Be Confused with Sandra Day O'Connor." *Washington Post*, December 17, 2013, http://www.washingtonpost.com/business/capitalbusiness/justice-ginsburg-happy-to-no-longer-be-confused-with-sandra-day-oconnor/2013/12/17/d8ba9c5c-6731-11e3-a0b9-249bbb34602c_story.html.

Holley, Joe. "Leading Texas Republican Anne Armstrong." *Washington Post*, July 31, 2008, http://www.washingtonpost.com/wp-dyn/content/article/2008/07/30/AR2008073002605.html.

Holmes, Oliver Wendell, Jr. "The Path of the Law." *Harvard Law Review* 10 (1897): 457, http://www.gutenberg.org/ebooks/2373.

Hopkins, Ann. "*Price Waterhouse v. Hopkins*: A Personal Account of a Sexual Discrimination Plaintiff." *Hofstra Labor & Employment Law Journal* 22 (2005): 357, http://law.hofstra.edu/pdf/academics/journals/laborandemploymentlawjournal/labor_hopkins_vol22no2.pdf.

Izadi, Elahe. "Ruth Bader Ginsburg's Advice on Love and Leaning In." *Washington Post*, July 31, 2014, http://www.washingtonpost.com/news/post-nation/wp/2014/07/31/ruth-bader-ginsburgs-advice-on-love-and-leaning-in/.

Johnson, Darragh. "Sandra Day O'Connor: Well Judged." *Washington Post*, March 7, 2006, http://www.washingtonpost.com/wp-dyn/content/article/2006/03/07/AR2006030700008_2.html.

Kearny, Robert A. "The High Price of *Price Waterhouse*: Dealing with Direct Evidence of Discrimination." *University of Pennsylviania Journal of Labor and Employment Law* 5 (2003): 303–33, https://www.law.upenn.edu/journals/jbl/articles/volume5/issue2/Kearney5U.Pa.J.Lab.&Emp.L.303(2003).pdf.

Kennedy, Randall. "The Case for Early Retirement." *The New Republic*, April

28, 2011, http://www.newrepublic.com/article/politics/87543/ginsburg-breyer-resign-supreme-court.

Kerr, Virginia. "Supreme Court Justice O'Connor: The Woman Whose Word Is Law." *Ms.*, December 1982.

Kiernan, Laura. "Feminist Picked for U.S. Court of Appeals Here." *Washington Post*, December 16, 1979.

Klarman, Michael J. "Social Reform Litigation and Its Challenges: An Essay in Honor of Justice Ruth Bader Ginsburg." *Harvard Journal of Law & Gender* 32 (2009): 251–302.

Kohn, Howard. "Front and Center: Sandra Day O'Connor." *Los Angeles Times Magazine*, April 18, 1993.

Kurland, Philip B. "'*Brown v. Board of Education* Was the Beginning.' The School Desegregation Cases in the United States Supreme Court: 1954–1979." *Washington University Law Quarterly* (1979): 309, 313, 316.

———. "The Equal Rights Amendment: Some Problems of Construction." *Harvard Civil Rights–Civil Liberties Law Review* 6 (1970–1971): 243.

———. "Foreword: Equal in Origin and Equal in Title to the Legislative and Executive Branches of the Government." *Harvard Law Review* 78 (1964): 143.

Labaton, Stephen. "Senators See Easy Approval for Nominee." *New York Times*, June 16, 1993, http://www.nytimes.com/1993/06/16/us/senators-see-easy-approval-for-nominee.html.

Lane, Charles. "Courting O'Connor: Why the Chief Justice Isn't the Chief Justice." *Washington Post*, July 4, 2004, http://www.washingtonpost.com/wp-dyn/articles/A16332-2004Jun29_3.html.

"The Law: Ten Teachers Who Shape the Future." *Time*, March 14, 1977, http://content.time.com/time/magazine/article/0,9171,947277,00.html.

Lewis, Anthony. "Abroad at Home: How Not to Choose." *New York Times*, May 10, 1993, http://news.google.com/newspapers.

Liptak, Adam. "Honoring O'Connor's Legacy at the Supreme Court." *New York Times*, April 12, 2012, http://thecaucus.blogs.nytimes.com/2012/04/12/honoring-oconnors-legacy-at-the-supreme-court/?_r=0.

———. "Kagan Says Her Path to Supreme Court Was Made Smoother by Ginsburg's." *New York Times*, February 10, 2014, http://www.nytimes.com/2014/02/11/us/kagan-says-her-path-to-supreme-court-was-made-smoother-by-ginsburg.html.

———. "Sotomayor Finds Her Voice Among Justices." *New York Times*, May 6, 2014, http://www.nytimes.com/2014/05/07/us/politics/sotomayor-finds-her-voice-among-the-justices.html?smid=pl-share&_r=0.

Lowe, Rebecca. "Supremely Confident: The Legacy of Sandra Day O'Connor." Guardian Legal Network, August 30, 2011, http://www.theguardian.com/law/2011/aug/30/us-supreme-court-george-bush.

Lukas, J. Anthony. "Playboy Interview: Bob Woodward." *Playboy*, vol. 36, no. 2 (February 1, 1989): 51.

Margolick, David. "Meet the Supremes" (review of Toobin, *The Nine*). *New York*

Times, September 23, 2007, http://www.nytimes.com/2007/09/23/books/review/Margolick-t.html?pagewanted=print&_r=0.

————. "Sex Bias Suit Perils Law Firms' Methods of Picking Partners." *New York Times*, April 23, 1983, http://www.nytimes.com/1983/04/23/us/sex-bias-suit-perils-law-firms-methods-of-picking-partners.html.

————. "Trial by Adversity Shapes Jurist's Outlook." *New York Times*, June 25, 1993, http://www.nytimes.com/1993/06/25/us/trial-by-adversity-shapes-jurist-s-outlook.html?pagewanted=all&src=pm.

Mauro, Tony. "Lifting the Veil: Justice Blackmun's Papers and the Public Perception of the Supreme Court." *Missouri Law Review* 70 (2005): 1037–47, http://scholarship.law.missouri.edu/cgi/viewcontent.cgi?article=3674&context=mlr.

Mayeri, Serena. "'When the Trouble Started': The Story of *Frontiero v. Richardson*." In *Women and the Law Stories*, edited by Elizabeth M. Schneider and Stephanie M. Wildman (New York: Foundation Press, 2011).

Miller, Margaret A. "Justice Sandra Day O'Connor: Token or Triumph from a Feminist Perspective." *Golden Gate University Law Review* 15 (2010): 493–525, http://digitalcommons.law.ggu.edu/cgi/viewcontent.cgi?article=1373&context=ggulrev.

Moberg, Eva. "Kvinnans villkorliga frigivning." In *Unga Liberaler: nio inlägg i idédebatten* (Stockholm: Bonnier, 1961).

Motluk, Alison. "US Abortion Policy: A Healthy Strategy for Whom?" *New Scientist*, October 6, 2004 (retrieved September 29, 2007).

Murphy, Michael. "Conservative Pioneer Became an Outcast." *Arizona Republic*, May 31, 1998, http://archive.azcentral.com/specials/special25/articles/0531goldwater2.html.

Myers, Linda. "Justice Ruth Bader Ginsburg Weighs In on Women's Progress in the Law Profession—and What Kept Them Out for So Long." *Cornell Chronicle*, July 1, 2004, http://www.news.cornell.edu/stories/2004/07/justice-ruth-bader-ginsburg-womens-progress-law.

Ness, Susan. "The Bench: Where Are All the Women?" *Los Angeles Times*, April 4, 1979.

————. "A Sexist Selection Process Keeps Qualified Women off the Bench." *Washington Post*, March 26, 1978.

Ness, Susan, and Fredrica Wechsler. "Women Judges—Why So Few?" *Graduate Woman*, November/December 1979, 46–49.

Newman, Jon O. "Probing and Allegations in the Confirmation of Federal Judges." *Journal of Civil Rights and Economic Development* 7 (1991): 15, http://scholarship.law.stjohns.edu/cgi/viewcontent.cgi?article=1520&context=jcred.

Novick, Sheldon M. "What Makes a Great Judge, His Reasoning or His Vision?" *Los Angeles Times*, April 22, 1994, http://articles.latimes.com/1994-05-22/books/bk-60553_1_learned-hand/2.

O'Brien, David M. "Holding the Center: As Thomas and Scalia Stake Out the Far Right, O'Connor Takes the Moral High Ground." *Los Angeles Times*,

March 8, 1992, http://articles.latimes.com/1992-03-08/opinion/op-5987 L justice-clarence-thomas.

O'Connor, Sandra Day. "Foreword." *New England Law Review* 18 (1982–83): ix.

———. "Introduction: Achievements of Women in the Legal Profession." *New York State Bar Journal* 57 (1985): 8.

———. "Legal Education and Social Responsibility." *Fordham Law Review* 53 (1985).

———. "Portia's Progress," Madison Lecture, 1991. *New York University Law Review* 66 (1991): 1546.

———. "Professional Competence and Social Responsibility: Fulfilling the Vanderbilt Vision." *Vanderbilt Law Review* 36 (1983): 1.

Pantazelos, Elizabeth. "Women at Work: Articles from the '70s, '80s, and '90s Address the Ongoing Obstacles that Career Women Face." *The Atlantic*, May 2006, http://www.theatlantic.com/magazine/archive/2006/05/women-at-work/304944/.

"Preview: Female Force: Ruth Bader Ginsburg #1." June 24, 2013, http://www.comicbookresources.com/?page=preview&id=17037.

Primus, Richard A. "Canon, Anti-Canon, and Judicial Dissent." *Duke Law Journal* 48 (1998): 243, http://scholarship.law.duke.edu/cgi/viewcontent.cgi?article=1040&context=dlj.

"The Reality of Ideas," *Stanford Review*, May 29, 2009, http://stanfordreview.org/article/reality-ideas/.

William H. Rehnquist. "Isaac Parker, Bill Sykes and the Rule of Law." *University of Arkansas Little Rock Law Journal* 6 (1983): 485.

Rosen, Jeffrey. "The Book of Ruth." *The New Republic*, August 2, 1993, http://www.newrepublic.com/article/politics/the-book-ruth and http://www.holy-smoke.org/sdhok/fem02.htm.

———. "Disgrace." *The New Republic*, December 24, 2000, http://www.newrepublic.com/article/politics/disgrace.

———. "The New Look of Liberalism on the Court." *New York Times Magazine*, October 5, 1997, http://www.nytimes.com/1997/10/05/magazine/the-new-look-of-liberalism-on-the-court.html.

———. "Ruth Bader Ginsburg Is an American Hero." *The New Republic*, September 28, 2014, http://www.newrepublic.com/article/119578/ruth-bader-ginsburg-interview-retirement-feminists-jazzercise.

"Ruth's Greatest Hit's [*sic*]: Ledbetter v. Goodyear." Ruth Bader GinsBlog, August 15, 2012, http://ruthbaderginsblog.blogspot.com/2012/08/ruths-greatest-hits-ledbetter-v_15.html.

Sassower, Doris L. "Women's Rights Ignored." *American Bar Association Journal*, October 1971.

Schlafly, Phyllis. "Women's Libbers Do NOT Speak for Us." *Phyllis Schlafly Report*, February 1972, reprinted in Siegel and Greenhouse, *Before Roe v. Wade*, pp. 218–19.

Schafran, Lynn Hecht. "Sandra O'Connor and the Supremes." *Ms.*, October 1981.

Schatz, Phil. "Judicial Profile: Hon. Ruth Bader Ginsburg." *Federal Lawyer*, May

2010, available at http://www.wandslaw.com/phils-book-reviews/90-judicial-profile-hon-ruth-bader-ginsberg.html.

Scherer, Nancy. "Diversifying the Federal Bench: Is Universal Legitimacy for the U.S. Justice System Possible?" *Northwestern University Law Review* 105 (2011): 587.

Schulder, Diane. "Women and the Laws." *Atlantic Monthly*, March 1970, http://www.theatlantic.com/magazine/archive/1970/03/women-and-the-laws/304923/.

Sherry, Suzanna. "Civic Virtue and the Feminine Voice in Constitutional Adjudication." *Virginia Law Review* 72 (1986): 543.

Shulman, Alix Kates. "A Marriage Agreement." *Up from Under* (August/September 1970); reprinted in *A Marriage Agreement and Other Essays: Four Decades of Feminist Writing* (New York: Open Road Integrated Media, 2012), available at http://jwa.org/sites/jwa.org/files/mediaobjects/a_marriage_agreement_alix_kates_shulman.jpg.

Slavin, Sarah, ed. *U.S. Women's Interest Groups: Institutional Profiles* (Westport, Conn.: Greenwood Press, 1995).

Sotomayor, Sonia. "A Latina Judge's Voice" (2001). *New York Times*, May 14, 2009, http://www.nytimes.com/2009/05/15/us/politics/15judge.text.html?pagewanted=all&_r=0.

Stewart, David O. "Holding the Center—Sandra O'Connor Evolves into Major Force on Supreme Court." *ABA Journal* 79 (1993): 48.

Stolberg, Sheryl Gay. "Ginsburg Leaves Hospital; Prognosis on Cancer Is Good." *New York Times*, September 29, 1999, http://www.nytimes.com/1999/09/29/us/ginsburg-leaves-hospital-prognosis-on-cancer-is-good.html.

Stoll, Ira E. "Ginsburg Blasts Harvard Law; Past, Present Deans Defend School." *Harvard Crimson*, July 23, 1993, http://www.thecrimson.com/article/1993/7/23/ginsburg-blasts-harvard-law-pin-testimony/.

Strum, Philippa. "Do Women Belong in Military Academies?" *Historic U.S. Court Cases: An Encyclopedia.* 2nd ed., edited by John W. Johnson (New York: Routledge, 2001), vol. 2, pp. 779–83.

"Supreme Court Runs Financial Gamut." *New York Times*, June 11, 2010, http://www.nytimes.com/2010/06/12/us/12scotus.html?_r=0.

"Symposium Honors and Roasts Professor Monaghan." *Columbia Law School Magazine*, Winter 2010, http://www.law.columbia.edu/magazine/153298/symposium-honors-and-roasts-professor-monaghan.

Tang-Martinez, Zuleyma. "The Curious Courtship of Sociobiology and Feminism: A Case of Irreconcilable Differences." In *Feminism and Evolutionary Biology: Boundaries, Intersections, and Frontiers*, edited by Patricia Gowaty (New York: Chapman and Hall, 1997).

"10 Things You Didn't Know About Antonin Scalia." *US News and World Report*, October 2, 2007, http://www.usnews.com/news/national/articles/2007/10/02/10-things-you-didnt-know-about-justice-antonin-scalia.

Thomas, Evan, and Michael Isikoff. "The Truth Behind the Pillars." *Newsweek*, December 25, 2000, 46.

Thomas-Lester, Avis. "A History Scarred by Lynchings." *Washington Post*, July 7, 2005, http://www.washingtonpost.com/wp-dyn/content/article/2005/07/06/AR2005070600637.html.

Totenberg, Nina. Introduction to *The Legacy of Ruth Bader Ginsburg*, edited by Scott Dodson (New York: Cambridge University Press, 2015).

"The Trailblazers." *Rutgers Magazine*, Winter 2013, http://magazine.rutgers.edu/features/winter-2013/the-trailblazers.

Tribe, Laurence. "The Roberts Court: New Frontiers in Constitutional Doctrine." *Washington Post*, June 6, 2014, http://www.washingtonpost.com/news/volokh-conspiracy/wp/2014/06/06/by-prof-laurence-tribe-the-roberts-court-new-frontiers-in-constitutional-doctrine/.

Von Drehle, David. "Conventional Roles Hid a Revolutionary Intellect: Discrimination Helped Spawn a Crusade." *Washington Post*, July 18, 1993.

———. "Ruth Bader Ginsburg: Her Life and Her Law." *Washington Post*, July 18–20, 1993.

Ward, Stephanie Frances. "Family Ties." *ABA Journal*, October 1, 2010, http://www.abajournal.com/magazine/article/family_ties1/.

Warren, Samuel D., and Louis D. Brandeis. "The Right to Privacy." *Harvard Law Review* 4 (December 15, 1890): 193–220, http://www.english.illinois.edu/-people-/faculty/debaron/582/582%20readings/right%20to%20privacy.pdf.

Wechsler, Herbert. "Toward Neutral Principles of Constitutional Law." *Harvard Law Review* 73 (1959): 1.

Weisberg, Jessica. "Supreme Court Justice Ruth Bader Ginsburg: I'm Not Going Anywhere." *Elle*, September 23, 2014, http://www.elle.com/life-love/society-career/supreme-court-justice-ruth-bader-ginsburg.

Weiss, Debra Cassens. "Ginsburg Defends Sotomayor, Calls 'Wise Latina' Flap Ridiculous." *ABA Journal*, July 9, 2009, http://www.abajournal.com/news/article/ginsburg_defends_sotomayor_calls_wise_latina_flap_ridiculous.

Weitzman, Lenore J. "The Economics of Divorce: Social and Economic Consequences of Property, Alimony and Child Support Awards." *UCLA Law Review* 28 (1980–81): 1181.

Wolf, Richard. "Justice Ginsburg Has Stent Implanted in Heart Procedure." *USA Today*, November 26, 2014.

Wood, Ann. "Pat Lindh Says She 'Nags a Lot' as Special Assistant to President." *Toledo Blade*, November 17, 1975, http://news.google.com/newspapers.

Yalof, David Alistair. *Pursuit of Justices: Presidential Politics and the Selection of Supreme Court Nominees* (Chicago: University of Chicago Press, 1999).

ONLINE RESOURCES AND BLOG POSTINGS

"Abortion—Twentieth-Century Abortion Law Reform," law.jrank (website), http://law.jrank.org/pages/447/Abortion-Twentieth-century-abortion-law-reform.html.

"All about Bernice Sandler," http://www.bernicesandler.com/id2.htm.

"Andrew McBride: Political Campaign Contributions, 2010 Election Cycle," CampaignMoney.com, http://www.campaignmoney.com/political/contributions/andrew-mcbride.asp?cycle=10 (accessed November 17, 2014).

Appleton, Mike. "Connick V. Thompson and Prosecutorial Impunity," Jonathan Turley (blog), April 10, 2011, http://jonathanturley.org/2011/04/10/connick-v-thompson-and-prosecutorial-impunity/.

"The Arizona Republic: An Overview," azcentral.com, http://www.azcentral.com/help/articles/about2.html.

"Aryeh Neier," ACLU ProCon.org, June 27, 2012, http://aclu.procon.org/view.source.php?sourceID=002205.

Baxter, Brian. "Justice O'Connor Dings Gibson Dunn on Letterman Show," *Am Law Daily* (blog), June 24, 2009, http://amlawdaily.typepad.com/amlaw daily/2009/06/oconnor-on-letterman.html.

"Before there was Sotomayor, before even Ginsburg and O'Connor . . . there was Mildred Lillie," *Peter Jennings Project*, August 3, 2009, http://peterjennings project.blogspot.com/2009/08/before-there-was-sotomayor-before-even.html.

"Bill Clinton on Abortion," OnTheIssues.org, http://www.ontheissues.org/celeb/Bill_Clinton_Abortion.htm (accessed November 18, 2014).

Biskupic, Joan. "Ginsburg 'Lonely' without O'Connor." *USA Today*, January 25, 2007, http://usatoday30.usatoday.com/news/washington/2007-01-25-ginsburg-court_x.htm.

———. "Ruth Bader Ginsburg Resists Retirement Pressure." Reuters, July 4, 2013.

Bruno, Debra. "Justice Ginsburg Remembers Her First Steps in the Law." *LegalTimes*, November 13, 2007, www.law.com/jsp/article.jsp?id=1194861838591.

"Chief Justice Peters Dinner," C-SPAN, October 17, 1994, http://www.c-span.org/video/?60896-1/chief-justice-peters-dinner.

Coyle, Marcia, Tony Mauro, and Todd Ruger. "Clinton Docs Reveal Concerns About Court Nominees." *LegalTimes*, July 18, 2014, http://www.nationallawjournal.com/legaltimes/id=1202663790913/Clinton-Docs-Reveal-Concerns-About-Court-Nominees#ixzz3IsohEp8v.

Doran, Jamison. "19 Reasons Ruth Bader Ginsburg Is Your Favorite Supreme Court Justice: R.B.G. is a complete and total boss. Plain and simple." BuzzFeed Commuity, July 30, 2013, http://www.buzzfeed.com/jamisond/19-reasons-why-ruth-bader-ginsburg-is-your-favorit-7fxd.

Francis, Roberta W. "The History Behind the Equal Rights Amendment." *Equal Rights Amendment* (website), http://www.equalrightsamendment.org/history.htm.

Garrow, David. "The Brains Behind Blackmun." *Legal Affairs*, May–June 2005, http://www.legalaffairs.org/issues/May-June-2005/feature_garrow_mayjun05.msp.

"George W. Bush on Abortion" and "George W. Bush on the Constitution," OnTheIssues.org, http://www.ontheissues.org/Celeb/George_W__Bush_Abortion.htm#Supreme_Court_+_Constitution (accessed November 18, 2014).

Ginsburg, Ruth Bader. "A Woman's Voice May Do Some Good," *Politico*, September 25, 2013, http://www.politico.com/story/2013/09/women-oconnor-ginsburg-supreme-court-97313.html.

———. Oral history page. *Jewish Washington*, May 27, 2005, http://www.jhsgw.org/exhibitions/online/jewishwashington/oral-histories/ruth-bader-ginsburg.

"Ginsburg's Hobby Lobby Dissent, Song a Day #2007," YouTube, June 30, 2014, https://www.youtube.com/watch?v=GYiTJ8JazkQ.

Gorlick, Adam. "Former Justice Reflects on How Law Professor Helped Shape Her Life Philosophy," *Stanford Report*, April 23, 2008, http://news.stanford.edu/news/2008/april30/sandra-043008.html.

Hasday, Jill Elaine. "The Principle and Practice of Women's 'Full Citizenship': A Case Study of Sex-Segregated Public Education." University of Chicago Public Law and Legal Theory Working Paper no. 35 (2002), http://chicagounbound.uchicago.edu/cgi/viewcontent.cgi?article=1333&context=public_law_and_legal_theory.

Hoey, Mike. "A Short History of the Missouri Catholic Conference 1967–2007," http://www.mocatholic.org/wp-content/uploads/2012/10/MCC-Short-History-1.pdf.

"Hoops at the Supreme Court, Literally." *Baller-in-Chief* (blog), March 31, 2009, http://baller-in-chief.com/articles/hoops-at-the-supreme-court-literally/.

Imes, Birney. "Joe Hogan's Legacy." *The Dispatch*, March 14, 2009, http://www.cdispatch.com/opinions/article.asp?aid=678&TRID=1&TID=.

"Investiture of Judge Friedland." United States Court of Appeals for the Ninth Circuit, YouTube, June 30, 2014, https://www.youtube.com/watch?v=7D-8OhPjKHY.

"Jane Stromseth Contributions," FindTheBest.com, http://individual-contributions.findthedata.org/l/1010743/Jane-Stromseth (accessed November 17, 2014).

"Justice Sandra Day O'Connor Talks about Her Life on Valley Girl," AOL.com, July 12, 2012, http://on.aol.com/video/justice-sandra-day-oconnor-talks-about-her-life-on-the-valley-girl-517415204.

"Justice Sandra Day O'Connor Visits Duke Law," *Duke Law News* (website), http://law.duke.edu/features/news_oconnor/ (accessed November 18, 2014).

Lithwick, Dahlia. "Cruel but Not Unusual: Clarence Thomas Writes One of the Meanest Supreme Court Decisions Ever." *Slate*, April 1, 2011, http://www.slate.com/articles/news_and_politics/jurisprudence/2011/04/cruel_but_not_unusual.html.

———. "Search Me." *Slate*, April 21, 2009, http://www.slate.com/articles/news_and_politics/supreme_court_dispatches/2009/04/search_me.html.

"Melvin Wulf, LLB." ACLU ProCon.org, June 12, 2008, http://aclu.procon.org/view.source.php?sourceID=002223.

Naderi, Sahar, and Russell Raymond. "Pregnancy and Heart Disease." Center for Continuing Education, Cleveland Clinic, February 2014, http://www.clevelandclinicmeded.com/medicalpubs/diseasemanagement/cardiology/pregnancy-and-heart-disease/.

"Nineteenth Amendment to the United States Constitution," Wikipedia, http://

en.wikipedia.org/wiki/Nineteenth_Amendment_to_the_United_States_
Constitution#Proposal_and_ratification (accessed November 18, 2014).

"The Notorious B.I.G." Wikipedia, http://en.wikipedia.org/wiki/The_Notorious
_B.I.G (accessed November 19, 2014).

Notorious R.B.G.: Justice Ruth Bader Ginsburg in All Her Glory (blog), http://
notoriousrbg.tumblr.com (accessed November 19, 2014).

"Paradise Valley Country Club." A People's Guide to Maricopa County (website),
May 2, 2011, http://peoplesguidetomaricopa.blogspot.com/2011/05/paradise-
valley-country-club.html.

Peacock, William. "Friday Frills: The Jabot (or Neck Doily)." *Findlaw Supreme Court* (blog), February 7, 2014, http://blogs.findlaw.com/supreme_
court/2014/02/friday-frills-the-jabot-or-neck-doily.html.

Polakova, Veronika. "Predicting Anthony Kennedy." *The Monkey Cage*, American Enterprise Institute blog, July 13, 2012, http://www.aei.org/article/politics-
and-public-opinion/judicial/predicting-anthony-kennedy/.

Post, David G. Beasley School of Law, Temple University faculty website, http://
www.law.temple.edu/pages/faculty/n_faculty_post_main.aspx (accessed November 18, 2014).

"Ruth Bader Ginsburg," *Miriam's Cup*, http://www.miriamscup.com/Ginsburg-
Biog.htm.

Sacks, Mike. "Women Supreme Court Justices Celebrate 30 Years since Court's
First Female." *Huffington Post*, April 11, 2012, http://www.huffingtonpost
.com/2012/04/11/supreme-court-women-justices_n_1419183.html.

"Sandra Day O'Connor." Biography.com, http://www.biography.com/people/
sandra-day-oconnor-9426834?page=1#early-life-and-career.

"Sandra Day O'Connor—Member." *Iraq Study Group Report*, Future of the Book,
http://www.futureofthebook.org/iraqreport/sandra-day-oconnor/index.html.

Scherer, Nancy. "Why Has the Lower Court Appointment Process Become So
Politicized and What We Can Do about It?" *Jurist* (online journal of the
University of Pittsburgh Law School), 2004, http://www.jurist.law.pitt.edu/
forum/symposium-jc/scherer.php.

Schizer, David M. Columbia Law School faculty website, http://www.law
.columbia.edu/fac/David_Schizer (accessed November 18, 2014).

Schlanger, Margo. University of Michigan Law School faculty website, http://
www.law.umich.edu/FacultyBio/Pages/FacultyBio.aspx?FacID=mschlan
(accessed November 18, 2014).

"School Desegregation." *West's Encyclopedia of American Law* (2005). http://www
.encyclopedia.com/topic/School_integration.aspx.

"Senators Decry 'Racism' of Exclusive Country Club." *Prescott Courier* (Associated
Press), April 3, 1990, http://news.google.com/newspapers.

Shapiro, Alexandra. A. E. Shapiro Arato & Isserles biography, http://www.shap-
iroarato.com/person/alexandra-shapiro/ (accessed November 18, 2014).

"Sherri Finkbine's Abortion: Its Meaning 50 Years Later." Planned Parenthood
Advocates of Arizona blog, http://blog.advocatesaz.org/2012/08/15/sherri-
finkbines-abortion-its-meaning-50-years-later/.

"Susan Deller Ross." ACLU Women's Rights Project, http://www.aclu.org/files/womensrights/tribute/3.html (accessed November 14, 2014).

Testicular Cancer Resource Center. "Testicular Cancer Treatments: Chemotherapy," http://tcrc.acor.org/chemo.html.

Texts from Hillary, April 11, 2012, http://textsfromhillaryclinton.tumblr.com.

Towle, Andy. "Gay 'Texts from Hillary' Creators Get Invite to State Department Meeting with Hillary." *Towleroad* (blog), April 10, 2012, http://www.towleroad.com/2012/04/gay-texts-from-hillary-creators-get-invite-to-state-department-meeting-with-hillary.html.

"Tribute: The Legacy of Ruth Bader Ginsburg and WRP Staff." ACLU.org, March 7, 2006, http://www.aclu.org/womens-rights/tribute-legacy-ruth-bader-ginsburg-and-wrp-staff.

"A Tribute to Lewis F. Powell, Jr." *Washington and Lee Law Review* 56 (1999): 6, http://scholarlycommons.law.wlu.edu/cgi/viewcontent.cgi?article=1532&context=wlulr.

Valentin, Iram. "Title IX: A Brief History." Womens Equity Action League, Equity Resource Center, August 1997, http://www2.edc.org/WomensEquity/pdffiles/t9digest.pdf.

Wermiel, Stephen. "Dissenting from the Bench." *SCOTUS for Law Students*, July 2, 2013, http://www.scotusblog.com/2013/07/scotus-for-law-students-sponsored-by-bloomberg-law-dissenting-from-the-bench/.

Westberg, Jenny. "D&X: Grim Technology for Abortion's Older Victims." LifeAdvocate.org, 1997, http://lifeadvocate.org/arc/dx.htm.

TELEVISION AND INTERNET BROADCASTS

Blackburn, Bradley. "Justices Ruth Bader Ginsburg and Sandra Day O'Connor on Life and the Supreme Court." *ABC News*, October 26, 2010, http://abcnews.go.com/WN/diane-sawyer-interviews-maria-shriver-sandra-day-oconnor/story?id=11977195.

Brokaw, Tom, and Lisa Myers. "Reaction to Nomination of Ruth Bader Ginsburg to Supreme Court." *NBC Nightly News*, June 14, 1993, https://highered.nbclearn.com/portal/site/HigherEd/flatview?cuecard=3734.

"Chief Justice Peters Dinner." C-SPAN, October 17, 1994, http://www.c-span.org/video/?60896-1/chief-justice-peters-dinner.

"A Conversation with Justice Ruth Bader Ginsburg." C-SPAN, September 15, 2009, http://www.c-span.org/video/?288900-1/conversation-justice-ruth-bader-ginsburg.

"Ginsburg Supreme Court Nomination." C-SPAN, June 14, 1993, http://www.c-spanvideo.org/program/42908-1.

"Sandra Day O'Connor Pt. 2." *The Daily Show*, March 3, 2009, http://thedailyshow.cc.com/video-playlists/rldluj/daily-show-14030/8twc80.

LEGAL CASES

Adarand Construction v. Pena, 515 U.S. 200 (1995), http://www.law.cornell.edu/supremecourt/text/515/200.

Akron v. Akron Center for Reproductive Health, Inc., 462 U.S. 416 (1983), http://www.law.cornell.edu/supremecourt/text/462/416.

Atkins v. Virginia, 536 U.S. 304 (2002), http://www.oyez.org/cases/2000-2009/2001/2001_00_8452/.

Baehr v. Lewin, 74 Haw. 530, 852 P.2d 44 (1993), reconsideration and clarification granted in part, 74 Haw. 645, 852 P.2d 74 (1993).

Barnes v. Costle, 561 F.2d 983 (1977).

Black v. Wilson, 198 So.2d 286 (1967) (Alabama Supreme Court), http://law.justia.com/cases/alabama/supreme-court/1967/198-so-2d-286-1.html.

Burwell v. Hobby Lobby, 573 (2014), http://www.law.cornell.edu/supremecourt/text/13-354#writing-13-354_OPINION_3.

Bush v. Gore, 531 U.S. 98 (2000).

Coleman v. Maryland Court of Appeals, 566 U.S. 12 (2012).

Connick v. Thompson, 131 S.Ct. 1350, 563 (2011), http://scholar.google.com/scholar_case.

Craig v. Boren, 429 U.S. 190 (1976).

Davis v. Monroe County Board of Education, 526 U.S. 629 (1999).

Duren v. Missouri, 439 US 357 (1979).

Easley v. Cromartie, 532 U.S. 234 (2001), http://www.oyez.org/cases/2000-2009/2000/2000_99_1864.

Ellereth v. Burlington Industries, 123 F.3d 490 (1997) (United States Court of Appeals, Seventh Circuit).

Ferguson v. Charleston, 532 U.S. 67 (2001).

Fisher v. University of Texas, 133 S.Ct. 2411, 570 (2013).

Gebser v. Lago Vista Independent School District, 524 U.S. 274 (1998).

Gonzales v. Carhart, 550 U.S. 124 (2007), http://www.law.cornell.edu/supct/html/05-380.ZO.html.

Grutter v Bollinger, 539 U.S. 306 (2003), http://www.oyez.org/cases/2000-2009/2002/2002_02_241/.

Harris v. Forklift Systems, 60 Empl. Prac. Dec. (CCH) 74,245, 74,247 (M.D. Tenn. 1990).

Harris v. Forklift Systems, 510 U.S. 17 (1993), http://supreme.justia.com/cases/federal/us/510/17/case.html.

Hishon v. King & Spalding, 467 U.S. 69 (1984), http://www.oyez.org/cases/1980-1989/1983/1983_82_940.

Jackson v. Birmingham Board of Education, 544 U.S. 167 (2005), http://www.law.cornell.edu/supct/pdf/02-1672P.ZO.

J.E.B. v. Alabama ex rel. T. B. (92-1239), 511 U.S. 127 (1994).

J. Mcintyre Machinery v. Robert Nicastro, 131 S.Ct. 2780, 564 (2011).

Johnson v. Transportation Agency, 480 U.S. 616 (1987), http://www.law.cornell.edu/supremecourt/text/480/616#writing-USSC_CR_0480_0616_ZC1.

Kahn v. Shevin, 416 U.S. 351 (1974).

Kaplowitz v. University of Chicago, 387 F.Supp. 42 (1974), http://www.leagle.com/decision/1974429387FSupp42_1422.xml/KAPLOWITZ%20v.%20UNIVERSITY%20OF%20CHICAGO.

Kelo v. City of New London, 125 S. Ct. 2655 (2005).

Lawrence v. Texas, 539 U.S. 558 (2003).

Lilly Ledbetter v. Goodyear Tire and Rubber, 550 U.S. 618 (2007).

Lujan v. Defenders of Wildlife, 504 U.S. 555 (1992), http://www.law.cornell.edu/supremecourt/text/504/555.

Meritor Savings Bank v. Vinson, 477 U.S. 57, 60 (1986).

Michael H. v. Gerald D., 491 U.S. 110 (1989).

Michael M. v. Superior Court of Sonoma County, 450 U.S. 464 (1981).

Miller v. Albright, 523 U.S. 420 (1998).

Moritz v. Commissioner of IRS, 469 F.2d 466 (1972), http://law.justia.com/cases/federal/appellate-courts/F2/469/466/79852/.

Nevada Department of Human Resources v. Hibbs, 538 U.S. 721 (2003).

O'Connor v. Ortega, 480 U.S. 709 (1987).

Oncale v. Sundowner Offshore Services, 523 U.S. 75 (1998), http://supreme.justia.com/cases/federal/us/523/75/case.html.

Planned Parenthood v. Casey, 505 U.S. 833 (1992).

Price Waterhouse v. Hopkins, 490 U.S. 228 (1989).

Ring v. Arizona, 536 U.S. 584, 609 (2002).

Rostker v. Goldberg, 453 U.S. 57 (1981).

Shelby County Alabama v. Holder, 133 S.Ct. 2612 (2013).

Skinner v. Oklahoma ex rel. Williamson, 316 U.S. 535 (1942).

Stanton v. Stanton 421 U.S. 7 (1975).

Stenberg v. Carhart, 530 U.S. 914 (2000).

Tuan Anh Nguyen v. INS, 533 U.S. 53 (2001), http://supreme.justia.com/cases/federal/us/533/53/case.html.

United States v. Virginia, 518 U.S. 515 (1996), http://www.oyez.org/cases/1990-1999/1995/1995_94_1941.

United States v. Virginia, 766 F. Supp. 1407 (W.D. Va. 1991).

University of Texas Southwestern Hospital v. Nassar, 570 (2012), http://www.supremecourt.gov/opinions/12pdf/12-484_0759.pdf.

Vance v. Ball State, 133 S. Ct. 2434 (2013).

Vieth v. Jubelirer, 541 U.S. 267 (2004).

Vorchheimer v. School District of Philadelphia, 430 U.S. 703 (1977).

Webster v. Reproductive Health Services, 492 U.S. 490 (1989), http://www.oyez.org/cases/1980-1989/1988/1988_88_605.

Weinberger v. Wiesenfeld, 420 U.S. 636 (1975).

ARCHIVES AND MANUSCRIPT COLLECTIONS

American Civil Liberties Union Records, Princeton University Library

Arizona Memory Project, Arizona State Archives, http://azmemory.azlibrary.gov

Harry A. Blackmun Papers, Library of Congress

Civil Rights Movement in Kentucky Oral History Project, Kentucky Historical Society, Frankfort (accessed September 16, 2010)

Ginsburg Archive, Library of Congress, box 20, folder: ERA correspondence 1974
Thurgood Marshall Papers, Library of Congress
Personal and Political Papers of Senator Barry M. Goldwater, Arizona State University Libraries Arizona Collection
Lewis F. Powell, Jr. Archives, Washington and Lee University School of Law
O'Connor files, Arizona History and Archives
Byron R. White Papers, Library of Congress
Correspondence between Ginsburg and Wiesenfeld is in the possession of Stephen Wiesenfeld.

INTERVIEWS AND CORRESPONDENCE WITH THE AUTHOR

Frank Askin, June 18, 2013
Barbara Babcock, March 9, 2014
Hugh Baxter, June 24, 2014
Susan Berresford, November 5, 2013
Pat Cain, March 21, 2014
Penny Clark, December 27, 2013
Wilbur Colom, November 11, 2014
Kelly Cosby, August 13, 2014
Norman Dorsen, June 18, 2013
John and Gail Driggs, January 25, 2014
Paul Eckstein, April 16, 2013
Ann Freedman, October 29, 2013
Michelle Friedland, June 20, 2014
Elizabeth Gavin, October 31, 2014
Steven M. Gelber, April 2013
Stephen Gilles, March 28, 2014
Harvey Goldschmid, November 4, 2013
Janice Goodman, July 11, 31, 2013
Sandra Grayson, November 8, 2013
Joan Greco, April 4, 2014
Marilyn Haft, June 19, 2013
Josh Johnson, August 11, 2014
Joel Klein, May 21, 2014
Shana Knizhnik, August 11, 2014
Loretta McCarthy, June 1, 2014
Ruth McGregor, January 23, 2013
Rita Menkes, October 2013
Henry Paul Monaghan, October 14, 2013
Aryeh Neier, July 8 and 11, 2013
Bernard Nussbaum, June 2, 2014
David G. Post, June 3, 2014
Harriet Rabb, October 15, 2013

Akila Radhakrishnan, August 13, 2014
Paul Rosenblatt, February 7, 2014
Lynn Hecht Schafran, March 22, 2014; October 9, 2014
Margo Schlanger, May 28, 2014
Mary Schroeder, February 27, 2014
John Setear, April 1, 2014
John Paul Stevens, July 21, 2014
Geoffrey Stone, September 12, 2013
Nina Totenberg, September 6, 2013
Stephen Wiesenfeld, October 14, 2013
Michael Li-Ming Wong, July 17, 2014
Mel Wulf, June 20, 2013
Tom Zemaitis, April 17, 2014

OTHER INTERVIEWS

Ruth Bader Ginsburg, interview, Academy of Achievement, August 17, 2010, http://www.achievement.org/autodoc/page/ginoint-3
Ruth Bader Ginsburg, televised interview with Brian Lamb, C-SPAN, July 1, 2009, http://supremecourt.c-span.org/assets/pdf/RBGinsburg.pdf
Harriet Haskell, interview with Phoenix History Project, January 31, 1980
Sandra Day O'Connor, taped interview with Phoenix Oral History Project, 1980
Suzy Post, interview by Betsy Brinson, January 6, 1999, American Civil Liberties Union Records, Princeton University Library, Catalog no. 20
Stuart Spencer, "Interview with Stuart Spencer," 2005, Ronald Reagan Oral History, Miller Center, University of Virginia, http://millercenter.org/president/reagan/oralhistory/stuart-spencer

SPEECHES

Ginsburg, Ruth Bader. Speech, New York Historical Society, October 28, 2014.
——. Oklahoma Bar Association Women in Law Conference Banquet Address, 1997, Ginsburg Archive, Library of Congress, Box 146.
——. "Realizing the Equality Principle," Ginsburg Archive, Library of Congress, Box 12.
——. "Remarks on Women's Progress in the Legal Profession in the United States," Speech at July Institute on World Legal Problems in Innsbruck. Ginsburg Archive, Library of Congress, Box 151 F Seminars 1995.
——. "Sex and Unequal Protection: Men and Women as Victims," keynote address, Southern Regional Conference of the National Conference of Law Women, Duke University, October 1, 1971, published in *Journal of Family Law* 11 (1971): 347.
——. "U.S. Supreme Court Justice Nomination Acceptance Address," American Rhetoric Online Speech Bank, June 14, 1993, http://www.americanrhetoric.com/speeches/ruthbaderginsburgusscnominationspeech.htm.

O'Connor, Sandra Day. "Surviving Cancer." C-SPAN, November 3, 1994, http://www.c-span.org/video/?61342-1/surviving-cancer.

———. "What Individuals Can Do to Improve the Courts" (remarks at Commencement Address at Stanford University), June 21, 1982, *Los Angeles Daily Journal* 4 (1982).

Palme, Olof. "The Emancipation of Man," address to the Women's National Democratic Club (June 8, 1970), http://www.olofpalme.org/wp-content/dokument/700608_emancipation_of_man.pdf.

Rathbun, Harry J. Audio recording, 1955, Stanford Digital Repository, http://purl.stanford.edu/qq737wt2311.

OTHER SOURCES

"Arizona's Expenditure and Tax Limitation Proposal: An Analysis of Proposition 106," Arizona State University Papers in Public Administration, 1974, O'Connor files, Arizona History and Archives, 5:2.

The Nomination of Ruth Bader Ginsburg, to Be Associate Justice of the Supreme Court of the United States: Hearings Before the S. Comm. on the Judiciary, 103d Cong. 127 (1993), http://www.loc.gov/law/find/nominations/ginsburg/hearing.pdf.

William H. Rehnquist, "A Random Thought on the Segregation Cases," 1952, http://www.gpo.gov/fdsys/pkg/GPO-CHRG-REHNQUIST/pdf/GPO-CHRG-REHNQUIST-4-16-6.pdf.

"Sandra Day O'Connor House," Tempe Preservation on Flickr, http://www.tempe.gov/city-hall/community-development/historic-preservation/tempe-historic-property-register/sandra-day-o-connor-house.

"Supreme Court Justice Sandra Day O'Connor and Chief Justice Warren Burger on Steps of Supreme Court, Washington DC," image, Ron Bennett Photography, http://ronbennett.photoshelter.com/image/I0000Del5UB91v3M.

"Uniform Disposition of Community Property Rights at Death Act," National Conference of Commissioners on Uniform State Laws, August 21–28, 1971, http://www.uniformlaws.org/shared/docs/disposition%20of%20community%20property%20rights/udcprda%201971.pdf.

Welborn, Angie A. *The Law of Church and State*: *Selected Opinions of Justice O'Connor*. Washington, D.C.: Congressional Research Service, Report for Congress, July 20, 2005, http://congressionalresearch.com/RS22201/document.php?study=The+Law+of+Church+and+State+Selected+Opinions+of+Justice+OConnor.

Index

✳

Note: Page numbers in *italics* indicate a photograph.

Abernathy, Charles, 72
abortion issue
  overview, 204–5
  doctors' awareness of women dying from illegal abortions, 78–79
  D&X or partial birth abortions, 250–53, 268–70
  and feminist movement, 79–80
  and Ginsburg, 60, 61, 80–81, 184–85, 204, 205, 209
  and health of the pregnant woman, 79–80, 152–54, 185, 194, 250–52
  and O'Connor, 60, 131, 134, 150–54, 184, 251
  prohibition on giving foreign aid for abortions, 259
  separation from feminism, 78–79
  and Supreme Court, 61–62, 82–83
  and thalidomide, 79
  undue-burden standard, 153–54, 194–96, 251–52
  U.S. military attempt to force an abortion, 61–62, 188
  Webster v. Reproductive Health Services, 186–90
  women asking their husbands before an abortion, 191, 194–95, 268
  See also anti-abortion movement; *Roe v. Wade*
abusive work environment, defining, 218
ACLU (American Civil Liberties Union)
  and ERA, 37–38, 39
  and Ford Foundation, 61
  and Ginsburg's Harvard professorship, 56–57
  and *Moritz* case, 33–34, 39, 43
  and *Planned Parenthood v. Casey*, 191
  policy on women's equality, 55–56
  and *Reed v. Reed*, 34–35
  resistance to integration of women, 58
  women's caucus, 38–39, 58
ACLU Women's Rights Project
  overview, 62–63
  agenda-setting conference with NOW, 63–66
  areas for action, 59–60
  creation of, 57–58
  and Ginsburg, xvii, 58
  offices in midtown Manhattan, 59
  and *Reed v. Reed*, xxi
  See also Ginsburg's cases before the Supreme Court
Adams, Abigail, 38
affirmative action
  and ERA, 85
  Fisher v. University of Texas, 285–87
  and Ginsburg, 170–71, 208–9, 286–87
  and O'Connor, 119, 171–72
  resistance to, 169–70
  Scalia on, 119
  Sotomayor's dissent on Roberts's roll back, 301
  Supreme Court on, 170–72, 286–87

Akron v. Akron Reproductive Center, 152–54, 184–85
Alabama
  African Americans voting in, 287–88
  Frontiero v. Richardson, 69–77, 97, 142–43
  J.E.B. v. Alabama, 224–28
  Lilly Ledbetter v. Goodyear Tire and Rubber, 274–76
Albright, Miller v., 246–47
Alexander, Michelle, 228
Alito, Samuel
  appointment and confirmation, 259, 268
  Burwell v. Hobby Lobby, 293, 294
  and Third Circuit ruling on *Planned Parenthood v. Casey,* 190, 268
American Bar Association, 51, 66, 110, 160–61
American Civil Liberties Union. *See* ACLU
American Law Institute (ALI), 79
American Nurses Association, 143
anti-abortion movement
  Akron v. Akron Reproductive Center, 152–54, 184–85
  and Bush, George W., 252, 257, 259
  in Missouri, 150–52, 186–90
  and O'Connor, 131
  Planned Parenthood v. Casey, 190–96, 295
  states' hurdles to abortion, 60, 186–90, 195–96
  and States' rights, 251
  Webster v. Reproductive Health Services, 186–90
Arizona
  abortion issue, 60
  Burger's trip to, 127–29
  law limiting women's work hours, 47
  O'Connor as Arizona Court of Appeals judge, 129
  O'Connor as Arizona State Senator, 23–24, 25, 45–50, 122–24, 134
  O'Connor childhood, xviii–xix, 3–5
  politics in, 19–20, 119–20
Armstrong, Anne, 126–27
Armstrong, Tobin, 126
Askin, Frank, 22–23, 25

Atlantic Monthly special issue on women, 45–46

Babbitt, Bruce, 129, 200
Babcock, Barbara, 147–48, 205
Bader, Celia (mother), xix, 6, 7, 200
Bader, Kiki, 7. *See also entries beginning with* "Ginsburg, Ruth Bader"
Bader, Nathan (father), 5–6
Baker, Jim, 137
Bakke, Allan, 170
Ballard, Schlesinger v., 89–90, 227
Ball State, Vance v., 284
Barnes, Paulette, 163
Barr, Burton, 123–24
bathing suit (wet T-shirt) contest at King & Spalding, 157–58, 162
Baxter, Hugh, 218–19, 222
Bellagio Center, Lake Como, Italy, 108
Bemiss, Fitzgerald, 137
Benshoof, Janet, 289
Berkeley Law School, Berkeley, California, 87–88
Berresford, Susan, 63
Berzon, Marsha, 87–88, 99
Biden, Joe, 134
"bird shit" case (*F.S. Royster Guano v. Virginia*), 43–44
Birmingham Board of Education, Jackson v., 265–66
birth control and health insurance case, 292–95
Biskupic, Joan, 3, 133
Black, Hugo, 41
Blackmun, Harry, *197*
  appointment, 41–42
  and Ginsburg, 225, 226, 227–28
  Harris v. Forklift Systems, 217, 218
  J.E.B. v. Alabama, 226
  on legal feminism, 75–76
  and O'Connor, 151, 225–26
  Roe v. Wade, 78
  and strict scrutiny of sex discrimination, 76
  Webster v. Reproductive Health Services, 186–90
  Weinberger v. Wiesenfeld, 98, 100
Blank, Diane, 156–57

Board of Education, Brown v., 40, 117–18, 140, 144–45, 273
Bolton, Doe v., 80
Boren, Craig v., 105–8, 142
Bork, Robert, and borking, 208
Born, Brooksley, 160–61
Bowen, Catherine Drinker, 45
Bradwell v. Illinois, 92, 269–70
Braibant, Guy, 176
Brandeis, Louis, 40, 273
Braun, Carol Moseley, 199
Brennan, William
  Berzon as clerk, 87–88, 99
  on *Califano v. Goldfarb*, 104
  and *Craig v. Boren*, 107
  and Ginsburg's argument for strict scrutiny of sex discrimination, 75–76, 77
  Hishon v. King & Spalding, 159
  Johnson v. Santa Clara Transportation Authority, 171–72
  and O'Connor, xxi
  Price Waterhouse v. Hopkins, 182
  raising the standard for sex discrimination laws, 107
  refusing to hire a female clerk, 21
  on *Weinberger v. Wiesenfeld*, 100
Breyer, Stephen, 176, 205–6, 240–41
Brown, Shirley, 261, 262
Brown v. Board of Education, 40, 117–18, 140, 144–45, 273
Burger, Warren, *115*
  appointment, 41
  Arizona trip, 127–29
  Craig v. Boren, 107
  Hishon v. King & Spalding, 159–60
  Hogan v. Mississippi, 145
  Meritor Savings Bank, FSB v. Vinson, 166
  and O'Connor, 128–31, 135, 168–69
  on women on the Supreme Court, 47
Burwell v. Hobby Lobby, 292–95
Bush, George H. W., 154, 187
Bush, George W., 252, 257, 259
Bush v. Gore, 255–59

Califano v. Goldfarb, 104, 106
Califano v. Westcott, 111–12
Cannon, Mark, 127

Carhart, Gonzales v., 268–70, 274
Carhart, Stenberg v., 250–53, 296
Carr, Robert, 10
Carter, Jimmy, 109, 110–11
Casey, Planned Parenthood v., 190–96, 295
Catholic Church and abortion, 150
centrism as philosophy, 221
Charleston, Ferguson v., 261–62
childbearing and special privileges, 246–50, 262–64
children born in a foreign country to American fathers vs. America mothers, 248–50, 262–64
child support case jury in Alabama, 224–28
child support for boys vs. girls, 105
Christopher, Warren, 12
Citizens Advisory Council on the Status of Women, 48–49
Civiletti, Benjamin, 112
"Civil Liberty After the War" (Cushman), 10
Civil Rights Act (1964)
  overview, xvii
  applicability to partnerships, 157, 158–60, 161
  Marshall's strategy, xvi
  and sex discrimination, 246–47, 275–76
  and sexual harassment, 164–68, 217–19
Clark, Penny, 88–90, 91, 98–99, 102–3, 105, 144
Cleary, Goesaert v., 26
Cleveland, Sarah, 218
Clinton, Bill, 6, 199–200, 206–7
Clinton, Hilary Rodham, 160–61
Coleman v. Court of Appeals of Maryland, 282–83
colleges and universities, integration of, 55–56, 138, 139–40, 141
Collins, Gail, xiii
Colom, Wilbur, 140, 146
Colonial Williamsburg, Virginia, 136
Columbia Law School, New York, New York, 16, 21, 57, 66, 109
Commissioner of Internal Revenue, Moritz v., 33–34, 39, 43, 55

Commission on Women in the Profession, American Bar Association, 160–61
"Conditional Emancipation of Women, The" (Moberg), 21–22, 26, 27
Congress of the United States
on abortion issue, 251–52
Family and Medical Leave Act, 265, 282–83
and Ledbetter, 275–76
Lilly Ledbetter Fair Pay Act, 276
Religious Freedom Restoration Act, 293
Voting Rights Act, 287–88
See also Civil Rights Act
Congress on Racial Equality (CORE), 38
Conlan, John, 48
Constitution of the United States
discrimination protection, 35
judicial interpretation of, 36–37, 209, 210
See also Fourteenth Amendment
Cooper, George, 84
Cornell University, Ithaca, New York, 7, 9–11, 14
Cosby, Kelly, 290–91
country club elites, 137–38
Court of Appeals
Coleman v. Court of Appeals of Maryland, 282–83
D.C. Circuit, 112–14, 163–64, 207, 231
Fourth Circuit, 238–39
Second Circuit, 110–11
Third Circuit, 190–91, 268
Cox, Bill, 150
Craig v. Boren, 105–8, 142
criminal sodomy laws, 260
Cuomo, Mario, 200
Cushman, Robert, xx, 9–11

Davis v. Monroe County Board of Education, 247–48
Day, Ada Mae Wilkey (mother), 3
Day, Alan (brother), 4
Day, Harry (father), xviii–xix, 3, 4–5
Day, Sandra. *See entries beginning with* "O'Connor, Sandra Day"

death row inmate exonerated, 279, 280–82
Dershowitz, Alan, 215
difference feminism, 201–4, 229, 234–35
different-voice theory, 203–4, 234, 300
discrimination
affirmative action as reverse discrimination charge, 170–71
constitutional protection against, 35
employment discrimination cases, 284–85
gains lost after Ginsburg goes to the bench, 139
Internal Revenue Code on men as caretakers, 32–33
redefining sexual harassment as, 163–68
in welfare law, 112
See also sex discrimination
Doe v. Bolton, 80
Domingo, Placido, 282
Donahue, Sean, 211, 212
Dorsen, Norman, 33, 39
Douglas, Les, 137
Douglas, William O., 42, 85–87
Draper, Bill, 137
Driggs, John, 19, 127, 133, 168–69
drinking age in Oklahoma, 107
Duren v. Missouri, 111, 227

Edwards v. Healy, 90
Egan, Michael, 110
"Emancipation of Men, The" (Palme), 22, 26
employment discrimination cases, 284–85
Equal Employment Opportunity Commission (EEOC) and sexual harassment, 164, 216, 217
equality. *See* affirmative action; Civil Rights Act; women's equality
Equality Committee of the ACLU, 55
equality feminism. *See* Ginsburg's strategy for equality feminism
equal-protection clause and women's equality, 40–44, 88–89, 95, 104, 264. *See also* Fourteenth Amendment

equal protection, *Harvard Law Review* article on, 37
Equal Rights Amendment (ERA)
  overview, xvii, 30
  abortion rights equated to, 186
  and ACLU, 37–38, 39
  affirmative action aspects, 85
  Fourteenth Amendment vs., 35–36
  and Ginsburg, 26, 27, 50–52, 53–55, 108
  and O'Connor, 47, 48–50
  opposition to, 41, 118
  and same-sex marriage issue, 64–65
Ervin, Sam, 52–53
evolution into self-realization concept, 7, 8–9

Family and Medical Leave Act, federal, 265, 282–83
Feigen Fasteau, Brenda, 59, 72
Feinstein, Dianne, 199
feminist movement
  overview, xiv, xvi–xvii, 101–2, 300
  abortion as separate from feminism, 78–79
  Atlantic Monthly special issue on women, 45–46
  birth control and health insurance case vs., 292–95
  and country club membership, 137–38
  difference feminism vs. equality feminism, 201–4, 229, 234–35
  and different-voice theory, 203–4, 234, 300
  and Ginsburg, xvi, xvii, 66
  law school as part of, 131
  and lesbianism, 64–65
  models for, xiv
  and O'Connor, xv–xvi, xvii, 123, 134
  and protective legislation for women, 28
  and redefining workplace sex-based harassment, 162–64
  and Republican Party, 131
  and Shulman's "A Marriage Agreement," 27–28
  social change in 1960s, 24, 25–30
  in Sweden, 21–22, 26

See also abortion issue; ACLU Women's Rights Project; Ginsburg's strategy for equality feminism; law firms and women; sexual equality
Ferguson, Plessy v., 118, 144
Ferguson v. Charleston, 261–62
Ferrari, Mary, 59
Finkbine, Shari, 79
Fisher v. University of Texas, 285–87
Florida
  Bush v. Gore, 256–58
  Hoyt v. Florida, 36, 90, 91–93
Ford Foundation, 61, 63
Fordham University School of Law, New York, New York, 149
Forklift Systems, Harris v., 215–19, 220–22, 223–24
Fortas, Abe, 41
Fourteenth Amendment
  and choice availability, 145
  ERA vs., 35–36
  and jury selection, 228–29, 230
  legal scholars criticism of, 54
  and substantive comparability, 239
  Title IX, 247, 265
  and women's equality, 40–44, 88–89, 95, 104, 264
France, American jurists in, 176
Frankfurter, Felix, 21
Freedman, Ann, 39–40, 42
Freund, Paul, 53
Fried, Charles, 188
Frontiero, Sharron, 69–70
Frontiero v. Richardson, 69–77, 97, 142–43
F.S. Royster Guano v. Virginia, 43–44
FWOTSC (first woman on the Supreme Court), xi. *See also* O'Connor, Sandra Day
Gaines, Ebersole, 137
Gavin, Elizabeth "Beth," 290–91
gay rights, 292
Gebser, Alida Star, 247
Gebser v. Lago Vista Independent School District, 246, 247
Geller, Steven, 8
George Washington Law School National Conference on Women and the Law, 154–55

Gibson, Dunn & Crutcher legal secretary position offer to O'Connor,
xiv, xix, 13–14
Gilbert, Fred, 106
Gilles, Stephen, 167–68
Gilligan, Carol, 202–3, 234
Ginsburg, Ruth Bader, *1*, *67*, *197*, *271*
and abortion issue, 60, 61, 80–81,
184–85, 204, 205, 209
and affirmative action, 170–71,
208–9, 286–87
awakening to women's rights issues, 11, 25–29
and Clinton, 6, 206–7
and Constitution of the United
States, 26–27, 28, 30–31
and criminals or poor people, 210
criticism of, 210–11
delegation to France, 176
and ERA, 26, 27, 35–36, 50–52,
53–55, 108
and *Hoyt v. Florida*, 91–92, 93
lobbying Congress for women's
rights, 30
and MacKinnon, 202, 203
and near-beer case in Oklahoma,
106–8
and O'Connor, 115, 222–24, 231–
33, 270
on O'Connor's cancer survivor
speech, 178
and *Reed v. Reed*, 39–44
on sex discrimination, 56, 102,
241–43, 283, 301
supporters for seat on the bench,
84–85, 109–10, 112–13
on Voting Rights Act preclearance
process, 288
whites-only country club membership, 138
See also ACLU Women's Rights
Project; Ginsburg on the Supreme Court; O'Connor and
Ginsburg comparisons
Ginsburg, biographical information
childhood, 5–7
as clerk for Palmieri, 21
at Columbia Law School, 16, 21, 57, 66
at Cornell, 7, 9–11, 14

demeanor, 76, 95, 102–3, 113, 207,
282
at federal Court of Appeals for the
D.C. Circuit, 112–14, 207
at Harvard Law School, xix, 14,
15–17, 56–57
health issues, 253–54, 277, 297
as newly-graduated lawyer, 20–23
pregnancy prevents promotion, 14
pre-Supreme Court, xvii, xix, xx
at Rutgers Law School, 22–23, 25–
30, 57
and Swedish feminist movement,
21–22, 26
as wife and mother, 14–15, 17–18, 22
Ginsburg's cases before the Supreme
Court
Craig v. Boren, 105–8, 142
Edwards v. Healy, 90
Frontiero v. Richardson, 69–77, 97,
142–43
Kahn v. Shevin, 85–87, 96–98, 99
Stanton v. Stanton, 105
United States v. Virginia, xi–xiii
See also Ginsburg on the Supreme
Court; *Weinberger v. Wiesenfeld*
Ginsburg's strategy for equality feminism
overview, 30–31, 70–72, 107–8, 253,
300
applying Civil Rights Act to sexual
harassment cases, 217–19
case selection, 59–60, 63–64
and *Craig v. Boren*, 106–7
difference feminism vs., 201–3
gains lost after Ginsburg goes to
the bench, 139
and *Kahn* setback, 97
Kennedy vs., 252–53
O'Connor's use of in *Hogan v. Mississippi*, 141–43
and *United States v. Virginia* opinion, 235, 241–43
See also sex discrimination in jury
service; strict-scrutiny vs. rational
basis standard of review
Ginsburg on the Supreme Court
overview, xv, 69, 220–22, 230, 273,
298–99

Burwell v. Hobby Lobby, 292–95
clerks, 211–12, 213, 273
consideration for nomination, 200–207
dissents read out loud, 274–76, 279–82, 284–88, 292–95
Gonzales v. Carhart, 268–70, 274, 296
"happy face dissents," 218–19
J.E.B. v. Alabama, 224, 225, 226–27
and Kennedy's opinion for *Planned Parenthood v. Casey*, 193–94
Lilly Ledbetter v. Goodyear Tire and Rubber, 274–76
nomination and confirmation, 6–7, 91–92, 199, 207–11
office, 210
retirement suggestions, 278–79, 296–97
Shelby County v. Holder, 287–88, 289
summer travel and public speaking, 244–45
swearing-in ceremony, 213–14
United States v. Virginia, 240
Ginsburg, James (son), 22, 108
Ginsburg, Jane (daughter), 14, 15, 102, 108, 213
Ginsburg, Martin "Marty" (husband)
cancer and death of, 277
cancer diagnosis, 17–18
courtship and marriage, 14–15
and Harvard vs. Columbia for Ruth, 16
lobbying for Ginsburg's appointments, 110–11, 112, 205, 278
as loving husband, 23, 278
and Moritz case, 32
teaching at Columbia, 109
Goesaert v. Cleary, 26
Goldberg, David, 212
Goldfarb, Califano v., 104, 106
Goldfarb, Leon, 104
Goldwater, Barry, xxii, 49, 123, 131, 181
Gonzales v. Carhart, 268–70, 274
Goodman, Janice, 39–40, 66
Goodyear Tire and Rubber, Lilly Ledbetter v., 274–76
Gore, Bush v., 255–59

Greco, Joan, 175
Greenburg, Jan Crawford, 267
Grimké, Sarah, 28, 75
Griswold, Erwin, 15–16, 62, 206
Gunther, Gerald, 20–21

Haft, Marilyn, 112
Hand, Learned, xix, 21
Hardy, Charles, 215–16
Harlan, John Marshall, 41, 273
Harlan, Malvina, 273
Harris, Barbara, 161
Harris, Teresa, 215–16
Harris v. Forklift Systems, 215–19, 220–22, 223–24
Harvard Law Review, 12, 37
Harvard Law School, Cambridge, Massachusetts, xix, 14, 15–17, 56–57
Harvard Law School dean and Ginsburg place in law school, xiv–xv, xix
Hatch, Orrin, 113
Hazeltine, Sherman, 120
health insurance and birth control case, 292–95
Healy, Edwards v., 90
Hess, Stephen, 200
Hibbs, Nevada v., 265, 282–83
Hibbs, William, 265
Higginbotham, Patrick, 110
Hirshman, Linda, xiii, xiv
Hishon, Elizabeth Anderson "Betsy," 157
Hishon v. King & Spalding, 157, 158–60, 161
Hobby Lobby, Burwell v., 292–95
Hochschild, Arlie, 28
Hogan, Joe, 140, 146
Hogan v. Mississippi
overview, xii–xiii, 233
decision and opinions, 138–39, 141–46, 232, 237
outcome, 146
prosecution and defense, 140–41
Holder, Shelby County v., 287–88, 289
Holes, Harry, 137
Holmes, Oliver Wendell, Jr., 273
Hopkins, Ann, 178–79

Hopkins, Price Waterhouse v., 178–80, 182–83, 285
House Un-American Activities Committee, 10, 11
Hoyt v. Florida, 36, 90, 91–93

"If" (Kipling), 8
Illinois, Bradwell v., 92, 269–70
immigration and parentage, 246–50
INS, Nguyen v., 263–64
Internal Revenue Code on men as caretakers, 32–33
Internet blog: *Notorious R.B.G.*, 289–90, 292, 295, 299

Jackson v. Birmingham Board of Education, 265–66
James Madison High School, Brooklyn, New York, 6
J.E.B. v. Alabama, 224–28
Jewish lawyers and "The Year of Our Lord" on certificates of admission, 213
Johnson, Josh, 292
Johnson v. Santa Clara Transportation Authority, 170–72, 208–9
judiciary and politics, xvi, 53, 183
Junior League, 20
juries, defendant's right to shape, 228–29, 230
jury service, 224. *See also* sex discrimination in jury service
Kagan, Elena, 278, 298–99
Kahn, Melvin, 85, 94
Kahn v. Shevin, 85–87, 96–98, 99
Keith, Judith, 233–34
Kelly, Mary F., 39–40, 156
Kennedy, Anthony, *197*
  appointment, 174
  Bush v. Gore, 256
  Ferguson v. Charleston, 262
  Gonzales v. Carhart, 296
  Jackson v. Birmingham Board of Education, 266
  Nguyen v. INS, 263–64
  Planned Parenthood v. Casey, 192–94, 250–51, 295
  post-*Bush v. Gore* liberal votes, 260
  and Scalia, 193

Stenberg v. Carhart, 250, 251, 253
  as swing vote, 279
  University of Texas Southwestern Hospital v. Nassar, 284
  and women's equality, 219–20, 252–53, 260–61, 262–65, 269–70
Kennedy, Cornelia, 151
Kennedy, Edward, 133
Kenyon, Dorothy, 38
King & Spalding, Atlanta, Georgia, 157–58
King & Spalding, Hishon v., 157, 158–60, 161
Kipling, Rudyard, 8
Kiser, Jackson, 237, 238
Klain, Ron, 208
Klein, Joel, 207–8
Knizhnik, Shana, 289–, 299
Kolbert, Kathryn, 191, 192
Kozinski, Alex, 215
Krauskopf, Joan, 54
Kurland, Philip, 52–53, 102

Lago Vista Independent School District, Gebser v., 246, 247
law firms and women
  Ginsburg's dead-end summer job at Paul, Weiss, 20
  Hishon v. King & Spalding, 157, 158–60, 161
  lawsuits for equal treatment, 156–57, 158–60, 161
  O'Connor offered legal secretary position post-graduation, xiv, xix, 13–14
  O'Connor's rejections, 13
  women presumed to be incompetent, 160–61
Lazy B (O'Connor and Day), 3–4
legal equality, 102
legal profession and ERA, 51–53
legal social change movements, xvi, xx–xxi. *See also* Ginsburg's strategy for equality feminism; racial social movement
legal system in the United States, 36–37, 42
lesbianism, 64–65, 146
Levin, Joseph, 69–70, 71–73

Lilly Ledbetter Fair Pay Act (2009), 276
Lilly Ledbetter v. Goodyear Tire and Rubber, 274–76
Lindh, Patricia, 126–27
Lippman, Mark, 176
London, England, legal conference, 129–30
Louisiana, 90, 92–93, 280–81
Lutzker, Shelly, 59

MacKinnon, Catharine, 163, 202, 203
MacKinnon, George, 163
Madison, Dolly, 40
Madison Lecture series at NYU, 203–5
Mandil, Daniel, 187
Mann, Jonathan, 295, 296
"Marriage Agreement, A" (Shulman), 27–28
Marriage of Figaro, The (Mozart), 293
Marshall, Thurgood, xvi, 42
  Brown v. Board of Education, 40, 117–18, 140, 144–45, 273
  case selection, 65
Mary Baldwin College solution to VMI, 238–39
McBridge, Andrew, 187
McCain, John, 181
McCarthy, Joseph, and McCarthyism, 9–10, 11
McFeathers, Ann, 131
McGregor, Ruth, 132–33, 136, 138–39
McKissick, Floyd, 38
Mellor, Mary-Audrey Weicker, 136
Meritor Savings Bank, FSB v. Vinson, 164–68, 216
Michelman, Kate, 205
Miller, Charles, 246
Miller v. Albright, 246–47
Mill, John Stuart, 243
Mills, Cheryl, 205
Millstein, Ira, 110, 113
Mississippi University for Women (MUW, the W), 138, 139–40, 141. See also *Hogan v. Mississippi*
Missouri, 111, 150–52, 186–90, 227
Missouri Citizens for Life (MCL), 150, 186
mixed-motive cases, 284–85

Moberg, Eva, 21–22, 26, 27
Monaghan, Henry, 278
Monroe County Board of Education, Davis v., 247–48
Monsoor, Debra, 60
Moore, Frank, 112
Morgan, Charles, 158
Moritz, Charles, 32–33
Moritz v. Commissioner of Internal Revenue, 33–34, 39, 43, 55
Moynihan, Daniel Patrick, 200–201
Murray, Bob, 137
Murray, Pauli, 38, 65
Myrdal, Gunnar, 40

Nassar, University of Texas Southwestern Hospital v., 284–85
National Association of Law Women, 29
National Association of Women Judges, xxii, 208
National Conference on Women and the Law, George Washington Law School, 154–55
National Organization for Women (NOW), 63–66, 133–34
near-beer case in Oklahoma, 105–8
Nebraska, 250–51
Neier, Aryeh, 39, 57–58, 61, 63, 66, 108–9
Ness, Susan, 111
Nevada, 265
Nevada v. Hibbs, 265, 282–83
New England School of Law, Boston, Massachusetts, 149
Nguyen v. INS, 263–64
Nicastro, Robert, 281–82
Nixon, Richard, 42, 117, 121–22, 131
Notorious B.I.G., 289
Notorious R.B.G. Internet blog, 289–90, 292, 295, 299
Nussbaum, Bernard, 201, 206–7

Oberly, Kathryn, 180
O'Connor and Ginsburg comparisons
  abortion issue, 60, 184–85, 209
  affirmative action, 170–72, 208–9
  constitutional interpretation, 209, 210
  and ERA battle, 49–50

mentors, 8–11
pre-Supreme Court, xvii–xix
relationships with others, xxi–xxii
road to the Supreme Court, xv–xix
self-respect and regard for others,
    xx–xxii
speaking about Ellen Ash Peters,
    231–32
on Supreme Court, xxii–xxiii
visions of the present world, 210
O'Connor and Ginsburg differenti-
    ation with T-shirts, xxii, 208
O'Connor, Sandra Day, *115*, *197*, *271*
and abortion issue, 60, 131, 134,
    150–54, 184, 251
on blessings of marriage, 46
and Burger, 128–31, 135, 168–69
and Bush, George H. W., 181, 182,
    192
cancer diagnosis, 181
and cap on taxes issue, 123, 124
constitutional interpretation, 152–
    53, 189, 209, 210
criticism of, 196
delegation to France, 176
demeanor, xxiii
and different-voice theory, 203–4,
    233, 300
and ERA, 47, 48–50
family first philosophy, xviii, 46,
    131, 132, 147–48
and feminism, 118–19
and Ginsburg, 155, 178, 222–24,
    231–33, 270, 298–301
and Goldwater, xxii, 123, 131, 181
at Mormon church service, 133
and Nixon, 46–47, 117, 119, 122
and Reagan, xiv, 123, 130, 131–32
and Rehnquist, 118–21
and social change, 172
on women in the law profession,
    161–62
See also O'Connor and Ginsburg
    comparisons
O'Connor, biographical information
as Arizona Court of Appeals judge,
    129
as Arizona State Senator, 23–24,
    25, 45–50, 122–24, 134

as assistant attorney general, 23
cancer diagnosis, 176–78
childhood, xxiii, 3–5
as criminal trial judge, 124–25
legal secretary position offer, xiv,
    xix, 13–14
as newly-graduated lawyer, xiv,
    xix, 13–14, 18–19
photographic memory, 148
pre-Supreme Court, xv–xvi, xvii,
    xviii, xx
and Rathbun, 9, 258
at Stanford, 5, 7–9
at Stanford Law School, 12–14
on Supreme Court, xv, xxii, xxiii
as wife and mother, 20, 24–25
O'Connor on the Supreme Court
overview, 174–75, 183, 195–96, 219,
    221, 222, 230–31, 298, 299, 300
abortion issue analysis, 150–54
and affirmative action, 119, 171–72,
    208–9
all-female aerobics class, 147, 175, 244
appointment and confirmation hear-
    ings, xiv, 130–35
Bush v. Gore, 255–59
clerks, 174–75, 187, 222–23
on defendant's right to shape ju-
    ries, 228–29
Harris v. Forklift Systems, 217, 218
Hishon v. King & Spalding, 160
Hogan v. Mississippi, xii–xiii, 141–
    43, 145–46
*Jackson v. Birmingham Board of Ed-
    ucation*, 266
J.E.B. v. Alabama, 228–29
*Johnson v. Santa Clara Transporta-
    tion Authority*, 171–72, 208
legacy, 266–68
*Meritor Savings Bank, FSB v. Vin-
    son*, 165–66, 167–68, 216
office disorder on arrival, 136
Planned Parenthood v. Casey, 192–96
post-*Bush v. Gore* support for
    women's equality, 259–60
Price Waterhouse v. Hopkins, 182–
    83, 285
public speaking and events, 147–49
road to, xv–xix, 127–30

Stenberg v. Carhart, 251
swearing-in ceremony, 135, 146–47
United States v. Virginia, xii, 241–42
O'Connor, John, III (husband), 13, 18–19, 46, 132–33, 137–38, 255, 267
Ogg, Mary Fran, 124–25
Olson, Theodore, 240
Oncale v. Sundowner, 221, 222
O'Neill, John E., 96–97

Palme, Olof, 22, 26
Palmieri, Edmund, 21
"partial birth" abortions, 250–51, 268–70
Paul, Alice, xvii
Paul, Weiss, Rifkind, Wharton & Garrison, New York, New York, 20
Pennsylvania's sex-segregated schools, 237
Peratis, Kathleen, 65
peremptory challenges of state vs. defendant, 228–29
Perkins, Charles, 140
Peters, Ellen Ash, 231–32
Pickrell, Bob, 23
Planned Parenthood, 79
Planned Parenthood v. Casey, 190–96, 295
Plessy v. Ferguson, 118, 144
politics
  and abortion issue, 191, 204–5
  in Arizona, 19–20, 119–20
  of equal rights, 88–89
  and judiciary, xvi, 53, 183
  and makeup of the Supreme Court, 181–82
  O'Connor's, 255, 257–58
  women and Republican Party, 130
Posner, Richard, 215
Post, David, 211–12
Post, Suzy, 38
Powell, Lewis
  Califano v. Goldfarb, 104, 107
  Clark as clerk, 88–90, 91, 98–99, 105, 144
  ERA argument in *Frontiero v. Richardson* decision, 76–77
  Hishon v. King & Spalding, 160
  Hogan v. Mississippi, 143–46

Nixon's appointment of, 75
  and O'Connor, 135, 136–37
  as swing vote for Ginsburg, 90–91
  Weinberger v. Wiesenfeld, 98, 100–101
  and whites-only country club membership, 138
Powell, "Mims," 135
preclearance process, Voting Rights Act, 288
pregnancy discrimination, 14, 59, 60, 78, 81, 82, 261–62
Price Waterhouse, 178–79
Price Waterhouse v. Hopkins, 178–80, 182–83, 285
protective institutions, harm from, 143, 287
protective legislation for women, 28, 37–38, 47, 52–53, 86
P.S. 238, Brooklyn, New York, 6
psychological injury standard, 165–66, 216–17, 218
Pulliam, Eugene C., 19
Pyles, Carol, 60

racial social movement
  overview, xvi, 30–31, 169
  and affirmative action, 169, 286–87
  and Civil Rights Act, xvii
  and country clubs, 137–38
  discrimination allowed by Supreme Court, 70
  exclusion of women, 37–38
  and Fourteenth Amendment, 35
  Ginsburg on racial minority, 204–5
  and jury of peers concept, 90
  and jury service, 224
  Rehnquist vs., 117–18
  and schools, 144–45
  sex segregation as weapon against, 140
  Sotomayor's insights, 301
  whites-only club memberships, 137–38
  See also affirmative action; Civil Rights Act
Ragsdale, Lincoln, 137
Rasmussen, Irene, 48, 50
Rasmussen, Rachel, 50
Rathbun, Harry, 7–9, 258

rational basis of review. *See* strict-scrutiny vs. rational basis standard of review

"RBGuicy" video, 290–91

Reagan, Ronald, xiv, 123, 130, 131–32

Redding, Safford School District v., 276

Redding, Savanna, 276

Reed v. Reed, 34–35, 36, 39–44, 70, 71, 141–42

Rehnquist, William, *197*
  overview, 117–18, 121
  Bush v. Gore, 256
  clerkship and job, easily found, 18, 19
  and *Craig v. Boren*, 107
  on employees' right to sue employers for damages, 265
  and Ginsburg, 223
  Meritor Savings Bank, FSB v. Vinson, 166–67
  Nixon's appointment of, 75
  and O'Connor, 118–21
  Planned Parenthood v. Casey, 191, 192
  thyroid cancer diagnosis, 267
  Webster v. Reproductive Health Services, 188–89
  Weinberger v. Wiesenfeld, 96–97, 101

religion and abortion rights, 150–52

Religious Freedom Restoration Act (1993), 293

Reno, Janet, 206

reproduction, burden of, 82, 295

Reproductive Health Services, Webster v., 186–90

reproductive rights, 81, 185, 187–90, 193–94. *See also* abortion issue; anti-abortion movement

Republican Party
  anti-abortion shift, 130, 151
  and ERA, 49, 122–23, 130
  New Right, 186
  in Texas, 126

Richardson, Frontiero v., 69–77, 97, 142–43

Rigelman, Diana, 39–40

right-to-life movement. *See* anti-abortion movement

Roberts, John, 267–68, 287–88

Roberts, Sylvia, 63–64

Robinson, Spottswood, 163

Rockefeller Foundation award, 108–9

Roe v. Wade, 60–61, 62
  Court of Appeals for Third Circuit refusing to follow *Roe v. Wade*, 190–91
  and Ginsburg, 61
  Ginsburg on, 204–5
  and O'Connor, 60, 153–54, 184, 189
  religious organizations vs., 150–52
  and Stewart, 151–52
  Supreme Court decision, 62, 78, 80
  and *Webster v. Reproductive Health Services*, 188–90

Rogers, Judith, 231

Rosenblatt, Paul, 124–25

Rosen, Jeffrey, 256

Rossi, Alice, 46

Rutgers Law School, Camden, New Jersey, 22–23, 25–30
  integration of, 57

Ruth Bader Ginsburg archive, Library of Congress, 27

Sachs, Albert, 20–21

Safford School District v. Redding, 276

Salzburg, Austria, 19

same-sex marriage, 64–65

Santa Clara Transportation Authority, Johnson v., 170–72, 208–9

Scalia, Antonin
  and abortion issue, 188
  on affirmative action, 119
  and Bush, George W., 257
  Bush v. Gore, 256
  constitutional interpretation, 209–10
  on Fourteenth Amendment, 283
  and Ginsburg, xxii
  J.E.B. v. Alabama, 229
  and Kennedy, 193
  United States v. Virginia, 243

Schafran, Lynn Hecht, 113, 134

Schizer, David, 211, 212

Schlafly, Phyllis, 49, 83, 186

Schlanger, Margo, 211, 212

Schlesinger v. Ballard, 89–90, 227

schools
  Brown v. Board of Education, 40, 117–18, 140, 144–45, 273
  illegal search of a young girl, 276

integration of, 55–56, 138, 139–40, 141, 237

sexual harassment of students, 246–48, 276

See also specific schools

Schrag, Philip, 84

Schroeder, Mary, 129, 132

Schwab, Stewart, 158

Second Shift, The (Hochschild), 28

Secretary of Defense, Struck v., 61–62, 188

self-realization concept, 7, 8–9

Setear, John, 174–75

severe psychological injury standard, 165–66, 216–17, 218

sex discrimination
overview, 84, 163, 233–34

Brennan raising the standard sex discrimination laws, 107

burden of reproduction, 82, 295

and Civil Rights Act, 246–47

Clark's memo to Powell on upcoming Supreme Court cases, 88–90, 98–99

Craig v. Boren, 105–8, 142

drinking age in Oklahoma, 105–8

Frontiero v. Richardson, 69–77, 97, 142–43

in girls intramural sports, 265–66

Hishon v. King & Spalding, 157, 158–60, 161

J.E.B. v. Alabama, 224–28

and judicial interpretation of the Fourteenth Amendment, 209

Kahn v. Shevin, 85–87, 96–98, 99

at law firms/partnerships, 157, 158–60, 161

Lilly Ledbetter v. Goodyear Tire and Rubber, 274–76

men filing complaints, 143–44

for pregnancy, 14, 59, 60, 78, 81, 82, 261–62

presumption that women were dependent on spouses and men were not, 71

sex segregation as weapon against racial integration, 140

stay-at-home dads as indolent, 98–99

Supreme Court justices' refusal to hire women as clerks, 21, 37

Utah law on child support for boys vs. girls, 105

woman's responsibility for proving, 182–83

against women who contributed to Social Security and died, 98–99, 100–101

See also Ginsburg's strategy for equality feminism; *Hogan v. Mississippi; Reed v. Reed; United States v. Virginia; Weinberger v. Wiesenfeld*

sex discrimination in jury service
Duren v. Missouri, 111, 227

Edwards v. Healy, 90

effect of, 170–71

Ginsburg's strategy for equality, 90

Hoyt v. Florida, 36, 90, 91–93

J.E.B. v. Alabama, 224–29

sex-integration of schools, 55–56, 237. See also *Hogan v. Mississippi; United States v. Virginia*

sexual equality
overview, xiii–xiv

equating to racial equality, 40–44, 88–89, 95, 104, 264

for men, 22, 26

at Virginia Military Institute, xi–xii

See also feminist movement; sex discrimination

sexual harassment
overview, 162–68, 172–73

adoption of Ginsburg's standard, 221

clarifying abusive work environment, 218

and EEOC, 164, 216, 217

lower court opinions, 215, 216, 218

Meritor Savings Bank, FSB v. Vinson, 164–68, 216

severe psychological injury standard, 165–66, 216–17, 218

sex-based descriptions of how to get promoted, 178–80

of students, 246–48

Vance v. Ball State, 284

Shapiro, Alexandra, 212
Shelby County v. Holder, 287–88, 289
Shevin, Kahn v., 85–87, 96–98, 99
Shulman, Alix Kate, 27–28
slaves, women compared to in literature, 40
Smeal, Eleanor, 133–34
Smit, Hans, 21
Smith, Chesterfield, 110
Smith, William French, 131
social change
  in 1960s, 24, 25–30
  in 1970s, 65–66
  in 1980s, 148–49, 161–64
  in 1990s, 234–35
  and abortion battles, 185–90
  See also racial social movement
social revolution through law, xvi, xviii
Social Security widows preferences, 103–4. See also Weinberger v. Wiesenfeld
sodomy laws, 260
Sotomayor, Sonia, 277, 300–301
Souter, David, 190, 192–94, 197
Spaeth, Carl, 12
Spann, William, 111
Stanford Law School, Stanford, California, 12–14
Stanford University, Stanford, California, 5, 7–9
Stanton v. Stanton, 105
Starr, Kenneth, 132
Steinem, Gloria, 214
Stenberg v. Carhart, 250–53, 296
stereotypes and stereotyping
  overview, 252–53
  effect of women as caregivers, 283
  Kennedy on women as natural parents, 263–64
  O'Connor on, 264
  of parents' relationships to children, 249
  sex-role stereotyping vs. sexual equality, 26, 28–29, 83, 86, 100, 142, 234
Stern, Paula, 45
Stevens, John Paul, 197
  Califano v. Goldfarb, 104

Ferguson v. Charleston, 262
Hishon v. King & Spalding, 159
Miller v. Albright, 246–47
  nomination to Supreme Court, 127
  on O'Connor, xv
  Webster v. Reproductive Health Services, 186–90
  and women on the Supreme Court, 151
Stewart, Potter, 42, 137, 151
Stoessel, Mary Ann, 255
Stone, Geoffrey, 44, 75
Strausbaugh, Toni, 59–60
strict-scrutiny vs. rational basis standard of review
  overview, 36, 41–42, 70
  Ginsburg's argument in Frontiero v. Richardson, 75–77
  and tax break for widows, 86–87
  and United States v. Virginia school sex-segregation case, 239
  See also Ginsburg's strategy for building women's equality
Stromseth, Jane, 187
Struck, Susan, 61
Struck v. Secretary of Defense, 61–62, 188
"Subjection of Women, The" (Mill), 243
substantive comparability, 239
Sullivan and Cromwell, New York, New York, 156–57
Sundowner, Oncale v., 221, 222
Supreme Court. See U.S. Supreme Court
Suzman, Helen, 233
Svirdoff, Michael, 63
Sweden's feminist movement, 21–22, 26

Taylor, Billy, 92
Taylor, Sidney, 164–65, 168
Taylor v. Louisiana, 90, 92–93
Tennessee, 216
Term of the Woman, Supreme Court, 87–90, 102–3
Thomas, Clarence, 190, 197, 256
Thompson, John, 280–82
Time magazine, 108

Title IX, 247, 265
Title VII. *See* Civil Rights Act (1964)
Tocqueville, Alexis de, xvi
Toobin, Jeffrey, 257, 266
Totenberg, Nina, 41, 66, 113
Tribe, Laurence, 108
Troll, F. Robert, Jr., 165–66
T-shirts for Ruth and Sandra, xxii, 208

undue-burden standard for state
  laws on abortion, 153–54, 194–96,
  251–52
United States legal system, 36–37,
  42, 93
United States v. Virginia
  and *Hogan* precedent, 232, 237
  and landscape of sex discrimination, 233–34
  lower court rulings, 238–39
  rationalization for sex discrimination, 234–35, 238
  results of, 243–44
  Supreme Court ruling and opinion, xi–xiii, 239–43
  trial, 235
  VMI male-oriented rituals, 235–36
  VMI preemptive action, 237
  VMI resistance to race desegregation, 236–37
University of Chicago Law School,
  Chicago, Illinois, 25
University of Texas, Fisher v., 285–87
*University of Texas Southwestern
  Hospital v. Nassar,* 284–85
U.S. military
  attempt to force an abortion, 61–
  62, 188
  and dependence of male vs. female
  spouse, 69–77
  fear about integration of, 52, 55
  male soldier suing for unfair promotion opportunity for women,
  89–90, 227
U.S. Supreme Court, *197*
  overview, 246
  and affirmative action, 170–72,
  286–87
  days for decision and decision day,
  xi, xii–xiii

decision day, xii–xiii
  and dissents read out loud, 274,
  291–92
  dissents read out loud in, 291–92
  and equality of women, 282–83,
  295–97
  justices voting at conference, 230
  lawyers presenting before, 72, 111
  O'Connor's anticipated effect, 134–
  35
  political election betting pool, 181–82
  on pregnancy discrimination, 82
  raising the standard for sex discrimination cases, 107
  reviewing requests for case review,
  95–97, 138–39, 158, 191–92
  and sexual harassment, 163–68,
  172–73
  "split in the Circuit" cases, 158
  swing votes, 9, 90–91, 279
  Term of the Woman, 87–93
  and "The Year of Our Lord" on
  lawyers' certificates of admission,
  213
  See also strict-scrutiny vs. rational
  basis standard of review; *specific
  cases*
U.S. Supreme Court clerks
  Berzon, Marsha, 87–88, 99
  Blackmun's, 228
  Bush v. Gore effect on, 259
  Clark, Penny, 88–90, 91, 98–99,
  102–3, 105, 144
  Ginsburg's, 210, 211–12, 213, 273
  O'Connor's, 174–75, 187, 222–23
  pool procedure for reviewing case
  review requests, 95–97, 138–39, 158
  resistance to women as, 21, 37
  status attributed to, 12
  Stone, Geoffrey, 44, 75
  Term of the Woman, 87–93, 98–99
  See also specific clerks
Utah law on child support for boys
  vs. girls, 105

Vance v. Ball State, 284
Vietnam, children resulting from
  Americans in, 248–49, 262–64
Vinson, Mechelle, 164–65, 168

Vinson, Meritor Savings Bank, FSB v., 164–68, 216
Virginia, 43–44, 136, 144–45
Virginia Military Institute, xi–xii, 234–36. *See also United States v. Virginia*
volunteerism of O'Connor, xx

Wald, Pat, 160–61
Warren, Earl, 41
Washington Post, 113
Weber, Brian, 170
Webster v. Reproductive Health Services, 186–90
Wechsler, Herbert, 15–16, 52
Weddington, Sarah, 80, 112–13
Weinberger v. Wiesenfeld
  celebration party, 103
  as discrimination against women who contributed to Social Security and then died, 98–99, 100–101
  facts of the case, 94–95
  fallout from, 103–4
  Ginsburg's expectations, 99
  O'Connor's use of in *Hogan v. Mississippi*, 143
  ruling, 101–3, 227
  and Supreme Court pool procedure, 96–97
  trial, 99–100
Weitzman, Lenore, 28
welfare law discrimination, 111–12
Westcott, Califano v., 111–12
wet T-shirt (bathing suit) contest at King & Spalding, 157–58, 162
White, Byron, 42, 76, *197*, 205
White House special assistant for women, 126–27
widows vs. widowers, deferential treatment for, 85–87, 97, 103–4. *See also* Weinberger v. Wiesenfeld
Wiesenfeld, Jason, 100, 103, 213, 244–45
Wiesenfeld, Paula, 99
Wiesenfeld, Stephen, 94–95, 100, 103, 274. See also *Weinberger v. Wiesenfeld*

Wiley, John, 141
Wilkey, Ada Mae, 3
Williamsburg, Virginia, 136
"Will London Bridge? or Women's Lib?" (American Bar Association mock arbitration), 51
women's equality
  overview, 238
  and abortion rights, 185, 187–88
  Ginsburg on, 269–70
  "injury to women" and "legitimate state interest" standards, 89
  Mill's essay on, 243
  and O'Connor, 230–31
  Supreme Court rolling back the progress, 274–76, 279–83, 284–88, 292–95, 299
  See Ginsburg's strategy for building women's equality; sex discrimination
women's movement. *See* feminist movement
women's rights
  ACLU policy, 55–56
  Civil Rights Act's applicability to partnerships, 157, 158–60, 161
  Ginsburg awakening to issues, 11, 25–29
  harm from protective institutions, 143
  health insurance and birth control case, 292–95
  O'Connor as newly-graduated lawyer, xiv, xix, 13–14, 18–19
  protective legislation for women vs., 28, 37–38, 47, 52–53, 86
  test for gender-based classification, 142
  See also ACLU Women's Rights Project
Woodmont Country Club, Rockville, Maryland, 138
Wulf, Mel, xxi, 34–35

Year of the Woman, 199–200
Young Republicans, 19, 181

About the Author

LINDA HIRSHMAN, a lawyer and a cultural historian, is the author of *Victory: The Triumphant Gay Rights Revolution* and many other books. She received her JD from the University of Chicago Law School and her PhD in philosophy from the University of Illinois at Chicago, and she taught philosophy and women's studies at Brandeis University. Her writing has appeared in the *New York Times*, the *Washington Post*, *Slate*, *Politico*, *Newsweek*, the *Daily Beast*, and *Salon*.